ALT-LABOR AND THE NEW POLITICS
OF WORKERS' RIGHTS

Alt-Labor and the New Politics of Workers' Rights

Daniel J. Galvin

Russell Sage Foundation   NEW YORK

ROR: https://ror.org/02yh9se80

Library of Congress Cataloging in Publication Control Number: 2023028179

Text design by Linda Secondari.

RUSSELL SAGE FOUNDATION
112 East 64th Street, New York, New York 10065
10 9 8 7 6 5 4 3 2 1

CONTENTS

Figures

Tables

ABOUT THE AUTHOR

DANIEL J. GALVIN is professor of political science at Northwestern University and faculty fellow at the university's Institute for Policy Research.

ACKNOWLEDGMENTS

THIS BOOK WOULD not have been possible without the generosity of the leaders, organizers, and members of alt-labor groups who, despite having many more important things to do, gave liberally of their time to share their stories and insights with me. I hope this book is faithful to their experiences and helps bring attention to the difficult and essential work they are doing. I am deeply grateful to them.

Numerous colleagues offered valuable feedback on earlier drafts and papers. Special thanks go to Janice Fine, on whose seminal work this book seeks to build; her constructive comments and consistent support were indispensable. I am also especially grateful to Tim Bell, Laura Bucci, Jacob Hacker, Hahrie Han, Alex Hertel-Fernandez, Adam Kader, Benjamin Kreider, Matthew Lacombe, Robert Lieberman, Jack McGovern, Eden Melles, Larry Mishel, Benjamin Page, Joe Soss, Chloe Thurston, and Alex Tom for their helpful comments at various stages in the writing of this book. Some of the most invaluable feedback came from my three anonymous reviewers; I thank them and the Russell Sage Foundation's Suzanne Nichols for their keen insights. And I am indebted to my coauthors on related work, from whom I have learned so much: Jake Barnes, Janice Fine, Jacob Hacker, Jenn Round, Jason Seawright, Hana Shepherd, and Chloe Thurston.

I was fortunate to receive excellent research assistance from several students at Northwestern University: Sean Diament, Jack Garigliano, Aaron Gordon, Naomi Kostman, Matthew Lacombe, Jack McGovern, Warren Snead, Mara Suttmann-Lea, and Flora Tian. I thank them for their hard work and important contributions. For feedback and advice on different parts of this project, I am also grateful to Jeffrey Broxmeyer, Tess Forsell, Laurel Harbridge-Yong, Thomas Keck, Andrew Kelly, Layna Mosley, Herschel Nachlis, Michael Piore, Gretchen Purser, Kumar Ramanathan, Reuel Rogers, César Rosado Marzán, Philip Rocco, Diane Schanzenbach, Kathleen Thelen, Rick Valelly, Leah Vosko, Patrick Watson, and workshop participants at Northwestern University, the University of Chicago, Columbia University, the American Political Economy summer academy, Syracuse University, the Russell Sage Foundation, Rutgers University, the University of Illinois at Chicago, Swarthmore College, the University of Virginia, Yale University, Georgetown University, and numerous academic conferences. I also thank Suzanne Nichols, Jennifer Rappaport, Marcelo Agudo, and Bruce Thongsack at the Russell Sage Foundation. The standard disclaimer applies, of course: those who helped me along the way are not responsible for any errors, which are mine alone.

This work has been supported in part by award #77-18-02 from the Russell Sage Foundation and the W. K. Kellogg Foundation; any opinions expressed are those of the author alone and should not be construed as representing the opinions of either foundation. Northwestern University's Institute for Policy Research, Weinberg College, and the Farrell Fellowship program in the Department of Political Science also provided valuable support. Parts of chapters 1 and 2, as well as figures 2.2–2.4 and tables 2.1, A.3, and A.4, draw upon my article "From Labor Law to Employment Law: The Changing Politics of Workers' Rights," *Studies in American Political Development* 33, no. 1 (2019): 50–86, and are reproduced with permission from Cambridge University Press.

For their unwavering support and encouragement, I thank Irene, Tom, Pat, Rachel, and Daniel. To Katie, whose contributions to this project (and all else) are immeasurable, I am grateful beyond words. Eliza, Noah, Hannah, and Sadie inspire me daily with their inquisitive minds, strong convictions, and great senses of humor; I thank them for their boundless enthusiasm.

Finally, once again, I'd like to thank the workers and all those who work so hard on their behalf. This book is dedicated to them.

CHAPTER 1

Introduction: The New Politics of Workers' Rights

NORMAN GREEN, thirty-three, father of eight, arrived at the Most Valuable Personnel (MVP) temporary staffing agency in Cicero, Illinois, in his steel-toed boots, ready to work. It was 4:00 a.m. in early July 2014. Green, a Black man who lived in the adjacent East Garfield Park neighborhood of Chicago, knew that MVP assigned work on a first-come-first-served basis, so he wanted to be listed first on the sign-in sheet. As he waited patiently for his name to be called, he saw numerous Latinx workers arrive and receive work assignments before him. He even saw two MVP recruiter vans arrive and unload twelve to fifteen Latinx laborers from each van. They, too, were assigned work before him. After several hours, an MVP staff member told him to return the next morning, which he did about a dozen times over the next year only to experience the same humiliation each time. Green was not alone: "A lot of Black people just sitting there mad that they can't work," he said. Years of racial bias in the temp staffing industry had hardened racial resentments and fostered antagonism and mistrust between Black and Latinx workers. "I was starting to hate them," said a different Black worker at the MVP temp agency. "I knew that I shouldn't be thinking the way that I was thinking, but I was frustrated and angry."[1]

One of MVP Staffing's largest clients was Gold Standard Baking (GSB), known for producing millions of "melt-in-your-mouth croissants" each week for stores and supermarkets around the country.[2] GSB's demand for labor fluctuated wildly: sometimes GSB would hire more than a hundred temp workers through MVP in a single day. But as one MVP supervisor testified in the class-action discrimination lawsuit later filed by Green and others, "it was common knowledge that GSB did not want to have African Americans at the factory."[3] To evade legal prohibitions against racial discrimination in employment, MVP staff used thinly veiled code words to identify the races of potential workers for their clients. "Guapos" (pretty ones) referred to Black workers "who didn't want to work hard or get their hands dirty," whereas "feos" (ugly ones) meant Latinos, whom MVP's clients perceived to be harder workers.[4] The notion that Black workers did not work hard was not only "clear-as-day racist," but dead wrong, Green said. "Every time I walk into a temp agency I work my butt off."[5]

Anti-Black racism, however, was not the only type of bias in the temporary staffing industry. Many employers found Latinx workers easier to exploit and therefore cheaper to employ. Whether due to their immigration status, language barriers that limited their awareness of their legal rights, or the threat of retaliation, Latinx workers were viewed as less likely to complain when they were not paid what they were legally owed, injured on the job, or mistreated in other ways.[6] Given the immense pressure to reduce costs and cut corners on labor standards in the highly competitive labor markets in which temp agencies operate, the most easily exploitable workers were the most desirable, and temp agencies recruited Latinx workers vigorously.[7] Consequently, workplace injuries and wage-hour violation rates were consistently highest among Latinx workers.[8] Employers routinely assigned Latinx temp workers to dangerous tasks without basic safety training or the necessary protective gear, left them stranded at worksites many miles from home at the end of their shifts, threatened them with violence or deportation, and sexually or physically abused them.

Take Carlos Centeno, a Mexican immigrant who worked as a temp for Raani Corp, a skin cream and shampoo factory a few miles from GSB. During a shift in the spring of 2011, chemicals splashed into Centeno's right eye and blinded him for several days, but he did not report the incident. "I wanted him to quit," said his wife. "But, at the same time, we knew he hadn't found another job yet, and expenses continued, unfortunately, and he had to work."[9] Six months later, a hatch opened on a 500-gallon chemical tank, showering Centeno with 185-degree citric acid solution.

He was wearing no protection other than rubber boots and latex gloves. Centeno suffered scald and chemical burns on 80 percent of his body. Though he was screaming in pain, supervisors failed to call an ambulance or use the available safety shower to wash away residual chemicals and cool his skin; it took ninety-eight minutes for a coworker to finally get him to an emergency room. Three weeks later, Centeno died from the injuries. The temp agency that hired Centeno, Ron's Staffing Service, denied liability, arguing that Raani was responsible for conducting safety training. Raani argued that "by voluntarily undertaking to work with such substances, [Centeno] elected to accept such possible risks."[10]

For low-wage Black and Latinx temp workers in and around Chicago's West Side and Lower West Side, any job was better than no job, but the hazards, rampant discrimination, and multiple forms of exploitation they faced were intolerable. The state was of little help—its enforcement capacity was minimal, and regulators were nowhere to be seen. It had been eighteen years, for example, since the Occupational Safety and Health Administration (OSHA) had last inspected the Raani factory. Nor did temp workers have much recourse through direct economic interventions like strikes, walkouts, or protests, or by applying pressure at the point of production or up the supply chain; since they were viewed by employers as expendable, their labor market power was negligible. Given the transient nature of their jobs, most temp workers found it exceedingly difficult to build relationships with other workers—much less to build collective power to counterbalance the outsize authority of their abusive employers. Without some third-party intermediary to help them come together outside the workplace and organize in collective action, most temp workers remained isolated from one another and vulnerable to mistreatment by their employers.

The Chicago Workers' Collaborative (CWC) was founded in 2000 as a nonprofit, nonunion "worker center" to help fill this void. From the beginning, CWC offered a mix of individualized services, leadership and skills training, and organizing opportunities for mostly Latinx low-wage temp workers. It also sought to support and organize Black temp workers in the area, but built-up resentments between Black and Latinx workers made multiracial community building challenging. "Temp labor seems to have perfected keeping Latinos and African-Americans hating each other instead of working together for the common good," said former CWC executive director Leone Bicchieri.[11]

In 2015, in an effort to demonstrate solidarity with Black temp workers, CWC launched a policy campaign to fight discrimination in the temp industry. The group asked a supporter in the Illinois Legislative Black Caucus to introduce a bill requiring temp agencies to report the race, ethnicity, and gender of every temp worker applicant to the Illinois Department of Labor.[12] The effort received positive media coverage, but the bill was killed after temp industry lobbyists convinced key members of the Illinois Legislative Latino Caucus that the bill would cost Latinx workers jobs.[13] The temp industry had prevailed by yet again using race to divide the Black and Latinx communities. CWC was disappointed but not defeated; the group resolved to try again in the next legislative session.

CWC was but a small, scrappy organization, with only $240,000 in revenue in 2016. But what it lacked in resources it sought to compensate for with "resourcefulness."[14] Over the previous fifteen years, it had assiduously invested in its members, emphasizing deep relational organizing, popular education, and collective consciousness raising. Though its membership base was small, it had built a strong, passionate community; developed a committed cadre of leaders and activists; and forged a robust network of allied groups. It had also developed new organizational capacities, including Raise the Floor Alliance (RTF), a novel umbrella group that CWC, along with seven other Chicago-area worker centers, launched in 2014 to provide legal, communications, policy campaign, and fundraising support to all eight groups.

CWC started the next round of its campaign by redoubling its commitment to organizing. Through a series of racial and gender justice workshops, leadership development trainings, and picnics that brought together Black and Latinx temp workers, it sought to build solidarity across racial, ethnic, and gender lines. The group identified the source of Black and Latinx temp workers' shared problems as the asymmetry of power between employers and employees, the hypercompetitive structure of the temp industry, and the ways in which employers used race, ethnicity, gender, and class to divide, silence, and oppress workers. Feelings of community and solidarity across racial lines reportedly grew as workers developed a "common understanding" and found a "common language."[15] CWC fashioned a straightforward new argument: "Black workers are losing their jobs and Latinos are losing their rights. Only united can [we] hold temp agencies accountable."[16]

The group also sought to build cross-racial solidarity by expanding its policy agenda to include a host of issues that affected Black and Latinx temp workers alike. Workers brainstormed a wish list of policy reforms, including proper training on job hazards to prevent the kind of horrors that befell Centeno, equal pay and benefits for temp workers who did the same work as permanent employees, penalties for retaliation, and more. This wish list became the template for what was referred to colloquially as the Illinois Temp Workers' Bill of Rights.[17]

In coalition with RTF and fellow worker center Warehouse Workers for Justice (WWJ), CWC arranged for a racially diverse group of temp workers to travel to Springfield to testify and educate lawmakers: "We had some really talented women who spoke to the state legislators and were extremely convincing to them," said former executive director Tim Bell. "They were artists. They knew how to do it. They were magical, actually."[18] In meetings with the Latinx and Black caucuses, Latinx and Black workers "led with racial unity," demonstrating that "we don't have a beef with each other, we have a beef with our boss who's getting away with exploitation by using divide-and-conquer tactics to keep us from organizing to improve our conditions," explained Sophia Zaman, executive director of RTF.[19] The bill passed the Illinois General Assembly with supermajorities in both houses and was signed by conservative Republican governor Bruce Rauner without comment on September 22, 2017.[20]

Although the bill was watered down during the legislative process, it still mandated a number of important changes. It required temp agencies to report demographic data on temp placements (but not applicants); notify workers in writing what clothing, protective gear, and training they would need for a particular assignment; provide return transportation for workers brought to a job site; stop charging workers for background checks, drug tests, and credit reports; and, to combat the trend toward low-pay, benefit-free "permatemping," make good-faith efforts to move temp workers into permanent jobs. These amendments reportedly made Illinois's Day and Temporary Labor Services Act one of the "strictest" temp agency regulations in the country.[21]

CWC and its allies celebrated their victory, but they saw trouble on the horizon: because the Illinois Department of Labor did not have the resources or the administrative capacity to proactively investigate temp agencies, it relied on complaints to trigger enforcement. This was seen as a fatal flaw of the regulations. Two years after the law went into effect, one temp worker reported: "People are afraid to complain. . . . They don't want to lose their job."[22] Indeed, as research would soon demonstrate, health and safety practices were not much improved, and two-thirds of the temp agencies in the Chicago area continued to engage in racial discrimination.[23]

The law's shortcomings prompted CWC to pivot to a new round of organizing around enforcement of the law. CWC began by building a task force from a network of allies—labor unions, academics, attorneys, workforce development organizations, public officials, and allied worker centers. The task force set out to create a "Temporary Staffing Agency Seal of Approval" program—a public-private hybrid solution that would combine supply chain pressures and co-enforcement initiatives to improve compliance with the law.[24] The lynchpin of the program was that state, county, and municipal governments would use their purchasing power to create market-based incentives for temp agencies to comply with the law. Each layer of government would promise to contract only with vendors that exclusively used seal-certified temp agencies and to periodically conduct audits to ensure that their procurement systems and supply chains were free of abusive temp agencies. Seal certification for temp agencies would be contingent on demonstrated compliance: independent researchers would conduct periodic matched-pair testing to verify compliance, while worker centers (the "boots on the ground") would train temp workers (the "front-line monitors") on how to report violations. Worker centers would operate a complaint hotline and serve as intermediaries between workers, researchers, and the state.[25]

In other words, to fulfill the promise of the Temp Workers' Bill of Rights, a milestone legislative victory in Springfield was not nearly enough. CWC also had to jury-rig a novel public-private enforcement regime out of whole cloth that asked temp workers, government officials, independent researchers, and worker centers to assume weighty new responsibilities. The whole experiment resembled a Rube Goldberg machine—and it had an uncertain payoff. But what was the alternative? If CWC did not attempt the effort, the Temp Workers' Bill of Rights would be a hollow victory: a new set of protections on paper that had little consequence in practice.

Meanwhile, CWC continued to educate lawmakers and organize around abuses in the temp industry. "Unless we're really vigilant to what happens in state politics," Bell explained, "the temp industry can come and gut the entire law that we have on the books right now. That could happen any session. In fact, they've tried before. So we have to be monitoring it constantly."[26]

In sum, to protect the rights of workers like Norman Green and Carlos Centeno, CWC had undergone an organizational metamorphosis. Without shedding any of its organizing or service provision functions, the group had taken on multiple new obligations. Now, passing new policies, devising complex strategies to ensure compliance with those policies, and vigorously monitoring political conditions in Springfield had become central to its mission. To make workers' rights real, this small, nonunion, nonprofit alt-labor group had to be continuously engaged in politics and policymaking.

This was the new politics of workers' rights.

A New Terrain for Workers' Rights

The case of temp workers in Chicago brings into sharp relief structural shifts in the American economy that have fundamentally altered the nature and experience of work for low-wage workers over the last several decades. Most conspicuous is what has been dubbed the "fissuring" of the workplace, which has dovetailed with the growth of precarious, low-quality jobs at the expense of higher-quality jobs.[27] Amid heightened global economic competition, many U.S. firms have sought to maximize shareholder value by decentralizing employment to focus on core competencies. Through temporary staffing and related strategies—subcontracting, outsourcing, offshoring, third-party management, franchising, and other nontraditional employment models—many firms have passed off the costs and liabilities of employment to smaller companies operating on thin margins in highly competitive labor markets featuring an oversupply of labor.[28] Those smaller companies, facing strong pressures to reduce costs, often respond by failing to pay workers what they are legally owed, bypassing health and safety protocols, and violating other foundational employment laws—as illustrated in the cases of Green and Centeno. Such practices undercut labor standards across entire industries, creating a "race to the bottom" as businesses struggle to compete. Stubbornly high baseline rates of wage-hour violations, discrimination, and health and safety violations are often the result.[29] In addition to illegal employer practices motivated by racism, xenophobia, and sexism, noncompliance with labor standards is a systemic problem in low-wage labor markets—it is a feature, not a bug, of the modern fissured workplace.

The CWC case also spotlights two major historical developments—one institutional, one organizational—that, over the last half century, have transformed the nature of workers' rights and fundamentally altered the pathways available to low-wage workers to combat their exploitation and raise workplace labor standards. They also constitute the primary focus of this book.

The Growth of Employment Law

To combat systemic exploitation in the temporary staffing industry, Chicago-area temp workers turned to the Illinois state legislature. That they could not look to their union for protection was obvious to all because, of course, the temp workers had no union. Although they had a legal right to unionize, the structure of their jobs made unionization all but impossible under extant labor law.[30] So rather than turn to national labor law and seek to raise labor standards through collective bargaining agreements, CWC turned to state-level employment law to strengthen the state's capacity to regulate the temp industry and hold employers accountable to higher employment standards.

CWC's impulse reflected a broader trend: as chapter 2 documents, between the 1960s and the early twenty-first century, as union density declined and New Deal–era labor law became increasingly mismatched to a changing economy, employment laws flourished at the subnational level and expanded into new substantive domains. This development was marked by "a shift away from national labor and employment standards toward standards imposed by state and local governments"—what leading industrial relations scholars have dubbed a "new labor federalism." In contrast to textbook models of decentralization, in which national authority is devolved to local governments, or deregulation, in which governmental rules are removed or reduced, the new labor federalism involves "newly legislating aspects of employment that have seen little regulation at any level of government."[31]

As compared to labor law, employment law is clearly an inferior mechanism for protecting workers' rights. Instead of raising labor standards and establishing dispute resolution mechanisms through union-negotiated collective bargaining contracts, employment laws establish only the most minimal terms and conditions of employment and rely on the blunt mechanisms of regulation and litigation for enforcement. And because most employment laws put the onus on workers to report rights violations—by filing complaints with government agencies or initiating lawsuits—they make heroic assumptions about workers' capacities to root out systemic noncompliance with the law. For the complaint-based system to work, workers must be aware of their rights and enjoy unimpeded access to them. For those most likely to suffer labor standards violations, this is seldom the case. Many low-wage workers, already at higher risk of discrimination, abuse, or harassment due to their immigration status, race, ethnicity, or gender, understandably fear that if they assert their rights, they may be subject to retaliation, termination, or deportation.[32]

What's more, the regulatory and legal systems impose myriad additional costs, financial and otherwise, on workers who choose to pursue litigation or file complaints with government agencies; both paths of redress have been shown to reinscribe ascriptive hierarchies.[33] As shown in chapter 2, the laws are also geographically fragmented across the United States—dispersed unevenly across states and cities—and vary greatly in terms of their substantive content; employment law's complex, multitiered, federated structure adds to the challenges of worker-driven enforcement.[34] These challenges further diminish opportunities for workers to come together and organize. Whereas labor law explicitly promotes collective action in the workplace, employment laws contain no built-in mechanisms for generating solidarity or concerted action among workers or for exercising voice on the job.[35]

Complaint-based regulation is also inherently reactive, triggered only after a violation has occurred, which does little to deter employers from committing violations in the first place. Indeed, because most employment laws contain minimal penalties and government regulatory capacities are often weak, the expected cost of a labor violation from the employer's perspective is nearly zero; their incentive to comply with the law is therefore extremely weak.[36] Government regulatory capacity, moreover, is contingent on budgetary politics, administrative will, and the embrace of strategic enforcement practices by agencies—a combination that seldom materializes. Consequently, worker organizations often find themselves in CWC's position: they may achieve significant policy victories, but without clear paths to enforcement, they are left to fashion fragile public-private partnerships to ensure on-the-ground compliance.[37]

Employment laws, in other words, are not the ideal way to make workers' rights real. While such laws are better than nothing, they privilege those with information and resources (typically professional, high-income white-collar workers) and disadvantage most low-wage workers, among whom Black, Latinx, Asian, and Indigenous workers and immigrants are disproportionately represented. But until an overhaul of national labor law becomes possible, strengthening employment laws and improving their enforcement represents low-wage workers' best hope of recovering some legal protections in the workplace. This is why employment laws are now at the epicenter of the new politics of workers' rights.

The Emergence and Political Development of Alt-Labor

The CWC story also illustrates a major organizational development affecting the politics of workers' rights. As unionization became exceedingly difficult, the quality of low-wage jobs declined, and millions of new immigrants came to the U.S. seeking low-wage work, workers at the bottom of the labor market became increasingly vulnerable to exploitation, discrimination, and abuse in the workplace. With few unions or other existing organizations serving these workers, demand grew for new forms of organization that could offer support. It was in this context that nonunion, nonprofit worker justice organizations ("alt-labor groups") began to emerge to support primarily low-wage immigrant workers and workers of color.[38] These diverse organizations have long offered a variety of services, skills training, advocacy, and opportunities to act collectively with other workers. In a contemporary economy that alienates, atomizes, and physically disperses its workforce, alt-labor groups help low-wage workers come together, build community, and engage in concerted action to combat their exploitation. In analytic terms, they help workers overcome their collective action problems.[39] The number of alt-labor groups has grown from only a handful in the 1990s to between 250 and 300 today.[40]

Over time, a growing number of alt-labor groups have turned to public policy to strengthen workers' rights and protections on a larger scale— and they have been remarkably successful in these endeavors. Alt-labor groups have led hundreds of subnational campaigns to raise the minimum wage, combat wage theft, create paid sick leave, establish predictive scheduling (fair workweek standards), strengthen health and safety laws, fight discrimination and sexual harassment at work, and create domestic workers' and temporary workers' bills of rights. They have also successfully advanced non-workers' rights policies that are of pressing concern to their members— defending immigrants' rights, fighting for racial justice, promoting gender equity, pushing for quality affordable housing, and more. And during the lengthy Covid-19 pandemic, many alt-labor groups secured vital financial relief and new workplace protections for struggling low-wage essential workers and their families.

These policy successes present something of a puzzle. According to standard metrics, most alt-labor groups are severely disadvantaged relative to their opponents (such as employer associations, the business community, and wealthy conservatives), who are typically much larger, better funded, more mobile, and have stronger political connections.[41] Low-wage workers have historically lacked organized representation and are among the least likely to enjoy policy responsiveness from lawmakers.[42] Further, these workers are often socially, economically, and politically marginalized, with many unable to vote due to their lack of U.S. citizenship. When such workers speak out against their mistreatment, they are often subject to retaliation, discrimination, harassment, and threats of termination or deportation—forms of domination that intersect with and are compounded by workers' experiences in race-class subjugated communities, where they face daily threats to their lives and livelihoods from the state and state-backed authorities.[43]

As nonprofit organizations, alt-labor groups also face significant structural and legal limitations: they are prohibited from serving as their members' exclusive bargaining representatives with their employers, and their tax-exempt status limits the extent of their permissible political activities.[44] In addition, because alt-labor groups typically lack large dues-paying memberships, most have come to rely heavily on private philanthropic foundations and other external sources for funding—a precarious and capricious source of revenue that can abrade the groups' core commitments to being member-led, people-powered organizations.[45] How to remain authentically representative of, and accountable to, their membership in the face of such financial dependence is an ongoing challenge.

Given these myriad limitations, how have alt-labor groups managed to make gains for their members in the policymaking arena? As I will discuss, they have been working to augment and leverage their strengths: their deep roots in local communities and the racial and ethnic bonds that unite their members; their organizing skills and their members' fierce determination to fight for economic, racial, and social justice, fueled by their righteous indignation at their exploitation and marginalization; their unique position within the labor movement and in the broader ecosystem of progressive-minded groups; and the flexibility of their organizational forms. By tapping into, developing, and harnessing these strengths, alt-labor groups have been building sources of power they can draw upon to advance their goals.

Despite their impressive policy successes, however, alt-labor groups often find that they are severely constrained by the configuration of political forces in their states and localities. Some of their most significant policy accomplishments are so watered down in the legislative process, poorly enforced, or antagonizing to their opponents that they end up creating additional problems without resolving the very problems they were designed to address.

A growing number of alt-labor groups have responded to these constraints by becoming more politically engaged and undertaking concrete efforts to alter the contours of their political environments. Fastidious about staying well within the legal restrictions on nonprofit political activities, 501(c)(3) alt-labor groups have found that they can still undertake a wide range of permissible civic engagement activities that can alter political dynamics in their localities. In recent years, a growing number have also launched 501(c)(4) "social welfare" organizations that enable them to intervene directly in electoral politics. These groups endeavor to change politics by cultivating more active and engaged citizenries, altering policymakers' incentives, and creating conditions conducive to further policy changes— all efforts aimed at incrementally shifting the balance of power and giving low-wage workers greater influence over the decisions that shape their lives.[46]

Alt-labor's turn to policy and politics does not resolve their internal tensions, organizational challenges, or structural constraints; rather, it reflects and responds to those limitations—while creating new challenges and tensions. Indeed, in assuming the role of political intermediaries—in which they speak on behalf of all low-wage workers in their communities, not just their members—alt-labor groups are embracing a strategy that fits their limitations, accommodates their constraints, and maximizes their resources. However, the more they become like "nonelected neighborhood representatives," the more glaring is their lack of strong mechanisms of accountability.[47] The objective benefits they deliver to their communities may well outweigh the democratic tensions inherent in this model—but these are recent developments and organizers have only just begun to evaluate the trade-offs.[48] In practical terms, pushing the conflict out of the workplace and into the political arena has also added weighty new obligations onto alt-labor groups' already lengthy list of responsibilities—as illustrated in CWC's layering of new political functions on top of its preexisting commitments. Put simply, alt-labor groups have taken on far more work than they are built or equipped to do.

How to manage these tensions, build capacity, develop resilience, compensate for their limitations, and maximize their strengths while making progress for their members? That is the question that animates chapters 3 through 6 of this book.

The Other Half of the Story: Labor Law's Drift, Employment Law, and Alt-Labor

How did we get here? How did we arrive at a place where employment law—rather than labor law—now serves as the primary basis of workers' rights? And where small, under-resourced, overburdened nonprofit alt-labor groups—rather than well-funded, mass-based labor unions—are at the vanguard of organizing some of the most vulnerable workers in collective actions to raise labor standards for all workers?

This, after all, was not how it was supposed to be. The National Labor Relations Act of 1935 (NLRA, "Wagner Act," or "labor law"), one of the cornerstones of Franklin D. Roosevelt's New Deal, was to be the permanent solution to the perennial "labor question," the best way to redress the inequality of bargaining power between the employer and the employee.[49] In 1940, after the Supreme Court had upheld multiple challenges to the law, FDR declared that the "untrammeled right—not privilege, but right—to organize and bargain collectively," now "firmly imbedded in the law of the land . . . must remain as the foundation of industrial relations for all time."[50] Employment laws, such as the Fair Labor Standards Act of 1938, in contrast, were meant to be but a floor—"merely the foundation"—upon which collective bargaining could flourish, argued senator Robert Wagner, labor law's chief sponsor and namesake.[51] But despite strong popular support for unions in the present day, nine of ten U.S. workers—and 94 percent of workers in the private sector—do not belong to a union; they look not to labor law, but to employment law for their rights and protections in the workplace.[52] And for those workers most in need of support and representation—low-wage immigrant workers and people of color working in precarious, low-quality jobs in fissured industries—few labor unions have endeavored to organize them. Oftentimes, the only organizations that offer low-wage workers a chance to exercise their voice, vindicate their rights, and organize in collective action with other similarly situated workers are under-resourced nonprofit alt-labor groups (in the places where they exist) that face major challenges of their own. Clearly, the current workers' rights regime looks very different from the one envisioned by New Dealers.

In any accounting of these historic institutional and organizational shifts, the slow-motion collapse of the collective bargaining regime must play a central role: its failure to achieve its design purposes, after all, underlies our present discontents. Thankfully, the story of labor law's failure and organized labor's decline has been well told by experts writing from a variety of scholarly perspectives. We now have a good grasp of the relative weight of economic and political factors, institutional constraints, cultural shifts, self-inflicted wounds, critical historical junctures, paths not taken, and other complex forces precipitating the decline of the labor law regime.[53] This nuanced scholarship has informed the work of labor law reformers as well, who have in recent years developed ambitious and promising new plans for overhauling labor law based on fine-tuned understandings of what contemporary workers need if they are to build countervailing power and voice in the twenty-first-century workplace.[54]

Oddly, however, the other half of the story—the concomitant growth of the employment law regime and the increased political engagement of alt-labor groups—has not yet been fully told. The links between the decline of the labor law regime, the rise of employment law regime, and the political development of alt-labor groups have not been fully fleshed out or clarified analytically.

That is what this book aims to do. To unpack these developments and examine their significance, I draw upon diverse forms of data (including novel datasets of subnational employment laws, survey data on workers' hours and earnings, local newspapers and periodicals, and in-depth interviews with alt-labor leaders, organizers, and workers) and use a mix of methodological approaches (including both qualitative and quantitative analyses). There is a lot of ground to cover, and I do not endeavor to explain a single outcome; multiple outcomes and developmental processes are of interest. Thus, while some parts of the book inch toward drawing causal inferences, most of the book aims for thick descriptive analysis of alt-labor's development. All of the book seeks to deepen our understanding of a major historical transformation in the politics of workers' rights over the last several decades. But let us begin with the overarching theoretical framework.

The Political Effects of Policy Drift

The rocky, winding path low-wage workers must take to secure protection against exploitation and vindicate their rights will not surprise most observers of the American political economy. The United States, after all, has long been viewed as the quintessential "liberal market economy," featuring highly fluid labor markets, weak employment protections, and labor and employment relations that are regulated by market forces rather than by the strategic interaction of economic organizations. As compared to countries with "coordinated market economies," in which collaborative relations and formal institutional arrangements uphold employment protections and regulate the behavior of firms and unions, precious few such centripetal forces exist in the United States.[55]

Such macroscopic observations put the lack of adequate protections for "cheap labor" and the struggles of low-wage U.S. workers in a valuable comparative context.[56] But that framework is static and cannot explain the historical dynamics of interest here; nor can it provide insight into how and why the institutions and organizations of interest look and act as they do. The picture is helpfully filled out by Kathleen Thelen's important argument that since the 1970s, the United States has offered a "textbook case" of what she calls "deregulatory liberalization," one of three distinctive trajectories of change in which institutions designed for the collective regulation of labor relations—never very strong in the United States to begin with, as the "liberal market economy" categorization reminds us—are dismantled, coverage declines, and what remains is a set of "individualized" legal options that aggrieved workers can pursue.[57] Thelen gives most explanatory weight to the strategic offensive mounted by powerful business interests amid the economic turbulence of the 1970s and 1980s and the absence of a strong, cohesive, underlying coalition of support for the collective bargaining regime found in other countries. Her comparative analysis dovetails with Jacob Hacker's observation that both the government and the corporate sector have since the 1970s shed their midcentury commitments to providing workers with health insurance, pensions, and relative job security, which has contributed to rising income volatility, job instability, and the "privatization of risk."[58]

Deregulatory liberalism helps to explain the shift in the locus of workers' rights from labor law to employment law, and the privatization of risk aptly describes the outcome. But neither explains why labor law remains in force as the primary law governing labor relations in the United States despite its increasing impotence, why employment laws have proliferated despite being so problematic, or why alt-labor organizations have followed the trajectory they have. Nor do they unpack the connections between these developments. Deregulatory liberalism and the privatization of risk, in other words, are not all this is a "case of."

What I wish to argue is that these outcomes also represent a case of policy drift—and more specifically, how drifting policies can shape and constrain the behavior of those on the losing end. Policy drift is when a policy—in this case, national labor law—is not updated to reflect changing external circumstances, and this lack of updating causes the policy's outcomes to shift in sometimes dramatic ways.[59] Drift thus describes a substantial change in a policy's effects without a change in its formal rules due to a transformation of the external context. Scholarship on policy drift has grown considerably over the last two decades as the phenomenon has been observed across a wide range of settings.[60] An underappreciated aspect of policy drift, however, is its effects on those who seek to alleviate the problems that invariably follow in its wake. Looking into the political effects of policy drift across a range of policy domains, Hacker and I have found that drift is both motivating and constraining: it increases demands for policy innovation and organizational change while also limiting the range of possible paths forward and generating new problems and conflicts.[61] As we will see, labor law's drift has produced an environment of constraints and opportunities of which alt-labor groups are well positioned to take advantage, with a range of consequences for the policy regime moving forward. Put differently: policy drift has led to organizational and policy innovation, which has led to new rounds of policy feedback.

Let us begin with the factors producing policy drift. The United States' exceptionally fragmented institutional landscape—riddled with veto points and barriers to policy change—is particularly conducive to policy drift, especially in the context of partisan polarization and gridlock.[62] But drift is not inevitable: plenty of outdated policies get updated or are replaced as needed. Policy drift also requires political strategy—motivated political actors who are determined to leverage their institutional authority to block policy change.[63] When a minority coalition dislikes a policy that is gradually losing efficacy due to changing contextual conditions, it can facilitate the policy's further degradation by simply standing in the way of reforms that would enable the policy to keep pace with changing external circumstances. Given the low threshold to block change in our veto-ridden separation-of-powers system—a minority of forty-one senators to prevent cloture in the Senate, only thirty-four Senate votes to sustain a presidential veto, myriad rules that create choke points in each legislative chamber, and so forth—quieter, lower-salience political strategies like policy drift are unsurprisingly the favored approaches of minority interests (such as businesses) when they oppose popular policies (such as collective bargaining rights).[64] Aligned with a Republican Party that derives significant advantages from the rural bias of the constitutional system, minority business interests have been able to prevent badly needed updates to many regulatory policies without doing much of anything at all.

National labor law offers a case in point.[65] To this day, the NLRA remains the primary federal law governing union-management relations in the private sector. But despite ample evidence that the law has become unable to accomplish its primary purpose of "encouraging the practice and procedure of collective bargaining," the NLRA has not undergone any significant formal legislative revisions since 1959.[66] Despite multiple attempts by unions and their allies to redress deficiencies in the law, overturn restrictive interpretations by the Supreme Court and agencies, and help the law function more effectively amid a changing economy—including ill-fated campaigns during the first two years of the Lyndon B. Johnson, Jimmy Carter, Bill Clinton, Barack Obama, and Joe Biden administrations—opponents have successfully leveraged institutional veto points (mainly, the Senate filibuster) to block those reforms and keep labor law awkwardly fixed in place for over sixty years.[67] Designed for an industrial relations system that no longer exists, the NLRA's rules and procedures for union organizing and collective bargaining—structured around the firm-based "employer-employee dyad"—have become major obstacles for groups of workers who seek collective representation and protection against exploitation in the workplace.[68] By preventing labor law reforms from advancing to a floor vote—and through anticipated reactions, deterring additional reforms from materializing—opponents have ensured that the NLRA would, over time, become ever more mismatched to the changing economy.[69]

Most scholars now view national labor law as an outdated piece of machinery that has grown out of step with the realities of modern work: it has been described as "ossifying," "stagnating," "shrinking" in reach and significance, "ceas[ing] to accomplish its purpose," and "more and more resembl[ing] an elegant tombstone for a dying institution."[70] Through its lack of updating, a policy that was initially designed to enhance workers' bargaining power has been transformed into a policy that now serves business' interests better than those of workers.

The real-life consequences of labor law's drift are plain to see. Despite a recent uptick in the number of unionized workers in select industries, the percentage of all unionized wage and salary workers in the private sector has continued its historical decline—down from 24.2 percent in 1973 to a mere 6 percent in 2022.[71] And whereas the number of large work stoppages averaged over 300 per year between 1946 and 1980, the average dropped to only 17 per year between 2000 and 2021.[72] Most importantly, employees in all industries have become more vulnerable to exploitation and abuse, wage theft, discrimination, uncompensated workplace injuries, political pressure, and more, with those at the bottom of the income scale who have the least bargaining power most at risk.[73]

The direct effects of policy drift are usually widely acknowledged. Less understood is that policy drift also has characteristic political effects. Consider first the effects of policy drift on institutional arrangements.

Policy drift invariably gives rise to new problems; those new problems incentivize those on the losing end to develop new policies to alleviate those problems. But because the political forces that benefit from policy drift remain capable of blocking change, policy innovators are not likely to succeed by pursuing new policies in the same governing venue. Instead, they must seek out alternative political venues in which they are less disadvantaged.[74] In cases of policy drift at the national level, this often means turning to state and local government.[75] The radically decentralized federal system of governance of the United States—composed of fifty states, over three thousand counties, and about forty thousand local municipalities, each with its own governing authorities—offers myriad entry points for groups and interests to try to "organize into politics" new policies designed to mitigate the negative consequences of policy drift.[76] The groups harmed by policy drift should therefore be expected to try to exploit this "extremely complex, spatially dispersed, and decentralized multi-tiered, multi-venue space" to circumvent the drifting policy and build new policies in other venues that can operate alongside the drifting policy and compensate for some of its failures.[77]

But so long as the drifting policy remains in place and authoritative (even if less effective), certain paths forward are likely to be foreclosed or viewed as impractical. Policy innovators must therefore design creative solutions that work around the drifting policy's rules, structures, and procedures. This may require them to develop second-best solutions and design convoluted delivery mechanisms.[78] Moving to new venues, similarly, means confronting different political contexts featuring distinct policy levers, which further complicates the task facing policy innovators. Thus, while policy drift encourages certain kinds of strategies, it also delimits what is possible and may leave those seeking to reduce drift's adverse effects to pursue suboptimal, jury-rigged alternatives. Hacker and I have found that this is a common effect of policy drift, evident not only in the case of labor and employment law but also across a range of domestic social and economic policy arenas including health care, disability insurance, welfare, and housing.[79]

In the case of labor law's drift, one of the biggest constraints policy innovators have faced is the Supreme Court's *Garmon* doctrine, which for over sixty years has interpreted the NLRA as "preempting" states and localities from experimenting with stronger labor laws that might alleviate some of the NLRA's problems.[80] States were permitted to design their own labor laws only for those workers excluded from coverage under the Wagner Act, such as public-sector and agricultural workers.[81] To provide stronger rights and protections to a wider range of workers, states would need to find alternative routes for doing so; the Wagner Act was to be the primary, authoritative, centralized labor law in the United States that would enjoy an effective monopoly on the process of collective bargaining and unionization for the vast majority of workers. National labor law has thus long exerted a powerful, jealous, and continuous governing authority over its expansive domain even as it has declined in effectiveness. As Cynthia Estlund writes, labor law has been "essentially sealed off—to a remarkably complete extent and for a remarkably long time—both from democratic revision and renewal and from local experimentation and innovation."[82] This has effectively boxed in workers' rights advocates and limited their options, profoundly influencing the form and content of the new policies they have developed in response to labor law's drift.

As detailed in chapter 2, beginning in the 1960s, labor unions and other advocates adapted to labor law's drift by pursuing many of the same substantive outcomes that they had traditionally sought through collective bargaining—such as higher wages and better terms and conditions of employment—through alternative institutional vehicles in other venues. With reform blocked at the national level, they turned to subnational venues to further workers' rights; because labor law preemption prohibited the creation of new subnational labor laws to regulate labor-management relations, they turned to employment laws to mandate higher standards in employment relations. And because they could not create enforcement mechanisms via collective bargaining procedures, they turned to regulation and litigation to do so.

These efforts to circumvent national labor law have proved to be highly consequential, both for the substance of workers' rights and for the labor movement. As noted earlier, although employment laws are better for workers than nothing at all, they are inferior to labor law in almost every way: in terms of the strength of the protections they extend to workers, the costs they impose on workers who seek to redress their grievances, and their enforcement mechanisms.

In addition, the highly decentralized structure of governance in the United States has acted as a sieve for workers' rights, fragmenting them—and the movement to strengthen workers' rights—geographically. While some state legislatures have constructed stronger and more extensive employment law regimes, others have enacted only a handful of laws touching on a few substantive areas. Regional patterns have emerged over time: Southern and plains states, for example, lag far behind states in other regions; California, meanwhile, has enacted more than four times the average number of state-level employment laws. From place to place, workers' rights now vary wildly; when workers change jobs or move to a different jurisdiction, they can easily lose rights they may have previously long enjoyed. If a worker at the McDonald's in Chicago's East Side neighborhood were to transfer to the McDonald's in East Chicago, Indiana—a mere fifteen-minute drive down US-20 across the state border—she would lose more than half her hourly wages, all of her accrued paid sick leave time, her predictable work schedule, her anti-retaliation protection, and more.

Shifting to the subnational level also means that workers' rights advocates have had to contend with differing political dynamics and adversaries from state to state. In some states, reformers have found strong labor federations, robust worker-friendly coalitions of progressive groups, sympathetic governors, and favorable legislative majorities, usually controlled by Democrats. In other states, they have had to build new coalitions from scratch, search long and hard to find champions in government, and work to persuade reluctant governors to enforce new employment policies that managed to pass. In still other states—typically those controlled by Republicans—they have faced vigorous efforts to roll back workers' rights and preemption laws that block local worker-friendly policy initiatives. In such contexts, workers' advocates tend to assume a more defensive posture and must fight to preserve what few rights and protections still exist; some have creatively leveraged their support in more progressive cities and counties to develop innovative workarounds on issues that are not preempted by state legislatures. Again, comparing Chicago's East Side neighborhood with the nearby city of East Chicago, Indiana, is instructive: whereas workers' advocates in Chicago have long benefitted from a robust and broad-based workers' rights movement, more conservative political conditions in Indiana have hindered the labor movement in that state.[83] The constraints imposed by labor law's drift, in other words, have significantly influenced the content, form, and spatial distribution of protections extended through employment law while creating complex new problems for those seeking to improve the conditions of work.

The second characteristic political effect of policy drift involves political organizations: by creating new incentives and constraints, drift tends to alter the constellation of organized interests in the policy space.[84] Among other effects, it creates strong incentives for new groups to form to help those suffering from the adverse consequences of drift. As Paul Pierson writes in his seminal work on policy feedback, policies can "create niches for political entrepreneurs, who may take advantage of incentives to help 'latent groups' overcome collective action problems."[85] The same is true in the context of drift. As the drifting policy gradually ceases to function as intended, some groups of people are left behind; this creates a "niche" or void waiting to be filled, thereby presenting an organizing opportunity for enterprising actors.

But the environment created by policy drift is likely to be more hospitable to some groups than others; those that emerge in this context are likely to face a distinctive set of challenges. First, the new groups must find an alternate path around the drifting policy to address the problems facing the underserved groups. Second, they must identify reliable sources of organizational sustenance not already monopolized by old groups. And third, because there are usually multiple forces causing the "losers" amid policy drift to be left behind, those constituencies are likely to face multiple, intersecting challenges, and organizing and supporting them may require significant creativity and ingenuity.

In the late 1970s, as the effects of labor law's drift became increasingly apparent, millions of low-wage workers (including tens of millions of new immigrant workers seeking low-wage work) became increasingly vulnerable to exploitation and abuse.[86] Many of these workers found it exceedingly difficult to organize into unions given the fragmented nature of their occupations, their nonstandard employment status, or their geographic dispersion (such as temp workers, taxi drivers, and fast-food workers); others were denied collective bargaining rights under labor law's exclusionary provisions (such as domestic workers, independent contractors, farm workers, and day laborers); and still others did not know their rights or felt unable to assert them without fear of legal trouble (such as undocumented immigrants and some nonnative English speakers). Many sought help from preexisting organizations. But most labor unions, scrambling to survive amid labor law's drift, did not dedicate significant resources to organizing hard-to-reach low-wage workers in fissured industries, nor did they endeavor to foster new organizations that might help those who were being left behind amid a changing economy.[87] Beginning in the 1990s, new groups emerged to start filling the void. Some were formed by low-wage workers themselves, while others were founded by preexisting organizations that "backed into" organizing around workers' rights in response to low-wage workers' growing need for support and advocacy.[88] The first generation of alt-labor groups— experimental forms known as worker centers—thus "sprung from a common desire for a local organization that would provide services, conduct advocacy, and encourage organizing on the part of low-wage workers in the absence of anything else," writes Janice Fine in her seminal book.[89]

Because unionization has long been difficult or impossible for so many vulnerable low-wage workers, alt-labor's primary challenge, from the beginning, has been to identify solutions that circumvent labor law and do not involve unionization or collective bargaining. The first move in this direction was for alt-labor groups to select organizational forms that accommodated these constraints. Because the union form—501(c)(5) under the tax code—would have been of little help to the populations they sought to support in the context of labor law's drift, they gravitated toward the nonprofit organizational form under the tax code. Having nonprofit status suited their purposes for several reasons. First, it fit worker centers' commitment to organizing, service provision, and advocacy—all standard 501(c)(3) "charitable" functions.[90] Second, those that "backed into" workers' rights were already registered as "c3s"; they simply added new functions. Third, the nonprofit form was conducive to fundraising. Because unions rarely offered funding to alt-labor groups, and because those groups failed to build mass-membership dues-based systems of their own, alt-labor turned to alternative funding sources—such as philanthropic foundations, private donors, and the government—for which the nonprofit designation was necessary to receive grants. In recent years, a growing number of groups have also founded "sister" entities under the 501(c)(4) "social welfare" section of the tax code, in part because doing so offers a new and potentially lucrative funding stream. 501(c)(4) groups can raise unlimited amounts of money from anonymous donors and can spend a larger share of those funds on explicitly political purposes. Finally, the nonprofit form granted the groups significant flexibility. Although it forbade alt-labor groups from doing some things that unions could do (for example, serving as workers' exclusive bargaining representative in negotiations with employers), it enabled them to do other things that labor unions could not do (such as engage in secondary boycotts, picket to pressure employers, receive anonymous tax-deductible donations, and more).[91]

For all these reasons, the groups became nonprofit organizations and have remained that way since. Many leaders and organizers express discomfort with the "nonprofit industrial complex" and readily note the contradiction of pursuing transformative structural change from within a heavily state-regulated organizational form while receiving money from undemocratic, unaccountable foundations whose extreme wealth depends on the preservation of the status quo. But they are also acutely aware that the alternative to alt-labor nonprofit groups is probably not a vibrant poor people's movement—it is probably nothing.[92]

Nonprofit alt-labor groups have thus come to serve as the primary organizational vehicles for low-wage workers fighting for their rights outside the labor law regime. While many alt-labor groups encourage workers to unionize and take advantage of section 7 of the NLRA, which protects "concerted activities" (such as discussing shared problems with coworkers), their primary focus has never been unionizing individual worksites.[93] Wary of raising the ire of opponents who view them as "union front organizations," these groups have been careful to avoid even the appearance of serving as workers' exclusive bargaining representatives with employers.[94]

To help nonunionized workers, alt-labor groups have long offered a wide range of individual services, including support for workers as they navigate the employment law claims-making process and labyrinthine legal system. But because employment law remedies are often so woefully inadequate, the groups have also sought out more creative ways to help their members fight back against exploitation and oppression, such as helping workers organize collective actions in the public sphere. Their signature strategy is the "workplace justice campaign," also known as "direct action," wherein groups of aggrieved and allied workers gather at a particular worksite to bring maximal public attention to their employers' abusive or exploitative behavior and boost their leverage in demanding redress. They often orchestrate spectacular public demonstrations, disruptive actions, boycotts, and other public shaming strategies to bring their employers to heel. They also seek to disrupt production processes and apply leverage at pivotal points in supply chains in order to raise labor standards—best exemplified by the successful years-long campaign by the Coalition of Immokalee Workers (CIW) to pressure brand-name restaurants to add a "penny per pound" to their tomato orders to improve the labor conditions of farmworkers.[95]

But examples like the CIW campaign are incredibly rare. Although direct actions against individual unscrupulous employers are often successful, aggregating the effects of individual worksite campaigns has proved extremely difficult; workplace justice campaigns rarely have ripple effects across industries or geographies.

The limited reach and minimal impact of these strategies has therefore prompted many groups to turn to public policy and strategic political engagement to scale up their work. This turn to policy and politics—the central focus of the second half of this book—is thus a learned behavior that represents an attempt to step out of the shadow of the labor law regime and into an arena in which alt-labor groups can create meaningful, durable change "at scale" for their members. Thus, both in their organizational forms (the gravitation toward nonprofit status) and in the content of their activities (services, direct actions, policy campaigns, and political engagement), alt-labor groups' development has been shaped by labor law's drift.

Of course, it was not preordained that alt-labor groups would emerge to organize and advocate for low-wage workers who needed help. It is not inevitable that any enterprising actor or group will emerge to help those who are left behind by a drifting policy: demand for entrepreneurship does not automatically generate its own supply. Although many alt-labor groups have emerged to organize and support low-wage workers, the vast majority of these workers in the United States still lack organized support.

But when new groups do emerge to support those left behind amid policy drift, they face characteristic challenges, as previously noted: they must find ways to circumvent the drifting policy (this is alt-labor's emphasis on services, direct action, and public policy instead of collective bargaining), identify new revenue streams (this is alt-labor's turn to private foundations for funding), and develop creative strategies to address what are likely to be multiple, intersecting challenges facing their underserved constituencies (this involves alt-labor's power-building and political activities).

Who is likely to be left behind by policy drift? In a U.S. polity characterized by deeply embedded racial hierarchies and systems of oppression, there is a good chance that the groups on the losing end of policy drift are also some of the same groups of people who have been systematically disadvantaged by national and subnational policies that were designed (and/or administered) to discriminate against them on the basis of their race, ethnicity, citizenship status, and/or gender. Marginalized groups are rarely excluded from one policy alone; they are often excluded from multiple policies simultaneously on account of their ascribed characteristics.[96] Each exclusion—from, say, equity in education or access to credit and other wealth-building opportunities—can compound the effects of exclusion from other policies—say, social insurance or labor rights—causing long-lasting social and economic injustices for entire groups of people.[97] In the United States, of course, the compounded effects of these exclusions have hit Black communities hardest; they have also significantly harmed undocumented immigrants, women, Native Americans, and other communities of color.[98]

These cumulative inequalities and historically embedded power asymmetries are perhaps most evident in the places where many marginalized groups live and often work—in what Joe Soss and Vesla Weaver have termed "race-class subjugated" communities.[99] These communities are "positioned at the intersection of race and class systems," wherein "these two dimensions of power relations remain thoroughly entwined in experiences of civic ostracism, social and political oppression, economic marginalization, and state-led governance."[100] Residents of these communities are poor; they are members of marginalized groups; and they live under the constant threat of the coercive power of the state in the form of the police (through surveillance, coercion, containment, repression, and violence), Immigrations and Customs Enforcement (ICE) officials (via containment and deportation), and other powerful governmental and nongovernmental entities that are often backed up by the state, such as landlords, creditors, and employers.[101] Layered atop these oppressive power relations are the pernicious effects of occupational segregation, which result in persistent racial, ethnic, and gender wage gaps, inequalities of opportunities, and differential rates of wage theft that disproportionately harm communities of color and noncitizens.[102] Race-class subjugated communities thus experience the deleterious, historically constructed, and compounded effects of racial discrimination, economic exploitation, and social and political domination on a daily basis. Groups seeking to organize those on the losing end of policy drift, in other words, face the difficult challenge of responding not only to the direct negative policy effects of drift but also to the ways in which these effects compound the other challenges their members face.

All of this accurately characterizes the experiences of millions of low-wage workers who have been mistreated at work and the efforts of alt-labor groups to organize and support them. Exploitation and subjugation, however, is not the end of the story. As we will see, many of the same structural and historical forces that have compounded the challenges facing racially and economically marginalized low-wage workers are also conducive to new modes of power building, new forms of collective action, and new methods of redress. Indeed, my findings run contrary to the predominant scholarly view that the geographic concentration of disadvantage in race-class subjugated communities "leave[s] racial and ethnic minorities not only economically marginalized but also geographically isolated and politically disempowered."[103] As Jamila Michener and Soss and Weaver argue, by emphasizing the multiple sources of disadvantage that affect racially and economically marginalized communities, many scholars have overlooked the "democratic possibilities" of such communities and obscured the ways in which they can be "resourceful, creative, and deliberate political actors."[104] The evidence in this book supports this more hopeful take, pointing to several "wellsprings of political agency, resistance, and solidarity that emerge in response" to workers' marginalization.[105]

In sum, even as they alleviate some of policy drift's most harmful consequences, the new institutions and organizations that emerge in its wake tend to be riddled with complex problems. As second-best solutions, they reflect the constraints imposed by drift in their makeshift forms and functions, and they give rise to new problems without fully solving the problems produced by policy drift in the first place. The new groups that emerge in this context thus have strong incentives to develop innovative solutions that circumvent the drifting policy and address their constituents' problems, new and old—even if those strategies also bring new challenges of their own. That, in a nutshell, is the story of alt-labor's turn to policy and politics.

Alt-Labor's Turn to Policy and Politics: Challenges and Tensions

To be sure, even the earliest worker centers saw the appeal of public policy as a means of challenging employers' outsize power.[106] But only over the last dozen years or so have policy and politics become central to many alt-labor groups' day-to-day operations and forward-looking strategies. In certain respects, it is unsurprising that vulnerable low-wage workers, lacking economic power, would turn to the government for assistance. "It is the *loser* who calls in outside help," political scientist Elmer Eric Schattschneider wrote frankly in his classic 1960 text. "It is the weak, not the strong, who appeal to public authority for relief." More powerful interests "want *private settlements* because they are able to dictate the outcome as long as the conflict remains private," he wrote, whereas "it is the weak who want to socialize the conflict, i.e., to involve more and more people in the conflict until the balance of forces is changed. In the school yard it is not the bully, but the defenseless smaller boys who 'tell the teacher.' When the teacher intervenes the balance of power in the school yard is apt to change drastically. It is the function of public authority to *modify private power relations by enlarging the scope of conflict.*"[107] With relatively little bargaining power in the workplace, low-wage workers have done exactly this—appealed to public authority for relief. They have sought to change the balance of power by shifting the conflict with abusive employers out of the shadows of the "private government" of the workplace and into the public political arena, where they stand a fighting chance of influencing outcomes.[108]

Despite their myriad disadvantages and weaknesses, alt-labor groups have been remarkably successful in the policymaking arena. "Considering that most worker centers are tiny organizations with a handful of paid staff and modest financial resources," writes Ruth Milkman, summarizing the view of most observers, "their record of legislative and public policy accomplishments is extremely impressive."[109] To verify these impressions, I examined every minimum wage, paid sick leave, and fair workweek law enacted in 102 cities and counties between 2003 and 2019 and found that alt-labor groups were cited as leading advocates in 72 percent of these campaigns.[110] But as examples throughout this book attest, those three policies only scratch the surface of alt-labor's accomplishments. Alt-labor groups have also led dozens of successful policy campaigns to combat wage theft, strengthen health and safety laws, fight discrimination and sexual harassment, and create domestic workers' and temporary workers' bills of rights (as in the CWC case)—as well as to defend immigrants' rights, fight for racial justice, and combat other problems affecting their communities.

Given their many disadvantages and challenges—their diminutive size, their lack of resources, their marginalized, overworked members, and more—alt-labor groups' policy successes present something of a puzzle. How to explain the ability of these groups to make headway for their members in the political arena?

Part of the answer involves structural features of the American political system—such as its highly decentralized form of federalism and its largely inattentive public—that enable well-organized minorities to strategically select favorable local governing venues and seize windows of opportunity when they arise.[111] As Fine recognized, these features have long enabled low-wage immigrant workers, despite their disadvantaged status in American society, to build and exercise greater political than economic power.[112] Fine emphasized how these workers rely on organization, alliance, and public empathy to win unlikely policy victories; I endeavor to build on her first two insights here.[113] Most subsequent scholarship has tended to emphasize the third—the public empathy aspect—showing how across a range of contexts, marginalized workers have gained political traction by using "symbolic leverage," drawing upon their "moral authority," and raising public awareness of their plight to build empathy and popular support for policy change.[114]

To be sure, workers' stories of exploitation are critical ingredients in most successful policy campaigns—they are particularly helpful in generating favorable media coverage and in persuading legislators to support policy change. But that leverage often comes late in the game, once the groups have already gotten their issues on the agenda. Moreover, stories of exploitation are not especially empowering to members outside of those contexts. Not only are alt-labor groups loath to rely on the vicissitudes of public opinion to advance the cause of workers' rights, but they are not particularly eager to reinforce a narrative in which low-wage workers are framed as helpless victims dependent on the goodwill of others. As Marcela Diaz, executive director of Somos Un Pueblo Unido in New Mexico, explained, "Right now there's a public narrative about immigrants being incredibly vulnerable victims. But our members don't feel that way. In everything we do, we ask: Where are *we* coming from? How can we get people to support the *strength* in our community and to support organizations like ours and people like us who are actually moving things forward?"[115]

For a growing number of alt-labor groups, resolving this puzzle has become a central preoccupation: How to build and exercise power in the political arena without relying on the moral/empathy frame?

To learn how groups approach this difficult task, I conducted in-depth, semi-structured interviews (and direct observation, where possible) with over four dozen leaders and members of thirty alt-labor groups scattered about the country, using a diverse case-selection strategy to maximize variance along multiple dimensions of group characteristics and political contexts—a common case-selection technique for the purpose of exploratory and descriptive analysis.[116] Analytically, I seek to leverage this diversity to draw out patterns common to all (or most) groups. I studied younger and older groups; poorer groups and better-funded ones; groups in every region of the country; some with a local focus, some that work at the state level, and some that work across multiple states; groups in Democratic, Republican, or mixed states; organizations with a single industrial focus as well as those whose members span multiple industries; stand-alone groups, groups that are affiliated with one or more major alliance, and those that are, themselves, umbrella groups; groups that are registered under the tax code as 501(c)(3) organizations and those that are registered as 501(c)(4) organizations; and groups that self-identify as worker centers as well as those that do not (see tables 1.1 and A.1).

Despite significant variation in the groups and their contexts, some clear patterns emerge. First, all groups are deeply engaged in efforts to build power. But the type of power they build is different from the conventional understanding of power as power over others. They build generative or productive power—which also may be conceptualized as building capacity or the power to.[117] Their power-building strategies are diverse, fluid, and not easily parsed. But for analytical purposes, they can be thought of as operating on two levels—at the level of the individual and at the level of the organization. At the individual level, alt-labor groups undertake concerted efforts to empower members, develop their skills, build community, and formulate collective issue agendas. At the organizational level, they work to build coalitions with allies and develop organizational innovations that expand the groups' reach and magnify their influence. Both types of power building look to compensate for alt-labor's weaknesses by augmenting and leveraging its strengths. By tapping into, developing, and harnessing these strengths, alt-labor groups are building sources of power they can draw upon to ratchet up their political engagement.

The second pattern that stands out is that many of the factors that disadvantage low-wage workers in the labor market and in the political arena also provide them with the resources and opportunities to fight back. Consider: (1) the exploitation and discrimination they face, (2) the groups' local rootedness, and (3) the unfriendly political contexts in which many groups operate.

Exploitation and abuse in the workplace not only extract resources from vulnerable populations but take a large psychological and physical toll on those who are affected. Those costs are compounded by, and interrelated with, the racism, xenophobia, sexism, and social and political domination many low-wage workers experience on a regular basis. Taken all together,

Table 1.1 Variation among Alt-Labor Groups in Study

	Characteristic	Number of Groups
Age	Founded 2007 or earlier	13
	Founded after 2007	17
Region	Northeast	8
	Midwest	6
	West	11
	South	5
Geographic reach	Local	12
	State	11
	Multistate	7
State partisan context	Democratic	14
	Mixed	8
	Republican	9
Industrial focus	Single	6
	Multiple	24
Network affiliation	Yes	17
	No	9
	Own network	4
Annual revenue	Under $500,000	8
	$500,000–$2,000,000	15
	Over $2,000,000	7
Worker center	Yes	11
	No	12
	Amalgam	4
	Alliance	3

Source: Author's compilation.

Note: "State partisan context" indicates which political party controlled state government during most years of the group's existence, with emphasis placed on control of both houses of the state legislature. "Mixed" indicates divided/alternating control or that the organization works in multiple states with varying partisan contexts. "Geographic reach" indicates the group's organizing purview. "Worker center" indicates whether the group self-identifies as a worker center. For full list of groups included in the study, see table A.1.

these experiences can be debilitating.[118] But at the same time, alt-labor groups have found that bringing workers together and collectively unearthing shared experiences of mistreatment and subjugation can be empowering for individual workers and instrumental in building solidarity, formulating policy agendas, and fostering collective action among workers of different racial and ethnic backgrounds who work in diverse and dispersed occupations.[119] These community-building and issue agenda–building efforts—discussed in chapters 4 and 5—are critical to overcoming barriers to mobilization in the political arena. Experiences of oppression, in other words, can also be harnessed to build power with others who are similarly situated.

Alt-labor groups' local rootedness presents another challenge.[120] In part, the problem is their geographic dispersion: being physically scattered across the country makes it more difficult to combine forces, reduce redundancies, and learn from one another's successes and failures. One way groups are working to address this is by building coalitions and establishing national and regional capacity-sharing networks. Alliances and networks enable them to share knowledge across geographic boundaries, generate efficiency gains, and magnify their collective influence. Some groups are also experimenting with organizational innovations, including using new technologies to organize low-wage workers at scale, launching novel capacity-sharing entities, and creating regional multi-entity "movement hubs" to incubate new organizational forms and generate synergies across groups. In other words, through coalition and organization building, many groups are learning, growing, and reaching more broadly than their small size and local rootedness might suggest. These efforts are discussed in chapter 5.

Another challenge stemming from the groups' local rootedness is that they are forced to contend with potentially unfriendly political contexts in their states, counties, and localities. The preemption of local policies by hostile state legislatures is a related challenge that limits the groups' policy options and strains their capacities in many Republican-leaning (red) and politically mixed (purple) states.[121] But even groups in Democratic-leaning (blue) states often find it difficult to identify reliable champions in the Democratic Party, and their policy accomplishments often fall short of expectations. These constraints and frustrations have steeled the resolve of many alt-labor groups to become more politically engaged—to build civic power and take concrete steps to alter the political context in which they are situated. Although each group prioritizes different activities depending on its nonprofit status, political environment, proximate goals, and level of resources, some general patterns can be observed among the groups that have become more politically engaged. I find that all are working to build new electorates; influence candidate selection processes; and expand local government capacities to facilitate "policy fit."[122] Each of these political activities is elaborated in chapter 6.

In these ways and more, alt-labor groups are designing strategies around their disadvantages in ways that maximize their strengths. Some of their biggest limitations and constraints—their members' subjugation and exploitation, their local rootedness, and unfriendly political environments—offer the raw materials for developing what John Gaventa has called "consciousness of the needs, possibilities, and strategies of challenge."[123] In other words, while this is a case of systemic disadvantage and exploitation, it is also a case of creative adaptation and power building in the face of adversity.

Alt-labor's growing emphasis on policy and politics, however, has not resolved the internal tensions with which the groups continually struggle. In particular, their size and resource challenges have become mutually reinforcing. Due to their small, poor membership base, the groups have turned to philanthropic foundations for organizational sustenance, which has reduced the pressure to build a mass base from which to collect dues and forced the groups into a vicious cycle of external financial dependence. As I discuss in chapter 3, this dependency has created cross-pressures to be responsive both to their members and to their funders, testing their commitment to being people-powered organizations.[124]

The turn to policy and politics does little to address these accountability questions. Instead, by "enlarging the scope of conflict," it effectively shifts the burden of responsiveness to elected officials. The question of how closely the groups' activities align with their members' priorities as opposed to the priorities of foundations is sidelined and the key questions become whether government officials are responsive to the broader race-class subjugated communities in which their members live, whether the policy agenda reflects the community's most pressing concerns, and whether the state is properly and adequately enforcing the law. Alt-labor's role is to hold those officials accountable to their members and the broader communities in which they live. The extent to which alt-labor can authentically speak on behalf of the broader community, however, remains an open question.[125] In the role of political intermediary, alt-labor risks becoming more like a special interest group than a people-powered community-based organization—a possibility that threatens to pull the groups away from their core commitments while compounding their challenges of representation.[126] Most groups are struggling to fulfill both functions, and each wrestles with its challenges differently. The variation is described in chapters 3 through 6, while drawing out the common trends observed across groups.

In sum, constrained by an increasingly ineffective but obtrusive labor law, challenged by structural constraints, and frustrated by their limited ability to make gains at scale via traditional activities such as individual services and workplace justice campaigns, a growing number of alt-labor groups have turned to politics and policy to combat the systemic exploitation of low-wage workers. Taking the political path has required the groups to build up their own sources of power in order to increase their leverage in the political arena. Employing a variety of tactics, they have sought to compensate for their weaknesses by augmenting their strengths. As we will see, some groups have achieved surprising policy successes and have made incremental progress toward their long-term goal of shifting the balance of power toward low-wage immigrant workers and workers of color.

While their progress thus far has been impressive, especially given the disadvantaged position from which they started, it has also been geographically scattered and substantively limited. The American political economy remains heavily stacked against these workers. Their adversaries are far more powerful, far more resourceful, and far more likely to win in any open conflict. Alt-labor groups' members are fighting back after already "hitting rock bottom," as one organizer put it, with "nothing left to lose."[127] They have risked their lives working in dangerous and deadly conditions, had their wages stolen, been sexually harassed or abused, suffered physical violence, and been belittled and disrespected. They have worked in extreme heat, lost fingers, been badly injured, and seen friends die from Covid-19, which they contracted at work because they could not work remotely or afford to take time off. They have been terminated, deported, and seen their loved ones deported because they complained about their reprehensible conditions at work. The alt-labor groups that organize them, support them, and help them fight for their rights are small, relatively poor, and only number between 250 and 300. Most low-wage workers still lack support. In other words, alt-labor's political development is a fascinating new development but it does not give reason to be overly sanguine about the position of low-wage workers in the contemporary American political economy. The fight for workers' rights remains an uphill battle.

This chapter has sought to emphasize the structural features and historical factors that have shaped the current crisis facing low-wage workers and delimited their range of potential paths forward. These factors bring the core dynamics of the present case into sharp relief, revealing it to be a "case of" (1) the political effects of policy drift; and (2) locally rooted, scrappy non-profit groups designing strategies around their structural disadvantages to maximize their strengths. In their efforts to build power among low-wage immigrant workers and workers of color, alt-labor groups demonstrate the important role community-based organizations can play in helping such workers organize in collective action, even in the face of great adversity.

Before we explore further alt-labor's emergence (chapter 3), development (chapter 4), power building (chapter 5), and political engagement (chapter 6), chapter 2 explores the proliferation of subnational employment laws since the early 1960s—the flawed but indispensable institutions around which the politics of workers' rights now revolve. Before the 1960s, leading employment law scholars have written that "there was no such thing as employment law."[128] By 2014, states had enacted over 7,250 statutes governing aspects of the employment relationship that union contracts ostensibly would have covered had unions not entered a period of steady decline amid labor law's drift. Understanding this transformation in the nature of workers' rights, and how it came to be, is the question to which we turn our attention next.

CHAPTER 2

The Changing of the Guard from Labor Law to Employment Law

IN THE 1960S, as New Deal–era national labor law started to "ossify" and "drift" and labor unions entered a period of steady decline, employment law began to blossom, proliferating at the state level and expanding into new substantive domains.[1] In all fifty states, legislatures enacted laws to protect workers against exploitation and enable those who had been aggrieved to recover some recompense. Each subsequent decade, states passed a greater number of employment laws; between 1960 and 2014, an astounding 7,250 employment laws were passed. These laws established higher wages for workers, set ceilings on hours, protected workers' civil liberties on the job, barred multiple forms of discrimination, and improved the terms and conditions of work.

Through the legislative process, workers' advocates and their allies in state government thus found a way to circumvent the still authoritative but increasingly ineffective national labor law to create the same types of substantive rights and protections that might have otherwise been established through collective bargaining agreements. The main difference was that these employment laws provided workers with only the bare-bones minimums in terms of wages, hours, and terms and conditions of employment. With collective bargaining, what workers can accomplish is limited only by the extent of their unions' bargaining power. Employment laws also require workers to navigate labyrinthine legal and regulatory pathways to vindicate their rights—rather than turn to their union representative and pursue mediation.

Today, 90 percent of workers in the United States do not have collective bargaining agreements; they must look instead to this elaborate catalog of employment laws for their rights and protections. Though these laws are blunt instruments, scattered unevenly across the fifty states, and often woefully underenforced, they serve as the primary guardians of workers' rights in the early twenty-first century.[2] For most workers, they offer the only available legal pathways to redress wrongs committed against them in the "private government" of the American workplace.[3]

This state of affairs represents the complete inversion of the industrial relations framework envisioned by the founders of the New Deal labor law regime. Employment laws established "by government fiat" were meant to be "merely the foundation upon which can be built the mutual efforts of a revived industry and a rehabilitated labor," said Senator Robert F. Wagner, the chief sponsor of the NLRA. "The working out of most arrangements in the American industrial complex must be left in the field of private management-labor relations."[4]

This historic inversion of the primary institutional bases of workers' rights has had serious implications not only for the substance of workers' rights, but also for the new politics that have developed around them. This is because, as Schattschneider famously wrote, "new policies create a new politics"—not only are policies shaped by politics, but policies often shape subsequent political dynamics in turn.[5] As this chapter begins to sketch out—and subsequent chapters elaborate—workers and their advocates have directed a growing share of their attention to these laws at every stage of the game: to the legislative politics surrounding their enactment, the electoral politics lurking behind the legislative process, the organizational and behavioral politics that lie beneath those electoral and legislative processes, and the enforcement of the laws after they are passed. Indeed, a core argument of this book is that employment laws now serve as the locus of significant political organization and collective action, especially among low-wage workers most in need of the new laws' protection.[6]

And yet, there is a paradox at the heart of the new politics of workers' rights. Employment laws are predicated on a highly individualized conception of rights. Their growth has been part and parcel of the neoliberal turn in American politics—well captured by Kathleen Thelen's concept of "deregulatory liberalization" and Jacob Hacker's "privatization of risk"—involving the breakdown of institutions designed to socialize risk across citizens of varied circumstances "in favor of arrangements that leave individuals and their families responsible for coping with social risks largely on their own."[7] Employment laws leave individual workers to fend for themselves—each person must be aware of their rights, know when those rights have been violated, and be sufficiently motivated (and have sufficient resources) to activate regulatory or judicial processes to vindicate those rights. Consequently, as scholars, workers, and organizers have repeatedly found, employment laws tend to have an atomizing effect on complainants; they push aggrieved workers down isolating, alienating pathways of redress.[8] Ellen Berrey, Robert Nelson, and Laura Beth Nielsen find in their large random sample of discrimination case filings that 93 percent of cases were brought by a sole plaintiff; in only 4 percent of cases was a group claim of disparate impact made.[9] "This statistical reality sets up the individualized treatment of rights claims," they write, "in which defendants are likely to treat the claim of one individual as not credible or as an aberration within the organization."[10] To the extent that each worker's experience of exploitation in the workplace is viewed as private and distinct from all others, workers' abilities to perceive systemic abuses in their industries may be impaired as well, making collective action and organization more difficult. Unlike labor law, which aids in the creation of collective rights and steers workers toward collective organization and group action at nearly every turn, employment law steers workers toward individual legal solutions. "But that's antithetical to group action," one worker center director told me. "It's antithetical to organizing." Any effort to organize workers collectively around employment laws therefore requires a strategic approach that is attentive to this paradox. For example, as we will see, alt-labor groups almost always begin with community-building workshops that seek to break down the individualizing assumptions inherent in the employment law regime.

Before exploring further how alt-labor grapples with this paradox, this chapter lays important groundwork. First: What does this new institutional landscape look like—in what does it consist? How are state-level employment laws distributed spatially and how far do they reach substantively? These questions are tackled in the first part of the chapter. Second: How did this historic shift in the institutional basis of workers' rights come to be? What were the primary drivers of employment laws' growth? In particular, how should we understand the relationship between declining labor unions and burgeoning employment laws?

Empirically, I show that states with stronger unions passed more employment laws, but employment laws did not appear to cause or accelerate union decline. Even in poorly explained outlier cases, labor unions were consistently on the front lines campaigning for stronger employment protections for workers. In contrast to those who argue that the individual-rights regime invariably undermines collective action, I find that campaigns for new employment laws produced significant collective mobilization and group action. The evidence presented suggests that the employment law regime—which today stands at the center of the new politics of workers' rights—ought to be considered one of organized labor's most significant and durable legacies.

Employment Law as the Guardian of Workers' Rights

In 1988, law professor Clyde Summers observed a "changing of the guard" from labor law to employment law:

> The significant fact is that collective bargaining does not regulate the labor market. Unions and collective agreements do not guard employees from the potential deprivations and oppressions of employer economic power. The consequence is foreseeable, if not inevitable; if collective bargaining does not protect the individual employee, the law will find another way to protect the weaker party. The law, either through the courts or the legislatures, will become the guardian. Labor law is now in the midst of that changing of the guard. There is current recognition that if the majority of employees are to be protected, it must be by the law prescribing at least certain rights of employees and minimum terms and conditions of employment.[11]

This observation has since become common wisdom among legal scholars. Law professors broadly agree that the large body of employment law that developed in the decades since has effectively displaced the New Deal's labor law regime as the primary legal source of workers' rights. In her influential work, for example, legal scholar Katherine Van Wezel Stone writes that "the emerging regime of individual employee rights represents not a complement to or an embellishment of the regime of collective rights, but rather its replacement."[12] Likewise, Cynthia Estlund affirms that "the New Deal collective bargaining system has been supplemented, and largely supplanted, by other models of workplace governance: a regulatory model of minimum standards enforceable mainly by administrative agencies and a rights model of judicially enforceable individual rights." Echoing Summers, she writes that American society now relies on employment law "as the primary guardians of employee interests."[13] There has been a decided "shift of emphasis from labor law to employment law," writes Theodore St. Antoine, "from governmental regulation of union-management relations, with collective bargaining expected to set most of the substantive terms of employment, to the direct governmental regulation of more and more aspects of the employer-employee relationship."[14] Kate Andrias summarizes the main historical arc as follows: "as labor law became ossified and decreased in relevance over the last few decades, employment law grew increasingly important."[15]

Benjamin Sachs describes the shift from labor law to employment law as a "hydraulic" process driven in part by workers' search for legal cover for their collective actions, which he says they located in the anti-retaliation provisions of the Fair Labor Standards Act of 1938 (FLSA) and the Civil Rights Act of 1964.[16] The FLSA and Civil Rights Act, however, are only two of the most important employment laws; workers have also looked to other major federal employment laws for their substantive rights and procedural protections, such as the Occupational Safety and Health Act of 1970, the Equal Pay Act of 1963, the Age Discrimination in Employment Act of 1967, the Employee Retirement Income Security Act of 1974, the Americans with Disabilities Act of 1990, the Civil Rights Act of 1991, the Family and Medical Leave Act of 1993, and the more recent Lilly Ledbetter Fair Pay Act of 2009.

But the blossoming of employment laws was not limited to the federal level; in fact, the dozen or so significant laws enacted at the federal level represent only the tip of the iceberg. "The most important and dramatic development in employment law over the last couple of decades came at the state level, not the federal," writes St. Antoine.[17] State legislatures enacted statutes that paralleled federal statutes but did not stop there; they also passed legislation "protecting employees in a wide variety of other circumstances," notes Richard Bales, including in areas as diverse as wrongful discharge, whistleblowing, employee testing, and workplace violence.[18]

As a response to the decline of labor unions, labor policy scholars like Ken Jacobs have noted, worker advocates "have increasingly turned to public policy to legislate labor standards" that historically were thought to be in the purview of collective bargaining. They have been "remarkably successful" in this regard, raising the floor on labor standards across dozens of cities and states.[19] In their interdisciplinary symposium on the "new labor federalism," for example, Fine and Michael Piore note that while federal pathways have been "blocked," "enormous activity has taken place at the state and local levels in terms of substantive protective legislation, particularly by and for workers at the bottom of the wage hierarchy." Pointing to subnational minimum wage, paid sick leave, ban the box, family leave, and fair scheduling laws, as well as domestic workers' bills of rights, they write that "lower levels of government have begun to play an increasingly important role in both the passage of new employment laws and regulations as well as their administration and enforcement."[20]

Clearly, employment law's growth in volume, reach, and importance has not escaped the attention of scholars working across multiple academic disciplines. But to date, surprisingly little systematic empirical evidence has been marshaled to substantiate or comprehensively analyze these claims. While we have a good understanding of the major employment laws passed at the federal level, and several watchdog worker advocacy organizations track the enactment of certain local ordinances, most employment laws have been passed by state legislatures, and there exists no systematic study of employment law enactments at the state level.

Consequently, while we know state-level employment law has grown, we do not know for certain what it consists of, when it emerged, where it has grown most, or who has pushed for it. St. Antoine's claim that "part of the growth we have seen in employment law, as distinguished from labor law, is attributable to the decline of organized labor," is an empirical question that we have yet to answer.[21]

Part of the reason for this empirical lacuna is practical, given that tens of thousands of new laws are enacted every year at the state level, and systematically obtaining reliable, equivalent information on the many different types of employment laws passed in fifty states over many decades is a daunting task. Luckily, between 1960 and 2014, the United States Department of Labor continuously monitored, recorded, categorized, and summarized employment law enactments at the state level. At the end of each year, expert staff members published reports of all laws passed, including short descriptions of each law, in the Bureau of Labor Statistics' *Monthly Labor*

Figure 2.1 Average Number of Employment Laws Enacted per Year

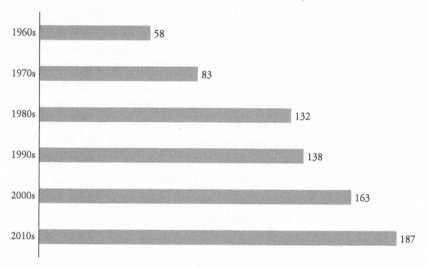

Source: Author's calculations based on Bureau of Labor Statistics 1960–2014.

Review (*MLR*).[22] The authorship of the reports was remarkably stable over time: across fifty-five years, the same five individuals authored more than 90 percent of the reports, with some overlap in the authorial transitions. The format of the reports remained the same throughout.

With a small team of research assistants, I used these reports to construct a dataset of every legislative enactment in all fifty states and Washington, D.C., between 1960 and 2014 (the last year of systematic recording) and coded the laws according to the categories listed in the reports (for example, "wages," "hours of work," "plant closings," "child labor," and "whistleblower").[23]

During this period, states enacted 7,256 employment laws in thirty-two distinct categories. The most striking feature of the data is the over-time growth of employment law. Every decade, states enacted a greater number of employment laws; on average, the number of employment laws enacted per year grew from 58 in the 1960s to 187 in the 2010s (figure 2.1).

Of course, new laws were not enacted in a vacuum: many built on previously enacted laws, modifying rules and addressing weaknesses that had become apparent over the course of time, and many were designed with the states' changing administrative capacities in mind. Once a given state passed a pay equity law, for example, it did not need to pass another law to establish the same standard, but it did often amend preexisting laws and enact new laws to bolster enforcement, expand the categories of covered or exempted occupations, modify the procedures for workers to seek relief, and so forth. Many new laws thus tweaked previous laws and altered their operations in ways big and small.

Substantively, the scope of the protections and rights covered by employment laws has grown significantly over time as well. New topics and issues were addressed each decade, indicating a gradually expanding issue space (table 2.1). Whereas in the 1960s the vast majority of employment laws dealt principally with wages and child labor, the 1970s saw a surge of attention to discrimination and equal employment opportunity, and the 1980s saw the emergence of new employment laws pertaining to parental leave, plant closings, privacy and drug testing, whistleblower protections, and more. In the 1990s, state legislatures expanded their attention to issues of genetic testing and the complex standards for discharging employees; and in the twenty-first century, legislatures have addressed new independent contractor issues, the eligibility of undocumented immigrants to work, workplace violence, and more.

State legislatures' relative attention to different categories of employment law also changed over time. For example, when laws are grouped into four broad but relatively distinct categories—wages, hours and leave, discrimination and retaliation, and terms and conditions of employment—it is apparent that employment laws dealing with wages became less common over the years relative to other types of laws, while those pertaining to terms and conditions of employment grew markedly (figure 2.2).[24] Attention to matters of discrimination and retaliation rose and then fell over the decades, consistent with the historical trajectory of the "rights revolution," while laws pertaining to hours and leave held fairly steady.[25]

These over-time trends reflect the emergence of new problems, worker needs, and vulnerabilities as the nature of the employment relationship changed and unions declined. Notice, for example, that laws dealing with wages and hours constituted a majority of all state employment laws in the 1960s and 1970s. Generally speaking, these laws raise the floor on wages and deal with procedural issues involving where, when, and how employees are to be paid. They establish a baseline above which unions could conceivably negotiate other terms and conditions of employment. But over time, with fewer workers represented by unions and a greater share of the workforce

Table 2.1 The Expanding Scope of Employment Law Protections over Time

1960s		1970s		1980s		1990s		2000s	
284	Wages[a]	569	Wages[a]	454	Wages[a]	473	Wages[a]	600	Wages[a]
119	Child labor	419	Discrimination/EEO[a]	367	Discrimination/EEO	264	Discrimination/EEO	350	Worker privacy
84	Discrimination/EEO[a]	186	Child labor	135	Child labor	181	Child labor	231	Discrimination/EEO
48	Women's laws	122	Employment agencies	95	Employment agencies	101	Worker privacy	160	Human trafficking
37	Employment agencies	36	Women's laws	83	Worker privacy	81	Family leave[a]	160	Child labor
5	Department of Labor	32	Hours of work	59	Hours of work	79	Employee testings	159	Prevailing wage
4	Immigrant workers[a]	28	Displaced homemakers	39	Plant closings	51	Whistleblower	127	Time off
		15	Immigrant workers[a]	35	Employee testings	50	Employment agencies	104	Employee testings
		10	Department of Labor	17	Family leave[a]	32	Hours of work	76	Immigrant workers[a]
				13	Whistleblower	32	Employee leasing	74	Family leave[a]
				8	Immigrant workers[a]	11	Garment industry[a]	67	Workplace violence
				7	Garment industry[a]	11	Plant closings	65	Independent contractor
				3	Displaced homemakers	6	Discharge of employees	63	Whistleblower
						6	Genetic testing	56	Employment agencies
						2	Immigrant workers[a]	49	Plant closings
								43	Hours of work
								41	Department of Labor
								36	Discharge of employees
								31	Workers with disabilities
								24	Employee leasing
								21	Offsite work
								19	Genetic testing
								7	Garment industry

Source: Galvin 2019.

[a] "Wages" includes wages (general), minimum wages, overtime, wages paid, and prevailing wages. "EEO" indicates equal employment opportunity. "Family leave" includes parental leave and family issues. "Immigrant workers" includes employment of immigrants, migrant workers, and undocumented workers.

Figure 2.2 Changes in Attention to Different Categories of Employment Laws over Time

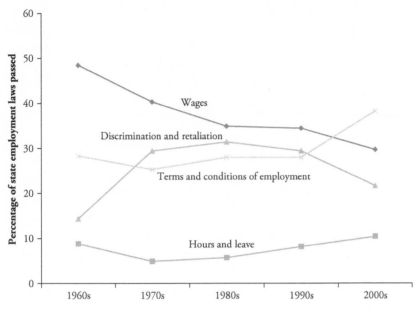

Source: Galvin 2019.

vulnerable to new forms of exploitation (such as gender, race, age, and disability discrimination; the use of genetic tests in hiring and firing; the privacy of employees at work; the growing use of independent contractors and the misclassification of employees), state legislatures shifted their attention to more complex issues regarding the terms and conditions of employment. The changing content of employment laws enacted at the state level thus reflected the changing nature of work and the growing demand for workers' rights and protections in areas that otherwise might have been guarded by unions and addressed through collective bargaining agreements.

To get a more granular feel for developments in state-level employment law over time, let us briefly review the legislative output in an average state—meaning one with an average number of employment laws and an average rate of private-sector union density decline during this period. New Jersey fits the bill, with 160 employment laws passed and a 57 percent rate of private-sector union density decline between 1960 and 2014.[26]

In the 1960s, New Jersey enacted only fourteen employment laws: eight dealt with wages, including raising the state's minimum wage and requiring overtime pay; three pertained to child labor, mainly adjusting the permissible work hours for teenagers; two involved discrimination, including one that added age discrimination to its fair employment practices law; and one amended a women's hours law (a holdover from the early twentieth century). In the 1970s, New Jersey enacted twenty-four laws: nine involved wages, including four minimum wage increases; five laws involved child labor, tweaking the hours and the list of special occupations in which minors were allowed to work; four involved discrimination—addressing affirmative action on public works projects and discrimination on account of nationality, blindness, and sex; two dealt with employment agency regulations and fees; and one repealed the state's "special work hours" law for women. In the 1980s, thirty-seven employment laws were enacted, twenty-three of which pertained to wages and child labor; eight addressed employment discrimination toward women, racial minorities, older workers, workers with disabilities, and workers with atypical hereditary cellular or blood traits; two involved employee stock ownership plans that would allow employees to purchase plants that were otherwise scheduled to be closed; others dealt with the use of lie detector tests when screening job applicants and regulation of the apparel industry and the temp industry. During most of the 1990s, Republicans controlled the state house and the governorship, and fewer protective employment laws were enacted. Among the twenty-four laws that passed during that decade, less attention was paid to child labor while greater attention was given to prevailing wage issues, gender equity, genetic testing, discrimination on the basis of disability or HIV/AIDS, smoking, and drug testing; the first laws pertaining to undocumented immigrant workers and family and medical leave were enacted; others dealt with industrial homework, the regulation of the apparel industry, and retaliation for whistleblowing. In the twenty-first century, Democrats retook control of the legislature and governor's office, and sixty-one employment laws were passed. Significant attention was paid to prevailing wage laws, especially in the construction industry; multiple laws dealt with wage payment, including illegal deductions; additional penalties were added for nonpayment of wages, and the labor commissioner was authorized to conduct extensive investigations; several laws dealt with employee rights pertaining to plant closings; hefty penalties were added for discrimination; religion and autism were added as protected categories; and additional regulation of the temp industry was codified.

States also responded to national trends, addressing new issues in waves. For example, in 1977, the *MLR* reported growing attention to age discrimination: "an emerging awareness of the valuable contributions of older workers and of the waste caused by arbitrary compulsory retirement based upon age has led to a reevaluation of such policies." Following the 1978 amendments to the Age Discrimination in Employment Act, ten states passed laws concerning arbitrary compulsory retirement based on age. When the U.S. Congress amended the Fair Labor Standards Act to increase the federal minimum wage, states tended to follow suit, as they did in 1978 and again in 2007; they also tended to raise their wages prior to a series of federal increases, putting pressure on the federal government to do the same. Similarly, in 1990, the *MLR* noted that "drug or alcohol abuse continued to receive considerable attention" from multiple states, reflecting ongoing concern regarding "employee right of privacy and workplace safety" as "thirteen states passed some form of legislation on this subject." *MLR* authors likewise noted the ebb and flow of trends in state-level employment law: in 1992, for example, they wrote: "breaking with the trend of the last few years, major laws were not enacted this year concerning drug, alcohol, or AIDS/HIV testing of employees. On the other hand, genetic testing emerged as an issue."[27]

Some state legislatures passed more employment laws than others—California, for example, enacted 512 employment laws over this period, more than 3.5 times the average. Comparing raw numbers across states can be misleading, however, as some states (especially California) were also far more legislatively productive than others in all policy areas, and many enactments were quite minor. As such, the enactment of a single employment law in a high-productivity state may not be as meaningful as the enactment of a new employment law in a state where each new law represents a hard-fought victory. Thus, the relative attention state legislatures paid to employment law—the number of employment laws enacted by session divided by the total number of laws passed that session—offers a more meaningful (and standardized) measure of a state's interest in employment law. It measures the state's attention to employment law relative to all other issues on the state's policy agenda and thus enables us to compare states on equal terms.

Figure 2.3 Employment Laws as a Share of All Enacted Laws by Session

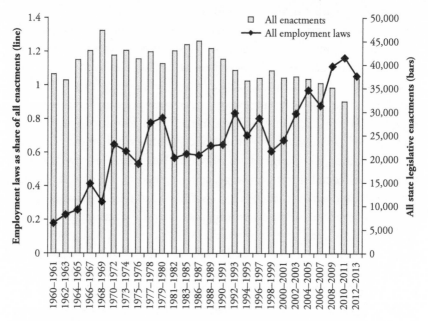

Source: Galvin 2019.

As figure 2.3 reveals, employment laws as a share of all enacted state bills more than quintupled over those fifty-five years. At precisely the same time that national labor law atrophied and private-sector union membership plummeted, state legislatures grew increasingly preoccupied with employment law.

But what of the "direction" of the laws? Were they all worker-friendly? Surely some must have favored the employer? A plain reading of the *MLR* employment law summaries indicates that the overwhelming majority of enacted laws were designed to advance workers' rights and provide statutory protections against exploitation. Still, the purposes of some laws are difficult to discern and other laws clearly aimed to reduce the regulatory burden on employers, such as by limiting their liability or making it more difficult for workers to sue. A qualitative effort at hand-coding the summaries in the *MLR* indicates that about 12 percent of laws enacted between 1960 and 2010 fall into this category.[28] As a share of all employment laws, these laws have grown slightly over time while roughly tracking partisan shifts

Figure 2.4 Employer-Friendly Laws as a Share of All Laws Enacted

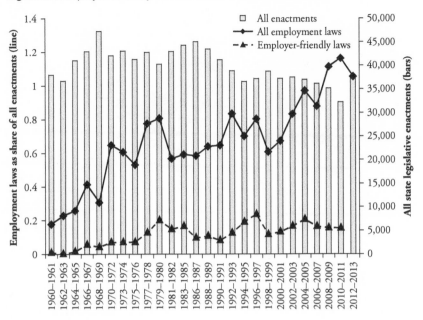

Source: Galvin 2019.

(as shown in figure 2.4), which is consistent with recent research on growing state-level policy polarization.[29] The peak years in the late 1970s and mid-1990s, for example, correspond to major Republican electoral gains at the state level (357 legislative seats in the 1978 elections and 514 seats in the 1994 elections). By state, the volume of employer-friendly laws is correlated with employee-friendly laws, however (correlation: 0.79), suggesting that some states are simply more legislatively active in this area than others and may be considered more lively sites of political contestation on employment issues.

In addition to strengthening workers' rights on paper, many employment laws grant state agencies greater authorities to enforce the law (for example, unfettered access to workplaces, subpoena power, or the power to make final judgments) and establish higher penalties to deter employers from breaking the law (including damages, fees, and civil and criminal penalties). As numerous scholars have shown, both the strength of the penalties and the extent of the state's enforcement capacities have a substantial impact on whether workers' rights are upheld in practice.[30]

Figure 2.5 Attention to Employment Law by State, 1960–2014

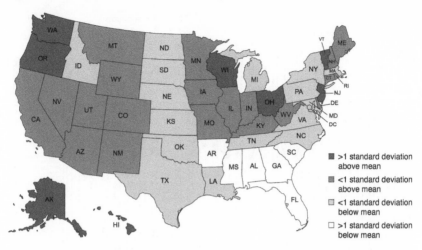

Source: Author's calculations based on Bureau of Labor Statistics 1960–2014.

Significant regional variation is evident as well (figure 2.5). In some regions, there has been precious little development of state regulatory capacity. In the Deep South, for example, the absence of state capacities and regulatory authorities has long enabled employers to exploit workers with impunity—undoubtedly a legacy of slavery and Jim Crow. In those states— Alabama, Arkansas, Florida, Georgia, Mississippi, and South Carolina— state legislatures paid significantly less attention to employment law than did all other state legislatures. In states along the Pacific coast, including Alaska and Hawaii, as well as some midwestern and northeastern states, legislatures paid far more attention to workers' rights; they were at the vanguard of creating new protections and enforcement capacities via public policy. Over the last sixty years, those states also tinkered consistently with these rights, protections, authorities, and capacities, fine-tuning and updating them to keep pace with changing industrial conditions.

Amid growing partisanship, red and blue states diverged further still. Red-state governors have taken steps to waive employer penalties, place moratoria on investigations, and dismantle enforcement capacities. Former Florida governor Jeb Bush, for example, dismantled his state's department of labor in the early 2000s, effectively eliminating enforcement of Florida's minimum wage.[31] Meanwhile, blue-state governors have appointed labor regulators who introduce innovative strategic enforcement practices, develop partnerships with community groups, and leverage obscure statutory authorities to improve the terms and conditions of work for workers in their states.[32] What this cross-state, cross-region (and within-region) variation reveals, therefore, is that workers' vulnerability to labor standards violations also has a geographic dimension: one's rights and protections vary greatly depending on the state in which one happens to live. This variation necessitates deeper examination of the causes and consequences of divergent subnational regulatory capacities since the 1960s and calls into question comparative frameworks that characterize the United States as a single regime type with a single historical trajectory.

In sum, as labor law became a case of policy drift, substantive issues that might have been addressed through collective bargaining processes were increasingly addressed through alternative mechanisms implemented through different processes, and enforced through different mechanisms. And yet, labor law continued to exert powerful constraints around what workers' advocates could do through those laws. This is perhaps most evident in what is conspicuously absent from the growing inventory of employment statutes. Due to labor law's preemption doctrine prohibiting virtually all subnational regulation of private-sector labor-management relations, state employment laws could not—and did not—address issues related to unionization or collective bargaining in the private sector. Otherwise, workers' advocates would have been able to strengthen union election procedures, increase the penalties for employer interference and intimidation, or construct other alternative arrangements that might have fortified labor law and promoted unionization.[33] Many states did, of course, enact a variety of extensive labor laws governing industries explicitly falling outside the Wagner Act's reach, especially in the public sector, where many states established collective bargaining rights for workers and set up elaborate regulatory frameworks modeled on the National Labor Relations Board. Some states created collective bargaining regimes for agricultural workers; more recently, some subnational governments have created special labor protections for independent contractors as well.[34] But as long as national labor law remained in place and exerted exclusive authority over private-sector labor relations, the possibility of regulating labor-management relations in the private sector through state-level labor laws was foreclosed.

Since the 1960s, the vast majority of workers' rights have therefore shifted to alternative venues (at the state level rather than the national level), taken on alternative institutional forms (employment law rather than labor law), and employed alternative enforcement mechanisms (regulation and litigation rather than collective bargaining). Instead of determining workers' wages, hours, and terms and conditions of employment through union-negotiated collective bargaining contracts (as labor law seeks to do), employment laws mobilize the regulatory instruments of the state to enforce higher standards and provide workers with a private right of action. That is, they pursue the same substantive outcomes as labor law but take different institutional pathways to get there. With respect to their timing, form, and content, employment laws reflect the delimiting force of the increasingly antiquated but still authoritative labor law.

Labor Unions and the Growth of State Employment Laws

How did this inversion of the New Deal labor law framework come about? Of particular interest is the relationship between declining labor unions and blossoming employment laws. Was the growth in employment law "attributable to the decline of organized labor," as St. Antoine posits and Summers implies?[35] If so, how? Did state legislators take the initiative while declining labor unions sat on the sidelines or did unions themselves play an important role in facilitating employment law's growth? Or did causation run in the opposite direction, with the growth of the individual rights–based employment law regime undermining unions and unionism? Or were these synchronous developments unrelated? The nature of the relationship remains unclear.

Because most existing scholarship in this area is preoccupied with explaining the causes of union decline, the proliferation of employment law is most often examined for its deleterious effects on unionism. Scholars have long treated employment law and labor law as "dichotomous, and in a fundamental respect incompatible, modes of intervention into workplace governance."[36] Whereas employment law provides highly individualized regulatory and legal proceedings for workers to vindicate their rights, labor law was designed to advance workers' rights by promoting collective bargaining, concerted action, and unionism. As employment law has proliferated, it is said to have eroded the underpinnings of the collective bargaining regime. These pernicious effects are generally said to operate at the level of ideas, institutions, and incentives.

In the ideational realm, some legal scholars argue that the growth of individual rights–based employment law has weakened commitments to collective action, especially in the workplace. "The dominant view among scholars," Sachs summarizes, "has long been that employment law's 'individual rights' regime at best provides no support for—and at worst is inimical to—collective organization and collective action. Employment law is thus charged with 'undermin[ing] the concept of group action,' and with 'foreshadow[ing] the eclipse of the collective bargaining model— indeed, of the centrality of collective action altogether.'"[37] By emphasizing individual rights over collective rights, the rise of the employment law regime has led to a "devaluation" of organized action, legal scholar James Brudney writes.[38]

Labor historians similarly argue that the growth of employment law, itself a product of the "rights consciousness" that began to blossom in the 1960s, has undermined many of the social norms and commitments on which trade unionism depends: namely, solidarity, collective action, and mutual support. "As the former [rights consciousness] became a near hegemonic way of evaluating the quality of American citizenship," Nelson Lichtenstein summarizes, "the latter atrophied. Indeed, in its most extreme interpretation, rights consciousness subverts the mechanisms, both moral and legal, that sustain the social solidarity upon which trade unionism is based." In this view, the growth of employment law reflects a historic shift in thinking away from the "collective institutionalism that stands at the heart of the union idea."[39]

Doctrinal and institutional frictions between employment law and labor law are said to have contributed to the decline of group action as well. For example, because union contracts usually mandate arbitration procedures for redressing grievances, membership in a union effectively deprives workers of their state employment law rights and the potential to win financial damages and civil penalty awards. Paradoxically, then, the emergence of two separate institutional orders may have divided union and nonunion workers and made it more difficult to forge a collective identity and mobilize in collective action. Employment law "functions to disorganize labor" and prevent "the very group-formation that is necessary to retain or improve the minimal terms," writes Katherine Van Wezel Stone.[40]

Tensions between individual-rights and collective-rights systems similarly underpin Paul Frymer's landmark study of the "bifurcated system of power that assigned race and class problems to different spheres of government."[41] Court interpretations of antidiscrimination employment laws, Frymer shows, "unintentionally weakened national labor law" and ultimately produced a more "diverse but weakened labor movement." What is more, employment laws are not adequate substitutes for labor law: as discussed, although employment laws provide workers with new substantive rights, they are also characterized by high barriers to access, and they force workers down highly individualized pathways of redress.[42]

Economists have also pointed to the dueling incentives emerging from the simultaneous operation of labor and employment law. In the "government substitution hypothesis" first posited by George Neumann and Ellen Rissman, state regulatory functions are said to reduce workers' incentives to unionize by providing for free what workers might otherwise get through their unions.[43] Scholars have examined empirically the effects of various "union-like" laws and social programs on union density, including social welfare expenditures, exceptions to at-will employment, and protective employment laws.[44] Statistical tests yield mostly null results, but the debate persists, in part because of anecdotal evidence that unions have perceived a substitution effect and worked to combat it—as when Los Angeles unions sought to exempt their members from a minimum wage law in 2016 or when the American Federation of Labor and Congress of Industrial Organizations (AFL-CIO) campaigned against a single-payer health care system in 1993.[45]

These theoretical frameworks are limited, however, by their preoccupation with explaining union decline. What of the reverse relationship? Might labor unions, even as they declined, have contributed to the growth of employment law?

Despite the many downsides of employment law, unions may have had multiple reasons to promote its growth. Perhaps some saw a benefit in taking wages and other terms and conditions of employment "out of competition," since a more level playing field could make competitive employers more likely to bargain with unions. Or perhaps by taking certain issues off the bargaining table, employment laws helped to limit the range of issues over which unions would have to negotiate with employers, thereby increasing their leverage over the issues that remained. Or perhaps unions were engaged in logrolling, exchanging their support for employment laws for policies that facilitate unionization.[46]

Of course, union behavior may be less instrumental and strategic than ideological and sincere. Many unions, viewing themselves as pillars of the labor movement, may simply have a wider purview than other interest groups and be inclined to promote priorities that transcend the interests of their members. As John Ahlquist and Margaret Levi have shown, some unions self-consciously expand their "communities of fate" to include "unknown others for whom the members feel responsibility."[47] Indeed, as William Moore, Robert Newman, and Loren Scott write, the organization director of the AFL-CIO "expressed relief, but not surprise" upon learning that the "government substitution hypothesis" was refuted by several studies. "He noted, however, that even if the evidence had supported that hypothesis, the AFL-CIO would continue to support social welfare legislation that aided the working men and the poor in this country."[48] In a similar vein, Richard Freeman and James Medoff, Bruce Western and Jake Rosenfeld, and Rosenfeld have found that although unions often fail to advance their own self-interests in legislative politics, they are far more effective in amplifying "the voice of workers and the lower income segments of society" more broadly.[49]

Debate over the relationship between employment law and labor unions, in other words, remains at a theoretical impasse, with reasons to think the causal arrows point in either direction. What the debate has lacked thus far is systematic empirical investigation of the posited relationships—in particular, whether unions were key players in the enactment of state-level employment laws or had little to do with employment law's growth.

Evidence that unions were integral to the legislative campaigns for new employment laws would not negate arguments about the potentially deleterious effects of employment laws on unionism more generally—unions may well have been shooting themselves in the foot. But if unions pushed for employment laws fully aware of their possible effects, it would raise new questions about whether, how, and in which ways employment law campaigns serve unions' purposes—perhaps providing an alternative route to galvanizing workers—and prompt further inquiry into the trade-offs. Before we can begin those discussions, the basic contours of the relationship need to be fleshed out.

Quantitative Analyses of the Relationship between Unions and Employment Laws

The relationship between employment law and union decline was probably most directly and comprehensively analyzed by the preeminent labor economist Richard Freeman in his 1986 examination of the "government substitution" hypothesis.[50] Analyzing both cross-national and cross-state data, Freeman found no support for the hypothesis; but in a surprising twist, he found much stronger empirical support for a "reverse causal link."[51] In his cross-national analysis, Freeman found a positive statistical relationship between union density and protective legislation for workers; he observed that "unions have fared better, not worse" in countries with more such laws.[52] In the United States, his cross-state analysis similarly showed that "more highly unionized states are, indeed, more likely to pass protective legislation." He concluded that "unionism leads to protective worker legislation, but such legislation does not have adverse feedback effects on union density."[53] Freeman's analysis was limited to basic regressions, however, and did not dig deeper into the nature of the positive relationship. And although his model improved on previous examinations of the substitution hypothesis, the dependent variable (a measure of each state's "level of statutory protection of workers") was simply a snapshot of state laws taken in 1985 by the now-defunct Southern Labor Institute.[54]

To probe the relationship further, I use the total number of state employment laws enacted in each legislative session over four decades (1973–2014), taken from my *MLR* dataset.[55] During this period, states enacted more than 6,000 employment laws. This more fine-grained measure permits the use of panel analysis to generate more precise estimates. I use the same independent variables as Freeman but add two more controls. The dependent variable is the number of employment laws enacted in each state-year (two-year legislative session). The main treatment variable is union density, which averages the state's percentage of nonagricultural workers in a union over each two-year legislative term.[56] A greater share of unionized workers may indicate a more politically powerful labor movement, which may (or may not) push for the enactment of stronger employment laws. Controls include the share of the nonagricultural workforce employed in manufacturing (because as a state's manufacturing industry declines, it may be encouraged to enact stronger protections for the workforce that remains);[57] per capita personal income (because economic modernization is related to policy innovation more generally, and states with richer populations may be more likely to enact employment laws);[58] and a dummy variable indicating whether the state adopted a right-to-work law (because those states may be less inclined to pass worker-friendly employment laws; right to work is also sometimes used as a proxy for the political strength of business).[59] I add legislative productivity to Freeman's controls, a measure of all laws enacted during the two-year term (since states with more productive legislatures may be more likely to enact employment laws).[60] I also include state policy liberalism to control for the state citizenry's economic liberalism (because states with populations that are more ideologically liberal on economic matters may elect representatives who are more inclined to enact worker-friendly employment laws).[61]

I conducted a time-series cross-sectional analysis and estimated the model with and without year and state fixed effects to account for unobserved temporal trends and time-invariant characteristics of the states that may confound the analysis, such as their political culture and history, economic structure, and workforce composition. Fixed effects "soak up" those more constant factors and allow us to better analyze dynamic factors like changes in union density. Results are reported from each specification in table 2.2.

Across all four models, union density is positive and statistically significant, which means that higher union density predicts the enactment of more employment laws. This relationship holds both within and across states, even when controlling for time trends. Legislative productivity and manufacturing employment are significant in the expected directions; the significance of personal income, mass economic liberalism, and right to work depends on whether one is looking within or across states. A variety of other statistical analyses (see the appendix) confirm the same strong, positive relationship between union density and employment law enactments, indicating that more unionized states are more likely to enact employment law protections for workers. Flipping the equation and regressing union density on employment laws plus controls, as in Freeman's analysis,

Table 2.2 Estimating the Relationship between Union Density and Employment Law Enactments (Panel Data, 1976–2013)

	(1)	(2)	(3)	(4)
Union density	0.115***	0.106***	0.132***	0.102***
	(0.0204)	(0.0152)	(0.0357)	(0.0335)
Manufacturing	−8.643***	−8.334***	−11.68***	−9.647**
	(2.193)	(2.251)	(4.327)	(4.286)
Income	8.61e-05***	7.81e-05**	7.10e-05***	−4.68e-05
	(1.25e-05)	(3.10e-05)	(1.86e-05)	(3.30e-05)
Right to work	−1.902***	−2.160***	1.184	0.747
	(0.201)	(0.268)	(0.748)	(0.836)
Legislative productivity	0.00566***	0.00585***	0.00358***	0.00317***
	(0.000633)	(0.000681)	(0.000429)	(0.000579)
State policy liberalism	−0.981***	−1.695**	0.431	2.989***
	(0.365)	(0.689)	(0.711)	(0.998)
Year fixed effects	No	Yes	No	Yes
State fixed effects	No	No	Yes	Yes
Constant	−0.440	0.121	0.544	1.100
	(0.738)	(0.655)	(0.839)	(1.020)
Observations	1,000	1,000	1,000	1,000
R-squared/within R-squared	0.405	0.431	0.116	0.176
Number of groups	50	50	50	50

Source: Author's calculations based on Bureau of Labor Statistics 1960–2014.

Note: Standard errors in parentheses.

* $p < .1$; ** $p < .05$; *** $p < .01$

reveals the same substantively strong and positive statistical relationship and undermines the notion that employment laws contributed to union decline (see the appendix).

Regression models, moreover, only capture basic relationships; they say nothing about causal pathways. They cannot rule out the possibility that overlooked factors might explain both union density and employment law activity; nor can they confirm that the standard measure of union density is a good proxy for unions' political strength. Higher levels of union density may correspond to a more fractious labor movement with less political influence, for example, while a state with lower levels of union density may still have powerful unions that exercise significant political clout. To move beyond blunt statistical associations and begin unpacking the relationships, case studies can be particularly helpful.

Qualitative Analyses of the Relationship between Unions and Employment Laws

One of the best ways to maximize analytical leverage from case study research is to carefully select cases that filter out the noise and allow the researcher to home in on what is most important. Rather than selecting cases randomly, choosing only "typical" cases, or comparing cases with similar and different characteristics, advances in qualitative methodology have pointed to the value of using statistical analysis to select cases that are least well explained by the regression model.[62] Relative to the overall cross-case relationship, these are the cases that have the most surprising values; they are the outliers. As political scientist Jason Seawright explains, such cases are particularly well positioned to illuminate problems with the model: they can reveal new information about the causal pathways that link the key independent variable (union density) to the outcome of interest (employment law enactments), sources of measurement error, omitted and confounding variables, and previously unknown sources of causal heterogeneity.[63]

In two published studies, I used two different case-selection techniques to identify cases that were the least well explained by the model. In one, I looked for "deviant" cases, identified by the extremity of their fitted values relative to their observed values (meaning they had the highest residuals). The model in that study pointed to one case with extremely high residuals on the dependent variable (Maine) and one case with extremely low residuals (Pennsylvania). Both cases were explored through systematic process tracing.[64] In the other study, my coauthor and I developed a new case-selection technique to identify "extreme cases" on the treatment variable, net of the statistical influence of the set of known control variables: a process we called selecting "surprising causes."[65] We sought to identify cases that exhibited extreme values of union density after filtering out the effects of the other covariates in the model (such as income, manufacturing, right to work, and policy liberalism). This method revealed sources of measurement error and helped us identify confounding variables; after addressing those problems and reconfiguring the model, Missouri emerged as our final outlier case.

Each case study set out to examine at least one policy area within each of four major categories of employment law (table 2.3). In Pennsylvania

Table 2.3 Employment Law Categories and State Scores

		Maine	Pennsylvania	Missouri
Wages	Minimum wage (DOL)	1	0	1
	Overtime (NCSL)	1	1	1
	Prevailing wage (DOL)	1	1	1
Hours and leave	Family/medical leave (NCSL)	1	0	0
	Meal/rest periods (DOL)	1	0.5	0
Discrimination and retaliation	Discrimination (NCSL)	1	1	1
	Drug and alcohol testing (NCSL)	1	0	0
	Whistleblower (NCSL)	1	0.5	0.5
Terms and conditions of employment	Child labor (NCSL)	1	1	1
	Employee misclassification (NCSL)	1	0.33	0
	OSHA state plans (DOL)	1	0	0
	Total points	11	5.33	5.5

Source: Author's calculations. DOL, Department of Labor; NCSL, National Conference of State Legislatures.

Note: A score of 1 indicates a major law on the books in 2014, 0 indicates no law, and fractions indicate partial coverage (for the following laws: *meal period*: 0.5 = only applies to minors; *child labor*: 0.5 = employer responsible for registration; *drug and alcohol testing*: 0.5 = public sector only; *whistleblower*: 0.5 = public or private sector but not both; *employee misclassification*: 0.33 for each: interagency taskforces; objective tests for employment status; sector-specific).

and Maine, I examined the minimum wage, employment discrimination policies, family and medical leave laws, and employee misclassification, irrespective of whether they resulted in legislative enactments. In Missouri, my coauthor and I looked at campaigns for the minimum wage, workplace discrimination policies, whistleblower protections, and child labor laws. Because each policy area was a politically contentious issue that featured multiple efforts over the years to establish new or amend preexisting employment laws, it was possible to identify multiple campaigns within each policy area, thus helpfully multiplying the number of "causal process observations" many times over.[66]

Using broad search terms, I examined hundreds of full-text searchable newspaper articles covering any and all campaigns relating to these policy areas. I looked for evidence that supported or undermined the hypotheses that labor unions were integral players in legislative campaigns for stronger employment laws (the primary hypothesis), that they were mere bystanders (for it was entirely possible that the statistical relationship revealed by the models was spurious), or that another causal pathway was worth exploring. If they were found to be integral political players, I also wanted to know how integral they were. Were they key actors in all legislative campaigns, or just some? How much leadership did they exert? What tactics did they employ? In other words, what does the causal pathway actually look like? Although close examination of these three outlier cases could not conclusively resolve the causal puzzle, it could turn up new information about how the supposed causal pathway actually worked.

The statistical models identified Pennsylvania, Maine, and Missouri as outliers for different reasons. Pennsylvania's puzzle was its very high level of union density but relatively few major employment laws; Maine's puzzle was its strong slate of employment laws despite merely average union density; Missouri's puzzle was its extremely low rate of union density in the public sector and a limited set of employment laws (we sought to test whether public-sector union density was a more revealing measure than the standard measure of composite union density). Each case therefore offered a different kind of leverage in addressing the question of how union density might be related to employment law enactments in the aggregate.

Across all three states, labor unions were found to be prominently and vigorously involved in almost every policy campaign to strengthen workers' rights. They were clearly campaign leaders, too: they lobbied lawmakers on behalf of legislation, testified in committees, organized rallies and protests, orchestrated letter-writing campaigns, wrote op-eds, funded advertisements, pressured governors, gathered signatures, spearheaded ballot initiatives, donated money, assembled coalitions, and participated in task forces; and when put on the defensive, they were no less vigorous in fighting the rollback of workers' rights.

In Maine, given its merely average rate of union density, organized labor outperformed expectations in all four policy arenas. Part of the unions' influence (expressed mostly through the Maine AFL-CIO) may have stemmed from their unusual clout within the Maine Democratic Party organization. But it also appears to have reflected the strong ad hoc coalitions they assembled to fight each policy campaign. The only organized group present in all four policy campaigns was organized labor, which suggests the centrality of labor unions within Maine's progressive networks. The Maine case also lends further support to the notion that a variable's causal effect need not be commensurate with its numerical value. Despite Maine's average rate of union density, labor unions appeared to exert outsize influence in the legislative process; their central role in party and progressive politics appears to have provided them with what we might view as a streamlined causal pathway to affecting legislative outcomes.

In Pennsylvania, voluminous evidence attests to the vital role played by the state federation of labor, which included a broad cross section of private- and public-sector unions, in advocating for stronger workplace regulation laws in three of the four policy areas I examined. Pennsylvania unions were prominent campaigners for a higher minimum wage at multiple junctures, for family and medical leave legislation, and for stronger laws around employee misclassification. The unions were notably absent, however, in efforts to expand antidiscrimination policies to include LGBTQ rights. Pennsylvania unions lost on the first three policies at almost every turn, but not for a lack of trying. Most bills supported by organized labor were either killed or watered down by the Republican-controlled Senate. Indeed, this seems to be the primary reason Pennsylvania registers as a deviant case, given its economic and political profile: the Republican Party exhibited unusual strength in the upper house, which gave it veto power over legislation. The evidence in Pennsylvania is therefore mostly consistent with the hypothesized causal pathway and helps to explain the state's surprising value on the dependent variable. The complete absence of organized labor in the area of discrimination, however, serves as a reminder of unions' mixed history on issues of diversity and inclusion.

Finally, the Missouri case lends further support to the hypothesis that unions were integral political players in campaigns for new employment laws. Like organized labor in Maine, unions in Missouri often worked in coalition with grassroots nonprofit groups, faith-based groups, women's groups, the NAACP, and others. As in Maine, the Missouri AFL-CIO was the only group that was consistently on the front lines in each of the dozen policy campaigns we examined across four major policy areas. Whether they won or lost, organized labor was consistently active, engaged, and integral to the policy debate in all four policy areas. But like unions in Pennsylvania, Missouri unions were often blocked by Republicans who controlled the state government; their only successes came through ballot initiatives that bypassed the state legislature and drew on broad public support (for example, Missouri's minimum wage increases in 2006 and 2018).

Again, the purpose of the case studies was not to explain policy outcomes or to make definitive claims about causal mechanisms—it was to use high-leverage cases to explore the nature of the causal pathway and assess the likelihood that the statistical relationship identified earlier was spurious. The evidence assembled renders the argument of spuriousness difficult to make. The case studies also identified important omitted variables and sources of measurement error, pointed to other valuable model refinements, and offered important lessons about unions' political engagement. Incorporating that new knowledge into an improved, better specified model featuring new and reconstructed control variables, I find further confirmation of the strong relationship between union density and state-level employment laws.[67]

In sum, analyses integrating quantitative and qualitative analyses turn up strong confirmatory evidence that labor unions, even in unexpected cases, were consistently on the front lines, employing myriad political tactics to create the state-level employment laws that largely structure the employment relationship today. The methodological approach taken here does not provide dispositive empirical evidence of a causal relationship or fully refute the notion that the relationship may yet be spurious in other cases. But the evidence assembled is difficult to square with alternative causal arguments and lends concrete support to the hypothesized causal pathway connecting labor unions to the growth of subnational employment laws.

In Maine, Pennsylvania, and Missouri, unions seemed motivated by a variety of nonexclusive reasons, including their abiding commitment to advocate for all working people, not just union members. Indeed, in most of the policy campaigns examined earlier, unions publicly trumpeted their role as guardians of all workers' well-being. An outstanding question is whether this inclusive public stance, and their ability to achieve policy victories, has been advantageous for unions, perhaps resulting in more favorable public views of unions, increased membership in certain states, or momentum for future organizing drives. This is a question that has loomed over the Fight for $15 (and a Union) movement: Whether, when, and how do campaigns for new employment laws complement unionization? To study this, future research should flip the model around and examine the various effects these employment law campaigns have had on unions and their ability to achieve their organizational objectives.

This analysis reveals that organized labor was a consistent contributing cause of these relatively durable, institutionalized workers' rights and protections lodged at the subnational level. Even as union membership continued its seemingly inexorable decline and labor's myriad "threat effects" vanished, these institutional achievements endured. These findings thus add a new dimension to the debate over what unions do and "no longer do."[68] Insightful recent scholarship has demonstrated that many of the positive effects unions once had have been disappearing alongside declining union density: union decline has been linked to rising income inequality and insecurity, wage stagnation, declining job quality, the deterioration of the moral economy, the magnified political influence of corporations and the wealthy, and more.[69] But it is worth bearing in mind that the positive socioeconomic effects of higher union density were always inherently ephemeral: union-threat effects only operate when unionization is viewed as a credible option. State-level employment laws, in contrast, endure even when unions decline. Notwithstanding their many inadequacies, employment laws constitute some of the only institutional protections workers have left to defend against exploitation. If unions were instrumental in their enactment, then the new federalism in work regulation may be considered one of organized labor's most significant and durable legacies.[70]

Subnational employment laws are not, of course, permanent—they can be amended or repealed—and they do not guarantee protection against exploitation. They can be (and often are) ignored by employers, under-enforced by regulatory agencies, and underutilized by workers.[71] Increasingly, they are circumvented by mandatory arbitration agreements, and local ordinances in many states are nullified by state preemption laws.[72] Their unequal distribution across states, as discussed, has created a new set of geographic inequalities in workers' rights. Although they do not appear to have accelerated union decline, neither have they fully compensated for labor's gradual disappearance or done much to redress the persistent power imbalance in the workplace. And while they do provide workers with valuable protections, the employment law regime is clearly inferior to the collective bargaining regime.

The limitations of employment law serve as an important reminder that labor unions and their allies did not have the luxury of starting over from scratch and designing state-level labor laws that are a better fit for modern economic conditions and industrial structures. Because national labor law remained fixed in place, exerting outsize authority in the field of labor-management relations, labor unions were not starting with a clean slate. They had to design workaround solutions in a crowded institutional landscape. Their solutions—employment laws—are highly imperfect and do not resolve the problems associated with labor law's drift. Extreme inequalities of power in the workplace persist and low-wage workers, in particular, remain highly vulnerable to exploitation, discrimination, harassment, and abuse. Employment laws do little to redress such problems.

This is precisely the point I wish to make in this book: addressing these challenges through organization and collective action, often around the enactment and enforcement of stronger policies in subnational venues, now lies at the crux of the new politics of workers' rights.

This chapter has helped us to more confidently point the causal arrows in the proper direction: we can state with greater confidence that the new federalism in work regulation constitutes one of organized labor's most significant and consequential legacies. It also enables us to move on to the next stage of analysis. We can now dig deeper into the role workers' rights organizations—including alt-labor groups—are playing in building, fixing, strengthening, and enforcing employment laws, which continue to be the primary sources of workers' rights and protections in the twenty-first century.

CHAPTER 3

Vulnerable Workers, the Rise of Alt-Labor, and the Funding Dilemma

DESPERATE FOR WORK during the height of the Covid-19 pandemic, six Latino construction workers traveled from Houston, Texas, to Cedar Rapids, Iowa, to help rebuild a senior living center after it was damaged in a powerful derecho storm. They were recruited by Pablo Ramirez, a subcontractor for BluSky Restoration Contractors, who promised them up to $250 in cash per day, housing, and $2,000 for travel expenses. For weeks, the men cleaned, painted, drywalled, repaired ceiling leaks, and installed plasterboard, moldings, and insulation. They slept on air mattresses in the rooms they were repairing, which lacked heat, were filled with roaches, and had only plastic sheeting as ceilings to protect them from the elements. They were given work boots and hard hats, but not goggles, masks, or gloves; they had to install fiberglass insulation with their bare hands, causing one worker to have an allergic reaction. Another was told to perform electrical wiring work, despite not being trained or certified; he accidentally split his finger open and did not receive medical care. Payment was made only once, in the second week: a lump sum averaging just over $200 per worker. Most of the men had planned to send money back home to their families; instead, they did not make enough to support themselves on the job. One man's mother, who lived in Mexico, sent money to help tide him over. The men continued working, but they soon ran out of funds for food; for several days, they didn't eat. Eventually, they walked off the job.

When the director of the nearby Grace Episcopal Church learned of their mistreatment, he took them in.

Their case was referred to a nearby worker center known as the Center for Worker Justice of Eastern Iowa (CWJ), which, together with a local carpenters' union, quickly assembled a coalition of allies—including clergy, politicians, local activists, and local union leaders—to advocate for the workers. Demanding recompense for the workers' wage theft, unsafe housing, and other illegal employment law violations, the coalition organized protests and generated local media coverage.[1] One complicating issue involved the identity of the workers' employer: Was it BluSky or the subcontractor who should have been paying them? BluSky insisted that the workers were under the employ of Ramirez, whom BluSky claimed it had already paid in full. Ramirez insisted that BluSky had only paid him a fraction of what he was owed, which was why he did not have the funds to pay the workers. CWJ argued that BluSky and Ramirez were joint employers; after all, the workers "were checked in for work by BluSky, were required to wear tee-shirts with the BluSky logo on the jobsite, and BluSky project director Wayne Gibson regularly reviewed their work."[2] After news outlets picked up the story and BluSky began to face public backlash, its chief operating officer and regional vice president flew to Cedar Rapids to settle with the workers. The company paid the full wages they were owed, as well as their travel costs home to Houston, on the condition that they sign a nondisclosure agreement.[3]

The last chapter showed that between the 1960s and 2010s, state legislatures, prodded consistently by labor unions, passed a growing inventory of employment laws to protect workers from exploitation and discrimination. These laws proliferated at precisely the same time that labor law was ossifying, union membership was declining, and the New Deal's collective bargaining regime was proving itself badly mismatched to the changing economy.[4] Subnational employment laws granted workers the right to sue their employers when their rights were violated; created penalties, damages, and fees to deter employers from violating the law; and empowered state agencies to enforce the new rights and protections. For higher-income workers and those working in larger firms, these laws alleviated some of the worst effects of labor law's drift by giving human resources departments new standards to follow and providing new pathways for eligible employees to vindicate their rights.[5] But for low-wage workers at smaller companies operating in highly competitive, fissured industries—such as residential construction, in the BluSky case—the deficiencies of the new employment law regime were evident from the start. Structural changes in the employment relationship and demographic changes in the low-wage workforce contributed to widespread uncertainty over who was entitled to which rights, and enforcement proved deeply problematic. Litigation was too expensive for most low-wage workers to pursue and tended to reinscribe social hierarchies, the regulatory complaint process was cumbersome and littered with obstacles, and state and federal enforcement capacity was woefully inadequate.[6]

Consequently, many employers ignored the new employment laws. Labor standards violations like those suffered by the construction workers in Iowa became rampant, particularly in decentralized and highly competitive industries such as food and beverage services, personal and laundry services, private households, and in highly informalized industries in which small companies and subcontractors like Ramirez were not registered with the state, paid their workers off-the-books, and operated on thin profit margins. Wage theft, unsafe and unhealthy working conditions, racial and gender discrimination, sexual harassment, and retaliation were common in these industries and disproportionately affected low-wage immigrant workers, people of color, and women. These workers lacked significant labor market power and often faced multiple, overlapping, and cumulative forms of discrimination.[7] Dispersed and disconnected in a modern economy featuring a "bewilderingly complex proliferation of employment relationships that structure work" and "layer after layer of subcontractors and vendors [which] make it exceedingly difficult for workers to organize on their own behalf," victims of labor standards violations often felt that they alone experienced the indignity and humiliation of their exploitation.[8]

In the absence of intermediary organizations (such as unions) that could bring low-wage workers together, attend to their urgent problems, and help them organize to challenge their subjugation, these workers were indeed on their own. Demand thus gradually grew for new forms of worker organization that could support and organize vulnerable low-wage workers. It was in this context that experimental, nonprofit alt-labor groups (like CWJ) began to emerge in the 1990s and 2000s.

Alt-labor groups have distinct advantages in the new legal, economic, and resource environment, but they also face significant challenges—not least, what might be called the membership/funding dilemma. No alt-labor group has successfully managed to build a large, robust membership capable of funding its operations through regular dues payments. Consequently, all groups have turned to generous but capricious external revenue sources such as private philanthropic foundations, individual donors, and government grants. Funding from external sources has reduced the pressure on the groups to build mass memberships; their small memberships, in turn, have reinforced their dependency on outside funders. For groups that strive to be member-driven, people-powered organizations, their financial dependency on external funders has raised difficult questions about mission and accountability that no group has yet fully answered—though all are actively trying. One especially consequential response to these tensions has been the embrace of public policy campaigns and political engagement by a growing number of groups. Such activities fit their existing capacities and deficiencies, minimize their weaknesses, and maximize their strengths. But before we explore alt-labor's turn to policy and politics (chapter 5), this chapter examines the context in which these nonprofit worker organizations emerged and discusses some of the central challenges they face.

Falling through the Cracks of Labor Law and Employment Law

Since the 1970s, the quality of low-wage jobs in the U.S. has deteriorated as many workers have lost pay, benefits, bargaining power, and dignity.[9] Although the growth in precarious, nonstandard work—including temporary, on-call, contract, independent contractor, and freelance work, as well as other "gig" jobs—may be somewhat overstated,[10] the declining quality of both standard and nonstandard work is a serious problem.[11] Part of the explanation for declining job quality involves changing business practices amid rising global economic competition. But much of it is also owed to the growing tendency of policymakers—beginning in the 1970s and 1980s—to embrace deregulatory policies that weakened state enforcement capacities and effectively neutralized workers' rights in the interest of "cutting red tape."[12] During this same period, tens of millions of energetic new migrants began to stream into the United States looking for work, creating an oversupply of cheap labor and further widening the power asymmetry in the workplace.[13] Between 1970 and 2017, in what the U.S.

Census Bureau would deem the "second great wave" of immigration, the foreign-born population in the United States grew from 9.6 million to 45 million people, or from 4.7 percent to 13.7 percent of the population.[14] This historical convergence of declining state enforcement capacity and an influx of low-wage immigrant workers caused millions of workers to fall through the cracks of extant labor and employment laws.

Some of the most vulnerable workers, of course, were excluded from cornerstone labor and employment law protections from the start. In efforts to preserve racial, class, and gender hierarchies in the South, collective bargaining rights and basic employment protections were intentionally denied to the overwhelmingly Black, female, and Latinx workers who were employed as farmworkers and domestic workers; those occupations were excluded from coverage under the NLRA and the FLSA at the behest of Southern members of Congress whose votes were needed to ensure the legislation's passage in the 1930s.[15] Also excluded were public-sector workers and those not technically considered employees—such as day laborers (who were also overwhelmingly non-White), those performing short-term and off-the-books work for cash, independent contractors, and so-called gig workers.

But low-wage workers in "standard" jobs covered under the NLRA and federal and state employment laws—including food and beverage workers, meat-packers, residential construction workers, warehouse workers, oil and gas workers, nail salon workers, car wash and auto repair workers, plant nursery workers, and building and grounds workers—have also found it exceedingly difficult to unionize. Their jobs often feature conditions that are conducive to labor violations, such as high turnover rates and unhealthy and dangerous working environments.[16] Whether intentionally excluded from labor and employment law or rendered particularly vulnerable to exploitation by the nature of their jobs, all low-wage workers in the United States have suffered from deterioration in the quality of their jobs and ineffective labor standards enforcement.

That said, some groups of workers are worse off than others. As Ruben Garcia points out, it is not a coincidence that people of color, women, and immigrants are most likely to be among those he calls "marginal workers," or those "who fall through the margins of different bodies of law that are supposed to protect them" and "are often unable to fully enforce their rights."[17] Black workers and other workers of color, for example, are significantly more likely to face discrimination in pay, hiring, firing, promotion, and quality-of-work assignments; they are disproportionately likely to work in jobs that are not covered by labor and employment laws; and they face uniquely high burdens in the litigation and complaint processes.[18] Women, similarly, often face discrimination and sexual harassment at work, are systematically paid less than men for the same jobs, and "shoulder a substantial burden of reproductive labor responsibilities that impact—and are impacted by—their work lives."[19] Although undocumented immigrants are technically covered by most employment laws and have access to most collective bargaining rights under the NLRA, many (correctly) fear retaliation if they complain or attempt to unionize; furthermore, language barriers leave many immigrants—documented and undocumented—unaware of their legal rights. During the Covid-19 pandemic, for example, new immigrants in New York City were "entering the workforce without knowing their rights, feeling powerless when it comes to confronting or asking for better working conditions . . . in fear of being retaliated [against] for asking personal protective equipment or for asking for a day off," reported Ligia Guallpa, co-executive director of the Worker's Justice Project worker center.[20] Many low-wage workers, of course, check more than one demographic box—for example, Black immigrant women—which means they not only face multiple and overlapping forms of discrimination but have unique experiences that are not reducible to the sum of their subgroups' collective experiences.[21]

Consider the largest constituency of alt-labor groups: low-wage immigrant workers. During the "second great wave" of immigration that began in the mid-1970s, the foreign-born share of the U.S. labor force climbed rapidly, both in real and relative terms. Whereas Black workers and women workers alike have seen their shares of the labor force grow by about 25 percent since the mid-1970s, the share of the total labor force that is foreign-born has grown by more than 300 percent during the same period (from 5.2 percent in 1970 to 17 percent in 2020).[22] Between 1990 and the mid-2000s, the estimated number of undocumented immigrants more than tripled, from about 3.5 million to 12.2 million, before declining to about 10.5 million by 2017 and then plateauing. Nearly a quarter of the foreign-born population in the United States is now estimated to be undocumented.[23]

The last comparable wave of immigration occurred between 1881 and 1920, when about 23 million new immigrants, many recruited by railroad companies and other large firms in need of laborers, came to the United States seeking work and a better life for their families. As Fine has pointed out, the vast majority of these migrants were White Europeans who received immediate work authorization and a pathway to citizenship; in contrast, undocumented migrants during the most recent wave—the vast majority of whom are non-White and hail from Mexico, El Salvador, Guatemala, India, Honduras, and China—have not, for the most part, been warmly welcomed into the workforce or the citizenry.[24] Support for immigration has polarized along partisan lines, with Republicans scapegoating undocumented immigrants for many social and economic discontents. In cities across the United States, undocumented immigrants have found themselves socially, economically, and politically marginalized. Often geographically clustered into race-class subjugated communities, they experience multiple forms of "civic ostracism, social and political oppression, economic marginalization, and state-led governance."[25]

Though the new arrivals may find greater economic opportunities in the United States than in their countries of origin, they also often find harsh working conditions; fierce competition for jobs; instability in employment; racial, ethnic, and gender discrimination; social exclusion; and significant barriers to accessing their legal rights—and they work under the constant threat of deportation.[26] Despite courts affirming many times over that undocumented workers are covered by wage and hour laws, antidiscrimination laws, and even the NLRA—such workers may file wage claims, initiate lawsuits, report dangerous and unhealthy working conditions, and unionize—their employers often retaliate against them for doing so, including by reporting them to U.S. Immigration and Customs Enforcement (ICE).[27] Since the costs of deportation far outweigh the expected benefits of recovering unpaid wages or receiving other forms of compensation for their mistreatment, many undocumented workers make the rational choice not to file complaints when they experience abuse in the workplace.[28]

With labor and employment law remedies either unused by workers or unenforced by the state, employers know they face a very low probability of detection and meager, if any, punishments for illegal behavior. Some unscrupulous employers therefore underpay (or fail to pay) their workers, cut corners on health and safety regulations, retaliate against workers who try to unionize, and exploit them in other ways in order to save on labor costs. Many employers, as noted in chapter 1, face such intense competition in their decentralized, fissured industries that evading labor standards has become baked into their business models.

One of the most common and pernicious problems low-wage workers face—alongside discrimination, health and safety violations, and sexual harassment and abuse—is wage theft, or the failure of employers to pay their employees the full amount they have earned to which they are legally entitled. Wage theft can take a number of different forms, including minimum wage and overtime law violations, off-the-clock violations, meal and rest break violations, illegal deductions, tip stealing, and the misclassification of employees as independent contractors.

To examine the prevalence of wage theft, I used Current Population Survey-Merged Outgoing Rotation Group (CPS-MORG) data to estimate rates of minimum wage violations over the last dozen years (for a discussion of methods, see the appendix). Minimum wage violations are not the most common or expensive type of wage theft (overtime violations probably are), but they are widespread and disproportionately affect the most vulnerable workers who can least afford to be underpaid.[29] When low-wage workers are underpaid by even a small percentage of their income, they face major hardships such as being unable to pay rent or childcare or put food on the table. In addition, minimum wage violations are deleterious to society, as they contribute to widening income inequality, wage stagnation, and reductions in the amount of tax revenue collected, which strains government budgets.[30]

Using the most conservative estimates possible, I find that between 2010 and 2021, 17 percent of low-wage workers were paid less than their state's minimum wage.[31] They lost about $1.86 per hour on average, or 20 percent of the minimum wage to which they were legally entitled.[32] Since these workers reported working roughly thirty-two hours on average per week, this amounted to a loss of over $3,000 per year for year-round workers, on average. Instead of collecting $15,611 per year at the applicable minimum wage (working thirty-two hours per week for fifty-two weeks), the average victim of this form of wage theft instead collected only $12,490. Since 77 percent of these workers were supporting at least one child (two on average), this loss of income would have caused them to fall well below the poverty threshold for two-person families each year.[33] All told, across all fifty states and Washington, D.C., over 50 million workers lost nearly $13 billion per year on average to minimum wage violations, or a total of $155 billion between 2010 and 2021 (table 3.1).[34]

Table 3.1 Estimated Costs of Minimum Wage Violations, 2010–2021

	Share of Eligible Low-Wage Workers (%)	Estimated Number of Workers	Share of Income Lost (%)	Average Hourly Underpayment	Average Weekly Underpayment	Average Annual Underpayment	Total Hourly Unpaid Wages (Aggregate)	Total Weekly Unpaid Wages (Aggregate)	Total Annual Unpaid Wages (Aggregate)
2010	15.4	3,645,181	20	$1.51	$47.96	$2,494	$5,503,115	$174,825,975	$9,090,950,694
2011	14.3	3,402,279	20	$1.51	$47.97	$2,494	$5,149,962	$163,196,055	$8,486,194,878
2012	14.4	3,550,441	21	$1.61	$52.21	$2,715	$5,702,795	$185,358,277	$9,638,630,408
2013	13.3	3,339,691	21	$1.59	$51.63	$2,685	$5,320,840	$172,412,630	$8,965,456,769
2014	14.4	3,683,129	20	$1.63	$53.21	$2,767	$6,017,498	$195,966,928	$10,190,280,270
2015	16.7	4,241,787	19	$1.60	$51.25	$2,665	$6,773,374	$217,389,618	$11,304,260,134
2016	16.9	4,309,827	20	$1.77	$57.12	$2,970	$7,625,421	$246,174,580	$12,801,078,144
2017	19.1	5,005,665	18	$1.71	$54.90	$2,855	$8,569,874	$274,798,910	$14,289,543,329
2018	18.7	4,931,461	19	$1.87	$59.98	$3,119	$9,219,692	$295,781,176	$15,380,621,164
2019	19.0	5,001,026	21	$2.16	$69.74	$3,626	$10,813,041	$348,762,407	$18,135,645,156
2020	18.4	4,483,770	20	$2.27	$72.76	$3,783	$10,159,306	$326,229,627	$16,963,940,598
2021	19.1	4,801,091	20	$2.42	$79.11	$4,114	$11,619,784	$379,807,967	$19,750,014,303
Total/Annual Average	16.6	50,395,348	20	$1.80	$58.15	$3,024	$92,474,700	$2,980,704,151	$154,996,615,848

Source: Author's calculations using CPS-MORG data.

Figure 3.1 Industries with the Highest Minimum Wage Violation Rates, 2010–2021

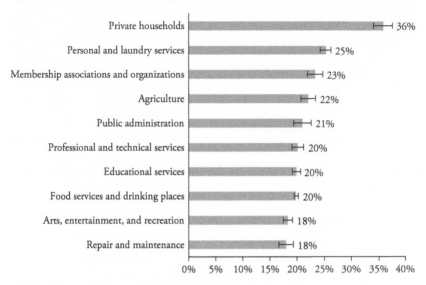

Source: Author's calculations using CPS-MORG data.
Note: Estimates represent predicted probabilities. 95 percent confidence intervals shown.
Average violation rate, all industries: 16 percent.

The highest rates of minimum wage noncompliance were in the following industries: private households (36 percent), personal and laundry services (25 percent), membership associations (23 percent), and agriculture (22 percent) (see figure 3.1).[35] The ten highest-violation industries, shown in figure 3.1, and their relative rankings, were remarkably stable year-to-year. Within those industries, the occupations with the highest violation rates included maids, housekeepers, and childcare workers (for private households); hairdressers, hairstylists, and cosmetologists (personal and laundry services); janitors, building cleaners, and secretaries and administrative assistants (membership associations); and miscellaneous agricultural workers (agriculture).

Across all industries, the highest violation rates were found in the following occupations: waiters and waitresses (32 percent); hairdressers, hairstylists, and cosmetologists (31 percent); bartenders (31 percent); childcare workers (23 percent); agricultural workers (23 percent); food preparation and serving workers (23 percent); and maids and housekeeping cleaners (19 percent) (see figure 3.2).[36]

Figure 3.2 Occupations with the Highest Minimum Wage Violation Rates, 2010–2021

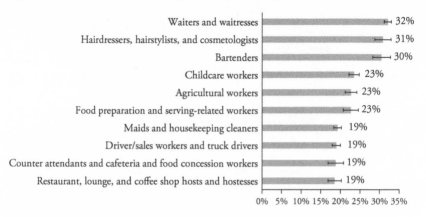

Source: Author's calculations using CPS-MORG data.
Note: Estimates represent predicted probabilities. 95 percent confidence intervals shown.
Average violation rate, all occupations: 17 percent. Includes occupations with $N > 500$.

Race, gender, and citizenship status are also key predictors of minimum wage violations. Among all workers, Black, Hispanic, and Asian workers were much more likely to experience minimum wage violations than were White workers.[37] Noncitizens and workers coded as Hispanic were nearly twice as likely as White workers to be paid less than the statutory minimum, Asian workers were 1.6 times more likely, and Black workers were 1.5 times more likely.[38] Women were 1.4 times more likely than men to be paid less than the statutory minimum. When the interaction of gender, race, and citizenship are taken into account, the effects of discrimination were compounded. Latina women who were not U.S. citizens, for example, were almost 4 times more likely to experience minimum wage violations than were White male citizens; noncitizen Asian women and noncitizen Black women were about 3 times more likely (figure 3.3).

In part, these disparities reflect the greater likelihood that people of color and noncitizens were working in jobs at the bottom of the wage distribution—which reflects, in part, occupational segregation, wage discrimination, and geographic segregation. If we look at only low-wage workers, violation rates across demographic groups were more similar, though Hispanic (18 percent) and Asian (23 percent) workers had higher

Figure 3.3 Demographics and Probability of Minimum Wage Violation by Group, 2010–2021

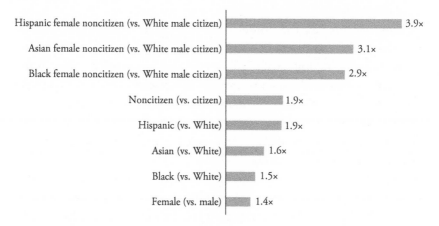

Source: Author's calculations using CPS-ORG data.
Note: All estimates are statistically significant. Error bars are too small to display.

predicted probabilities of experiencing minimum wage violations than White (15 percent) or Black (15 percent) low-wage workers. Although White workers and U.S. citizens experienced the greatest number of minimum wage violations overall, their relative risk of suffering this form of wage theft was lower than it was for workers of color and noncitizens. Specifically, White workers constituted 61 percent of the eligible (nonexempt, covered) workforce but suffered only 48 percent of all minimum wage violations; Hispanic workers, in contrast, made up only 19 percent of the workforce but suffered 28 percent of all violations. Black workers made up only 13 percent of the workforce but suffered 15 percent of all violations, and Asian workers constituted 6 percent of the workforce but suffered 7 percent of violations. Noncitizens, similarly, constituted 10 percent of the workforce but suffered 17 percent of violations.

Other risk factors can be identified as well: those who work part-time (3.3 times more likely), do not have a college degree (2.3 times), work in the service sector (2.1 times), are not unionized (2 times), are not veterans (2 times), are unmarried (1.9 times), are not paid by the hour (1.5 times), changed jobs in the last year (1.3 times), and live in metropolitan areas

(1.3 times) are all more likely to suffer minimum wage violations than their reference group, as well as workers younger than twenty-four or older than sixty-five.

These are precisely the workers who have fallen through the cracks of the labor and employment law regimes, as previously discussed. They disproportionately fill low-quality jobs in fissured industries or work in the informal, unregulated economy and live in race-class subjugated communities where they are vulnerable to multiple forms of social, economic, and political discrimination and coercion. Especially for new low-wage immigrant workers settling in the United States, language barriers, information asymmetries, and poor working conditions in low-wage jobs have amplified the urgent need for organized support, advocacy, and collective action. But these workers have found very few existing organizations dedicated to supporting them and helping them contest their exploitation. As the next section discusses, these dire problems and the lack of existing solutions have created incentives for new organizations to fill the void.

Enter Alt-Labor

A characteristic effect of policy drift is that as the policy gradually ceases to function as intended, new problems emerge that render the policy's target beneficiaries vulnerable. This in turn creates incentives for new groups to enter the field to support those who are left behind.[39] In this case, labor law's drift and the inadequacies of employment law left millions of low-wage workers without sufficient avenues of redress when their rights were violated at work. With few labor unions or other groups serving these constituencies, demand grew for new forms of worker organization. Alt-labor groups thus emerged to support, organize, and advocate for these vulnerable low-wage workers.

The term "alt-labor" primarily refers to nonprofit organizations that organize and support low-wage workers in their fight for their rights.[40] Sometimes, however, the moniker is used by journalists to describe any worker movement that is not explicitly union led—including the Fight for $15 movement funded by the Service Employees International Union (SEIU), online platforms such as coworker.org, and the wildcat teacher strikes of 2018. To keep the present analysis focused on dynamics within the organizational core of the alt-labor movement, I focus here on groups that are registered as nonprofit organizations who organize and support low-wage workers in their fight for their rights. The predominant type of alt-labor group is the worker center, defined by Fine as "community-based mediating institutions that provide support to and organize among communities of low-wage workers."[41] Alt-labor also includes community-based groups that do not self-identify as worker centers (or explicitly reject the worker center label) but pursue the same core priorities; groups that organize and operate at a regional or national scale; "sister" entities registered under the 501(c)(4) "social welfare" section of the tax code that employ different strategies and tactics than traditional worker centers; and "amalgams" such as Make the Road New York (MRNY) that tackle a wide range of issues while prioritizing workers' rights and economic justice.[42]

By definition, all worker centers conduct three core activities: service provision, advocacy, and organizing.[43] Services include assistance to workers in understanding and asserting their rights, documenting their grievances, filing formal complaints, interacting with regulatory agencies, and suing unscrupulous employers; language and skills training to boost members' job prospects; access to specific benefits such as insurance, bank accounts, and government assistance; and referrals to legal clinics, health clinics, and other nonprofits. Advocacy includes conducting and disseminating research on exploitative conditions in the workplace, calling for policy changes, monitoring employers' compliance with labor standards, and interfacing with enforcement agencies. Organizing involves leadership development, community building, and direct economic action to confront abusive employers.[44] As numerous scholars have shown, each worker center also undertakes additional activities specific to that group's context, culture, and membership needs.[45]

Alt-labor groups that do not consider themselves worker centers, including regional or national networks, either downplay or do not provide services; they primarily focus on organizing and advocacy. Amalgams typically offer all three worker center functions alongside a range of other activities. All alt-labor groups seek to empower workers and help them mobilize in collective action to demand justice.

In 2022, Thomas Kochan and colleagues identified at least 246 operational worker centers in the United States (figure 3.4).[46] Given that only a handful were in operation in the 1980s, this number reflects dramatic

Figure 3.4 The Fast Growth of Worker Centers, 1980–2021

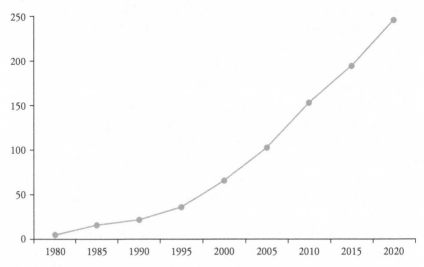

Source: Author's calculations from Fine, Narro, and Barnes 2018, 14, figure 2, and Kochan et al. 2022, 6.

growth in this organizational field. The proliferation of community-based alt-labor groups that do not consider themselves worker centers, the establishment of 501(c)(4) sister organizations, and the expansion of regional and national networks have increased the total number of alt-labor groups further still; alt-labor groups thus likely number between 250 and 300 today. The actual number is unknown; no formal registry exists. In addition, many groups enter and exit the field each year as some of the smaller, poorer groups do not survive and preexisting groups that did not previously tackle workers' rights issues take on those functions in response to the needs of their members.

The first worker centers were founded in the 1970s and 1980s by diverse groups in diverse locations for diverse reasons: by immigrant activists in New York City and in Southern California to support day laborers, restaurant workers, and domestic workers; by Chinese immigrants in San Francisco to support low-wage workers in their community; by immigrant advocates along the border in El Paso, Texas, to support Mexican immigrants; and by Black workers and their advocates in Southern states in response to anti-Black discrimination against nonunionized workers in the retail sector.[47]

The second wave of worker centers arose in the late 1980s and early 1990s in response to the stream of immigrants and refugees from Central America and Southeast Asia settling in large metro areas. Many focused on organizing and supporting domestic workers, garment workers, day laborers, construction workers, and taxi drivers, and many were founded by faith groups. In the third wave after the turn of the millennium, worker centers continued to emerge in urban areas, but a greater number appeared in rural and suburban communities, especially in southern states, where Mexican and Central American immigrants were lured by work opportunities in the food processing industries and in the agricultural and service sectors; new worker centers were also sprouted by and for Filipino, Korean, African, and South Asian immigrants.[48]

In the late 2000s, the Los Angeles Black Worker Center was founded—the first in a string of Black worker centers networked and "incubated" by the National Black Worker Center (NBWC) that today number around a dozen.[49] Offering an early model of intersectional organizing, Black worker centers aim not (only) to "train workers out of the [labor market] problems" they face—including unemployment, underemployment, and low-quality, low-wage jobs—but to organize them and build a "new kind of labor movement that could center racial justice and economic justice and bring [the two] together," explained Lola Smallwood-Cuevas of the NBWC.[50] In addition to combating labor market problems, Black worker centers fight discrimination, the barriers facing those formerly incarcerated, and the distinct challenges facing Black immigrants.

In the overarching main, however, immigrant settlement patterns have been the driving force behind the spatial dispersion of worker centers. In 2012, Fine and Theodore found a clear correlation between the places where the 212 worker centers they identified had taken root and places where the concentration of immigrants was highest.[51] However, the founding and proliferation of worker centers was not a coordinated movement. There was no centralized effort to develop these groups; nor was there a common organizational model or design (although second- and third-wave groups tended to take notes from earlier waves). Although some national networks such as the NBWC and the National Day Laborer Organizing Network (NDLON) have helped new groups get off the ground, most organizations have emerged independently, built from the bottom up in response to urgent problems facing workers in their localities. Some have been founded by immigrants and native-born low-wage workers with support from allied organizations; others by individuals associated with faith-based groups; and others by social service organizations, legal aid groups, immigrant nonprofits, or labor unions.[52]

In her groundbreaking study of worker centers, Fine found that most groups emerged in response to "the decline of institutions that historically provided workers with a vehicle for collective action," such as labor unions and immigrant advocacy groups.[53] "While worker centers have grown out of a range of institutions, they have sprung from a common desire for a local organization that would provide services, conduct advocacy, and encourage organizing on the part of low-wage workers in the absence of anything else."[54] One common thread running through most groups' origin stories, Fine found, was a catalyzing event of workplace exploitation or a labor market–related disruption that led workers to seek support from an existing nonprofit group. Because those groups had not typically focused on workplace justice issues, they either expanded their purviews to include such concerns or spun off new organizations. They "almost literally 'backed into' organizing and advocating for low-wage workers. They did so upon discovering that a service approach was simply not enough and that there was a void in terms of institutions for collective action among low-wage workers."[55]

Indeed, despite the centrality of service provision to many groups, they are not and have never been exclusively service-oriented nonprofits that deliver social services, as in Nicole Marwell's well-known study of nonprofit community-based organizations; nor are they like the professionalized nonprofit community-based organizations that plan and implement policy on behalf of the government, as in Jeremy Levine's important study.[56] They are grassroots groups that exist in the "shadow of the shadow state," in Ruth Wilson Gilmore's words, meaning that although they may receive some public funds, they are not primarily direct service providers; the government serves as both "the object of their advocacy and their antagonisms"; they have "detailed political programs and deep social and economic critiques"; and the "real focus of their energies is ordinary people whom they wish fervently to organize against their own abandonment."[57] In many ways, alt-labor groups best approximate social movement organizations that have developed heterogeneous "repertoires of contention," as I discuss further in chapter 5.[58] That said, although they engage in disruptive and transgressive forms of collective action, many groups also do undertake many conventional nonprofit behaviors and a growing number engage in activities more commonly associated with interest groups or political organizations.[59] They are, in short, experimental, almost improvisational organizational forms that have emerged and developed in response to the problems their members face. Fine aptly labeled them "hybrid organizations" for their combination of "elements of different types of organizations, from social service agencies, fraternal organizations, settlement houses, community organizing groups, and unions to social movement organizations."[60] Nonprofit worker organizations and immigrant advocacy organizations, of course, have a long history in the United States: in the Progressive Era, groups such as the Women's Trade Union League waged vigorous campaigns to expose sweatshops and unscrupulous employers; those early reformers also campaigned for workplace protections and unionization and offered services for immigrant workers from Southern and Eastern Europe in much the same fashion as contemporary worker centers do for immigrants from Latin America and Asia.[61]

Usually embedded in immigrant-majority neighborhoods or in majority-minority race-class subjugated communities, alt-labor groups typically have organizational identities that reflect their cultural contexts. Oftentimes, "ethnic identity and the experience of prejudice are central analytical lenses through which experiences in and the organization of the labor market as a whole are understood," write Victor Narro and Fine.[62] Race, ethnicity, country of origin, and language are also frequently the primary ties that bind workers together, foster collective action, and recruit new members, as the groups' tap members' social networks and fashion their outreach efforts to appeal to shared identities and backgrounds. From the beginning, the groups have integrated the rich heterogeneity of cultural traditions their members brought from their countries of origin into their organizing practices, while also drawing on the teachings of the U.S. civil rights movement, women's rights movements, Black nationalist movements, Latin American liberation and guerrilla movements, liberation theology, movements of the Global South, and immigrant rights struggles.

Most alt-labor groups organize predominantly within certain neighborhoods, cities, or counties. However, much of the growth over the last two decades has occurred among national alt-labor networks that organize workers along occupational or industrial lines: for example, NDLON,

National Domestic Workers Alliance (NDWA), Restaurant Opportunities Center United (ROC), and the retail-centered United for Respect (UFR).[63] Sector-focused community-based groups such as the Workers Defense Project (WDP), which focuses primarily on the construction industry, and Pineros y Campesinos Unidos del Noroeste (PCUN), which focuses on farmworkers, have also thrived. Precious few groups organize workers according to their employment status—such as CWC (for temp workers) and the Freelancers Union (gig workers). Most groups appeal to all low-wage workers in their communities. Those that organize along sectoral lines, however, have reportedly had an easier time forging partnerships with alt-labor's most important allies, labor unions.[64]

Relations with unions are discussed at some length in chapter 5. Suffice it to say, notwithstanding the steady decline of organized labor over the last half century, alt-labor groups operate in an arena in which some of the most significant resources (material and ideational) are still controlled by labor unions—the groups with the strongest stake in the labor law regime and whose own commitments and operations remain powerfully shaped by it. Although some unions have begun to forge ties with nonprofit worker organizations in recent years, and although the two types of worker organizations often stand shoulder to shoulder in public policy campaigns and street-level protests, their relationship has historically been rocky.[65]

But they are not competitors. As Tom Juravich argues, alt-labor groups and traditional labor unions have developed such different approaches that they are best understood as operating "in distinct arenas of power against fundamentally different adversaries."[66] Perhaps because of their different foci, unions have never significantly funded the alt-labor movement. Alt-labor organizations have therefore had to seek out their own resources, primarily from private foundations and other external sources—a dependency that has not come without serious trade-offs, as discussed later.

Alt-labor groups nevertheless have been profoundly influenced by labor unions. Many share the ideological commitments and long-term aspirations of social movement–oriented labor unions and see themselves as constituent parts of the labor movement—not as alternatives to it, as the term seems to imply. "There is nothing 'alt' about us," writes Adam Kader of Arise Chicago. "There is one labor movement, made up of workers asserting democracy and insisting on dignity."[67] From the beginning, worker centers have mimicked some labor union tactics while leveraging their flexibility as nonprofit organizations to experiment with new approaches. Like unions, they help workers to organize concerted action for "mutual aid and protection" (protected by section 7 of the NLRA) and train them to organize others; they also support workers in their confrontations with employers and pursue multiple strategies to improve workers' wages, hours, safety, and other terms and conditions of employment.

But alt-labor groups are not, and never have been, unions. As noted, they have emerged in an organizational environment that is particularly hostile to labor unions. While their organizational structure offers them certain advantages in the legal, political, and resource environments they face, it also comes with some important constraints.

As nonprofits registered under the 501(c)(3) or 501(c)(4) sections of the tax code, rather than the 501(c)(5) section designated for labor unions, alt-labor groups perform very different functions, must abide by different rules, and have different opportunities from those of unions. Though many do organize workers in specific industries and design campaigns that target individual employers, unlike labor unions, they are not anchored to individual worksites. This suits the groups' members, who often change industries or work in multiple industries simultaneously, making it much harder for them to unionize. Alt-labor groups do not (and cannot) seek majority representation at individual firms, nor do they engage in collective bargaining or serve as workers' exclusive bargaining representatives, as per the rules of national labor law. Nor have the groups focused exclusively on workers' rights, as many traditional labor unions do: to respond to their members' most urgent concerns, most alt-labor groups have enlarged the scope of their issue agendas to include immigrants' rights, racial justice, women's rights, gender justice, housing, criminal justice, and other issues affecting their communities and families.[68] While both unions and alt-labor groups undertake policy campaigns, alt-labor groups, as nonprofits, face significant legal restrictions on what they are able do in the political arena.[69]

Although alt-labor groups lack many of the advantages that labor unions enjoy, they have their own comparative advantages: they reach deeply into decentralized industries where unions have not successfully penetrated; many of their workers have in-depth "salient knowledge" of industry strategies and employer practices; and because of their flexible organizational forms, they are able to support and organize workers that unions have had difficulty reaching.[70] Whereas unions typically select targets for organizing campaigns carefully and strategically to advance long-term goals and maximize returns, alt-labor groups are more likely to expend what minimal resources they have to help vulnerable, needy workers that unions might otherwise view as "too risky to justify the time and expense of an organizing campaign."[71]

The nonprofit tax status of alt-labor groups also grants them some operational flexibility that unions lack. For example, whereas unions are forbidden to engage in secondary boycotts, alt-labor groups can and do pressure companies that do business with unscrupulous employers in order to increase their leverage on those employers. As most groups are 501(c)(3) nonprofits, they are also eligible to receive funding from philanthropic foundations, and the donations they receive are generally tax deductible and anonymous.[72]

Because they operate almost entirely outside the labor law regime, alt-labor groups have had to develop creative strategies to support their members and combat workplace exploitation. Their repertoires of action have long been heterogeneous. In addition to service provision, skills training, and referrals, all groups emphasize leadership development, community building, and organizing to help low-wage workers discover their agency and overcome their collective action problems. Their most well-known strategy is the workplace justice campaign, discussed in the next chapter, whereby groups of workers organize disruptive, confrontational actions, protests, and public shaming strategies to expose abusive employer practices and pressure employers to redress the wrongs they have committed against workers. Due to the limited scope and impact of these campaigns, however, a growing number of groups have made public policy campaigns an increasingly central strategy, also elaborated in the next chapter. Many also conduct research on exploitive conditions in low-wage industries, and several have developed sophisticated understandings of the role that financial actors play in structuring political and economic landscapes; many are now developing strategies to combat these private actors' oftentimes hidden uses of power. Some groups have also orchestrated complex supply chain strategies, best exemplified by the successful yearslong campaign by the CIW to pressure brand-name restaurants to improve labor conditions for low-wage agricultural workers.[73] Unfortunately, such examples are the exception rather than the rule.

In the overarching main, alt-labor groups have failed to use their members' economic leverage to improve working conditions across industries. This failure is perhaps best understood in contrast to the traditional labor union model of power. Whereas unions historically derived their clout in the economic and political realms from their structural and associational power (their members' strategic positions in production processes and their power in numbers), alt-labor groups have neither developed the ability to significantly affect production processes or supply chains nor managed to grow a mass base of dues-paying members.[74] Their members often work in low-quality jobs featuring high turnover, in fissured industries at the bottom of supply chains, on informal work assignments, or as temporary workers or (often misclassified) independent contractors. Their physical dispersion, job instability, and sometimes ambiguous employment status weaken their leverage with employers, limit the scope of their economic actions, and hamper their ability to unionize; indeed, in recent decades, there have been precious few examples of unionization among low-wage workers.[75] Although alt-labor groups have altered conditions at some firms by orchestrating successful workplace justice campaigns—and although the SEIU-funded Fight for $15 demonstrated low-wage workers' ability to organize on a mass scale within a fissured sector—alt-labor groups have struggled to exercise broader "structural power" in their members' industries.[76] Their limited ability to effect economic change helps to explain the arc of alt-labor's development, as the groups have sought out alternative methods of improving working conditions for their members.

The frustrations they have experienced in trying to effect change through economic action are owed, in significant part, to their failure to build a mass base of members. The dispersed nature of their members' jobs and the multiple demands these workers face have made it exceptionally difficult for alt-labor groups to build the kind of "associational power" that has historically powered labor unions. As Milkman writes: "Low-wage workers often work long hours, commute great distances, and have families to care for, which leaves them with little time to devote to membership activities in these organizations, particularly without the incentive of ongoing representation of the sort unions can provide."[77] Alt-labor groups thus lack two key sources of power—structural and associational—that labor unions have long used to their advantage.

The groups' membership challenges are inextricably related to their funding difficulties—and both raise questions about how to ensure that they will continue to represent and serve their members and the broader low-wage community effectively and authentically.

Tensions in the Alt-Labor Organizational Model: Membership, Dues, and Foundation Funding

The absence of a mass base is not an incidental problem for alt-labor: because a small membership creates financial challenges, it affects everything a group is able to do. Large memberships provide labor unions with power in numbers, which they can wield in the economic and political realms, but that is not all large membership rolls do. Formal dues payments—often made through automatic paycheck deductions negotiated through collective bargaining agreements—generate the lion's share of labor unions' revenue, fuel their operations, grant them independence from outside influence, and generate pressure for leaders to be accountable to members.

Alt-labor groups, in contrast, lack similar systems. A few do not charge dues; some have only "suggested" dues. Many technically have dues but have not developed formal processes for collecting them; some offer alternatives to dues payment (for example, participation in activities or progression through training programs) as a route to membership in good standing. None generate significant revenue through dues; in all the groups I studied, membership dues account for only a very small fraction of their revenue.

Among those that do ask members to pay dues—whether suggested or required—the fee is usually nominal. Groups typically charge a few dollars per month or between $20 to $120 per year. CWJ, for example, charges $20 for an individual and $25 for a family yearly membership. "We don't take a lot of dues from them because all of them are low income," explained cofounder Mazahir Salih. "And we are flexible: you can give us $10 now, $5 now, more later, until you finish it through the year."[78] This sentiment was echoed by Jessica Vosburgh, executive director of Adelante Alabama in Birmingham: "Nominally we have suggested donation dues, [but] I think because our membership is low wage to extremely low wage, we never wanted to even try to build a model where dues were a significant source of income for us—although a lot of our members do donate, and on an incredibly generous level relative to their income and wealth."[79] Typically, if a member fails to pay dues or fulfill membership obligations through other routes, that member is no longer eligible to vote on leadership—but can still attend classes and events and participate in actions.

Most alt-labor leaders argue that nominal, "symbolic" dues are important even if they do not fund the organization in any significant part. "Even if it's just a few dollars," explained Ursula Price, executive director of the New Orleans Workers' Center for Racial Justice (NOWCRJ), "it gives people a sense of ownership and it clearly defines decision-making."[80] Added Rachel LaZar, director of El Centro de Igualdad y Derechos in Albuquerque, New Mexico: "Even if it's nominal, there is something important about people saying, 'We're going to give our time, but we're also going to invest in this movement because it's that important to us.'"[81] As Gilmore notes, "when one owns something one cannot sell—such as membership in an organization—one is more likely to participate in it."[82] Most group leaders echo these sentiments, even if very few have well-established dues-based systems. At the time of my study, only a dozen did; but the revenue they generated was very small, and the regularity and formality of their collection processes varied.

Whether the groups can build—or ever could have built—mass dues-paying memberships sufficient to fund their operations is an open question. Perhaps members' low incomes make it impossible to rely heavily on dues; as some of the above quotes indicate, members' inability to fully fund the organization is often taken as given.[83] Some analysts, however, consider this point both condescending and incorrect: the Justice for Janitors movement, after all, has spurred tens of thousands of low-wage immigrant workers and workers of color to join unions, to which they regularly pay dues; the United Farm Workers, likewise, charged dues before it became a union, despite the low incomes of its members (but had trouble collecting them); in the 1970s, the Massachusetts Fair Share organization had over 100,000 working class members who paid $15 in dues; and low-income churchgoers similarly generated the bulk of the financial resources for many local civil rights movements in the 1960s.[84] Perhaps, then, dues-based systems have not taken root because leaders and organizers have been reluctant to ask for money from their members out of concern that a dues requirement would reduce the trust alt-labor groups have built or create a fee-for-service culture. "We don't want people thinking we're solving problems for a fee," said one director, "that we're professionals who can solve their problems. As soon as they're with the program for a bit, they see this is different: it's not a transactional payment, it's a solidarity payment."[85] But it could also be that the groups have simply failed to convince members that the organizations are worth paying for. Or perhaps the desire of many organizations to represent all low-wage immigrant workers and workers of color in their communities—not just serve "an exclusive club of members whose interests we represent," as one leader put it—makes establishing more rigorous membership systems a low priority. Some leaders point to the difficulty of collecting dues outside the workplace—for example, alt-labor's inability to automatically deduct dues from workers' paychecks, as unions typically do, or some members' lack of checking accounts—as an explanation for the lack of formal dues-based systems. Although some groups have attempted to implement innovative auto-payment systems, none have taken hold. Whatever the reason, the result is the same: few groups have well-established dues systems, and those that do cannot survive on members' dues alone.[86]

The minimal amount of revenue generated through dues has incentivized alt-labor groups to pursue alternative sources of funding. Most groups, in consequence, have become heavily reliant on external sources such as philanthropic foundations, individual donors, subgrants from other nonprofit organizations, and government grants (though some reject government funding on principle).[87] Although many alt-labor groups have formalized partnerships or strong informal alliances with labor unions, Leslie Gates and Kati Griffith find that labor union funding constitutes only a "minuscule portion" of the groups' revenue (1.1 percent).[88] In their comprehensive study of worker center revenue in 2012, they found that at least 80 percent of worker center revenue came from external sources, the bulk from foundations; only 1.8 percent of worker centers' revenue came from membership dues. Among the groups I studied, average reported revenue from dues was less than 1 percent.[89] Reported revenues are inexact, but interviews confirm that dues constitute but a "very small fraction" of overall revenues; the greatest share of the groups' income clearly comes from philanthropic grants, and the rest from "program services" and other internal programming (such as the arts and culture events and community radio station operated by South Florida immigrant worker enter WeCount!).

Scholars, organizers, and activists alike have expressed concern over alt-labor groups' reliance on external funding—especially private philanthropic foundations.[90] One of the primary concerns is the capriciousness of the funding: it is never guaranteed, and few grants last longer than a few years. Reliance on external funding therefore poses a threat to the groups' long-term sustainability and leaves them in a perpetually precarious state.

But perhaps the biggest concern centers on the ways in which foundations' priorities may affect the groups' organizational behaviors. Foundations are often reluctant to fund groups whose mission is to critique, confront, and dismantle the systems that support the highly unequal accumulation of wealth on which philanthropy is based.[91] And until recently, precious little funding was available for organizing, per se, and other power-building activities that do not result in short-term accomplishments and easily quantifiable results. Foundation funding has tended to flow more freely toward less controversial and confrontational work that fits funders' worldviews and standard metrics of evaluation.[92]

The relationship between foundations and grassroots groups thus features some problematic power dynamics that can create perverse incentives for group behavior. As Steven Teles writes, foundations' preferences and organizational practices can "filter down to the organizations they fund, shaping the strategies and resources that are deployed. . . . Grantee and grantor are playing a two-level game, the outcome of which determines which organizations are funded, which of the many activities they might engage in that they actually prioritize, and with what level of effectiveness they are able to act on their strategies."[93] The concern is that the pressure to attract foundation funding may cause alt-labor groups to emphasize programs and activities that are favored by their funders even if they abrade the groups' core commitments.

What is more, external funding may undermine the groups' membership-building efforts. A self-reinforcing cycle may emerge whereby the receipt of outside funding relieves the pressure to build a larger membership base from which to collect dues, which contributes to having a small membership, which increases the need for external funding. This cycle, furthermore, may be reinforced by the members themselves: some group leaders report a kind of path dependence, whereby their members resist efforts to move toward a dues-based model once they are accustomed to not paying dues.

At the center of these concerns is the question of accountability. If alt-labor groups had stronger dues-based systems in place, the argument goes, they would have stronger incentives to be responsive to members' concerns as opposed to foundations' priorities; if they depended on members' dues payments to stay afloat, leaders would have to be more accountable to members. Without strong systems in place, how accountable can they be to their members, in practice? As Fine writes, notwithstanding many groups' efforts to streamline their fundraising operations, "it is still worth contemplating what kind of capacity is lost when a low-wage worker organization relies upon external sources rather than internal sources (dues) for its core support; fundraising that requires constantly talking to workers creates a different type of culture, capacity, and accountability than fundraising that focuses on external sources."[94] Put more bluntly, an anonymous progressive leader told Robert Kuttner: "Billionaire funding liberates organizations from having to have a base. When you have a billionaire base, there is no incentive to do the organizing and get the feedback you need to be aligned with how real people feel about issues."[95]

Some, indeed, have questioned whether external funding has turned the groups into "paper tigers" that appear to represent low-wage workers but in actuality pursue the objectives set on high by foundations and other grant-makers. How autonomous and self-determining can the groups truly be if they rely heavily on foundation funding? This concern speaks not only to the groups' autonomy and authenticity but to their power-building capacities. As Hahrie Han, Elizabeth McKenna, and Michelle Oyakawa have noted, independence, flexibility, and commitment are the key resources people-powered organizations can cultivate in their constituency base that provide them with "a broader array of strategic choices" in future negotiations and conflicts.[96] When a group is "beholden to another person or group's assessment of value"—for example, when it is dependent on foundation funding—its independence may be compromised, its flexibility and freedom to maneuver may be restricted, and its capacity to adapt to changing conditions may be diminished.[97] Without a large membership base whose commitment to the organization is reinforced through regular dues payments, the groups' ability to activate or "deliver" their membership may be compromised as well. Reliance on foundation funding may therefore threaten the essential resources groups need to "exercise power in dynamic political environments."[98]

These concerns are compounded by the critique that the groups too often hire executive directors from outside the organization—attorneys, people with fundraising or nonprofit managerial experience, former labor organizers, and those with other types of expertise—in a parallel to the elite and middle class–led Progressive reform movements around the turn of the last century.[99] Although most of the executive directors I encountered emerged from within their communities and have racial, ethnic, and cultural ties to them—many are immigrants or the children of immigrants—most were never low-wage workers and some are White, which can revive the antiracist critique of Alinsky-style community organizations dominated by White staff.[100] Executive directors typically manage day-to-day operations, raise funds, provide direct services to members, and exercise visible leadership in the groups. While this can be a valuable arrangement, especially in helping new groups get off the ground, it can also exist in tension with the groups' goals of being member-driven organizations. Indeed, it can be unclear who is leading whom within the group—the members or the paid executive director? The answer depends on the group, the personalities involved, the decision at stake, and so forth. But in the absence of a strong dues-based system, it stands to reason that leaders (elected and hired) will have greater discretion and weaker incentives to be responsive to members, especially given the groups' dependency on foundations. As organizer Steve Jenkins wrote in his critical analysis of the worker center movement, to the extent that "the membership must rely on outside support, control of the campaign will pass to whoever has the most expertise about how to mobilize that support, and the demands and activities of the group will be altered to suit the requirements of their potential supporters."[101]

All the group leaders I spoke with acknowledged these tensions while noting that external funding, especially from philanthropic foundations, will likely constitute the largest portion of their revenues due to their members' low incomes and ingrained views on dues, their inability to collect automatic paycheck deductions, the lack of better alternatives, and their nonprofit status. Every leader also expressed a genuine desire to authentically represent their members and maintain the group's autonomy. But as Jenkins writes, "when the financial basis for building member power is based on other people's money, it is impossible to assert that the organization simply represents the voice of its membership."[102] How, then, to ensure that their agendas and priorities are primarily reflective of what their members, rather than their funders, want?

Most leaders readily acknowledge that they have not yet identified the perfect formula for balancing their groups' need for foundation funding with the groups' goal of being people-powered organizations—but this is not for a lack of trying. Although each group attends to this dilemma in its own way, most endeavor to be accountable to their members despite their external funding in three primary ways: (1) establishing democratic leadership selection processes and creating other formal internal structures to integrate the greatest number of workers in decision-making; (2) emphasizing activities that are directly responsive to members' greatest concerns, such as individual services and workplace justice campaigns; and (3) pursuing expansive issue agendas that commit the groups to tackling the wide variety of problems their members face.[103] The first strategy is addressed here; the second and third are examined in chapters 4 and 5, respectively.

Theoretically, internal democratic processes can provide alternative routes to accountability that do not depend on formal dues-collection systems.[104] But the devil is in the details, and most groups are still experimenting with different systems. In groups with formal membership systems, members in good standing can usually vote and stand for elections for leadership roles and for seats on the board of trustees. Adelante Alabama and CWJ, for example, both have about two hundred dues-paying, voting-eligible members who can become leaders. (They each also have several hundred people who occasionally participate in actions and are on email lists, as well as thousands of followers on social media.) Elections are held to determine the groups' boards of directors—and according to the bylaws for both organizations, a majority of board members must be members. Rules and norms, too, dictate that leaders rotate out of their positions after a certain number of years. Although their bases are small, alt-labor leaders often point to elections as an important mechanism of accountability.

Many groups have also sought to integrate leadership development into their membership structures. In 2020, for example, NOWCRJ began moving to a flat membership structure that was linked to a three-tiered leadership school. Members could graduate from the ground level (basic member) to become "developing leaders" before progressing to the advanced level, which included eligibility for elected leadership and board service.

Mandating dues, however, was not likely to be part of the plan. "It goes against the history of the worker center," its director Price explained. "And peoples' automatic reaction is always negative. If we go to a dues structure, it's going to take a while to make that turn."

PWC has for many years sought to develop leadership structures to ensure that the organization is controlled by its membership, even as it draws the vast majority of its financial support from private foundations. Like other groups, PWC members elect leaders to its primary decision-making body. But PWC has also developed a distributed leadership structure based on a small-circle model of organization—which it has retooled in several iterations over the years.[105] It has also added a worker fellow program, in which low-wage workers spend time on various staff teams and are integrated into all the organization's planning and evaluation processes. PWC's internal organizational structures have evolved over time: its processes reflect ongoing efforts to ensure that the organization is "owned by the members, versus the foundations," said cofounder and executive director Aquilino Soriano-Versoza.[106]

From its beginnings, MRNY was designed to be a member-driven community center whose issue agenda was built with a bottom-up approach by members participating in open dialogue in regular meetings. This is what MRNY calls the "high touch" model.[107] MRNY is internally structured around multiple issue programs, beginning with its workplace justice project; over time, committees were developed around education justice; health justice; housing and environmental justice; immigration, policing, and criminal justice; transgender, gender nonconforming, intersex, and queer justice; and youth power. Each program has its own community, although members often participate in multiple committees. Each committee is staffed and led by members; paid staff play a supportive role. MRNY deliberately mixes agenda-setting meetings with rice-and-bean dinners, socializing events, direct services, member-led presentations, and myriad other activities. Organizers joke about the endless meetings, but also readily acknowledge that those meetings are vital to how the organization operates—it is through meetings that members find fellowship, articulate grievances, plan collectively to address the many interconnected issues that shape their lives, and maintain ownership over the organization.

At any given moment, issue-based committees are typically running multiple mini-campaigns (for example, legislative policy campaigns, campaigns against abusive landlords, and workplace justice campaigns). Each campaign has its own leadership team comprising members who help to guide the campaign; those leaders are authorized by the other members to participate in decision-making on their behalf. Campaign leaders play a particularly vital role in the final phase of campaigns when the group is negotiating a deal and must make compromises while upholding the groups' priorities. At least twice a year, MRNY also holds leadership retreats centered on particular issue areas to discuss ongoing campaigns and plan new ones; the organization also holds regular leadership training programs. Members in good standing can vote to elect and run for the board of directors on the condition that they are active in the leadership team of a committee and have gone through MRNY's leadership schools.

The membership and leadership structures developed by Adelante in Alabama, CWJ in Iowa, NOWCRJ in New Orleans, PWC in Southern California, and MRNY in New York illustrate how alt-labor groups of different sizes, in different states and regions, catering to different racial-ethnic groups are trying to balance member responsiveness and account-ability with their need for external funding. From an analytic perspective, however, measuring the extent to which a group's priorities authentically reflect its members' interests (versus those of their funders) is difficult. For example, I did not speak with any members who expressed opposition to, or discomfort with, their organization's activities and campaigns, even in well-funded groups that receive large grants from foundations. Though many rank-and-file members mentioned the large challenges their orga-nizations face—both in terms of finances and in terms of confronting the powerful forces arrayed against them—members were uniformly proud and supportive of the work their groups were doing. Of course, they may not have told me if they felt otherwise! The bigger challenge in measuring responsiveness, however, may be self-selection, whereby those who approve of the groups' agendas choose to become members while those who would prefer a different agenda do not join; in both cases, the decision to become a member is shaped by the organization's preexisting priorities and the nature of its outreach strategies. Issues that are important to many low-wage work-ers may never even make it onto the groups' agendas; we may never know how many latent issues are being overlooked. Indeed, as Jenkins argues in his penetrating critique, "whether we are consciously aware of it or not, the construction of the membership is largely a product of the initial outreach process. Consequently, the views of the membership largely reflect the political vision of the foundations and the staff, regardless of the decision-making structures within the organization." As I discuss in chapter 5, many groups canvas extensively in their communities and endeavor to construct bottom-up issue agendas that authentically reflect the concerns of their members and their communities. But the critique is still valid that democratic structures may generate the appearance of authentic member-driven priorities while the groups' priorities are actually determined by staff and funders.

However, this critique is also unfalsifiable: Even concrete evidence of member responsiveness cannot be said to be a true reflection of members' interests if members self-select into groups that reflect staff and funders' priorities. Nor can we prove that the groups do not represent members' interests. Thus, whether the groups' internal structures, processes, and strategies help to generate authentic responsiveness and accountability to members remains an open question; while some groups may be more accountable to their members than others, one's view of their efforts in this regard may ultimately turn on the degree of skepticism one brings to the table. Whatever the truth may be, alt-labor groups are certainly aware of the tension and are working to achieve accountability through their internal decision-making processes and via the activities to which they devote time and resources.

Another way to gauge how well alt-labor groups are managing their membership/funding dilemma may be to look for patterns in the relationship between the groups' level of funding and their apparent responsiveness to members. My "diverse case" sample size is small, but it is notable that with the exception of MRNY and the Chinese Progressive Association (CPA), the most well-funded groups in my study were not community-based organizations but national networks structured in ways that limit member-driven decision-making—including the Center for Popular Democracy (CPD), NDWA, Center for Popular Democracy Action (CPDA), and ROC. That said, all but CPDA link together smaller community-based groups that have their own membership and leadership structures. Meanwhile, the groups in my sample with the least funding—including Worker Justice Wisconsin (WJW), Needham Area Immigration Task Force, CWJ, WeCount!, New Labor, Adelante, and El Centro—are independent and member-driven but are also the most constrained in what they can do by their limited budgets.

Some have struggled to cover basic operating expenses. With less organizational capacity and scale than better-funded groups, their ability to deliver results for their members is significantly more limited. Across the full sample, however, the relationship between funding levels and groups' responsiveness to members does not seem to correlate consistently: some well-funded organizations have strong democratic structures (for example, MRNY, CPA, WDP, and PWC) and some poorer organizations are still developing formal member-driven decision-making processes (for example, WJW, WeCount!, and El Centro). The relationship, in other words, does not reveal anything straightforward or predictive.

Perhaps the absence of a strong correlation between a group's funding and its accountability structures should not be surprising. The critique of foundation funding, after all, may be too blunt: the receipt of foundation funding does not necessarily mean that a group lacks autonomy or has blindly adopted the priorities of foundations. For example, as the following chapters discuss, alt-labor groups have often developed innovative programs on shoestring budgets, using "sweat equity" to get them off the ground, and then sought funding on their own terms (for example, at CPA, the Center for Empowered Politics (CEP), and Heartland Workers Center, discussed in chapters 5 and 6). Many funders, moreover, have moved away from "project-driven portfolios" in favor of grants for "general operating support" that either are not tied to specific projects or have vague stipulations that simply reiterate the groups' core objectives—a positive development that may lessen some of the "dependency and accommodation" that has long plagued the nonprofit-foundation relationship.[108] Between 2011 and 2019, for example, the Ford Foundation provided NOWCRJ an average of $854,000 per year for "general support to build the power and participation of workers and communities and project support for capacity building and organizational development."[109] The W. K. Kellogg Foundation likewise recently provided PWC with $300,000 in "general operating support to help the organization advance its mission to address issues faced by Pilipinx immigrant workers and their families in low-wage industries, through programs that meet immediate needs and organizing efforts to make collective, proactive, and long term changes."[110] NDWA also received $750,000 for "general operating support" to "enable the organization to achieve its mission of ensuring respect, recognition and inclusion in labor protections for domestic workers."[111] Adelante received "general support" grants from the Heising-Simons Foundation; Public Welfare Foundation likewise provided such grants to RTF, Interfaith Worker Justice, and MRNY.[112] Grants from the government are another story: One group leader explained that such grants tend to be "money in, money out—cost, reimbursement." Some groups only take government funding if a significant share is reserved for "overhead." Otherwise, it "doesn't build the base, doesn't build power—it's a failure from an organizing perspective."[113]

But even if most foundation funding is for "general support," concerns about accountability remain. If a foundation ceases to look favorably on a group's activities, its funding may disappear; groups therefore have an incentive to do things that please their funders. And because alt-labor groups compete with one another for funding, there is a constant pressure to promote each group's work as independent from all others', which can fracture the movement and encourage "niche marketing."[114] In other words, incentives to be responsive to funders' priorities are substantial, with potentially detrimental effects for the alt-labor movement. Compared to the ideal of a dues-based system, foundation funding is clearly a problematic source of organizational sustenance.

That said, although foundations are notoriously "undemocratic and unaccountable to the public," the personal relationships alt-labor leaders forge with funders may at times permit influence to flow in the opposite direction: group leaders may be able to persuade funders to support their ongoing work.[115] For example, there has long been ample funding for "upskilling," "workforce development," and "future of work" programs—neoliberal concepts that reflect many funders' contentment with the status quo.[116] Although some alt-labor groups seek out such funding and run side programs to help workers improve their market value (résumé classes, skills training, "job readiness," and so forth), many argue that less funding should go to "fixing the worker" and more to combating exploitation, confronting power inequalities, fighting for workers' rights, community organizing, and movement-building—that is, to supporting most alt-labor groups' core missions. The growth of general support grants may reflect the persuasiveness of this argument. Leaders can also highlight for funders connections between shared priorities. For example, when approaching foundations whose funding priorities center on defending immigrants' rights, groups can (and often do) explain that the top priority for low-wage immigrant workers is combating exploitation in the workplace, a priority heightened

by fears of deportation. The best way to improve the lives of immigrants—
who primarily come to the United States to work—is by transforming their
workplaces; funding should therefore go to groups that are fighting for
workplace rights and protections. Alt-labor groups can thus try to persuade
foundations to broaden their understanding of how best to serve the vulnerable populations they target and to make connections between their issue
priorities and the work alt-labor groups are already doing.

The problem, of course, is that influence only infrequently flows in
that direction. Foundations' funding priorities tend to be set from on
high, by those who are "reliant on capitalist systems to produce and maintain their wealth."[117] In an incisive critique of modern philanthropy, its
cozy relationship with capital, and its tendency toward what Megan Ming
Francis calls "movement capture," Francis and Erica Kohl-Arenas write that
"gilded philanthropy [is] wholly out of step with the causes it purports to
support and lacking in imagination about how to cede power" to assist
movements led by people of color. Although many funders claim to want to
fund "movement building," their grantmaking practices are rarely designed
around the actual needs of movements. Philanthropists, the authors argue,
ought "to engage deeply in the history of social movements, to shift how
they evaluate success, and to adopt longer time horizons." If funders are
serious about avoiding capture, they must take a critical look at their past
practices and trust "the vision of organizers from communities most affected
by an issue."[118]

For alt-labor groups, resisting "movement capture" likely requires
leaders and organizers to view current membership and funding structures
as temporary accommodations to an inhospitable system; the ultimate goal
should not be to perfect this jury-rigged system or even to ensure each
group's organizational longevity, per se, but rather to advance the larger
movement of which each organization plays but a supporting role.[119] To the
extent that foundation funding hinders the groups' ability to meaningfully
advance the broader labor movement, a reassessment of current strategies
and practices is clearly necessary. But the same question can be asked of
labor unions: to what extent do current strategies and practices advance
the long-term objectives of the labor movement? If labor unions decided to
provide greater financial support to alt-labor groups and other new forms,
would the labor movement as a whole benefit?

To date, alt-labor groups have had only sporadic success in convincing labor unions to financially support them. Most of this support has come via the Labor Innovations for the Twenty-First Century (LIFT) Fund, a foundation–labor union partnership whose mission is to "support new forms of worker organizing" by funding innovative collaborations between unions and alt-labor groups.[120] The LIFT Fund's funders include thirteen philanthropic foundations, the AFL-CIO, and SEIU. But as key leaders in the field have suggested, the time may be ripe for labor unions to undertake a more thorough reassessment of how they intend to "invest their resources in building for the future. Labor unions need to decide if they are going to scale their investments and deepen their engagement" in joint organizing efforts with alt-labor "or raise more resources from the broader labor movement that can in turn leverage larger amounts of money from donors and other sources to support the growth and sustainability of this field of worker organizations," write Laine Romero-Alston, cofounder and chair of the LIFT Fund and director of workers' rights initiatives at the Open Society Foundations, and Sarita Gupta, former executive director of Jobs with Justice and director of the Future of Work(ers) program at the Ford Foundation.[121] Combining revenue from labor unions, foundations, government, individual donors, and other sources, these authors argue, is likely the best path forward, both for alt-labor groups and for the broader movement, but it requires more "intentional coordination" and strategic thinking.[122] Alt-labor's struggle to align its need for financial support with its core purposes, in other words, reflects not only alt-labor's internal organizational issues but also deeply rooted challenges of coordination within and across the labor movement.

At present, alt-labor groups continue to face serious challenges stemming from their small membership bases and their reliance on external funding, especially foundations. External funding is an uncertain and unstable source of organizational sustenance that creates cross-pressures for the groups to be responsive to both their members and their funders. Without this funding, however, alt-labor groups would likely vanish, leaving many of the workers who fall through the cracks of labor and employment law to suffer silently.

How to balance alt-labor groups' existential imperative to secure funding against their desire to be member driven is both a source of ongoing discussion and a spur to experimental action. The previous section looked at one common approach: the groups' efforts to establish democratic internal structures and processes. Another way alt-labor groups respond to this tension is by devoting significant resources to providing individual services and organizing workplace justice campaigns—arguably the two most direct and authentic ways to respond to members' needs. But as we will see in the next chapter, notwithstanding their many benefits and virtues, services and direct actions are severely limited in scale and impact and bring numerous other downsides—which have encouraged a growing number of groups to gravitate toward alternatives such as public policy campaigns and deeper political engagement.

CHAPTER 4

The Logic of Alt-Labor's Political Development

THE LAST CHAPTER highlighted a key challenge facing alt-labor groups: how to achieve meaningful gains for their members while addressing the accountability questions that have arisen from their dependency on external funding? This challenge is rooted in the legal, economic, and social environment in which the groups find themselves. In the context of labor law's drift and employment law's inadequacies, options for redressing their members' most pressing problems are limited, funding is scarce, the groups are small and structurally constrained, and their members are socially, economically, and politically marginalized.

While these challenges may seem highly particular and idiosyncratic, they are not actually specific to alt-labor groups. Many nonprofit community-based groups face similar dilemmas and constraints.[1] But they are especially acute for the new groups that emerge in the context of policy drift to support constituencies that are left in the lurch. These groups tend to face three major challenges: they must identify alternative pathways around the drifting policy to redress their constituents' problems; they must identify sources of organizational sustenance that are not already monopolized by old groups; and they must be responsive to the multiple, intersecting challenges their underserved constituencies typically face.[2] These tasks are complicated and can require the groups to make difficult compromises.

As discussed in the last chapter, alt-labor's small membership numbers and their members' low incomes have made it exceedingly difficult for the groups to rely solely on dues to fund their organizations. Consequently, alt-labor groups have sought out external sources of funding, principally through private foundations. While this funding is relatively generous, relying on sources other than their members for their survival has created something of a legitimacy crisis for these groups as they seek to remain member-driven organizations. This helps to explain why many alt-labor groups go to great lengths to establish internal democratic structures (discussed in the previous chapter) and emphasize individual service provision and workplace justice campaigns (this chapter) as cornerstone strategies for supporting their members. Both services and direct actions are viewed as the most authentic ways to respond to their members' most pressing concerns; they also reflect and accommodate the groups' structural, size, and funding limitations. But as strategies to help low-wage workers combat exploitation, both are severely limited in scope and reach and can impose significant opportunity costs on the organizations.

The downsides of these strategies have prompted a growing number of groups to turn to public policy to scale up their work and maximize their impact. Public policy is attractive because it offers an alternate route to protecting workers' rights that circumvents drifting labor law, it draws the interest of funders, and it enables groups to respond to multiple issues facing their members simultaneously. It also plays to the groups' strengths while compensating for some of their deficiencies. Policy campaigns do not require a mass base of active member-participants; for vulnerable workers, they are also low-risk, high-reward activities that simultaneously serve as training grounds for leadership development, skill building, and organizing. As such, policy campaigns are a logical solution to several of the key challenges alt-labor groups face.

But policy is not a panacea. Policies enacted at the city or county level are geographically limited, enforcement is a perennial problem, and enacting strong policies is not easy: many alt-labor groups must contend with unfriendly political forces in their states and local contexts. Policy campaigns can also become exercises in "advocacy," in which workers are involved only indirectly or symbolically. In such cases, an alt-labor group may find itself playing the role of special interest advocacy group more than people-powered community-based organization. In other words, policy campaigns may pull the groups away from their core commitments while compounding their challenges of representation. Furthermore, the groups are often dissatisfied with the half-loaf compromises that result from the policymaking process. They have become painfully aware that their policy campaigns can achieve only what the powers-that-be find acceptable.[3]

Consequently, a growing number of alt-labor groups have resolved to confront these constraints and change the contours of their political environments. As I describe in this chapter and illustrate in greater detail in chapter 6, politically engaged alt-labor groups have sought to intervene in a variety of political and electoral processes. In particular, they have endeavored to build new electorates, influence candidate selection processes, and augment government enforcement capacities. These activities seek to enhance the groups' political power by cultivating more active and engaged citizenries, altering policymakers' incentives, and creating conditions conducive to further policy changes. They also reflect the groups' determination to play the long game and incrementally shift the balance of power toward low-wage immigrant workers and workers of color. Like policy campaigns, political engagement offers many benefits—it helps members develop their skills, attracts funding, builds their coalitions, and expands their reach—while accommodating members' precarity and vulnerability, their limited labor market power, the organizations' small membership bases, and their dependency on foundations.

In other words, many alt-labor groups have come to embrace a role in which they believe they can be most effective in the new legal, economic, and resource environment: as political intermediaries that speak on behalf of all low-wage workers in their communities (and not just their members).[4] But political engagement has its downsides, too. It does not resolve alt-labor's internal challenges; rather, it shifts focus to different challenges (such as holding elected officials accountable) and raises new questions about the groups' ability to legitimately represent the broader communities for whom they advocate. At present, there exist no obvious mechanisms through which the broader community can hold alt-labor groups accountable.[5] That said, it is important to underscore that the groups' goal is not only to speak on behalf of workers and their communities but also to organize and empower their communities. These power-building goals are pursued steadfastly and tirelessly, as discussed in the next chapter.

The political turn has also layered weighty new responsibilities atop the groups' already robust list of existing obligations. Now, alt-labor groups must remain politically vigilant and devise mechanisms to ensure political responsiveness for their low-wage, racially and economically marginalized communities while continuing to follow through on their existing commitments to their members. Their dockets, in short, are full.

In sum, alt-labor's political development has followed a discernible logic. From individual services to workplace justice campaigns to policy and politics, the groups have experimented with new ways to help those who have been left behind by labor law's drift. Each effort, in different ways, has been the result of learning and adaptation and has been designed to fit their limitations, accommodate their constraints, and maximize their resources and capacities. From a broader perspective, each effort has increasingly shifted attention away from the workplace and toward the political arena while raising knotty new questions and problems with which the groups are still struggling. This chapter examines the logic of this developmental trajectory.

Service Provision and Workplace Justice Campaigns

Most workers find their way into an alt-labor group after they have suffered wage theft, injuries, sexual harassment, verbal or physical abuse, discrimination, retaliation, or other forms of exploitation in the workplace. They seek practical support and assistance in redressing their grievances. Many are unaware of their legal rights and unacquainted with the bureaucratic and legal processes they must navigate to vindicate those rights.[6] Most expect the group to help them sue their boss or complain to the authorities. "They think, 'You are a nonprofit, you are here to help me,'" one worker-organizer noted.[7] Ultimately, most workers want a judge or state agency to order their employer to pay back the wages they stole, give them their job back, get their abusive supervisor fired, or otherwise rectify the wrongs committed against them.

Most groups respond to workers' grievances by helping them take advantage of their employment law rights—filing complaints with labor standards enforcement agencies and pursuing legal remedies in court—and by providing skills training and leadership development opportunities. These services are often referred to as core worker center functions. Throughout, alt-labor groups are sensitive to the fact that many low-wage workers are highly vulnerable. Many undocumented immigrants, in particular, correctly fear that if they complain or make their stories public, they may be deported; other workers find themselves in unsafe situations in which it may be costly for them to complain publicly. Explained Reyna Lopez, executive director of the PCUN in Oregon: "We don't like to pressure people into doing things because we know what the risks are. We have seen people come out and tell their story, and they have then been deported. We have seen people end up getting the short end of the stick. So we have to be able to provide that support and refer them to an attorney so they can make a choice. We know that a lot of our folks are really traumatized and a lot of their dignity has been taken from them."[8] Offering individual services—such as help with filing lawsuits and complaints—thus authentically responds to workers' pressing needs while respecting their particular situations and sometimes low tolerance for risk.[9]

Service provision also fits the groups' structural, size, and funding limitations. Although most groups report being overwhelmed by the number of workers seeking their services and assistance, it takes neither a mass base nor a self-sustaining membership structure to respond to individual workers' complaints—only an effective staff supplemented by volunteers. While funding is always scarce, alt-labor groups are usually able to cobble together enough money through grants to maintain their casework, classes, and other types of services. As nonprofit organizations, they are in these ways "built" for individual services.

Most leaders and organizers consider service provision central to their mission of helping low-wage workers. But many also have mixed feelings about it; some have even sworn it off. While they recognize the critical importance of assisting workers who have suffered abuse or exploitation at work and acknowledge the value services bring to the organization by drawing workers into the groups, they have also learned that employment law remedies are inefficient and ineffective pathways to redressing workers' grievances. It often takes years for workers to recover the back pay they are owed, and their chances of success are usually small; the legal system, likewise, throws up so many hurdles that the costs of filing lawsuits can outweigh the benefits.

Some leaders also worry that service provision, though highly responsive to individual members' concerns, is counterproductive for their groups' larger organizing and movement-building goals. This is because services effectively individualize workers' experiences. Complaints to state departments of labor are made by individuals; the private right of action permits legal action by an aggrieved individual worker against his or her individual employer; skills classes, too, focus on individual advancement. Ultimately, these individualized pathways can reinforce the isolation and alienation many workers already feel, in turn undermining groups' efforts to foster a collective consciousness and generate sustained collective action on behalf of all low-wage workers. "Part of it is a rational read on the part of workers," said Kader of Arise Chicago. "I'm being abused in the workplace? It's a legal problem and I need a legal solution. But that's antithetical to group action. It's antithetical to organizing."[10]

Consequently, before meeting with individual aggrieved workers to review their cases and explore their options in greater depth, most groups require workers to attend a workshop with other newcomers. Organizers typically walk the newcomers through the basics of federal, state, and local employment and labor law rights and protections, showing what employers can and cannot legally do and what options workers have. At that point, workers often learn to their disappointment that elements of their employers' behavior that may be most offensive to them—especially verbal abuse and disrespect (such as belittling, name calling, and shouting)—are rarely illegal. In order to challenge their employers' behavior, workers may need to consider alternatives to lawsuits and formal complaints. As Bell of the CWC explains, "You say: we're going to analyze an issue, through movement, and you're going to present this issue, and you're going to think with your compañeros about what is a solution to that issue. Who benefits from this? What can be done to change it? What will make you feel that it's a more just situation?"[11] Working collectively with a small group, they begin to explore what might be done. They explore where power really lies in their communities, how policy decisions are made, how pro-employer biases and loopholes get inserted into laws during the policymaking process, how laws are not self-enforcing, and why employers seem to have such outsize power and latitude to act as they please.

In these workshops, organizers emphasize to newcomers that "you're not alone; we've all been through the same thing; that's why we're here," explained Deborah Axt of MRNY.[12] Then, staff and trained memberleaders try to deconstruct the individualist premises and assumptions most workers bring with them, helping them see that their personal, individual grievance is actually a collective problem shared by others in the room. Explained Kader:

You think you're individually aggrieved, it's because of your individual identity alone, and you all want attorneys. Those are the three assumptions workers are bringing to the table. We quickly have to dismantle all three. First we say: OK, well look around—there's more than one of you. So this is not a personal problem. This is a social problem. Number two: You said the reason you're exploited is because your boss is Hindu and you're not. Well, the brother next to you said his boss is Mexican and he's been exploiting him too. So maybe your boss is racist against Mexicans, but that's not the *only* factor. Clearly exploitation is bigger than simply prejudice against a certain nationality. And third, you can only get from the law what the law provides. With organizing you can get whatever you want. It's a question of how much power you can build.[13]

Organizers thus try to help workers reinterpret their individual experiences as collective problems that reflect broader power imbalances in the workplace and in society and that require collective solutions. It may well be true that a particular worker's employer is unusually cruel and abusive, but that employer is a symptom of a broader problem, said Diaz of Somos Un Pueblo Unido: "No, we're not victims of wage theft because employers are thieves, although that is part of it. We're victims of wage theft because they're not accountable to anyone. There's no government holding them accountable. There's no culture in this community that's holding them accountable. We're victims of wage theft because we don't have power as workers. That's what we continue to drive."[14] Some workers become interested in digging deeper into the power analysis and learning more about the upsides of collective action; others are eager to move on to filing a complaint or initiating a lawsuit, depending on the nature of the exploitation they have faced.

Many group leaders and organizers resist service provision—what they refer to as the "worker center model"—because they argue that it breaks the "iron rule" of organizing made famous by Alinsky: "Never do for others what they can do for themselves."[15] For example, Heartland Workers Center in Omaha, Nebraska, downplays services in favor of community organizing, individual empowerment, and leadership development. Heartland's model directs attention to the painstaking work of one-on-one engagement with individual community members to foster collective action and build community. "Our concept of power is different. It's the difference between charity and social justice," said organizer Lucia Pedroza. "Doing charity is comfortable because you give somebody a service, and you see they actually use it. Going door to door and talking to people one-on-one, getting people to see that *they* have power—it's harder than giving them a service."[16]

While the majority of alt-labor groups still offer individual services and rely heavily on those support functions to recruit members, a growing number of groups have come to share Heartland's perspective. Many that once prioritized individual services have scaled back, outsourced, or ceased those offerings in favor of organizing and leadership development activities that they can channel toward either workplace justice campaigns or policy campaigns and political engagement.[17] "We've been very intentional about not doing direct service," said LaZar of El Centro de Igualdad y Derechos:

> If what you want to do is only resolve your wage case, then we're going to support you, but in a very limited way. What we're about is growing power. So if you want to join a movement to grow power with other low-wage workers, this is how you do that. . . . Of course, people are at different levels of being politicized: Not everyone's there, and so we try to recognize and work where people are at. . . . [But] our organizers should not be case managers. If that's what they're doing, we're really not doing anything to end wage theft, or shift dynamics of power, and that's what we need to be doing.[18]

Pedroza explains that leadership development begins with recognizing one's own agency—which is what organizers try to help workers accomplish through one-on-ones:

> I'm a good example of this. Before I started here as a [staff] organizer, I learned from experience what it means to change. And so I know that's what I want people to understand. You can be on the sidelines your whole life—go to work, come home, do nothing. But you wake up one day and you find out that there's an alternative—that you don't have to live that life. That's what we want to share— that there's an alternative. We know it's really hard to change that mentality, and that's the biggest challenge. Things won't get better overnight—but at least you're acting, you're doing something more. . . . So it's about teaching leadership skills. To develop themselves, to give the wakeup call. But many people—they don't want to move. It takes time. [And it's hard to quantify because] you can't measure individual success.[19]

Leadership development is conventionally viewed as the core of organizing: organizers seek to develop the capacities of ordinary people to be their own advocates, exercise their agency, and hone their organizing skills. Many groups offer such programs, though the concept of leadership development is favored more by foundations than grassroots organizers, who often prefer to emphasize skill building. Diaz explained that leadership development erroneously assumes that change would come "if only you had the right quote-unquote leadership skills. If only you knew how to tell your story before a city council meeting, or if only you were just a better leader and had stronger skills as a community organizer. . . . [But] we have lots of different kinds of skills in our community. Some people are never going to be able to tell their story, are never going to be able to understand a certain policy position. . . . But it takes all of us, right?"[20] Continually investing in members' diverse skill sets is therefore a high priority for all alt-labor groups, whether it is called "leadership development" or something else.

Individual empowerment and skill-building work, however, can be just as time and resource intensive as helping workers take advantage of their employment law rights—if not more so. Further, too much emphasis on developing workers' sense of agency threatens to reify such work's individualist premises. Most groups therefore do not stop with leadership development—they insist that skill building and individual empowerment must be linked to collective actions in which members work together to expose exploitative employers and bring them to justice.

The most prominent way alt-labor groups link individual services to collective action is through workplace justice campaigns, also known as "direct action" or "economic action organizing," in which groups of workers seek to gain leverage in demanding redress by bringing maximal public attention to their employers' abusive behavior.[21] A worker who seeks to organize such an action must compile information about the employer and their abusive practices: by conducting research on the employer, how that employer treats other employees, and the industry in which the company operates. The aggrieved worker then joins with a staff organizer to plan a face-to-face confrontation with their employer. Typically, the worker is tasked with recruiting as many coworkers as possible to join the effort—at least three or four, but ideally more. "That's really hard for workers to do in their worksites," one organizer told me—a sentiment echoed by many workers—"because employers are constantly dividing us in many, many ways." When the worker recruits a handful of coworkers, however, "that process is incredible for people. Already, they're becoming organizers."[22] Often, the group's staff organizer helps the worker draft a letter to the employer (called "love letters" by organizers at Worker Justice

Wisconsin) asserting that their "concerted activity" is protected by section 7 of the NLRA, which establishes the right "to engage in other concerted activities for the purpose of collective bargaining or other mutual aid or protection."[23] Often, the mere presentation of the NLRA letter or copy of a Department of Labor complaint to the employer creates leverage for the workers.

When employers are not responsive, the workers may choose to escalate their efforts; the culmination of the workplace justice campaign is highly public and combative. Workers protest in front of the storefront, conduct Alinsky-style disruptions, shame employers in their home neighborhoods and work communities, generate public outrage through the media, organize secondary boycotts, and exert other kinds of pressure to redress their grievances. They present their demands to the employer, and negotiation usually proceeds with staff playing a facilitating role. Although the workplace justice campaign often takes place after the aggrieved worker has already been fired or quit, it is usually successful in getting the worker rehired, winning back wages, getting a predatory manager fired, or creating structural changes in the workplace, such as improved safety procedures or changes to the terms and conditions of employment for all workers.

In a few standout cases, alt-labor groups have also won breakthrough successes via direct economic actions, adeptly leveraging the flexibility afforded by their nonprofit status to wage extensive secondary boycotts and using their symbolic power—which some scholars argue is their primary source of power—to successfully shift public narratives, alter public opinion, and win meaningful concessions that affect entire supply chains.[24] Perhaps the most inspiring and well known is the aforementioned campaign by the CIW in Florida to improve labor conditions for tomato pickers and establish a joint monitoring and enforcement program to raise labor standards.[25] Also notable is PCUN's orchestration of a massive, decade-long boycott of NORPAC Foods, the largest processor of fruits and vegetables in the West, in an effort to win collective bargaining rights for workers on NORPAC farms. Although the campaign failed to result in an agreement, it successfully brought NORPAC to the bargaining table, raised the visibility of farmworkers' poor working conditions, and helped to grow the movement.[26] Such cases are the exceptions rather than the rule, however.

Still, as the NORPAC boycott illustrates, even when a workplace justice campaign does not result in major changes, it often advances the group's organizing and movement-building goals, generating what sociologist Rachel Meyer has termed "collective efficacy" and Meyer and Fine call "grassroots citizenship."[27] "Just having to rely on your coworkers for a successful process . . . it builds solidarity within the workplace, it allows us to expand our base of workers. . . . That really intense worker committee process makes them all really incredible leaders," explained Bell of CWC.[28] By transforming individual experiences of abuse, victimhood, and isolation into a sense of empowerment and collective efficacy—and by helping workers develop their organizing and leadership skills—workplace justice campaigns transform workers from victims into activists. Even small-scale workplace justice campaigns can be exhilarating for workers and provide them a real sense of power over their employers—which can encourage workers to help others do the same when their rights are violated. "We see it as the seed for the next campaign," said Kader of Arise Chicago. "We are arming people going forward. Each time, they're smarter, more prepared, and they know that we have their back."[29]

Most groups choose their battles carefully. Workers and organizers discuss and evaluate every potential action for how effectively it will empower members, build their skills, strengthen their campaign capacities, and bolster the group's collective efficacy. While achieving workers' proximate purposes (for example, winning back wages owed, getting an abusive supervisor fired) is important, the primary goal is to build their collective power, not solve individual problems. As Diaz of Somos Un Pueblo Unido explained:

> It's not actually our job to solve all these problems. It's our job to utilize problems to grow power. It's how can we *use* these problems—*exploit* these problems—to continue to build power. . . . You go to one of our meetings and the first thing people do is say OK, what's our number-one goal? And it just rolls off the tongue of our members: Build power for immigrant families and low-wage workers. OK, so everything we do in this meeting has to meet that goal. So if we're doing a vigil, we're not doing a vigil just to do a vigil, we're not doing an action just because it's some kind of day of action somewhere. . . . If we're doing a this, if we're doing a that—who can explain how this is going to build power for us?

Successful models of direct economic action have diffused across the country over the years as groups have learned from one another and through experience what models best build power; each tends to adapt those strategies and tactics to suit their local contexts.[30] Leveraging modern communication technologies and seizing opportunities to meet, leaders and organizers often confer with their counterparts in different states and share best practices. In consequence, workplace justice campaigns have become increasingly effective; they are undoubtedly the signature strategy of the alt-labor movement.

But while workplace justice campaigns offer myriad benefits for low-wage workers and alt-labor groups, they also have several downsides. For starters, campaigns demand an enormous amount of time and resources from workers and organizers. While the benefit of seeing justice served is hard to quantify, the cost of a campaign can be significant. Spending days off and evenings organizing and protesting is not easy for low-wage workers. And as noted, exposure to public scrutiny can be risky for undocumented immigrants and others in precarious situations. Furthermore, though the campaign can be exhilarating, after it is over, it can be difficult to sustain momentum and keep workers engaged. Once workers have won their settlement, they often disappear. "Early on I used to joke that if there were one hundred workers [involved in a workplace justice campaign] and we got even ten to stay behind and continue, that would be a win," said Alex Tom, former executive director of CPA. "But often it was just one or two that were super committed."[31] For CPA, the goal of campaigns ultimately became less about maximizing the size of its membership base and more about deepening workers' commitments and enlarging the organization's scope across the working class—"bringing workers from factories *and* restaurants, for example, to support each other—to broaden our reach a little bit more" in each campaign.[32] But there is no escaping the fact that campaigns are resource intensive, and the movement-building gains they generate are often modest and difficult to sustain in a political environment in which low-wage workers are kept in a perpetually precarious state, scapegoated, exploited, threatened, and pressured to remain quiescent.

Second, because campaigns respond to labor violations that have already occurred, they are inherently reactive—fundamentally backward-looking, seeking redress for past abuses—and offer no concrete mechanism through which to deter future exploitation. Once the campaign is over, the employer retains his or her outsize authority and may well continue to exploit workers. (The same may be said for the downstream effects of filing complaints or lawsuits.) Many organizers refer to workplace justice campaigns as "band-aids" because they are reactive fixes rather than proactive deterrents. To be sure, direct actions, regulatory complaints, and lawsuits are all important tools for achieving justice for the wrongs committed against workers—especially when used in combination. But confronting employers after abuses have already occurred has not had much of a deterrent effect on future behavior, partly because negotiated settlements are inherently unenforceable. Lacking the legal standing of an employment contract, collective bargaining agreement, or formal mediation settlement, workers must take it on faith that the employer will carry out their end of the bargain. If the employer reneges on the agreement after the workplace justice campaign has wound down, the campaign must start up all over again.

Third, direct actions impose significant opportunity costs on under-resourced alt-labor groups. When groups choose to devote staff and members' time, resources, and attention to orchestrating workplace justice campaigns, other projects must receive less attention. For underfunded nonprofit groups, this choice may ultimately prove to be counterproductive if it spends down their resources without advancing their larger goals. If direct actions do little to alter the pervasive power imbalance in the workplace, they may inadvertently exacerbate the problem, because they drain the organization of precious resources without making a dent in the employment relationship. As Kader explained: "If you devote all of your resources to hand-to-hand combat, that's actually making things worse, because you've used all your resources and it still doesn't change the calculus of whether [the employer is] going to exploit their workers. . . . You didn't change the nature of this relationship at all."[33]

Indeed, this is surely the biggest limitation of workplace justice campaigns: they spend down the groups' resources without tackling the root causes of why so many bad low-wage jobs exist, why workers are so vulnerable to exploitation, and why the power asymmetry persists in the American workplace. Successful direct actions often feel like winning small battles on the periphery while losing the war spectacularly everywhere else. Indeed, if the abusive employer is small and has little market power, the effect of a successful workplace justice campaign will likely be confined to that individual worksite alone. There will always be more exploitative employers that need to be confronted. Workplace justice campaigns can become an endless game of "Whac-A-Mole," said CPD co-executive director and former MRNY co-executive director Andrew Friedman.[34] In order to create ripple effects across industries and regions, campaigns need to be far more strategic than they usually are. As Axt of MRNY explained:

> I spent a lot of time in the early years feeling angsty about these mini-campaigns: how many thousands of hours are we going to spend beating up on the local bodega owner for not paying the minimum wage? If we're not careful, we can get really stuck in that space. We have really struggled over the years to figure out how to have a fight with Amazon instead of the local small business that's going to be out of business any minute anyway because of Amazon, and to connect our analysis of who's driving the economy with who we're capable of picking a fight with at that moment and who our members see as the ones actually doing the exploitation.[35]

Given alt-labor groups' limited resources, those sorts of more sophisticated, strategic calculations matter a great deal. Where best to devote attention? How to weigh the urgency of members' needs against the feasibility of winning and the potential impact on the imbalance of power in the economy, in society, and in politics? Given the groups' small memberships, local rootedness, limited reach, and legal and financial constraints, determining how best to mobilize their limited resources to serve their members is an urgent, essential, and extremely difficult task. Individual services and workplace justice campaigns are arguably the best way to respond directly and authentically to members' concerns, but they are also inefficient and relatively low impact. The groups must weigh the trade-offs.

As alt-labor groups grow in size and organizational capacity, these trade-offs shrink, and devoting significant resources to mini-campaigns is less taxing on the organization. MRNY, for example, has 5 offices, dozens of staff, a large legal team, over 25,000 members, and approximately $24 million in annual revenue. It is therefore in a better position to run multiple workplace justice campaigns and simultaneously pursue a wide range of other campaigns. Another mature and well-resourced alt-labor group is ROC, which as Marnie Brady details, spent its early years emphasizing direct actions against abusive employers but ultimately concluded "that they could not respond to every group of indignant restaurant workers in the city, however much they were underpaid, not paid at all, or discriminated against. To maximize their impact on the broader restaurant industry, ROC's leaders decided to zero-in on fine dining ("tablecloth") restaurants in New York City. Because upscale restaurants were standard-setters across the entire industry, they realized that victories at that level would trickle down to benefit workers all across the industry, including at casual dining and fast-food establishments."³⁶ In 2013, ROC's cofounders and codirectors launched One Fair Wage, a separate 501(c)(4) that runs policy campaigns at the local, state, and federal level to abolish the subminimum tipped wage and establish a "full, fair minimum wage with tips on top" for all workers.³⁷ Saru Jayaraman of ROC and One Fair Wage explained how her groups have sought to choose their battles: "Choosing a campaign has to be both about what workers want and making sure that what we're fighting for is getting at the heart of our ultimate mission, which is changing the power dynamic between the industry and the workers. If we choose an issue that doesn't get at changing the power balance, it doesn't actually fulfill our long-term mission. Workers want a lot of things—but among those things, what are the most strategic to get at the power dynamic?"³⁸ ROC and MRNY are two of the most well-funded alt-labor groups in the nation. For less well-funded alt-labor groups, the question of how to advance their goals and maximize their impact with limited resources is a perennial challenge.

A growing number of alt-labor groups have thus come to the conclusion that their goal cannot simply be to win recompense for small groups of exploited workers. As much as they would like to be able to respond forcefully and courageously on behalf of every exploited worker—to channel their members' deep sense of anger and righteous indignation into disruptive workplace justice campaigns—many organizers have accepted that direct action is ultimately not the most productive path forward. Even if workplace justice campaigns were conducted on a daily basis and were uniformly successful, they would do precious little to combat the persistent and systemic exploitation that occurs across entire industries. Exploitation is a feature, not a bug, of the fissured workplace and the informal economy; it is not simply a problem of a "few bad apples."³⁹ Services and workplace justice campaigns are critically important to their members, but they do not significantly alter the behavioral calculus of employers, deter future abuses, or make meaningful change in basic power relationships. The effects are too limited, low-wage workers remain too powerless, and employers retain too much power.

After years of emphasizing casework and workplace justice campaigns, many groups have thus grown frustrated with finding themselves perpetually back where they started—as if in the movie *Groundhog Day*—still fighting exploitative employers over basic labor standards violations and seeing virtually no change in the (im)balance of power in the workplace. This is a big part of why so many alt-labor groups have turned to public policy to combat workplace exploitation and strengthen workers' rights. But there are other reasons as well. The next section provides evidence of the policy turn; the following section examines the broader logic behind the groups' growing attention to public policy.

The Turn to Policy

As early as 2005, Fine observed that worker centers "had greater success at raising wages and improving working conditions via public policy rather than direct labor market intervention."[40] In periodic updates to her seminal book on worker centers, she has argued that the balance of worker centers' activities was shifting toward ever-greater engagement in the policymaking process. In 2011, for example, Fine wrote that the role worker centers played in promoting higher labor standards via state and local public policy initiatives was becoming more widely acknowledged. Whereas in the early 2000s, unions tended to remark that worker centers "only enforce existing laws, they don't raise standards," Fine noted this was no longer the case. "Over the past few years this work has moved out of the margins . . . [as] worker centers have mounted a compelling case for a rejuvenated state role in governing the labour market."[41] And in 2018, Fine, Narro, and Jacob Barnes argued that the "most successful worker center campaigns for improvements have focused on winning policy change rather than pressuring companies directly through strikes or consumer boycotts."[42]

Over the last two decades, alt-labor groups have indeed led hundreds of policy campaigns at the state and local levels to combat wage theft, raise the minimum wage, strengthen health and safety laws, fight discrimination and sexual harassment, create domestic workers' and temporary workers' bills of rights, establish a right to paid sick leave and advance scheduling, and more. The groups have also pushed for public policies that respond to their members' concerns outside the workplace: defending immigrants' rights, fighting for racial justice, promoting gender equity, establishing Covid-19 relief funds, and more. Wage and hour issues are still their "bread and butter," however, and policies such as minimum wage increases and anti-wage-theft laws have figured prominently in their policy campaigns. For example, in a quantitative study, Marc Doussard and Ahmad Gamal find a strong and statistically significant relationship between the number of worker centers in a state and the number of state-level anti-wage-theft laws introduced prior to 2012. I similarly find that most of the major anti-wage-theft laws passed between 2006 and 2013 were the result of vigorous advocacy by worker centers and allied groups.[43]

To further investigate the extent of alt-labor's involvement in local policy campaigns, I scoured local newspaper coverage of every successful minimum wage, paid sick leave, and fair workweek law enacted in 102 cities and counties between 2003 and 2019 and tracked instances in which alt-labor groups were cited as leading advocates in the policy campaigns. As shown in table A.2, alt-labor groups were integral players in 72 percent of all campaigns (61 percent of minimum wage campaigns, 92 percent of paid sick leave campaigns, and 100 percent of fair workweek campaigns).[44]

Alt-labor groups were almost never solely responsible for getting these laws passed, nor would any group claim all credit for themselves. They almost always worked in coalition with other alt-labor groups as well as labor unions, women's groups, family advocates, faith-based groups, and various other community-based groups. But alt-labor groups were high-frequency repeat players: while dozens of other types of advocacy groups were instrumental at particular times and in particular places, only alt-labor and traditional labor groups (active in 73 percent of the successful policy campaigns) were consistently on the front lines.

Stepping back, we can understand this growing attention to policy as an effort to alleviate the problems associated with labor law's drift by fashioning workaround solutions to help those who have been left behind. Alt-labor groups have thus sought to build on the state-level work of labor unions discussed in chapter 2 by shifting the focus of employment law campaigns downward to the city and county level.

The policy campaigns listed in table A.2, however, represent only the tip of the iceberg; they do not include all the campaigns that failed to result in new policy enactments. Alt-labor's engagement in the policymaking arena has, in fact, been much more extensive. Most groups do not maintain a formal, running list of the policy campaigns they have run. Nor do they always publicize their campaigns—partly out of fear of drawing the ire of the opposition, which is intent on delegitimizing alt-labor.[45] But even within the relatively small, diverse sample of groups I studied, each group's list of policy accomplishments was long. Let us consider a few examples.

Somos Un Pueblo Unido cut its teeth in the policy arena fighting for immigrant rights in the 1990s, when the group successfully persuaded the

New Mexico state legislature to condemn California's Proposition 187, which forbade undocumented immigrants from using state-run services. In those early years, Somos also helped undocumented students gain access to valid drivers' licenses and in-state tuition rates and financial aid for state colleges, pressured the Santa Fe City Council to prohibit police officers from asking residents about their immigration status, and led a campaign to prevent a for-profit segregated immigrant prison from opening in Santa Fe County. But its agenda evolved with its members' needs and, by the mid-2000s, began to include workers' rights more prominently—a natural development, as the group's members were low-wage immigrant workers who consistently faced exploitative conditions at work. In 2003, Somos and its allies successfully prodded the city of Santa Fe to enact the first citywide living wage ordinance in the country (raising the minimum wage for all workers higher than the federal level), indexed to the cost of living. In 2007, Somos helped raise the state minimum wage. In 2009, it led a campaign to pass one of the strongest statewide anti-wage-theft laws in the country, adding treble damages—amounting to three times the back wages owed—for minimum wage noncompliance and extending the statute of limitations from one to three years. Around that time, it also began to emphasize racial justice issues, working with the NAACP and the Drug Policy Alliance to ban racial profiling and other bias-based policing practices in New Mexico. In 2019, it successfully secured green-energy jobs for rural workers in places impacted by coal plant closures—such as in Hobbs, New Mexico, where Somos had opened an office—as part of the state's Energy Transition Act of 2019. At that time, it participated in the large-scale Citizenship Now! campaign to naturalize Santa Fe residents eligible for citizenship and boost their civic engagement. All the while, Somos worked to expedite wage theft litigation through state courts, shorten the time it took to recover back pay, enhance the state's enforcement capacities by hiring additional wage theft investigators, and fight for immigrants' rights.

PCUN's beginnings were similar. Early on, it focused exclusively on securing amnesty for undocumented workers and providing services for farmworkers and tree planters; gradually, PCUN began tackling wage-hour and workplace justice issues as well. Its early forays into the policymaking arena emphasized pesticide exposure, establishing collective bargaining rights, and securing affordable housing for low-wage farmworkers. In 2000, PCUN and the United Farm Workers union came close to getting national legislation passed through Congress that would have granted legal status to over two million farmworkers and their families, having reached an agreement with major national agribusiness associations on the terms of the proposal. The bill's progress was ultimately thwarted by renewed concerns about border security in the wake of the September 11, 2001, terrorist attacks. In 2004, PCUN successfully won the right to paid rest breaks in Oregon. Four years later, it began to try to influence electoral politics by organizing nonpartisan voter mobilization drives within the Latinx community. By 2013, PCUN had won driving privileges for undocumented immigrants, and in 2016 it helped to secure a large minimum wage increase in Oregon and to elect Teresa Alonso León, the first Indigenous migrant Latina to the Oregon legislature. In recent years, PCUN helped pass Oregon's Voting Rights Act in 2019, secured legislation in Oregon to entrench driving rights for undocumented immigrants, and successfully persuaded the U.S. House of Representatives to pass the Farm Work Force Modernization Act. It was also instrumental in establishing the Oregon Worker Relief Fund, a private-public partnership that provided more than $30 million to workers excluded from federal Covid-19 relief programs and unemployment insurance.

Another group whose policy agenda has expanded over time is ROC. Initially formed in the wake of the 9/11 terrorist attacks to organize and support surviving restaurant workers from the Windows on the World restaurant, which was located on the top floors of the North Tower of the original World Trade Center, ROC now has local chapters in the Bay Area, Chicago, Los Angeles, Detroit, Minneapolis, Jackson (Mississippi), New Orleans, New York, Philadelphia, and Washington D.C. As the primary organized voice for the more than thirteen million low-wage workers employed in the food preparation and service occupations, ROC has long fought both exploitative restaurant owners and the national corporate restaurant trade lobby—the National Restaurant Association ("the other NRA")—on multiple fronts. In addition to eliminating the tipped wage and raising the minimum wage, ROC's policy agenda includes combating racial segregation in the industry; fighting discrimination in hiring, promotion, and training; ending sexual harassment in the restaurant, leisure, and hospitality industries; securing paid leave, vacation leave, health care, childcare, and other employment benefits; and establishing fair scheduling to end unpredictable work scheduling practices. ROC's efforts have contributed to significant change and created forward momentum for more: it has helped end the tipped minimum wage in more than ten states and twenty cities, and it pushed the U.S. House of Representatives to pass the Raise the Wage Act in 2019, which would have raised the federal minimum wage for all workers, tipped and non-tipped, to $15 an hour. During the pandemic, ROC and One Fair Wage helped financially support workers who refused to return to work until they had higher wages and safer, healthier working conditions.[46]

Beyond the examples provided throughout this book, a non-exhaustive list of envelope-pushing policy campaigns organized by the alt-labor groups in my study also includes efforts by the small community-based group New Labor to enact New Jersey's $15 minimum wage, earned paid sick time, and anti-wage-theft laws; to secure the right of frontline workers to refuse unsafe working conditions; and to expand access to drivers' licenses; along with its current campaigns for a Temp Workers' Bill of Rights and a Domestic Workers' Bill of Rights. It also includes the successful campaign of another small, underfunded group, WeCount!, to pass an anti-wage-theft ordinance in Miami-Dade County granting hearing examiners subpoena and enforcement powers and providing for liquidated damages; its ¡Que Calor! campaign to win heat stress protections for outdoor workers; and its efforts to stop ICE's detention policies in Miami-Dade County, end its collaboration with local police, and secure other protections for immigrant workers.

Also included are Living United for Change in Arizona's (LUCHA) successful 2016 campaigns to increase Arizona's minimum wage and create a right to paid sick leave via ballot initiative and to defeat the Republican governor's ballot referral to constitutionally ban sanctuary cities in 2020; El Centro's effective campaign to cover domestic workers under New Mexico's minimum wage law and to pilot a guaranteed basic income program for mixed-status immigrant families; Heartland Worker Center's successful campaign for a Nebraska wage collection law providing workers with a private right of action; NOWCRJ's successful living wage campaign in 2019; MRNY's formative work on the landmark New York State anti-wage-theft law of 2010, paid sick leave in New York City in 2014, the blocking of major banks' financial backing for private prison and immigrant detention companies, and stopping Amazon from opening a headquarters in Queens; CPD, CPD Action, and UFR's fair workweek initiative, which has produced advance scheduling laws in nine different states and cities thus far; ROC and UFR's work on the Paid Leave for All campaign; CWJ's success in raising the minimum wage in Johnson County, Iowa, to $10.10 and raising the minimum wage for Iowa City employees to $15 an hour by 2021; and bold Covid-19 relief efforts organized by Adelante, Somos, CWC, CPD, PCUN, New Labor, WDP, WeCount!, NDWA, El Centro, Heartland, CWJ, Needham, NOWCRJ, and WJW.

Considering the myriad challenges facing these typically small community-based groups, their record of public policy accomplishments is surprisingly long and objectively admirable. As Milkman writes, "unions also routinely engage in public policy organizing, but considering that most worker centers are tiny organizations with a handful of paid staff and modest financial resources, their record of legislative and public policy accomplishments is extremely impressive."[47]

Why Policy?

Although alt-labor groups have long viewed stronger employment laws as a way to challenge employers' outsize power and recover a modicum of workplace rights and protections in the context of labor law's drift, only over the last dozen years or so have policy and politics become central to their day-to-day operations and forward-looking strategies.[48] Whether big or small, relatively well-funded or poor, in red states or blue states, working in one or more sectors, and regardless of whether they represent mostly Latinx, Black, Asian, or Indigenous workers, alt-labor groups have mostly been moving in the same direction. Why?

Public policies are attractive for multiple reasons. One of the most important is that they promise to address the problem of scale that has long frustrated these small, locally rooted, and otherwise severely constrained groups. Whereas individual services can improve conditions for a small number of workers and successful workplace justice campaigns can change the behavior of individual employers, stronger public policies can affect the behavior of thousands of employers in one fell swoop by raising the floor on labor standards across entire geographic regions and altering practices within all industries at once. "That's how we scale up our efforts," explained Kader. "Our path to scale is via policy. We go over the heads of all these employers. Then, theoretically, we've changed every workplace in the entire region."[49] Regarding the Temp Workers' Bill of Rights discussed in chapter 1,

Zaman of RTF said: "We organized a group of temp workers in the Chicago area. But the [bill] is impacting over 800,000 temp workers across the state of Illinois. So legislative change, especially in industries where workers have been excluded from exercising collective bargaining rights, allows you to have a much broader impact."[50]

Another way alt-labor groups expand their reach through public policy is by durably altering laws that have long excluded entire categories of low-wage workers from protections—disproportionately people of color, immigrants, and women—and prevented them from enjoying rights that others take for granted. By amending existing regulatory frameworks, policies such as the Temp Workers' and Domestic Workers' Bills of Rights, for example, extend wage-hour, antidiscrimination, and health and safety coverage to thousands of workers who had been previously excluded, often due to the institutionalized legacies of slavery and racism. By tackling structural sources of discrimination and exploitation, public policies can achieve greater impact than strategies that confront employers one at a time.

The attraction of public policy may also be understood as a rational response to alt-labor's weaknesses. When the groups push for stronger employment laws, they effectively ask the state, via laws and regulations, to intervene in the employment relationship and put a thumb on the scales in favor of workers—to bring the power of public authority into what would otherwise remain a private and highly unequal relationship between the employer and the employee. In her instant classic *Private Government*, philosopher Elizabeth Anderson characterizes the employment relationship in the United States as fundamentally "authoritarian" and akin to a "private government" in which employers exercise "sweeping, arbitrary, and unaccountable" authority over their workers—an authority that is, in most cases, "not subject to notice, process, or appeal."[51] By injecting public authority into the equation, alt-labor groups seek to delimit and check employers' outsize authority. In 1960, Schattschneider wrote that the main storyline of U.S. employment relations was best described along precisely these lines—as a perpetual struggle between employers who wished to keep employment relations private and employees who hoped to make them a matter of public concern. The push and pull between the two interests, Schattschneider argued, illustrated fundamental dynamics of politics:

> Since the contestants in private conflicts are apt to be unequal in strength, it fol-
> lows that *the most powerful special interests want private settlements* because they

are able to dictate the outcome as long as the conflict remains private. If A is a hundred times as strong as B he does not welcome the intervention of a third party because he expects to impose his own terms on B; he wants to isolate B. He is especially opposed to the intervention of public authority, because public authority represents the most overwhelming form of outside intervention. Thus, if A/B = 100/1, it is obviously not to A's advantage to involve a third party a million times as strong as A and B combined. Therefore, it is the weak, not the strong, who appeal to public authority for relief. It is the weak who want to socialize the conflict."[52]

Sometimes, alt-labor group leaders conceptualize public policy as an alternative way to recreate the semblance of a collective bargaining agreement, enforced by the state, for nonunion workers who would otherwise lack concrete protections against exploitation. "We are trying to fill the holes of what a collective bargaining agreement can get workers, for the workers who don't have a collective bargaining agreement," Axt told Jane McAlevey. "For the many workers in the informal economy, we are trying to put as many pieces together as we can to offer protections as if they had a contract."[53]

At their most aspirational—when asked to sketch their boldest vision for the future—many group leaders paint a similar picture: Each new policy contributes in piecemeal fashion to building a different kind of state, one that views the employment relationship from the perspective of workers at least as much as from the perspective of employers and business owners— one with operations geared toward protecting workers' rights and raising the floor on labor standards at least as much as toward promoting economic growth. Ideally, this reconstituted state regulatory apparatus will work hand in glove with a reformed national labor law and revived unions, with each helping to fortify the other.[54] At the end of the day, Kader suggested, new state capacities might someday result in "the kind of robust welfare state guaranteed by local governments that we typically never had, in a way that Western Europe has traditionally had, that isn't negotiated through contracts, but is state-based. . . . To me, that's the end game of all this policy talk. I want, for example, paid paternity leave and maternity leave for every low-wage worker in Cook County. And I don't care who is the guarantor of it. If it's not the employer, fine—we'll go on and we'll make the county make you do it. That's the aspiration."[55]

Leaders and organizers hasten to point out the limitations of employment law. They emphasize that employment law is a last resort in the context of declining unions and widespread exploitation of low-wage workers—it is a workaround solution to raise the floor on labor standards in industries that are likely always going to be rife with violations. But they are highly attuned to how powerfully disruptive new employment laws can be for the employment relationship. Consider the paid sick leave and paid time off ordinances that have spread rapidly around the country over the last decade. Rigid schedules and fear of retaliation have long discouraged workers from seeking time off. Now, in places where workers have guaranteed paid leave, if they wish to take time off, they can: their employers cannot make them work. By handing workers a measure of control over their work lives that they did not previously have, the ordinances fundamentally alter the terms of the employment relationship. They give workers a legal right to put their health and their family's health ahead of their employers' interests. Fair workweek policies do something similar; by imposing legal constraints on employers, they chip away at employers' power of at-will scheduling.

Public policy campaigns are also attractive because they are relatively low-risk, high-reward endeavors for low-wage workers who lack significant economic and social power. Whereas workplace justice campaigns can be risky undertakings for workers who hold a precarious position in the labor market and may be doubly vulnerable on account of their immigration status, criminal record, or other reasons, public policy campaigns do not necessarily require workers to put their jobs on the line or to risk deportation. Only a few select workers are typically needed to share their stories with policymakers; a few courageous workers can speak on behalf of the many exploited workers who may choose to remain anonymous. The policies that are enacted, however, benefit all.

Policy campaigns are also low-cost in terms of participation. For those who do not testify or educate lawmakers in person, the bulk of the work involves canvassing neighborhoods, organizing communities, and attending mass protests—flexible, relatively low-profile activities that do not ask members to walk off the job or expend precious resources on prolonged workplace justice campaigns. Little of value is put on the line for the policy campaign, and participation is often flexible. For vulnerable workers with severely limited time to devote to such activities outside the workday, this is a major advantage to policy campaigns over workplace justice campaigns. And for all low-wage workers, winning a higher minimum wage, the right to paid sick leave, and new health and safety regulations, are of outsize benefit.

The low-risk, low-cost nature of policy campaigns ties into what is perhaps their main draw: campaigns for stronger laws can be undertaken without a large membership base.[56] Planning and implementing policy campaigns is staff-heavy work: the burden falls not on a large membership but on a small cadre of leaders and organizers and a small group of workers. Policy campaigns thus do not depend on the kind of associational power that unions need to generate economic leverage for workers. Much of the responsibility, moreover, can be spread across coalitions with other groups; as elaborated in the next chapter, alt-labor can lean on better resourced allies through alliances and coalitions and develop valuable efficiencies. Likewise, through organizational innovations, alt-labor groups can extend their reach, project greater power in the political arena, and magnify their impact.

But policy campaigns are also a draw for workers. They are exciting to be a part of: the timetable of a legislative campaign creates pressure, urgency, and momentum, and protesting or speaking with legislators can be empowering and can motivate further activism. High-profile policy campaigns can therefore swell the groups' membership numbers; although attrition almost invariably follows the campaign's conclusion, there is no denying that policy campaigns can help to build the groups' membership bases.

The campaigns can also serve as important leadership development and movement-building opportunities. They provide rallying points for collective action, and they build solidarity and advance the broader labor movement. Indeed, many organizers view policy campaigns as primarily useful for movement-building purposes. As Bell of CWC explained: "The policy campaigns are very useful for mobilizing workers. That's the major use for them. The regulation that you get out of them can create tools for building power around enforcement of the regs. But the biggest use you get out of them is that it's an opportunity for workers to have movement, and it's an opportunity for them to have a voice in something. . . . So what this does is it gives us a vehicle to bring all those workers together."[57]

As noted, workplace justice campaigns, too, offer organizing and leadership development opportunities for workers and provide rallying points, build solidarity, and foster collective action. But whereas workplace justice campaigns are squarely focused on achieving recompense for abuses that happened on the job, public policies offer vehicles for addressing a wide range of members' other concerns that intersect with, but are not confined to, workplace justice issues. Groups can devise policies to fight wage theft, workplace discrimination, sexual harassment, or health and safety violations—or all the above—but if their members demand it, they can also organize policy campaigns around getting drivers' licenses for undocumented immigrants, fighting racially discriminatory stop-and-frisk policies, improving police accountability, bolstering tenants' rights, securing economic relief for low-wage workers during a pandemic, and more. Public policy allows them to intervene in any number of policy issues that touch their members' lives and shape their communities. In this way, public policies help alt-labor groups respond to one of their core challenges—how to help constituents overcome the multiple, often intersecting, and mutually reinforcing challenges they face. As I discuss in the next chapter, the process of issue exploration, problem articulation, and collective agenda formation is crucial in breaking through barriers to mobilization, pushing against the individualist premises many exploited workers hold, and authentically representing members' interests.

Policy campaigns also suit alt-labor's financial model—indeed, the policy turn may be understood in part as a response to the groups' financial weaknesses. Foundations are usually willing to fund policy-centered civic engagement activities, and individual donors are often enthusiastic about the prospect of bringing about policy change. To the extent that alt-labor groups' policy campaigns dovetail with funders' interests, then, they present significant fundraising opportunities. Indeed, the new 501(c)(4) side organizations launched by many groups, which offer a new channel for revenue generation and permit a wider range of political activities, are both a cause and a consequence of the groups' policy turn: the opportunity to raise funds around policy campaigns encourages their growth, while their existence further reinforces policy as a strategy. The challenge is to ensure that policy campaigns reflect the priorities of the groups' members rather than their funders—an issue to which we return later.

The final impetus for turning to public policy is perhaps the most obvious: well-crafted and vigorously enforced stronger employment laws offer important means of deterrence, altering employers' behavior via the threat of penalties for noncompliance. Of course, even the strongest policies will not prevent all abuses from occurring. As shown in chapter 3, certain industries and occupations consistently see higher rates of labor standards violations than others despite changes over time to state and federal laws. But generally speaking, as economists and others have shown, the higher the penalties for noncompliance and the higher the probability of detection (through vigorous enforcement), the lower the likelihood that employers will engage in illegal behavior.[58]

Indeed, in a study of the dozen state anti-wage-theft policies enacted between 2005 and 2014, I found that the states that significantly increased their penalties for noncompliance with the minimum wage—especially those that raised their penalties to treble damages—saw a statistically significant decrease in the incidence of minimum wage violations. Likewise, states with stronger enforcement authorities and capacities had statistically lower minimum wage violation rates.[59] Policy reformers, aware of this relationship, have introduced new employment laws featuring tougher penalties, including large criminal penalties and jail time for employers who commit wage theft; the Wage Theft Prevention and Wage Recovery Act, most recently introduced in the U.S. House and Senate in 2022, for example, adds treble damages to the FLSA.[60] The draw to public policy, in other words, is driven in part because there is evidence that it works.[61]

Focusing on deterrence has other benefits as well. For example, it can be empowering for workers to shift from always being on the defense to "playing offense." In their casework and direct actions, alt-labor groups act in a wholly reactive fashion: they seek to help workers rectify past wrongs. Public policy campaigns alter the groups' temporal position relative to the laws: now they are getting in front of worker exploitation, combating it before it happens. The Minneapolis worker center Centro de Trabajadores Unidos en la Lucha (CTUL) pursued a similar logic when it gradually shifted to embrace public policy solutions. As one of their original board members put it, "By responding to wage theft cases one at a time after they'd happened we were behaving like firefighters rushing around putting out fires. Instead we decided we must catch the pyromaniac who's lighting these fires, to stop the harm before it occurs."[62] Sergio Sosa, renowned organizer and executive director of Heartland Workers Center, similarly recalled: "So many workers came through here, always fighting unpaid wages, fighting against contractors and companies. And we got some money back. But at a certain point, I told the organizers and the workers: I am tired of continually fighting this. Because all we are doing is putting on band-aids, and we have to fight again next year, and the next year. How about if we pass legislation: then it would be a better thing that would help workers across the whole state."[63]

Public policy thus offers a solution for many of the challenges alt-labor groups face. But as a strategy for advancing workers' rights and as a means of responding authentically to their members' concerns, it is also limited in several respects.

For starters, the fact that most alt-labor groups are anchored in their local communities and have a relatively limited reach means that policy campaigns usually take place at the state or local (county or city) level—which means that they must contend with whatever political forces hold sway in those locations. In conservative and mixed political contexts, they tend to face pro-business policymakers who oppose new workers' rights and protections; many Republican-controlled legislatures have also preempted key employment policies by, for example, prohibiting cities and counties from setting minimum wages higher than the state wage floor or from implementing fair scheduling, project labor, prevailing wage, paid leave, or gig economy regulations.[64] Under those conditions, alt-labor groups must identify circuitous routes around preemption. In chapter 6, we will see how some of these efforts unfolded in the red states of Texas and Iowa. Local workaround policies, however, tend to be fragile, as they are vulnerable to changing local political tides or to repeal by state-level legislation. They are also inherently limited in reach—indeed, the more local a group's policy campaign is, the smaller the number of workers it is able to help. Local policies thus exacerbate the patchy geography of workers' rights described in chapter 2, which can cause confusion regarding the rights and protections workers have and undermine the policies' effectiveness.

Local policy enforcement is also always a challenge. Because policy effectiveness is contingent on there being sufficient government capacity to implement and enforce the laws (and the political will to defend them against repeal), the highly variable enforcement capacity of local government is a persistent problem. Although some policies may alter certain employers' behavior through deterrence alone, most require vigorous enforcement. In places where local governments lack the enforcement capacity or political motivation to implement their legal mandates, alt-labor's policy wins may prove to be hollow victories—rights on paper that are ineffective in practice. This creates incentives for alt-labor groups to launch additional campaigns around strengthening the government's enforcement capacity—as we saw in the CWC case in chapter 1 and will see in San Francisco and elsewhere in chapter 6.

The questions previously raised about responsiveness and accountability also plague alt-labor groups' policy campaigns. Some have questioned whether such campaigns respond more to funders' priorities than to those of members. Although most groups formulate their policy agendas through bottom-up, collective processes (see chapter 5), the campaigns they organize are invariably shaped by forces outside their members' control. Campaign leaders must make strategic decisions jointly with coalition partners, they must discuss what is legislatively possible with policymakers, and their capacity is largely determined by the extent of the resources their groups have to devote to their campaigns (which is usually influenced by the amount of support they receive from foundations and other external sources). For these reasons, even if procedures are in place to involve members centrally at various stages, group leaders still must have significant discretion to manage strategic considerations as they arise. Policy campaigns can therefore potentially come to reflect the priorities of staff, allies, funders, and politicians more than the membership.

Whereas alt-labor groups' best response to questions of responsiveness and accountability to their members involves the establishment of democratic decision-making structures and an emphasis on activities that directly address individual workers' grievances (such as service provision and workplace justice campaigns), public policy campaigns can only ever be indirectly responsive to members' concerns. To be sure, members are often involved directly in policy campaigns via media engagement, meetings with legislators, public protests, neighborhood canvassing, and the like. But policy campaigns can easily become exercises in advocacy in which professional staff, supported by external partners and entities, mobilize elite institutions to help their constituents achieve certain changes. In Jenkins's critique, workers "function primarily as objects, as symbolic representations of the injustice in question. . . . [Their] role is to help advocates convey the human impact of a given problem to people in power."[65] Jenkins distinguishes between a campaign in which workers have the power to "force changes from the institutions they are confronting" and campaigns in which workers stand as "a group of people as symbols who attempt to convince elite sources of power to correct a given injustice."[66]

Moreover, policy campaigns are inherently constrained by the configuration of political power in each context. Whereas workers can demand virtually anything they want from their employers in workplace justice campaigns, in the policy arena, "the changes that can be achieved are limited to those that are palatable to elite decision-makers."[67] This is true virtually everywhere. In Republican-dominated political environments, alt-labor groups typically find themselves on the defensive, holding the line against efforts to roll back workers' rights. Things are not always much improved in heavily Democratic settings—as well as in evenly balanced partisan contexts—where groups often find themselves "captured" by Democratic politicians who are not adequately responsive to their interests; they are often forced to settle for what those in power are willing to support.[68] And of course, the perennial need for legislative compromise can cause policy outcomes to fall short of the groups' ideals and ultimately leave their membership dissatisfied. This contrasts unfavorably to the (idealized) workplace justice campaign in which, through sustained militancy, workers may be able to force the changes they seek without having to significantly compromise. While such outcomes may be the stuff of fantasy, the (oft-discussed) prospect of creating change wholly on workers' terms can make the strategic twists and turns and substantive compromises necessitated by the policymaking process seem disappointing.

Beyond Policy: Altering the Political Context

The limitations and constraints of policy campaigns impel alt-labor groups to look beyond short-term policy wins. Disappointed by half-loaf policy outcomes and frustrated by the emphasis the policymaking process places on advocacy over participation, many groups have gravitated toward greater political engagement. To be clear, "political" is not a synonym for "partisan" or "electoral." None of these groups' work is partisan, and only 501(c)(4) groups engage in electoral politics. I examine how some 501(c)(4) alt-labor groups try to impact electoral dynamics in nonpartisan ways in chapters 5 and 6—but most alt-labor groups are registered under the 501(c)(3) section of the tax code. Their political work typically centers around building civic power—developing an active and engaged citizenry in low-wage workers' communities by focusing on issues, not candidates, personalities, or parties.

Drawing on their organizing skills, the groups seek to create stronger incentives for government officials to respond to their members' concerns, and they strive to hold those officials accountable. They aim to shape the terms of debate, alter the policy agenda, and influence the identities and calculations of the decision-makers. In other words, their political efforts are aimed at altering the political environment in which policy decisions are made—at reshaping the contours of the political terrain and laying the groundwork for more favorable outcomes over the long term. To borrow Hacker and colleagues' terminology, alt-labor groups seek to influence the "long transit" that leads to "last mile" politics—their efforts are aimed at "the many, many previous miles that shape the substance and scope of conflict, the venues where decisive authority over policy reside, the key political actors who operate in these venues, and the balance of power among those actors."[69] Specifically, they seek to build new electorates, influence candidate selection processes, and bolster state capacities to facilitate "policy fit."[70] Each strategy is illustrated and elaborated in chapter 6.

The efforts of 501(c)(3) alt-labor groups to build civic power and those of 501(c)(4) groups to influence electoral politics are relatively late-breaking developments in the alt-labor field. Although a number of worker centers were already engaged in policy advocacy when Fine first studied them in the early 2000s, few were focused on politics. She found that "they could seldom answer questions about overall numbers of voters in a district, or more fine-grained questions about the margin of victory of a specific city councilor or state representative they were seeking to influence."[71] Although organizers understood the connection between mobilizing voters and persuading elected officials, they "seemed to think that these workers were so vulnerable and these organizations so weak that such questions were, for the moment, irrelevant."[72] Although Fine identified a few exceptions (Casa de Maryland and Voces de la Frontera in Wisconsin), she found that "few worker centers have developed focused voter participation programs and very few, despite their pursuit of public policy change, have undertaken detailed electoral analyses of their communities and developed strategies on the basis of this information."[73] This dovetails with Jennifer Gordon's observation in the 1990s that the worker center she directed in New York lacked strategic acumen; it would engage in "strategizing-by-outrage" and "strategizing-by-what-presents-itself" without "looking carefully at its components, its political and economic context, or the ways it can expect to exert power for change on that issue."[74]

This is clearly no longer the case. Not only are the specific indicators Fine mentioned—knowledge of the size of the electorate in a given district and elected officials' margins of victory—often referenced by leaders and organizers offhandedly, but the majority of groups in my study have well-developed, routinized voter engagement programs. The legislative calendar and the rhythm of the electoral cycle factor into virtually all their strategic planning. Many group leaders have personal relationships with elected officials and have prior campaign management experience. Every year, more groups are spinning off 501(c)(4) groups, enabling them to endorse candidates, devote significantly more time and resources to legislative lobbying, and raise more money from undisclosed donors for their political and policy-focused activities—so long as electoral work does not constitute the group's "primary purpose" or make up more than 49.9 percent of its expenditures (rules that the groups in my study have followed conscientiously). Some groups, large and small, have even contracted with public opinion polling firms to conduct surveys of voters in their area. A growing number of groups have formed coalitions with other issue-based progressive organizations to run voter education and mobilization campaigns during election seasons; and CPDA is even a "national member organization" of the Working Families Party.[75] Of course, not every alt-labor group is equally politically engaged: some, such as Worker Justice Wisconsin, have intentionally sworn off electoral work. But all recognize the importance of thinking politically and strategizing to win, and most groups are moving in the same direction: toward deeper and more sophisticated political engagement in order to reconstruct their political contexts.

Of course, alt-labor groups are not conventional political organizations. As noted, neither 501(c)(3) or 501(c)(4) groups can engage in partisan activity or coordinate with party campaigns or candidates' electoral campaigns.[76] They do not seek to influence politics by donating large sums to their favored candidates' campaigns, hiring teams of lobbyists, or orchestrating splashy campaigns. Although some of the largest 501(c)(4) groups in my sample have run more extensive electoral campaigns as their revenues have grown and their political operations have expanded, most groups are still small, under-resourced, constrained by their nonprofit status, and aware that they can only do so much in open, conventional political conflict.

These constraints are why alt-labor groups' political activities tend to be subtle and indirect, and why groups seek to alter aspects of the political environment—politicians' incentives, their pathways to power, and government's capacities—rather than confront their adversaries head-on in open conflict. Their goal is to "tilt the playing field," as it were; to bias outcomes in their favor. This is not to say that they are shrinking from the fight—to the contrary, their strategy reveals their grand ambitions. Rather than resign themselves to working within the confines of the political system as they find it, politically engaged alt-labor groups are determined to change the system in which they operate.

In Jenkins's well-known critique of the worker center movement, policy-focused campaigns are disparaged for their reliance on advocacy: "the social change that can be achieved through advocacy work is limited because it does not alter power imbalances between oppressed people and the institutions that dominate their lives."[77] Milkman similarly notes that "the accomplishments of the [worker] centers do make a difference, and advocacy may be the best use of their limited resources; yet their self-conception as agents of radical social change belies the inherent constraints of advocacy."[78] The critique of policy-campaign-as-advocacy rings true when those campaigns are not accompanied by parallel efforts to reshape the political landscape. But in their ambitious efforts to alter their political confines, alt-labor groups are directly confronting the power structures that constrain and oppress them. In their political and electoral activities, in other words, the groups reveal that they recognize the limitations of traditional advocacy campaigns as highlighted by Jenkins and Milkman and are working to expand their range of possibilities. Whether they will ultimately be able to accomplish the kind of structural political change they seek in the short- or medium-term is another question, and it is fair to ask whether they are selecting the optimal strategies to achieve their goals. But alt-labor groups have only just begun to experiment with political engagement (see chapter 6), and they are learning and adapting quickly. It is clearly a work in progress.[79]

Given the myriad weaknesses of alt-labor groups and the many ways in which the American political system is stacked against low-wage workers, their ambitions to change the political system may seem overly idealistic or even fantastical. But these organizers and activist workers are not easily deterred. Many are immigrants who have overcome great hardships to get where they are, and their disposition remains the same as it ever was: they seek to confront and change the conditions that cause them suffering. Many have been deeply influenced by radical organizing traditions as well, and they do not view inherited, status quo power arrangements as fixed or immutable. Working toward political reconstruction is not viewed as a stretch—it is the objective.

Political engagement, moreover, offers a number of upsides for alt-labor groups' members, who play a vital role through their canvassing and organizing efforts. As in policy campaigns, their active participation is empowering and builds leadership and organizing skills. During election seasons, campaigns to build civic power, shape the issue debate, and alter electoral incentives provide excellent opportunities for groups to recruit new members—though attrition is usually high after the election is over. Voter engagement through neighborhood canvassing also provides an opportunity for noncitizens who lack access to the voting booth to have a political impact.[80] And for racially and economically marginalized workers and their allies, these activities enable them to proactively redress inequalities of representation and to begin shifting the balance of power toward their communities.

Thinking about alt-labor groups' political engagement in terms of their structural, size, and funding limitations is also helpful. Political activism requires more member participation than policy campaigns, but it, too, is staff-heavy work. It attracts funding from foundations and individual donors and is conducive to coalition building and organizational innovation. Such activism therefore advances groups' ongoing power-building activities while complementing (and perhaps reinforcing) their decision to not build mass dues-based membership systems and to rely on external funding.

Political activism is also partially (and unintentionally) a response to the perennial questions of responsiveness and accountability that come with foundation funding. When groups focus on developing the political capacities of the broader community of low-wage workers and their families and neighbors, they shift the focus away from questions about how closely their activities align with their members' priorities as opposed to the priorities of foundations. With political engagement, the key question becomes whether politicians and government officials are being responsive to the broader community. The role of alt-labor groups in this process is to facilitate that responsiveness. They become, in short, political intermediaries. Clearly, this shift in role does not resolve lingering concerns about member power and group responsiveness. Rather, it adds new questions and tensions, piling them on top of the old ones. Now, questions of political representation are thrust to the forefront: How representative of their broader communities are alt-labor groups? Through what mechanisms can they hold elected officials accountable? Through what mechanisms can their communities hold them accountable? How should groups manage their growing list of responsibilities?

Again, I want to emphasize that the extent of alt-labor groups' political activities varies significantly. Some groups intentionally avoid policy and political engagement due to their different theories of change (usually involving community organizing and building economic power), their deeply rooted distrust of government, or their fear of potential audits and lawsuits brought by their opponents. A group's level of resources matters somewhat, too—better-funded groups (such as MRNY, CPD, NDWA, LUCHA, and ROC) tend to have 501(c)(4) side organizations, are more likely to be part of resilient coalitions that are also politically engaged, and have more capacity to devote time and attention to politics. But the correlation between political activism and a group's resources is not very strong: some less-funded groups are just as deeply engaged in political work (for example, Somos Acción, PCUN, WDAF, and New Labor). Other factors such as industry, race/ethnicity, group age, or region do not seem predictive either. The only clear pattern is that more groups are moving in this direction every year. The growing number of groups spinning off 501(c)(4) side organizations offers perhaps the most concrete evidence of this trend.

But a looming puzzle remains: Given groups' significant limitations of structure, size, and resources, how are they able to punch above their weight in the political and policymaking arenas? What steps are they taking to build and exercise power? That is the question to which we now turn.

CHAPTER 5

Building Power, Forging Capacity

THE PREVIOUS CHAPTER elaborated the logic of alt-labor's turn to policy and politics and noted the impressive record of subnational policy achievements alt-labor groups have racked up over the last two decades. Their success in the policymaking arena, however, presents something of a puzzle: according to standard metrics of political strength, they are remarkably weak compared to their adversaries. Employers and business groups are typically better organized, better funded, and socially dominant, and they enjoy access and influence in government.[1] Most alt-labor groups, in contrast, tend to employ only a few modestly paid staff, and the law imposes strict limits on the types of political activities in which they can engage. Their members—who typically number only in the hundreds—include mostly socially, politically, and economically marginalized immigrants and Black, Latinx, Asian, and Indigenous low-wage workers. Many are not citizens and are unable to vote. Due to occupational segregation and their members' employment on the bottom rungs of the labor market, alt-labor groups have limited structural power and lack the key sources of leverage that labor unions have long used to their advantage—power in numbers and their members' strategic position in production processes. Most groups also have limited budgets and are reliant on capricious external funding sources such as private foundations for their organizational sustenance. The political system, moreover, features high barriers to entry; pathways to power in American politics are often structured in ways that sustain and reproduce existing power imbalances. In short, alt-labor groups seem to be among the least likely to have their voices heard in the political arena.

Even if they manage to get their issues on the agenda, the extent of what alt-labor groups can accomplish through policy is often limited by elite decision-makers who typically do not have their members' best interests in mind. Further, what many consider to be alt-labor groups' greatest asset in the political arena—their members' stories of inhumane treatment at work and the moral outrage their accounts can generate—only works by generating sympathy among politicians, interest groups, and key segments of the public. The "symbolic" or "moral" power they can generate, in other words, still leaves them dependent on others. What is worse, the sympathy route to political influence necessarily casts alt-labor group members as victims rather than as part of a strong community of workers who have legitimate claims to policy change and political responsiveness.

Given these myriad challenges and weaknesses, how are alt-labor groups managing to disrupt existing political dynamics and influence policymaking processes? How are they working to build and exercise their own sources of power?

Although each alt-labor group approaches its power-building work differently depending on its organizational culture and history, its size and resources, the political context, and the experiences and inclinations of its leaders and organizers, some clear patterns emerge across the cases. I find that all alt-labor groups are deeply engaged in efforts to build power on two levels: at the individual level (in their people) and at the group level (in their organization). At the individual level, they help their members reject oppressive and historically entrenched structures and expressions of power, develop their own individual and collective political capacities, and formulate alternative issue agendas. At the group level, they forge coalitions with other groups and develop new organizational capacities to expand their reach and magnify their influence. That is, they seek to build *gen*erative or productive power, sometimes conceptualized as building capacity, energy, or the power to.[2] As Jo Rowlands has written, generative power is "the power to create and participate in new forms of activity"—and is concerned with "the processes by which people become aware of their own interests and how those relate to the interests of others, in order both to participate from a position of greater strength in decision-making and actually to influence such decisions."[3]

Put differently, alt-labor's power-building efforts generate resources the groups can draw upon to intervene in and, they hope, shape policymaking and political processes. The next two sections unpack commonalities in how groups are building power in their people and in their organizations.

Individual-Level Power Building

Alt-labor groups have found that the first and most crucial step in building power for low-wage workers is ideational: it involves transforming the outlook of low-wage workers who have suffered exploitation in the workplace. Most workers view their exploitation as an isolated event and come to the groups asking for help in resolving their individual problems; they are not necessarily seeking out community or looking to join in a collective movement for political and policy change. Lacking the wherewithal to change their situation, many workers feel disempowered or embarrassed by their mistreatment, as well as vulnerable on account of their immigration status, race, ethnicity, gender, sexuality, language skills, or job status. Although they seek redress for the wrongs committed against them, they do not often view themselves as activists or organizers who are capable of effecting broader change.

Transforming this outlook is no easy task—but it is arguably the most essential power-building step and a precondition of all subsequent efforts. In their classic texts on power and domination, John Gaventa and Steven Lukes argue that the first stage of rebellion—moving from a state of powerlessness to an active posture of mobilization against constraints—involves breaking down conceptual and psychological barriers to action.[4] Traversing this stage involves reckoning with what is sometimes known as the "third dimension" or "third face" of power: the weaker party must reject the myths, ideologies, and internalized, taken-for-granted scripts that have produced— and reproduced—its sense of powerlessness. Only then can the less powerful group—whom Gaventa and Lukes call "B," to distinguish from the more powerful group "A"—formulate an alternative agenda and develop strategies to mobilize on it. The less powerful must expose and delegitimize structures and expressions of power they once accepted without question if they are to begin to see themselves as agentic actors who, in concert with others similarly situated, can articulate their own set of demands and develop strategic plans to countermobilize in the public arena. As Gaventa writes: "Several steps in overcoming by B must occur before the conflict is on competitive ground. B must go through a process of *issue and action formulation* by which B develops consciousness of the needs, possibilities, and strategies of challenge. That is, B must counter both the direct and indirect effects of power's third dimension." This is a prerequisite to the next step: "the process of *mobilization of action upon issues* to overcome the mobilization of bias of A against B's actions."[5]

Alt-labor's individual-level power-building work consists primarily of three types of efforts: (1) helping workers develop a sense of power and agency within themselves; (2) building a sense of community among low-wage workers and fostering a collective consciousness; and (3) constructing broad issue agendas that link workers' experiences of exploitation and oppression to a positive program of action. By transforming exploited, disempowered workers into empowered activists and organizers who work in concert with other similarly situated workers to achieve shared objectives, they provide a vital service for individuals and their communities while building resources they can draw upon in their various campaigns.

Transformational Organizing and Community Building

Although a few select alt-labor groups have grown their membership rolls into the thousands, most have a smaller number of reliably active members—usually in the low hundreds—and an even smaller number who serve as leaders and help train others. Group leaders readily acknowledge that they lack the kind of associational power upon which labor unions have long relied. Their groups' strength, leaders believe, comes not from the size of their membership or the extent of their financial resources, but from the passion, solidarity, and determination of their members; from their members' creativity, resourcefulness, and diversity of skills; and from the courage and fearlessness members bring to their collective actions. "If we only have 200 members, but if those 200 members are really solid, they're politically conscious and they know how to run their campaign, that's a lot of people," said Joanna Concepción, executive director of the Filipino Migrant Center. "And so, it may be small, but in terms of quality of the leaders, it means so much more."[6]

To build their membership bases on shoestring budgets, alt-labor groups draw upon the traditions and practices of community organizing and emphasize what political scientist Hahrie Han has called "transformational organizing": they work to transform the "motivations and capacities of their members to cultivate greater activism."[7] Their goal "is not only to get work out of the activist in the short term but also to invest in developing the activists' capacity to act."[8] This kind of organizing seeks to alter the "affects, outlooks, and other orientations of individuals and groups."[9] Organizers encourage workers to transcend the confines of their own self-interest and recognize their abilities, when working together, to affect change. Organizers also help members become autonomous leaders and activists and provide pathways for them to take on leadership roles in the organization (as chairs of committees, lead organizers on key projects, board members, and the like).[10] In other words, rather than trying to "go broad" and build power in numbers, organizers "go deep" by empowering individual workers, investing in their skills, and giving them ownership over the organization.

Notwithstanding many other differences between them, all the community-based alt-labor groups I examined practice some variant of "popular education"—a model developed by Paulo Freire that emphasizes critical thinking, experiential learning, power analysis, collective action, and high participation; everyone serves as a teacher, and the group collectively builds issue agendas out of members' genuine concerns.[11] Groups explore the structure of work in their industries and learn the history of workers' rights, organizing, and power and oppression in the United States; they examine the nuts-and-bolts of community organizing and formulate strategies of action. Following the "train the trainer" method, trained workers then go out into their communities and conduct further training sessions for other workers. Most groups also have committees that conduct their own outreach focused on specific issues, such as exploitative practices in extraction industries, agriculture, or domestic work, or problems of local governance. Participatory education workshops, organizing training sessions, and community outreach are thus some of the primary ways in which groups recruit members and help them see their own power to affect change.

When executed well, transformational organizing supercharges alt-labor groups' work in the political and policymaking arenas. After the 2016 election, Arizona Center for Empowerment (ACE) director Alex Gomez recalled an undocumented woman member who stood up after a training session and said: "I've never felt like I can be the president before. But after this, I feel like I can, because I'm with a community and I feel like I'm supported and backed up." To Gomez, this was an illustration of power effectively being built. "Power," Gomez said, "is that individual person feeling their agency and being able to translate that and activate themselves and call their neighbors and call their family—and show up to fight."[12]

Empowered and dedicated workers who become leaders and organizers also infuse the groups with an intensity, determination, and tenacity that is needed to persevere through challenging circumstances. As Han, McKenna, and Oyakawa write, having a self-directed, committed, knowledgeable base lends groups the resilience and adaptive capacities they need to operate amid uncertainty, weather ups and downs, and carry out a wider range of unknown activities in the future, even in the absence of substantial financial resources.[13]

Member recruitment is pursued differently depending on the group's composition, history, and context. Some groups, such as Heartland Workers Center, recruit workers through door knocking and use classic community organizing techniques as discussed in chapter 3; they reject the service-provision model as a method of drawing in new members in favor of what they call "the Latin America formula," emphasizing issue-based committees and "core teams." Other groups, such as Arise Chicago, the Congress of Day Laborers at NOWCRJ, and Adelante Alabama, have a steady stream of workers who come through their doors seeking individual services; they therefore do not devote precious resources to the costly work of outreach through neighborhood canvassing. Irrespective of how they arrive, prospective members are invited to participate in a variety of training sessions, workshops, and meetings and are warmly welcomed into the community.

Another critical component of the groups' power-building efforts involves community building: cultivating meaningful, authentic relationships among members, a sense of mutual accountability, and a collective identity within and across race, class, gender, and country of origin. Community building has long been central to the practice of organizing, which #BlackLivesMatter cocreator and organizer Alicia Garza describes as "the messy work of bringing people together, from different backgrounds and experiences, to change the conditions they are living in. It is the work of building relationships among people who may believe that they have nothing in common so that they can achieve a common goal."[14] As the sociologist and organizer

Marshall Ganz has noted, "Through the process of coming together, individuals learn to move beyond their narrow self-interest. They move toward an enlightened self-interest and a broader understanding of common interests and common purpose. . . . Equality of voice can translate into the power or the capacity to achieve common purpose."[15]

Organizers typically describe the low-wage workers they meet through door-to-door canvassing, community outreach events, or intakes at the office as unhappy with their jobs, discouraged by their station in life, and feeling relatively powerless to do anything about it. The task of the organizer is to listen, emphasize that they are not alone, and encourage them to meet with other similarly situated workers to talk, offer mutual support, and develop plans to collectively improve their communities and work lives. As Sosa of Heartland Workers Center explained:

> You need to understand that they are forgetting—they are not human beings anymore. Because they are living under the social amnesia: I wake up, go to work, finish work, drink, go to bed. And do that over and over again. . . . [So you ask]: "Why are you unhappy?" You get the anger out of the people. "OK, I'll tell you why I'm unhappy. I'm unhappy because I was treated like shit today by my supervisor. I have been told again that if I don't do my job, if I don't work like a dog, there are so many like me who can take my place. I'm unhappy because I don't have money to pay the rent. I'm unhappy because I don't have money to go back to Mexico. I'm unhappy because I don't have papers to walk [down the street without fear]." "OK, well if you are unhappy because of all of that, I know a lot of unhappy people you can meet. Have a meeting with unhappy people, and drink a beer. To celebrate our unhappiness."[16]

The simple act of bringing people together and providing an opportunity to forge meaningful relationships is viewed as fundamental. Ana Maria Archila, co-executive director of the CPD and previously co-executive director of MRNY, put it this way:

> Powerlessness is so inside people's bodies—or like the glasses we can't take off—and we practice it so much in our society that I think a lot of our work is actually like doing interventions, creating the space for people to peel away a little bit the layers of that so that they can get to a place of creativity and fearlessness, tap into courage. . . . Basically just a room with someone to facilitate a conversation, some food, and some space for socializing—that was the basic formula for building a membership organization [Make the Road New York] that is now 25,000 people or so. The space for people to take off the many layers of accumulated experience of not being powerful.[17]

Fostering authentic relationships among members generates a critically important, if often overlooked, form of power, argues Vosburgh of Adelante Alabama: "There are things you can do that build alternative power structures around personal-level interconnectedness while ignoring really corrosive and negative forms of power: that is building power—just not in a 'I'm going to go lobby the city council' kind of way."[18] Gomez similarly explained: "At the core of all of the work is the relationship building. It's never glossed over. . . . We genuinely know who our members are. I know our members by name, they know me. . . . You have to have organizers that come from the community, that understand the community and can constantly foster and cultivate that relationship with people."[19]

CWJ, located in Iowa City, a purple city in a red state, prioritizes the building of authentic relationships between its racially diverse, primarily immigrant base and longtime Iowa City residents—many of whom are White liberals—who support the center's work. Its efforts to build relationships across race, ethnicity, class, and citizenship have created highly resilient mutual support networks. These efforts are not complicated, nor do they require much in terms of funding. On the last Friday of every month, for example, the center hosts Sudanese, Latina, and White women for tea and dessert. "They start talking, they start having programs, they dance," explained Salih. "They say, 'Now it's a Sudanese dance; now an American dance.' They're just building relationships."[20]

Periodically, the center also hosts open-invitation potluck dinners for the community. One, held in the wake of former president Donald Trump's "Muslim ban," attracted five hundred people—a strong demonstration of community solidarity with the Muslim immigrant community in Iowa City. Attendees were encouraged to sit and converse with someone they did not know. By the end, Salih reported, playdates had been scheduled for attendees' children, longtime residents had volunteered to help English language learners, and other forms of mutual support and social connection had been forged. "People just start making relations. Which is so important. If this community becomes one community, it will help. Discrimination will not be happening, people can advocate for people. We cannot change the state level or even the federal level. We cannot. So we have to improve our community here. Because this is where we live."[21] In Marwell's terms, CWJ's community-building work has therefore aimed to create both "organizational adherents" and "community participants"—both of which the group views as essential to its mission.[22]

Despite Iowa's preemption of local minimum wages and the minimal resources the state dedicates to enforcing state employment laws, CWJ has accomplished a great deal for workers simply by channeling the strength it has built in its community. One of the center's main activities involves hunting down employers who fail to pay their employees what they are owed. Wage theft complaints are read aloud at membership and allies' meetings. Participants discuss the case, ask if anyone knows the employer, and brainstorm ways to pressure the employer to pay up. "We don't have a lawyer, we don't go to court to hold business accountable," Salih says. "We just have community pressure." Salih starts by calling the employer and asking them to pay their workers the back wages they are owed. If they do not comply, Salih gathers community members and allies to visit the employer "at a busy time of day." They go "like a delegation" to the place of business, hand the employer a formal letter demanding payment, loudly retell the worker's story, and set a deadline for the payment of back wages—or else they promise to escalate. Most of the time, the worker gets paid: "That's how we have recovered over $80,000 of unpaid wages. Just by putting community pressure."[23]

For more homogenous groups, shared racial and ethnic identities and common languages are extremely useful for building community and forging a collective consciousness among members who might not otherwise interact because they work in disparate occupations and industries. This is the case for ACE in Arizona, which primarily organizes undocumented Latinx workers; Chinese Progressive Association in San Francisco, whose members are predominantly Chinese; PWC in Southern California, a majority of whose members are Filipino; and NOWCRJ's Stand with Dignity project, which is predominantly Black (and an affiliate of the National Black Worker Center network). In these and other cases, alt-labor groups serve as "meso-level" mechanisms that activate linked fate—the sense of racial/ethnic solidarity among group members that produces political cohesion. As Reuel Rogers and Jae Yeon Kim write, such meso-level mechanisms "interpret what these shared racial experiences mean; advocate collective action strategies and policies for addressing them; and convey these messages to the rest of the group. In addition, leaders organize individuals to prepare them to act in unison."[24]

Many groups, however, organize a diverse set of workers representing a range of racial and ethnic backgrounds, countries of origin, languages spoken, and occupations. Members of CWJ, for example, speak nearly a dozen languages; the most common other than English are Spanish, Arabic, and French. Members of Adelante Alabama speak a half dozen languages as well—mostly Indigenous languages from Mexico and Guatemala, as well as Spanish and English—and represent a wide range of ages, as well as gender identities, sexualities, and belief systems. Arise Chicago organizes mostly Latinx and Polish immigrants. This diversity presents both a challenge and an opportunity. The variety of spoken languages among members can create logistical challenges for the groups, as multiple translators are often required. And racial resentments, both preexisting and fostered by discriminatory employers (as we saw in the temp workers' case in chapter 1), can make bridge-building difficult.

One way alt-labor groups work to build community among diverse groups of workers is through social events in which members can bond over the traditions they share as well as the traditions they do not—they compare experiences, share stories, and build friendships. But perhaps the most powerful force for generating a collective identity among diverse workers involves members' shared experiences of exploitation, discrimination, and harassment. Sharing and deconstructing experiences of abuse is difficult for most workers. But it can also be empowering and conducive to formulating collective issue agendas.

Issue Formulation

Moving from individual-level grievances to collective consciousness—and then to collective action—is no easy task. It is made all the more complicated by the diversity of workers' grievances: the day laborer's wage theft, the meat-packer's unhealthy and unsafe working conditions, the domestic worker's sexual harassment, discrimination in placing temp workers, retaliation against farm workers who dare to complain. Although these forms of exploitation are widespread and affect millions of workers, they are experienced individually by people who are usually isolated from one another and scattered across industries, geographies, and workplaces. One of the functions of alt-labor groups is to help otherwise atomized workers draw out the connections between their situations; identify, name, and reject power structures they may have taken for granted; build community around their shared interests and issues; and collectively formulate agendas for action.

As they construct a forward-looking policy agenda, members invariably link the racism, xenophobia, and sexism they face inside the workplace to the same oppressive forces they, their families, and their neighbors face outside the workplace. Organizers seek to bring greater visibility to these linkages in much the same way that Jane McAlevey describes "whole worker" organizing, which "seeks to engage 'whole workers' in the betterment of their lives. To keep them consistently acting in their self-interest, while constantly expanding their vision of who that self-interest includes, from their immediate peers in their unit, to their shift, their workplace, their street, their kids' school, their community, their watershed, their nation, their world."[25] When discussing the low quality of their jobs, members often link their feelings of precarity at work to the ways in which public policies affect their employment prospects and compound their vulnerability to exploitation—such as unequal access to educational resources and mandatory disclosures of prior felony convictions. Likewise, members recognize how their lack of health insurance owing to their immigration status or the housing discrimination they face affects their ability to attend work regularly and perform well. Members note that even driving to work is a high-risk activity due to racially biased policing, "show me your papers" laws, and high barriers to acquiring valid drivers' licenses.

Although these sorts of institutionalized and intersecting forms of subjugation are obvious to many members, they are not plainly evident to everyone. Some write off their experiences as isolated problems or as the consequences of neutral market forces. Alt-labor groups thus provide spaces for workers to explore the similarities across their experiences, make their collective goals concrete, and take their first steps toward mobilizing for policy change. In Gaventa's apt framework, for the first stage of rebellion to occur, "the powerless must be able to explore their grievances openly, with others similarly situated. They must develop their own notions of interests and actions, and themselves as actors."[26] Only then can they mobilize on those issues and press for change.

Alt-labor groups primarily determine which policy campaigns to pursue through bottom-up democratic processes and open discussions among members and organizers.[27] Such processes ensure that the groups are responsive to, reflective of, and accountable to their members rather than foundations and other external funders. These freewheeling deliberative processes often lead to the construction of broad, multifaceted issue agendas. Rather than single-mindedly seeking to combat wage theft, for example, groups construct agendas that also include fighting anti-immigrant policies, racial discrimination, gender discrimination, and other challenges specific to their communities.

Despite significant variation in alt-labor groups' histories, cultures, and programming, one common trend across all groups is that the scope of their issue agendas has grown in response to the challenges their members face. Groups that started as predominantly workers' rights organizations (for example, WDP, Arise, CWJ, and Adelante Alabama) now fight on the front lines for immigrant rights, criminal justice reform, and more; groups that began as predominantly immigrant rights organizations (such as CPA, Somos, El Centro, Needham Area Immigration Task Force, and the PWC) have increasingly focused on workers' rights, racial justice, and other topics; and groups that initially organized around a specific issue such as wage theft (for example, CWC, NOWCRJ, MRNY, and WeCount!) have gradually expanded the scope of their agendas to confront the broader range of challenges their members face, both inside and outside the work-place. "We made a decision to have a much more intentional fight," Merle Payne, a cofounder of CTUL, told Michelle Chen, "not just about work-place conditions and looking at it from a class perspective, but also fighting around racial justice and gender justice, really looking at the three prongs of exploitation, from capitalism to patriarchy to racism."[28]

From a broader perspective, one may understand this process of issue expansion as a characteristic outgrowth of policy drift. As discussed in chapter 1, the people who are left behind by policy drift often face multiple crosscutting challenges, and one of the primary tasks of the new groups that emerge to support them is to help them identify means of addressing those multiple challenges simultaneously. Consider alt-labor groups that organize domestic workers. In the United States, domestic workers are overwhelmingly female (97 percent), non-White (77 percent), and foreign born (78 percent), and almost half are estimated to be undocumented (47 percent).[29] In addition to regularly experiencing wage theft and work-place abuse, domestic workers often face racial discrimination, sexual harass-ment, and assault; immigrant domestic workers face threats of deportation.

NDWA's policy agendas thus reflect the multiple challenges its members face as immigrant women of color. Explained Anna Duncan, NDWA director of affiliate engagement:

> Because of who our members are, we have a much more intersectional approach than some organizations that might choose to have a narrower focus. If more than half of our membership are immigrant women being harmed by current immigration policies, we can't stand on the sidelines as an organization. Not only is it impacting people's work situations because it's making them afraid of demanding their rights at work because they're afraid of retaliation—their employer is telling them they're going to call ICE—but you can't do domestic worker–specific organizing if people are either too afraid to speak out or they are not able to focus on that because they're trying to get their partner out of detention.[30]

NDWA has consequently become a leader in numerous immigrants' rights campaigns, in addition to fighting for stronger protections in the workplace. It has also joined in campaigns around sexual harassment and assault, gender-based discrimination, and modern slavery, partnering with Time's Up Legal Defense Fund and anti-trafficking groups. It also helped start the We Dream in Black initiative to empower and uplift Black women's stories of triumph. And it launched Caring Across Generations to spotlight the "elder boom" and advocate for family support, better jobs for caregivers, and better choices for seniors. In other words, rather than dedicate resources only to a single set of issues—for example, wage theft or discrimination—NDWA and its local affiliates push forward on multiple fronts simultaneously.

Broad policy agendas, in addition to responding authentically to members' manifold intersecting concerns, undeniably offer the groups instrumental, strategic benefits as well. They enable alt-labor groups to expand the scope of the conflict, reach out to new constituencies, and generate additional points of pressure on the political system. Issue breadth also allows their campaigns to tap into a wider range of members' experiences, forge allies with a wider range of groups, and expand their political footprint. By formulating agendas that transcend workers' rights and tackle multiple issues simultaneously, groups can also pivot from one fight to the next; adjust to the different tempos of different campaigns; mix and match bolder, more ambitious goals with smaller, more winnable fights; and shift focus from a demoralizing loss along one front to an uplifting victory on another.

Multidimensional issue agendas thus provide alt-labor groups with a greater number of pathways along which to challenge—and to chip away at—oppressive economic, social, and political power structures. But broadening the scope of the agenda also presents significant challenges, including how to set priorities, allocate resources, and build unity and solidarity within diverse membership bases while pursuing campaigns along multiple fronts.

Many groups have found that the best solution to those challenges is to center their analysis on power and its manifestation. Organizers encourage members to view their problems as flowing from the same underlying source: their adversaries' outsize power and their own lack of influence over the decisions that shape their lives. Each issue on the groups' policy agendas is understood as a separate door onto the same fight: an opportunity to chip away at the broader power imbalance in society and politics.[31] As Price of NOWCRJ explained:

> To me, intersectionality is not about trying to be in every fight—it's about understanding the connections between every fight. We have to do the analysis to understand the connections. With that analysis, we will shape our demands in a way that hits the intersections. . . . In our moment of crisis, it's natural for human beings to get focused on the immediate problem in front of them, which are separate issues [such as housing, immigration, policing]. But if we do the work to dig down a layer, then we find a common target, we find a common fight.[32]

The key, Price says, is to "dedicate resources to political education" and engage in "constantly renewing the politic" so that members can conduct new political analyses as conditions change, draw out issue linkages, and "center the analysis on us fighting together."[33]

The agenda-building work of alt-labor groups constitutes one of the most fundamental components of their power-building efforts. But it is only a first step: like transformational organizing, agenda building, by itself, cannot bring about institutional change or alter the balance of power in the workplace. Alt-labor groups must also develop the capacity to act on their high-priority issues. Thus, whereas the first stage of power building—comprising individual empowerment, community building, and issue formulation—focuses primarily on building power in people, the next two stages involve building power in the organization. Coalition building and organization building develop the groups' capacity to counteract the organizational and institutional biases that influence which issues get "organized out" of politics so that the groups can countermobilize sufficiently to "organize in" alternatives.[34]

Group-Level Power Building

If alt-labor groups are to exercise autonomous power in the political arena, they must develop the capacity to act, both on their own and in concert with others. Although they are disadvantaged due to their small size and precarious funding, the groups have two key assets: first, their unique position in the labor movement and in the broader ecosystem of progressive groups, which affords them ample opportunities to build coalitions and forge alliances with like-minded organizations; and second, their legal status as nonprofit organizations, which provides significant flexibility in what to do and how to do it. Although both advantages can sometimes also be constraints—alt-labor groups are often junior partners in their coalitions and their nonprofit status prohibits them from undertaking partisan activity or collective bargaining—these assets provide the raw materials for expanding alt-labor's organizational capacity and help the groups to punch above their weight in the political arena.

Building Coalitions

There is significant variation in the types of coalitions groups join, the reasons for joining them, and their durability and strength. Some coalitions are temporary and ad hoc, aimed at achieving specific policy outcomes, while others are more durable and formalized, featuring more institutionalized arrangements. The most highly valued, reliable, and durable alliances are with other workers' rights groups. These include affiliations with nationally federated organizations that concentrate on specific industries such as NDWA, NDLON, and ROC (NDWA has "chapters" and "affiliates," ROC has "chapters," and NDLON has "member organizations"); individual labor unions, the AFL-CIO, and local labor councils; Interfaith Worker Justice, a national network that nurtures alliances between alt-labor groups, faith-based groups, and labor unions; the NBWC network, which links groups organizing Black low-wage workers; and CPD, which networks politically progressive community-based nonprofit groups.[35]

Informal alliances are also common among fellow progressive community-based groups in the same city, county, or state; such partnerships reflect alt-labor groups' efforts to collaborate with other nonprofit organizations that work on issues that affect their members. Examples include CWC's partnerships with immigrant rights groups, civil rights groups, and women's rights groups; El Centro's alliance with Somos and NM Comunidades en Acción de Fe to promote immigrants' rights in New Mexico; and Alianza Poder, which counts PCUN as one of nine "sister" organizations and seeks to organize and serve Latinx, Indigenous, and Black workers and their families in Oregon.

The impulse to ally with other groups is also, of course, a rational response to weakness. For groups that are at a decided disadvantage when working alone, membership in a coalition enables them to generate synergies, share resources, reap efficiency gains, borrow power from stronger partners, and magnify their collective influence.[36] Leaders and organizers readily acknowledge that the best way for small, poor groups to build collective power is "through the creation and nurturing of alliances," as Bill Okerman of the Needham Area Immigration Justice Task Force in Massachusetts put it.[37] WJW, for example, has prioritized coalition building since its beginnings in the late 1990s, when the Interfaith Coalition for Worker Justice of South-Central Wisconsin (ICWJ) started as a collaboration between faith leaders, unions, low-wage workers, and local nonprofits to study and publicize the exploitation of low-wage Latinx workers in Dane County. ICWJ spun off a worker center in 2007, but sustaining it as a stand-alone entity proved challenging, and in 2018 the two decided to formally merge as WJW, which now serves as both a worker center and a centralized hub for coalition building and generating collective action among interfaith, labor, and community groups. WJW executive director Rebecca Meier-Rao explained: "We're aware that we're small and by ourselves, we're fairly powerless, especially as we devote a lot of our resources to taking care of workers that are coming to our worker center. The only way we get the word out is to build partnerships and coalitions. . . . Our sense is that if we are not in coalition, our impact will be limited. And even if we grow, we won't be powerful enough to go against strong forces alone."[38]

But coalition building is not only undertaken by small, poor groups. The largest group in my sample, CPD—which reported almost $29 million in revenue in 2019, has 95 staff members in 9 states and 3 large cities, and which nurtures 55 affiliated partner groups in 131 cities—was similarly founded to "aggregate institutional resources and relationships," said co-executive director Friedman.[39] CPD seeks to institutionalize linkages between base-building groups across the country, disseminate resources, share best practices, and build collective political capacities to advance a "pro-worker, pro-immigrant, racial and economic justice agenda."[40] Several of CPD's affiliates maintain their own coalitions and networks— for example, PCUN, UFR, Make the Road, and Casa de Maryland— which, in partnership, extend each group's reach further still. CPD also regularly partners with still other independent groups and forms ad hoc coalitions around specific issues.

For younger groups moving into issue domains in which they lack expertise or strategic relationships, joining in coalition with more experienced nonprofit groups can be extremely valuable. When the relatively young Adelante Alabama (founded in 2014) launched a campaign to end police coordination with ICE and push for criminal justice reform— an agenda formulated by its overwhelmingly Latinx membership base— its partnerships with organizations that had strong ties to faith-based and Black communities proved indispensable. "Even if it's just them willing to put their name on certain things, or if we do—it makes a difference. . . . We couldn't do the work we were doing if we weren't both leading certain coalitions and participating in other ones," said Vosburgh, Adelante founder and executive director.[41]

The degree to which a group actively participates in a coalition-run campaign varies by issue: for instance, some groups may join coalitions around issues they deem not to be priorities, and their participation may be more apparent than real—lending their name, contributing some resources, and perhaps putting in a small amount of effort. The strength of each ally's contribution toward the campaign is difficult to discern from the outside. In addition, the simple existence of a coalition does not necessarily imply political strength; coalitions comprising weak groups will be weak, too. Coalitions can also conceal adversarial relations between groups, paper over frictions, and obscure power differentials in the alliance.

But even when coalitions project greater strength than they actually have, they signal to elected officials a breadth and intensity of support for a particular issue, which can make risk-averse policymakers more likely to adopt their position.[42] Because "the result of political contests is determined by the scope of public involvement in conflicts," alt-labor's impulse to demonstrate a wider base of support reflects the fundamental impulse of weaker groups to "enlarg[e] the scope of conflict."[43]

In Amanda Tattersall's seminal study of community unionism, the most effective coalitions were those built on trust that featured mutually beneficial ("positive-sum") relations.[44] Trust and personal relationships are particularly helpful in places where labor and progressive movements have historically struggled. For example, in the Republican-dominated state of Texas, which has a historically low union density, the progressive infrastructure remains relatively inchoate, with a small (but growing) number of young groups working toward similar goals. Genuine personal relationships established between the leaders of key economic and social justice groups—including WDP, Texas Organizing Project (TOP), Texas Civil Rights Project, and the Texas AFL-CIO—are pivotal to fostering collective action on behalf of shared goals. "We've all become friends," explained José Garza, former co-executive director of WDP. "That's the only way you get six people to raise money together that's not going to their own organizations. It's the only way you get people to lift each other up and say to their donors, 'You really need to hear what TOP is up to: They're badasses.' And TOP to be able to say, 'You know, Workers Defense are our ride-or-die partners, you need to go see, they do this really well.' And to allow us to have honest conversations with each other about strategy."[45]

In any given moment, alt-labor groups are likely to be in multiple coalitions with many partners. But coalitions can be difficult to maintain and challenging to operate in equitable ways.[46] Practically speaking, this can make for some difficult choices about which campaigns to prioritize. It can also spread groups thin, deplete their resources, and strain alliances when partners in other coalitions are adversaries. For example, although most alt-labor groups view themselves as steadfastly engaged in a long-term struggle to fight exploitation, White supremacy, patriarchy, and neoliberalism, groups with specific sectoral foci sometimes seek to build alliances with organizations they and their allies might otherwise oppose in order to make progress in reforming industrial practices. High-road employers and business associations with an interest in leveling the playing field, for example, can make useful allies for alt-labor groups in policy campaigns, demonstrating to elected officials the breadth of support for reform. In politics, "you have to have unlikely alliances," Price of NOWCRJ explained. "You have to find common ground with people you don't agree with."⁴⁷ Sometimes those alliances offend those with whom the groups are partnering on other campaigns; this is a tension these groups try to manage.

But for industry-focused groups, "unlikely alliances" are often viewed as necessary. The NDWA, for example, has deliberately tried to treat domestic worker employers as potential allies rather than targets. ROC, too, has put considerable effort into forging partnerships with high-road employers and local restaurant associations that support higher wages and other protections for restaurant workers in order to level the playing field. By 2021, ROC's "high-road employer association" had grown to more than nine hundred members who supported a $15 minimum wage with tips on top (eliminating the subminimum wage), paid sick days, and racial and gender equity. Given the strength of the National Restaurant Association—which argues forcefully that wage increases will lead to job losses, that employees will lose tips altogether, and that wage increases will bankrupt small businesses—ROC executive director Sekou Siby argues that "it is vital to answer the attack. The wage increase campaign must feature both workers and small business owners. . . . We make the case that a good salary and better working conditions will lead to employee job satisfaction, which will increase their performance and is good for business. So therefore, for us improving wages and working conditions is good for the working people [and] it is a win for employers."⁴⁸

Changing the restaurant industry, ROC leaders argue, requires support from all stakeholders. "Without allies it cannot work," explained Fekkak Mamdouh, cofounder and former co-executive director, now senior director at One Fair Wage. "You need the restaurant owner, you need the consumer, you need the city council people, you need the Congress people, and you need tourists, too." ROC encourages its restaurant-owner allies not to leave their local restaurant associations but to "stay inside and fight from within. . . . You have to be in it to change it. Our members should be on the board."⁴⁹ Jayaraman, ROC cofounder and former co-executive director, now president of One Fair Wage, agreed: "We've expanded our definition of who's most affected—we've come to understand it's not just workers, it's employers too—and built a broader social movement organization based on that."⁵⁰

PCUN, similarly, has joined in coalition with corporate retail firms, farm owners, and consumers, as well as other workers' rights groups, in the

Equitable Food Initiative (EFI), a coalition that seeks to transform the agriculture industry by bringing together multiple players in the food supply chain in common cause. PCUN has at times been criticized by other workers' rights organizations for its participation in the EFI. But by setting higher labor standards collectively and offering a certification for products from employers who agree to key labor standards, EFI has met with some success. As the label has gained positive attention, more industrial entities have sought it out. A similar example is CWC's Temporary Staffing Agency Seal of Approval Program described in chapter 1, designed to ratchet up employment standards and reward high-road temp agencies.

But alt-labor's most common allies outside the nonprofit world are not businesses—they are labor unions. In fact, many alt-labor groups and labor unions are formally allied. In 2006, thanks to the efforts of Pablo Alvarez and other NDLON organizers to build relations with AFL-CIO leaders including president John Sweeney, the national labor federation launched the AFL-CIO National Worker Center Partnership to strengthen ties to worker centers; the network has grown in the intervening years.[51] Informal alliances are also quite common. Within my sample alone, eleven of the twenty-four 501(c)(3) groups have ties to labor unions that range in formality from memberships on local labor councils with voting rights to courtesy affiliations and solidarity relationships.

Examples of partnerships between alt-labor groups and unions are found all around the country. Unions in Los Angeles worked closely with the Koreatown Immigrant Workers Alliance and the Los Angeles Alliance for a New Economy to persuade the Los Angeles City Council to raise the minimum wage to $15 an hour; SEIU helped launch a worker center known as the Awood Center in Minnesota to engage the East African community; worker centers seeded by the Interfaith Worker Justice network have partnered with unions across the nation; the United Steelworkers joined in alliance with several worker centers in the well-known CLEAN Carwash Campaign; and in 2011 the AFL-CIO and several foundations launched the LIFT Fund, which has distributed more than $1 million in grants to encourage worker center–labor union alliances.[52]

These partnerships notwithstanding, the relationship between unions and alt-labor has often been described as a "mismatch" in practice.[53] In part, the explanation is structural: whereas traditional unions typically focus on organizing bargaining units within companies in targeted sectors for the purpose of engaging in collective bargaining, worker centers tend to focus on "raising labor standards community-wide . . . [and] building a grassroots social movement that can transform society."[54] But the lines are blurry. As we saw in chapter 2, unions, too, have fought to raise community-wide labor standards, and some are very social-movement oriented. In addition, many alt-labor groups focus on specific industries and encourage their members to unionize; they often consider union contracts the best possible outcome of any workplace organizing campaign. (Collective bargaining agreements are often called "the gold standard" of worker protections.)[55]

Still, unions and alt-labor groups have substantial cultural differences. Within some unions, discussion of immigration and alt-labor are "still quite fraught" and "marked by misconceptions and misunderstandings."[56] For example, some union organizers believe that undocumented workers undercut labor standards in their industries—especially in construction and other building trades. And because employers have historically used temp workers as replacements during strikes, some union leaders view low-wage temp workers with suspicion.[57] Some temp workers, in turn, consider unions to be corrupt and likely to make "sweetheart" deals with management that harm nonunion workers. Alt-labor groups are also frequently frustrated by unions' lack of interest in organizing "hot shops" where low-wage workers are eager to unionize.

But relations can change. After years of work collaborating on campaigns against exploitative employers, the temp worker–focused CWC and the Chicago Federation of Labor, for example, have built a strong and reciprocal partnership. In 2018, the two organizations formed the Temp Worker Union Alliance Project, comprised of union staff, temp worker organizers, academics, and labor activists, to build solidarity between union members and temp workers.[58] CWC often works to ensure that temp workers do not cross picket lines, and its members have picketed with the SEIU and the Teamsters Union. Back at Gold Standard Baking (discussed in chapter 1), CWC and Workers United joined together to turn two hundred temp workers into permanent, unionized employees.[59] From the unions' perspective, collaborating with CWC's temp workers promised to invigorate their organizing efforts. "A lot of our locals are busy doing collective bargaining and defending their contracts, and organizing is the last thing on their agenda," the Chicago Federation of Labor's secretary-treasurer admitted.

"A lot of these industries are heavily temped out. By building these bridges with worker centers, it helps us to organize."[60]

Some alt-labor leaders, however, continue to feel that unions turn a blind eye to the exploitation of low-wage immigrant workers and workers of color. Some complain about union complacency, arguing that they have lost their edge: "They forgot to be the Knights of Labor," one leader told me. "Their fights are more around money." Another stated plainly that although they work together regularly, "we're small and scrappy and uninfluential in their eyes." And one explained that while alt-labor has "moved unions in a more radical direction, they take offense to the notion that we're influencing their agenda. The power dynamic is definitely unequal." Such frictions notwithstanding, many unions and alt-labor groups have built constructive, mutually beneficial relationships with one another. "We are all part of the same movement," said Zaman of RTF. "We flex different organizing muscles, but we share the same goals: healthy and dignified work for all. Robust worker organization—composed of labor unions and worker centers alike—is the best vehicle for the working class to wield a greater degree of control over their work lives, and by extension, their non-work lives."[61]

Whereas alt-labor groups are young and still growing, traditional labor unions have decades of experience and established networks from which alt-labor groups can benefit—a point stressed by scholar and organizer McAlevey, whose experiences and writings have influenced alt-labor and traditional labor organizers alike.[62] In many cases, coalitions with labor unions may therefore be more about borrowing unions' power than building power together. Alt-labor groups often ride the coattails of more established, well-funded, politically connected labor unions, especially in state-level policy campaigns where state labor federations have established clout. In city- and county-level policy campaigns, alt-labor groups are able to exercise more independent political power.

The cultural differences between labor unions and alt-labor groups may have dissipated somewhat in recent years as their members' demographics and worldviews have converged. Some of the more diverse, growth-oriented labor unions, like UNITE HERE and SEIU, have publicly recognized that business-style unionism is no longer as effective as it once was and have experimented with innovative campaigns like Fight for $15 and sectoral bargaining strategies.[63] In that well-known broad-scale campaign, SEIU partnered with alt-labor and other community-based groups across dozens of cities and states while providing funding for the massive protests. Unions increasingly recognize that the labor movement needs to be more bottom-up, led by empowered members and energized by dense networks of mobilized allies at the grassroots.[64] In this spirit, a growing number of public-sector unions have advanced Bargaining for the Common Good initiatives in which coalitions of unions and community groups employ a diversity of tactics and organizing models to deepen ties and collectively push for improvements to their communities.[65] During the Covid-19 pandemic, many teachers' unions interested in broadening their base of community support followed suit. The union-rights organization Jobs with Justice serves a similar purpose, bringing local labor and community groups together in common action. The goal is to build a "flourishing ecosystem" in which allied groups are fighting existing power structures from all corners, through different tactics, and by employing a diversity of models. As numerous scholars have argued, in the new economy, no one size fits all.[66]

Although the labor movement, broadly conceived, has experienced its share of internecine conflicts, one of the advantages to building partnerships and alliances across different forms of worker organizations is that each group can play different but complementary roles in the same policy campaign. Sometimes unions are the agitators and worker centers are the peacemakers; sometimes they swap roles. "We're able to play off each other and strategically use those roles," one leader told me. "More often than not, we're the bad cop, they're the good cop. . . . But because our membership are the ones who are often the most directly affected by the [policy] issue, we're able to bring those authentic stories to the table." When their interests converge, the synergies can be substantial.[67]

Coalition building is thus the primary way alt-labor groups build power with others; it enables small, under-resourced groups to accomplish far more than they could ever accomplish alone. Coalitions provide groups with myriad benefits, though some conceal frictions and project more unity and breadth of support than really exists. Coalitions are not costless; some partnerships have been challenging to develop and maintain— especially those with employers and labor unions—but in the political arena, those alliances are some of the most valuable, helping alt-labor groups to mobilize around expansive issue agendas and more effectively intervene in the policymaking process. Another way is through organizational innovation.

Organization Building

In part, alt-labor groups compensate for their lack of resources with "resourcefulness," to borrow from Ganz's well-known formulation.[68] By experimenting with different organizational models, the groups seek to expand their capacity to act. Rather than replicate familiar organizational templates designed for other purposes in other contexts, alt-labor groups have been iteratively developing new models and learning as they go. "Everything that we've done, all of these strategies, started with throwing mud at the wall," said Diaz of Somos Un Pueblo Unido. "And then we keep doing it, figure out what works, what doesn't. . . . And *then* we can be deliberate and create a model that ends up working. But it always shifts."[69]

Leveraging Technology

UFR offers an intriguing case of capacity building through experimentation. Originally called OUR Walmart and funded by the United Food and Commercial Workers Union to help Walmart workers organize and push for changes to the corporation's infamously harsh labor practices, UFR now targets the entire retail sector and has morphed into a radically different kind of workers' rights organization—both from its original form and from the more familiar community-based worker center model.[70] As Dan Schlademan, cofounder and former co-executive director, explained: "The way we started OUR Walmart and then what OUR Walmart ultimately became is different. We learned things along the way and kept an eye on doing things not because we thought they were the right things but because they were creating power and having real outcomes. We don't have the answer to the question of what we're ultimately trying to build, but we feel like we're on the path of building it."[71]

UFR relies heavily on online interaction to engage workers. It has no physical offices: most work is done remotely, leveraging online tools and apps. It reports hundreds of thousands of retail workers in its online network who regularly interact, sign petitions, take surveys, and so on. It also reports thousands of "activists" who take part in UFR campaigns; hundreds of "leaders" who organize those campaigns; and about fifteen paid staff organizers, roughly ten of whom work primarily on training leaders (who then train activists). With its primary corporate targets, Walmart and Amazon, spanning multiple states and frequently opening and closing locations, an organizational model rooted in a particular geography would be counterproductive, they argue. UFR's goal is to remain nimble and be capable of swooping into specific locations when campaigns need to be organized in a hurry.

UFR's organization draws inspiration from the multileader, decentralized "starfish" model described in *The Starfish and the Spider* by Ori Brafman and Rod Beckstrom.[72] "If you cut a starfish in half, you get two starfish. You cut a spider in half, it's dead," said Schlademan.[73] In an industry where workers and organizers must always react to corporate management decisions regarding store closings, wages, benefits, and so on, UFR has sought to develop a model that can adapt and regenerate when its limbs are severed. When Walmart closed seven stores in Southern California in early 2016 as part of a "global restructuring"[74] (arguably in response to worker agitation for improvements in wages and working conditions), "it had a huge impact on workers in LA but it didn't destroy our national networks," Schlademan said. "When a company attacks us it has an impact, but it doesn't kill us."[75]

The 2017 response of laid-off Toys "R" Us workers to their unfair treatment offers an illustrative example.[76] After the well-known toy store declared bankruptcy and unceremoniously fired 33,000 workers without severance pay or benefits—while its executives made off with multimillion-dollar bonuses and payouts and private equity firms made hundreds of millions— UFR considered organizing the laid-off workers, dedicating two paid staff to a month-long organizing effort. Using a combined online-offline strategy, UFR discovered thousands of workers who wanted to sign petitions and act collectively to demand severance pay, and it identified leaders in several Toys "R" Us communities who were eager to organize their coworkers. Whereas the traditional organizing model would have required workers to organize at locations around the country one store at a time, UFR's strategy enabled it to build a network online, identify key people, and move quickly to take advantage of workers' outrage while emotions were still high and the media was still attentive. Reflecting on how the group's organizational model "lowers the price of taking risks," Schlademan noted that its initial investment in the campaign was so minimal that if the campaign had failed, the cost to the organization would have been negligible.[77] The campaign was successful, however, as laid-off workers pressured private equity firms to create a $20 million severance fund.

After the Toys "R" Us campaign, UFR, as part of a coalition, urged lawmakers in New Jersey (where Toys "R" Us was headquartered) to enact a severance-protection bill to preempt similar crises in the future; the bill was successfully enacted in 2020. When Toys "R" Us eventually reopened two stores in 2019 in New Jersey and Texas, UFR also helped to create a "mirror board" of Toys "R" Us employees that persuaded the company to rehire as many former workers as possible and use UFR's principles for quality jobs as a guide for employment relations.[78] UFR's public policy work was also instrumental in getting the Stop Wall Street Looting Act introduced in both houses of Congress in 2019 and 2021—a law to prioritize worker protections in the bankruptcy process and close legal loopholes that enable private equity firms to reap large profits from bankrupting the companies they invest in while insulating themselves from risk.[79]

UFR is now working to pass severance protection laws in other political contexts. This points to what is arguably one of the primary advantages of UFR's flexible model: whereas geographically rooted worker organizations are often dependent on having friendly governing majorities in their localities to get policies passed, UFR is able to choose where to campaign in order to achieve gains for workers wherever and whenever opportunities arise. Its corporate focus also enables it to make gains for workers in deep red states: when Walmart responded to worker pressure to raise its base wage to $10 an hour in 2015 and introduce more worker-friendly pregnancy policies, beneficiaries included thousands of Walmart workers in states where statutory minimum wage hikes would have been next to impossible to achieve.

Notably, UFR is the only alt-labor group thus far to adopt a mostly virtual, industry-specific, distributed-network model while pursuing both policy change and industrial transformation through direct economic intervention. For what it trades off in terms of base building and member engagement, it has earned some serious detractors.[80] The other industry-specific groups in my sample—ROC, WDP, CWC, NDWA, and PCUN—also pursue a combination of public and private actions, but most of their work is geographically rooted in their local communities, and most of their power and resilience comes from their base of committed members and the solidarity they have cultivated. Thus, what UFR gains in nimbleness and efficiency it may sacrifice in terms of human connection, mutual commitment, and community power. Conversely, what community-based groups gain in resilience and solidarity they may lose in terms of scope and agility.

Resource-Sharing Umbrella Groups

Alt-labor groups typically develop informal coalitions with allied groups when running discrete policy campaigns, but increasingly, they have sought to institutionalize those relationships as well. More durable, formal partnerships have been developed in Boston (Immigrant Worker Center Collaborative), San Francisco (Workers' Rights Community Collaborative), Los Angeles (LA Wage Theft Coalition), Santa Clara County (Wage Theft Coalition), Minneapolis, and Seattle and across the state of California (Coalition of Low-Wage and Immigrant Worker Advocates). The most advanced form of institutionalized collaboration developed to date formalizes resource sharing, collaboration, and coordination in an umbrella-like organization. Although such umbrella organizations are still rare, the experience of Raise the Floor Alliance in Chicago suggests that the model may be attractive to groups in other contexts as well.

Since the late 1990s, worker centers in the Chicago area had informally worked together to promote various state- and municipal-level policy campaigns. In 2009, three worker centers and a legal clinic decided to join forces to form a more durable coalition around their shared goal of combating wage theft, which they called the Just Pay for All Coalition (JPAC). By joining in a more permanent coalition and centralizing their litigation work, the groups hoped to improve coordination and achieve efficiency gains. In 2014, the remaining five Chicago-area worker centers were invited to join with the members of JPAC to form a more durable umbrella organization that would focus on raising revenue and combating shared problems collectively.[81] They named the new group Raise the Floor Alliance. Its purpose was to develop strategies to combat the four most common problems affecting members of all eight groups (wage theft, discrimination, unhealthy and unsafe working conditions, and retaliation) and to build shared organizational capacity similarly to the way the union movement created central labor councils. RTF now has six permanent staff: an executive director, two staff attorneys, a communications and development director, a policy director, and a paralegal. This "backbone" organization helps coordinate the groups' policy campaigns, facilitate and centralize litigation strategies, and further each group's ongoing base-building efforts. On a day-to-day basis, the legal division is perhaps the most valuable resource for the worker centers; groups can contact RTF attorneys for quick, free consults. Executive directors from each of the eight groups compose a board of directors that meets monthly at the RTF office to plan and coordinate collective campaigns. Whereas in the past the groups would duplicate their efforts, compete over scarce resources, and collaborate only intermittently and spontaneously, RTF offers efficiency gains, helps to resolve the groups' collective action problems, and enables them to plan more extensive and well-strategized campaigns. Benefits also include deeper relationships, collective learning, and the ability to leverage each organization's specific areas of expertise in joint campaigns. "RTF is a way of scaling up," Kader of Arise Chicago explained. "It's also a way of covering all the gaps that we don't cover. We can't be effective if we're trying to do everything."[82] Executive director of RTF Zaman explained: "Each organization in our coalition has a unique set of strengths, whether its specific industry expertise, tactical knowledge, or organizational relationships. When we bring all that wisdom together . . . it allows us to really punch above our weight and have a more transformative statewide presence."[83]

One of RTF's most critical functions is fundraising. Because philanthropic foundations tend to favor statewide networks over local organizations, RTF provides the community-based groups with entrée into a wider range of funding streams. By generating additional funding and passing it to the eight alt-labor groups, typically taking a small percentage for overhead, RTF helps each group grow its operations. Although the reverse—supporting RTF and helping it grow—has created yet another set of responsibilities for already overburdened groups, the benefits of the arrangement are viewed as outweighing the costs.

Whereas several of the groups have developed strong relationships with policymakers and stakeholders in Chicago and in Cook County, RTF provides the groups with the ability to speak on behalf of low-wage workers and alt-labor groups at the state level. In 2017, it helped lead the campaign for the Temp Workers' Bill of Rights discussed in chapter 1; in 2018, it led the charge for HB 4324, the Wage Protection Act. After winning a national grant to spearhead a campaign for "just cause" legislation, RTF began work in 2020 on a statewide legislative campaign to curb at-will employment in Illinois.[84] RTF was also involved in city-level policy campaigns around raising Chicago's minimum wage, enacting fair scheduling laws, and establishing a new Office of Labor Standards; and in 2023 it spearheaded the state-level campaign to pass the Illinois Work Without Fear Act (HB 361) to strengthen whistleblower protections for immigrants and contributed to campaigns to strengthen the Temp Workers' Bill of Rights. Its leaders ultimately hoped that RTF would become the nonunion companion to the state federation of labor, such that legislators would feel obliged to consult with RTF on new state-level labor and employment policies affecting low-wage workers.

501(c)(4) Organizations

One of the most consequential organizational innovations alt-labor groups have made in recent years involves the formation of sister organizations under the 501(c)(4) "social welfare" section of the Internal Revenue Code. These groups can explicitly endorse candidates for public office, devote unlimited resources to legislative lobbying, and conduct overt electioneering for or against candidates, so long as election work does not constitute the 501(c)(4) group's primary activity (as a rule of thumb, less than 50 percent of its resources). The rest of the groups' resources can, of course, be devoted to civic engagement, issue education, leadership development, and the many other activities in which 501(c)(3) groups are also engaged. The formation of 501(c)(4) groups also opens another fundraising stream, enabling groups to raise money for these activities from (undisclosed) donors and political action committees. As Kim Fellner writes, some groups are still figuring out how to "mesh" the 501(c)(3) model with the developing 501(c)(4) model; in some cases, the 501(c)(3) side's community organizing work reportedly suffered. Yet most groups recognize that "venturing into legislative and electoral politics seems like a natural next step, a sign of maturity and capacity" as they reach the limits of what they can accomplish under 501(c)(3) restrictions.[85]

Workers Defense Action Fund (WDAF), for example, was launched in 2014 as the sister 501(c)(4) organization to WDP, a 501(c)(3) organization founded in 2002 and headquartered in Austin, Texas. After more than a decade of organizing low-wage workers and pursuing its agenda through workplace justice campaigns and periodic policy campaigns, WDP organizers began to feel that the group's 501(c)(3) status was forcing it to remain on the sidelines while others exerted greater influence over the policy agenda and critical decision-making processes. Despite WDP's growing, passionate base, elected officials were not seen as sufficiently responsive to their needs. "What we started to understand," explained former co-executive director José Garza, "is that we really needed to start changing the people at the table."[86] WDP directors launched WDAF, therefore, as a means of deepening the group's impact in the political and electoral arenas (discussed further in the next chapter).

Other 501(c)(4) groups in my study were founded for similar reasons. Organizers at Somos Un Pueblo Unido in New Mexico contemplated applying for 501(c)(4) status for many years but felt most of their objectives were being achieved effectively through their issue education and nonpartisan voter mobilization (registration, get-out-the-vote) work on the 501(c)(3) side. As Somos expanded into more rural parts of the state, however, the group decided to apply for 501(c)(4) status (creating Somos Acción) so that it could conduct more explicitly election-focused work in the run-up to the 2018 midterm elections. PCUN in Oregon, too, founded its 501(c)(4) organization, Acción Política PCUNista, to give its community greater voice in the 2016 elections. And PWC launched its 501(c)(4), Pilipino Action Center, at the end of 2020 to deepen PWC's electoral work. In 2021, for example, Pilipino Action Center fought the recall of Gavin Newsom and campaigned to keep the Filipino vote from being diluted in the redistricting process. Looking ahead, it planned to undertake more intentional interventions in candidate selection processes—holding candidate forums, endorsing candidates, and using its new funding stream to support new types of political engagement. PWC was also learning from its close partnership with NDWA, which in 2017 founded its own 501(c)(4). That group, Care in Action, endorsed seventy-three women of color candidates with pro-worker platforms in 2020. During the 2021 Senate runoff elections, in which two Georgia Democrats won in close elections that handed control of the Senate to that party, Care in Action ran what was considered "one of the largest voter contact programs in Georgia."[87]

LUCHA in Arizona provides an illustrative case of how 501(c)(3) and 501(c)(4) side organizations, working in tandem, can build power for a community of workers. LUCHA's 501(c)(3) and 501(c)(4) side organizations

(ACE and LUCHA, respectively, though together they are often referred to as LUCHA) were founded by the same codirectors (Gomez and Tomas Robles) in 2010. Each has different core tasks: ACE is focused on civic engagement and leadership development—it emphasizes individual empowerment, community building, and political-consciousness raising. LUCHA, meanwhile, coordinates the group's more overtly political activities, including candidate endorsements, electoral campaigns, policy campaigns, and lobbying—though it also undertakes issue education, community building, and leadership development. In pursuing all these activities under the same umbrella yet under the auspices of formally separate organizations, the group has managed to generate organizational synergies and win significant policy and electoral victories, such as raising Arizona's minimum wage in 2016, creating a right to paid sick leave via ballot initiative, and dramatically driving up Latinx turnout in the 2018 and 2020 elections.

The 501(c)(4) organization Make the Road Action (MRA) performs the same explicitly political, electoral function for the 501(c)(3) MRNY. Although MRNY has long fought for social and economic justice for poor and working immigrants and people of color, its 501(c)(4) group enables the community to generate the "electoral power" it needs to support the "same values that MRNY is working on from a (c)(3) perspective," Axt explained.[88] MRA, which has a separate board of directors and funding stream, is codirected by the same codirectors of MRNY. It works to register voters, enact favored legislation, influence redistricting, and "hold electeds accountable by mobilizing the vote against them if necessary and supporting folks from our community and other allies to run for office as well."[89] Specifically, MRA formulates a policy platform to flesh out its issue agenda, "sends out candidate questionnaires, does endorsement interviews, endorses candidates, [and] mobilizes volunteers in support of candidates that we're committed to," usually in alignment with the Working Families Party, with which MRA is a national and state affiliate.[90]

MRA uses a set of political metrics and benchmarks to measure its success. It tracks the number of people it helps register to vote, how many protests it organizes and the number of people it encourages to show up, how many events it disrupts, how many elected officials or powerful elites it pressures to move toward a position more favorable to the organization, and so forth. Much of that "soft" political work can be legally done through MRNY, which without endorsing candidates, is legally able to hold candidate forums, pepper candidates with questions about what they're going to do, raise the salience of its issue agenda, and so on. In most places, organizers explained, that was all that was needed. But when MRNY's 501(c)(3) work is harmonized with MRA's 501(c)(4) work—coordinated to maximize the hours staff spend on civic engagement on the 501(c)(3) side to stay well within legal lobbying limits and to confine all explicitly candidate-centered work to the 501(c)(4) side (as all such organizations in my study conscientiously did)—the combination generates synergies for the group's membership base.

Regional Multi-entity Movement Hubs

By investing in new organizational infrastructures dedicated to political election-focused work, alt-labor groups are making a critical turn toward politics. This turn has not, however, come without its challenges. Indeed, as some of the older, more mature groups have created side 501(c)(4) political operations and increased the number of politically engaged allies with whom they are in coalition, they have faced growing administrative challenges—especially around legal compliance, workforce development, organizational management, and funding. At the same time, growing threats to immigrants and people of color and to the health and safety of low-wage workers during the lengthy Covid-19 pandemic spurred many grassroots progressive groups to develop stronger mutual support networks among groups clustered within discrete geographic regions.

One of the most significant capacity-building innovations to emerge in response to these challenges is what has been called regional multi-entity "movement hubs," which in practical terms involves uniting 501(c)(3)s, 501(c)(4)s, political action committees (PACs), and corporate structures to build power and sustain leadership within a network. Within such hubs, dedicated pathways are established for leadership development and training; supervision, coaching, and mentorship; incubation support for emerging organizations; and a consolidated operations back-end to provide human resources/administration, finance/accounting, legal/compliance, and technology assistance across entities. Multi-entity movement hubs are still rare in the alt-labor world—examples in my sample only include the Center for Empowered Politics (CEP) in San Francisco and PCUN's Alianza Poder in Oregon. Let us consider CEP, which grew out of CPA.

Between 2000 and 2010, CPA launched several projects on shoestring budgets, including the Workers' Rights Community Collaborative (an alliance with other local worker centers that focused on minimum wage enforcement in collaboration with the newly established San Francisco Office of Labor Standards Enforcement), San Francisco Rising (a multi-racial alliance of community-based groups determined to shift the political balance of power in San Francisco toward low-income communities of color), and the Progressive Workers' Alliance (an alliance of low-wage worker organizations in San Francisco). "None of us had money to do this," recalled Alex Tom, former executive director of CPA and founder of CEP. "This wasn't funder driven; it was a movement strategy to build regional power."[91] Determined to fight austerity-motivated cuts to social services in San Francisco during the Great Recession and to ensure that San Francisco's minimum wage ordinance was properly enforced, CPA and its allies sought to aggregate their collective resources. In 2010, CPA's growing list of allies in the Progressive Workers' Alliance cofounded Jobs with Justice-SF, which helped the group build power with progressive unions in San Francisco and marked an important step toward greater civic engagement. Equally important was the emergence of San Francisco Rising Action Fund (SFRAF), a 501(c)(4), as a visible and valuable organization in 2012. After it helped lead several local candidates to surprise victories with substantial margins, candidates began to seek out SFRAF's endorsement. "We were not resourced to do any of this. But we built a center of gravity that was distinct yet connected to labor," explained Tom.[92]

Currently, the hub consists of over thirty organizations, a majority of which are based in the Bay Area, and includes multiracial, Asian American, Black, and Latinx organizations. Within the hub, CEP, a 501(c)(4) group, and the Center for Empowered Politics Education Fund (CEPEF), a 501(c)(3) group, provide organizational capacity alongside Resilient Strategies, which provides back-end operations support. The purpose of CEP and CEPEF is to build capacity within the hub by helping the groups build partnerships and deepen relationships, build pathways for leadership, develop organizational capacity, and continue to experiment and innovate, especially in the political realm.[93]

The main impetus to create the regional multi-entity hub was the realization that many of the constituent organizations were growing fast but lacked a sufficient number of trained and developed organizers. In the 2010s, leaders and organizers began to envision and develop a "workforce development" approach for training and sustaining the next generation of organizers across entities and the broader ecosystem. The problem, Tom writes in an important white paper, is that "with weak and fragmented leadership development pathways, and poor recruitment and retention of skilled and experienced leaders, organizers and directors, we are not able to address the rapid growth, evolution and needs of the [racial justice organizing] sector. . . . We need robust leadership development programs and pathways for leaders at all layers of society (from pre-apprentice programs for grassroots leaders and organizers to career ladders and lattices for senior leadership and executive directors)."[94] To begin addressing these issues, in 2010 CPA founded Seeding Change, a summer program to train young Asian Americans interested in community organizing that is now operational in six states at sixteen host sites. An overwhelming majority of CPA's organizers come through the program. Other similar initiatives include Youth MOJO (Movement of Justice and Organizing), a leadership development program that focuses on low-income Chinese American high school students, and Tenant Worker Center, which educates and organizes low-wage immigrant workers. The hub offers the "wraparound support" of coaching and mentoring for directors and organizers across its entities.

The lynchpin of the hub is Resilient Strategies, which provides human resources/administration, finance/accounting, legal/compliance, and technology assistance for all the entities. Some organizations are still relatively small, and some staff and organizers work across multiple 501(c)(3), 501(c)(4), and PAC organizations; the administrative burden is quite large. Entities thus contract with Resilient Strategies as a vendor to handle all back-end operation issues for each organization.

Although CEP's "movement hub" experiment is still relatively young, it seems to be operating effectively. Organizations have navigated leadership changes, onboarded new organizers, and mentored new directors. CEP views its role as "flanking" or providing "lateral support"—emphasis is placed on building independent partnerships. "This approach builds mutuality and reciprocity" between networked groups, Tom explained.[95]

Particularly notable is that the origins of the hub were not foundation driven or funded. The impetus to build this kind of structure grew out of existing alliances, the necessity of the moment, the commitment to building working-class power, and the collective vision that evolved. Seeding Change, likewise, was an experiment undertaken by two CPA organizers who poured their free time and extra energy into launching the project. Eventually, the group was able to raise money to support what it was already doing—but funders did not influence its development. Self-determination is a core value shared by the groups in the ecosystem, reported Tom:

> Indigenous folks and people in the Black South have been doing this for hundreds of years. We are resilient, knowing how to do things for very little money. . . . We started doing a lot of innovations to set the trend of what can be funded—now we're in a position so the funding that comes in now is just a little bit more on our terms—from the city, from labor, from philanthropy, there are just fewer strings attached. . . . So I think the question is: How do we create "risk capital" to experiment? And the way we did it was we all took collective losses, collective cuts. Some people took on more based on their own interests and innovations which aligned with movement needs. Instead of relying just on the traditional models of the nonprofit industrial complex, we see ourselves building self-determination.[96]

In sum, innovative new organizational models—such as UFR's distributed-network model, RTF's resource-sharing umbrella organization, 501(c)(4) sister groups, and regional multi-entity movement hubs—illustrate some of the ways alt-labor groups are scaling up their operations, building flexibility and resilience, and generating greater organizational capacity.

This chapter has shown that alt-labor's power-building work at the individual and group levels comes in many shapes and sizes. The examples offered here constitute only a sampling. As a growing number of groups turn to policy and political engagement, they draw on this work in equally diverse ways. The next chapter illustrates these efforts and explores the variation.

CHAPTER 6

Policy and Politics: Illustrations

THE LAST CHAPTER discussed some of the ways alt-labor groups are build-ing power by investing in their people and in their organizational capacities. Although not every alt-labor group conceives of this power-building work as primarily political—as redounding to its benefit in the policymaking and electoral arenas—a growing number have found that it equips them to intervene in politics in consequential ways. Many groups now undertake this work with an eye to its policy and electoral impacts.

In the political arena, groups draw upon their individual- and group-level power-building investments in several ways. From their small but dedicated, empowered, and politically conscious communities of members, they draw the capacity to sustain year-round campaigns and weather set-backs. From their formal and informal coalitions, they draw the capacity to wage multiple campaigns, learn from more experienced partners, share resources and knowledge, and project a wider base of political support. And from their organizational innovations, they gain the capacity to extend their reach and adapt to change. These capacities—to persevere, grow, and adapt—are invaluable in politics, where uncertainty is a constant and the groups must be resilient and nimble if they are to overcome obstacles and make progress for their members.[1]

The first part of this chapter uses two policy campaigns in California and Texas to illustrate how alt-labor groups have drawn upon their capacity-building work to pass stronger employment laws at the state and local levels. In both cases, alt-labor groups were successful and they celebrated their accomplishments; but they soon found that the policies they fought for either fell short of their objectives or were blocked from being implemented by more powerful forces in their states. Such disappointments are precisely what motivate alt-labor groups to become more politically engaged and to take concrete steps to alter their political environments. The second half of the chapter thus illustrates how groups in settings across the partisan spectrum have endeavored to change their political contexts— by building new electorates, influencing candidate selection processes, and expanding government capacities to create conditions conducive to further policy changes.

Alt-labor's progress in passing policies and altering their political contexts has thus far been relatively modest and generally confined to their localities. Their victories, however, defy the conventional notion that low-wage immigrant workers and workers of color living in race-class subjugated communities are subdued, defeated, or rendered "politically disempowered" by their exploitation at work or by their social, economic, or political marginalization.[2] As this chapter's first section demonstrates, low-wage Filipino domestic workers in California and low-wage Latinx construction workers in Texas scored significant policy victories through organized collective action, strategic coalition building, and organizational innovation. The chapter then examines several ways in which marginalized low-wage workers in those states as well as in urban and rural communities in Nebraska, New Mexico, Iowa, Arizona, Oregon, Georgia, Virginia, New York, Pennsylvania, New Jersey, Connecticut, Nevada, and Illinois are working to alter their political environments and give their members greater voice in politics and government. Rather than evidence "political deficits," these communities of workers evidence dynamic political activism.[3]

Policy Campaigns: Two Illustrative Cases

Let us first consider policy campaigns in two very different settings that resulted in similar outcomes: a decade-long campaign waged by PWC and its allies for a Domestic Workers' Bill of Rights in California, and a series of policy campaigns by WDP culminating in the creation of a right to paid sick leave for all workers in three of the biggest cities in Texas.

Pilipino Workers Center and the California Domestic Workers' Bill of Rights

For many years, PWC devoted the vast majority of its resources to individual services and workplace justice campaigns. Said cofounder and executive director Soriano-Versoza: "We started doing case, case, case, case—and we had some bigger public [educational know-your-rights] campaigns that we launched—but none of it was making an overall impact on the standards in the industry. It was just too few and far between. . . . We had little leverage and we couldn't launch full-scale organizing campaigns against every single employer in the industry, in which it seemed like almost everyone was committing wage theft. So we really took a step back from those and started reflecting on: Where are we getting with this strategy alone?"[4] A key advantage of PWC's emphasis on services and direct action, however, was that it helped to build a relatively large, committed, active base of members who were trained in organizing. The disadvantage was that the group's work was frustratingly limited in scale. To extend its reach, PWC began to explore how certain public policy changes might help improve working conditions for its members.

The vast majority of PWC members are Filipinas who emigrated to the United States from the Philippines, and the remainder are Latina immigrants; almost all work in private households. They often work long shifts and many are live-in caregivers. Although they are "doing the work that makes all other work possible," as Soriano-Versoza put it, they have long been excluded from cornerstone U.S. labor and social policies such as the NLRA, the FLSA, the Social Security Act, the Occupational Safety and Health Act, and Title VII of the Civil Rights Act.[5]

Despite the 1974 amendments to the FLSA that extended minimum wage and overtime protections to many domestic workers, those deemed "companions" for the elderly and disabled remained exempted under specific conditions. The complex criteria to determine who was covered under the law proved too much for many employers—and workers, and agencies, and courts—to handle; consequently, many home care workers continued to suffer egregious labor violations, including wage theft, unsafe and unhealthy conditions, sexual abuse, and other forms of exploitation.[6]

A California wage order in 1976 brought many domestic workers under the state's wage and hour laws, but "personal attendant" caregivers who spent less than 20 percent of their time on general housekeeping duties were exempted from coverage. This exclusion was owed to "the erroneous belief that these workers were primarily young or elderly persons doing the work to supplement income received from their parents or social security benefits, respectively."[7] Swept up in the personal attendant category were many nannies, childcare providers, caregivers, housekeepers, cooks, and other household workers.[8] In 2001, personal attendants were finally granted full coverage under California's minimum wage law—but they remained ineligible for overtime protection. Since many domestic workers worked most days of the week and frequently took twenty-four-hour shifts, the lack of access to overtime pay presented a significant hardship.[9]

In 2005, PWC and several other community-based organizations came together for the purpose of extending overtime protection to all domestic workers in the state. The alliance, which called itself the California Household Worker Coalition, began by trying to move its issue onto the state legislature's agenda. Organizers soon learned, however, that policymakers were extremely uninformed about the issues facing domestic workers in the state. Because the work took place behind closed doors, and because many of the workers were undocumented and often did not complain when their rights were violated, the deplorable conditions facing domestic workers simply were not on policymakers' radars. Confused lawmakers would often ask: "you mean domestic *violence*?"[10] Organizers would patiently educate lawmakers about the history of domestic workers' exclusion and exploitation, emphasize that domestic work was work and not help, and try to link those understandings to the need for policy reform.

Their primary goal was not to build public sympathy or to activate the charity impulse in others, but rather to

> build public *solidarity* to support the leadership of the workers. . . . Our narrative is really centered around the workers themselves having the agency to make change and be leaders not only in their industry, but in the overall society. . . . It is an empowering process and workers are at the center of that. So it's not like, "you should not exclude these workers because look at them, you should feel sorry for them"—it's, "we demand that this work has value; we as workers have value; we are doing the work that makes all other work possible; so you should value it and recognize our rights as well." So it's a very different framework. I mean, you can

show the gravity—we have workers who are working for $2 an hour, and this is why they're in that situation—but they're actively the agents in terms of saying: "we don't want to put up with this anymore."[11]

The coalition succeeded in getting the California State Senate and Assembly to take up and pass their bill, but it was strongly opposed by home-health agencies and disability-rights advocates and was ultimately vetoed by Republican governor Arnold Schwarzenegger in 2006.[12] The coalition recognized that as long as Schwarzenegger was in office, further efforts would likely be futile. Though organizers were disappointed, the campaign served a vital movement-building purpose: it helped workers develop their organizing skills, grew the domestic worker coalition in California, and successfully put the issue on the legislative agenda.

While waiting for the political context to change, PWC continued to build its organizational capacities and forge relationships with allies in Sacramento. For example, PWC joined the Women's Policy Institute of the Women's Foundation, which connected PWC with elected officials who helped it hone its campaign strategy. In 2007, the NDWA was formed, with PWC as a founding group.[13] And in 2010, the growing California Household Worker Coalition was renamed the California Domestic Workers Coalition (CDWC) and formalized as a nonprofit organization.

Through a bottom-up agenda-building process, the CDWC expanded its list of policy demands beyond overtime protection to include removing domestic worker exemptions from all labor, health and safety, and workers' compensation laws; guaranteeing workers eight hours of uninterrupted sleep, meal and rest breaks, and the right to use kitchen facilities; and ensuring that all pertinent laws covered all domestic workers, including those hired by third-party agencies. In New York, a similar policy campaign resulted in the landmark New York Domestic Worker Bill of Rights of 2010, which included one day of rest per week, three days of paid time off per year, and overtime protection—but it exempted workers hired by agencies to provide (poorly defined) "companionship services." Because agency hires accounted for 53 percent of all domestic workers in California (and 74 percent New York), the California coalition felt it critical that these workers not be exempted from coverage.[14]

When Democrat Jerry Brown replaced Schwarzenegger as governor in 2011, the CDWC tried again, this time pursuing its full slate of policy changes and calling the proposal the California Domestic Worker Bill of Rights. PWC and its allies redoubled their efforts to educate policymakers on the challenges of domestic work, brought members to Sacramento to share their stories with lawmakers, and trained others in phone banking, fundraising, and petition drives. The coalition reached out to opponents from the last round—especially disability-rights advocates—to build support and identify compromises that would make home care affordable for people with disabilities while still providing workers with the rights and protections they sought. This bridge-building work successfully won over some individuals and organizations, but not enough to soften the industry's opposition.[15] The bill, consequently, was watered down in committee and ultimately vetoed by Governor Brown, who cited the negative impacts it would have on people with disabilities and the elderly who needed twenty-four-hour care, as well as on domestic workers, who he argued would see a reduction in work opportunities.

The coalition tried again in the next session, this time winnowing its list of priorities to its original core issue: extending overtime protections to domestic workers who worked longer than nine hours a day or forty-five hours a week. The legislature passed the bill in short order but gave it a three-year sunset provision to satisfy the governor's concerns. Brown's signature on the narrower bill remained uncertain, however. The coalition focused its attention on persuading the governor by meeting in person with Brown's staff and even wooing his priest.[16] It also lined up the support of the AFL-CIO, which helped draw attention to the policy campaign by giving a high-profile human rights award to domestic workers, and the *Los Angeles Times* editorial board expressed support for the bill. The governor signed the bill (AB 241) on September 26, 2013.

The sunset provision, however, meant that advocates had to continue their campaign to make the law permanent. PWC conducted a large-scale study of the bill's effect on families and workers, coauthored a report on domestic work employers, and helped members file wage claims with the state enforcement agency to ensure that the new measure was enforced. At the end of the three years, Brown agreed to make the new law permanent, finally guaranteeing overtime pay eligibility to all 350,000 domestic workers in California, including previously excluded personal attendants.

Having a Democratic legislature and governor was obviously critical to the ultimate success of the policy, but even still, Brown proved very difficult to move; the key ingredients, rather, seemed to be the CDWC's tenacity and political acumen, which it had developed over the course of the nine-year campaign.[17] For its part, PWC drew heavily on its individual- and group-level power-building work while simultaneously using the campaign to build more capacity: it mobilized its small but dedicated base of workers, centered their lived experiences, and used the campaign to foster leadership development and individual empowerment; it reached out to allies and forged a broad coalition of support; and it established a durable, formal network of domestic workers' groups across the state to coordinate the effort and magnify their collective influence in the future. Other crucial factors included the growing national visibility of domestic work, thanks to the NDWA, and parallel campaigns that took place during the same period in New York and Hawaii.

Our analytical goal, however, is not to definitively sort out the factors that explain the law's passage but to use this case to illustrate how small, under-resourced alt-labor groups can draw upon their capacity-building efforts to break through barriers and thrust onto the policy agenda issues that were previously ignored or considered beyond the pale.

But this case also reveals the limits of traditional grassroots policy campaigns. Despite a nine-year, multifaceted campaign, the final bill was so watered down by the legislative process that it left the majority of issues identified by the coalition unresolved. Domestic workers in California were still without coverage under the state's health and safety laws and workers' compensation laws, and they still lacked rights to eight hours of sleep each night, rest and meal breaks, and access to kitchens. What was more, in its research study, PWC found that only a third of employers knew about the California Domestic Worker Bill of Rights, and only 11 percent of domestic workers who worked overtime in the month prior to the study had earned the premium pay to which they were now entitled. To fulfill the promise of the bill and ensure ongoing responsiveness from policymakers, PWC vowed to deepen its political engagement. It began to strengthen its field operation and launched its own 501(c)(4) group to facilitate its strategic electoral work—as discussed later in this chapter.

Workers Defense Project and Paid Sick Leave

In less worker-friendly states such as Texas—where conservative Republicans have controlled both houses of the state legislature and the governorship since 2003—alt-labor groups have found that advancing workers' rights requires the development of innovative policies that circumvent state government and creatively leverage local governing authorities. Finding a friendly city government is not always sufficient, however: as WDP's campaign for paid sick leave in three cities illustrates, state-level actors still have the power to thwart local initiatives and undo years of hard work. As we will see, those frustrations can provide the impetus for alt-labor groups to launch long-term campaigns to transform their political contexts.

WDP traces its origins back to a service-oriented "wage recovery project" at the University of Texas at Austin legal clinic in 2002. Finding that many workers wanted to remain involved in organizing even after their complaints were resolved, WDP officially became a membership-based organization in 2005. The group emphasized community building while offering its members (mostly low-wage immigrant construction workers) leadership development training, a range of individual services, and the option of organizing workplace justice campaigns. The group was an early mover in the policy space as well, regularly looking for creative policy hooks to improve working conditions for low-wage workers in Austin.

WDP's first major policy campaign involved a vital yet often under-the-radar issue: rest breaks for construction workers in Texas.[18] In a survey of more than 300 construction workers in Austin, WDP found that while 71 percent of respondents worked overtime, often in over 100 degree heat, 41 percent were not permitted rest breaks and 27 percent said they were not even provided with drinking water.[19] This contributed to Texas's dubious distinction of having the highest number of construction worker deaths of any state in the previous year—142—nearly twice as many as the next state (California). After a series of WDP-orchestrated protests at city hall (including a symbolic thirst strike), engagement with the media, and testimony from workers, the Austin City Council unanimously passed the first right to rest breaks for construction workers in the nation in 2010: 10 minutes for every 4 hours worked, with employers facing a $500 fine for each day a violation occurs.[20] The same year, WDP also persuaded the city to adopt OSHA's 10- and 30-hour safety training for all public contracts and for much of its affordable housing portfolio.

Wage theft, rampant in the construction industry, was another top concern of WDP members. But with the state's enforcement agency—the Texas Workforce Commission—not reliably enforcing the state's payday law, WDP had to look elsewhere for support. Ingeniously, it identified a relatively obscure law, the theft of service law, under which wage claims against unscrupulous employers could be pursued by local law enforcement. WDP was able to fashion a collaborative partnership with the Austin Police Department whereby WDP would conduct investigative work, police officers would serve the arrest warrant to the employer, and WDP would help to prosecute the employer.[21] But when it realized that some employers could avoid the law's criminal penalty by paying workers only a portion of their back wages owed rather than the full amount, WDP resolved in 2011 to close that loophole, launching a state-level policy campaign in coalition with high-road construction companies eager to level the playing field. The proposed change to the law, billed as a small technical fix, passed both houses of the Republican-controlled state legislature unanimously and was signed by the state's Republican governor.

In another innovative local policy initiative, WDP sought to compensate for Texas's weak health and safety regulations by developing a program to incentivize construction companies to adopt higher labor standards—and prevent abuses before they occur. Companies that voluntarily signed on to its trademark Better Builder certificate program promised to pay their workers a living wage, offer workers' compensation, provide rigorous OSHA training, implement the Department of Labor's hiring goals and local craft training programs, and subject themselves to third-party on-site monitoring.[22] For years, the program operated with success—but was not backed up by any governmental entity. In 2016, WDP persuaded the Austin City Council to require companies that sought city contracts or expedited permits for large public construction projects to comply with Better Builder standards; Travis County followed suit, as did the mass transit system.[23] By 2023, 34 percent of the 41,000 workers that had participated in Better Builder projects reported receiving workers' compensation for the first time, 40 percent received OSHA training for the first time, and roughly $100,000 in stolen wages was recovered through the program.[24]

Over time, WDP's issue agenda—until then focused overwhelmingly on wages, hours, and health and safety in the construction industry—broadened in response to attacks on immigrants in the state. In 2017, the Texas legislature passed Senate Bill 4, which banned sanctuary cities and empowered police officers to question the citizenship status of people who were detained, even during traffic stops. Working in coalition with immigrant rights and civil rights groups, WDP successfully persuaded the city council to enact the Freedom City Policy, which charged the Austin police department with reducing racial disparities in arrests and, in a clever twist, required officers to inform individuals of their right to remain silent when asked about their immigration status; officers also had to file a report about any such encounter that explained why they asked individuals for their immigration status. The first year of the Freedom City Policy's operation saw a 63 percent reduction in arrests for class-C misdemeanors (the least serious misdemeanor classification).[25]

Each policy victory encouraged WDP to build its organizational capacity with an eye to expanding its potential policy impacts. In 2012, the group opened an office in Dallas, and in 2017 it opened another branch in Houston—both of which could serve as launching pads for parallel policy campaigns in those cities. "We have a very clear formula," said former co-executive director José Garza. "We march policies around the state to local jurisdictions where we are building power in an attempt to build an alternate vision of what governing could look like in the state of Texas."[26] The first fruits of this strategy were realized in 2015, when WDP ran a successful campaign for rest breaks in Dallas, making that city the second after Austin to offer such protection. WDP also funded its 501(c)(4), WDAF, and commenced year-round organizing efforts in the predominantly Latinx areas of Austin, Dallas, Houston, and San Antonio, providing the group with a beachhead in Texas' biggest cities.

In three of the four cities, the group resolved to push a policy that did not yet exist anywhere in the South: paid sick leave. Said José Garza:

> Here in Texas, Republicans control the entire state apparatus of power. They control our legislature, they control every executive office. And so the only way that we could effectively fight back against that blanket of power was to fight from our base of power in our cities in a connected, strategic way. And so that was where [paid sick leave] was born: Let's pick a fight of our choosing. And [let's] do it in multiple cities at the same time to leverage our power. So that when it got to the legislature, they weren't just picking a fight with crazy hippy liberal Austin, they were picking fights with cities across the state.[27]

Starting in Austin, WDP built a diverse coalition that included local business owners, medical professionals, labor unions, socialist groups, women's groups, policy researchers, and survivors of sexual assault and domestic violence who, under the new policy, would receive time off to seek the help and attention they needed. It filmed a number of videos with workers telling their stories; held public health fairs to educate city residents about the benefits of paid sick time, drawing upon its original research; and ran dozens of community canvass campaigns. It vilified the policy's opponents as out-of-state corporate interests funded by the Koch brothers (which some of them were), persuaded a popular politician to record robocall patch-throughs to city council members' offices, and sent talking points and opposition research to every city council member.[28] In early 2018, the ordinance passed handily.[29]

WDP then translated the Austin policy into ballot initiative language for San Antonio and Dallas and ran massive canvassing drives with allies to gather petition signatures in those two cities. The requisite 70,000 signatures were validated in San Antonio, ensuring that the ordinance would either be placed on the ballot in the 2018 midterm elections or taken up by the city council, which, on August 16, 2018, voted 9–2 in favor of the ordinance.[30] In Dallas, the campaign needed 53,765 valid signatures from registered Dallas voters; although WDP collected over 119,000 signatures, the Dallas city secretary's office validated only 52,885 of them. As a result, the campaign fell 880 signatures short.[31] Nevertheless, the Dallas City Council responded to the wave of support the measure had received from constituents by passing a paid sick leave ordinance in a 10-4 vote on April 24, 2019.[32]

In response to these successful policy campaigns in Austin, Dallas, and San Antonio, Republicans in the Texas Senate passed a bill to add paid sick leave to the list of local policies "preempted" by state law.[33] Since 2003, Texas had forbidden local governments from raising the minimum wage higher than the state wage floor (and since 2015 local governments also were preempted from regulating transportation network companies such as Uber). As the bill moved through the legislative process, it grew in scope, ultimately preempting local governments from "requiring any terms of employment that exceed or conflict with federal or state law relating to any form of employment leave, hiring practices, employment benefits, or scheduling practices." If passed, the bill would have killed not only paid sick leave but also the rest break ordinances in Austin and Dallas while putting Better Builder in jeopardy.[34] WDP and a number of progressive groups formed the Coalition Against State Interference, which ran a vigorous lobbying and media campaign to oppose the bill. The bill ultimately failed to advance in the Texas House of Representatives when Democratic lawmakers staged a dramatic last-minute walkout to block a Republican voter suppression bill.[35]

Nevertheless, all three paid sick leave ordinances were indefinitely enjoined by three courts (Texas state courts in the case of Austin and San Antonio and a federal court in the case of Dallas), all of which concluded that each ordinance "increases the pay of those employees who use paid sick leave," thereby "establish[ing] a wage" and conflicting with Texas's Minimum Wage Act, which "preempts local regulations that establish a wage."[36]

Disappointed by its losses in the courts and alarmed by the increasingly aggressive offensives mounted by Republican state legislators against local worker-friendly policies, WDP resolved to devote more attention to altering the political context in Texas. Although the paid sick leave policies the group had championed were blocked, the campaigns had shown what was possible to accomplish in Texas and had succeeded in "expanding what people's rights are," said Emily Timm, co-executive director of WDP.[37] Large constituencies in the three biggest cities in Texas now felt that they were entitled to paid sick leave and were outraged by the rulings, which, coming in the early weeks of the Covid-19 pandemic, prevented workers from taking their accrued leave in their moment of greatest need.[38]

Frustration with the rulings and with state preemption was something the group believed it could organize around going forward. Indeed, organizing around setbacks seemed likely to become increasingly important as the group looked to the future. In 2023, as this book was going to press, the Texas legislature passed what was dubbed the "Super Preemption Bill" (HB 2127) to prevent localities from adopting or enforcing local ordinances relating to any activity governed by state codes (in the areas of labor, natural resources, agriculture, insurance, property, and more) unless expressly permitted by state law—thus dealing a significant blow to WDP's many local policy innovations.[39]

Before the court rulings were handed down and the broad preemption bill was passed, José Garza said presciently: "At Workers Defense, what we say is there are no such things as losses. There are just organizing opportunities. By losing, you can win. You can build public outrage, you can draw more attention that readies you for [the next fight]. We're not afraid to lose. You can't be."[40] Explained Timm: "We're in a long-game fight here in Texas. When I say we're making this a voting issue—this is on the (c)(4) side [the WDAF]—we are thinking about how are we long-term shifting who holds power in Texas? How do we have our elected officials better represent people of color, better represent our working communities?

[Paid sick leave] is an issue that voters will continue to be energized to engage around. That will contribute towards that long-term vision of shifting Texas."[41] Motivated by its successes as well as its failures, WDP ratcheted up its efforts to alter the contours of the political landscape, leveraging its new 501(c)(4) to expand its political operations throughout Texas—as discussed further in the following pages.

These two policy campaigns differ on a number of important dimensions. Whereas PWC organized primarily domestic workers in the Democratic state of California, WDP organized primarily construction workers in the Republican state of Texas. Whereas PWC's policy campaign focused on changing the state's regulatory policy for overtime protection to include domestic workers, WDP's campaign took place at the city level, aiming to provide paid sick leave to all private sector workers in Austin, Dallas, and San Antonio. Despite these differences, both cases illustrate how alt-labor groups draw on their individual- and group-level power building, as described in the last chapter. Both groups leveraged their small but active membership bases to run large and successful policy campaigns, drawing on their members' organizing skills, links to the broader community, and courage and determination to share their stories of exploitation. Both groups forged coalitions to magnify their influence, generate synergies, and project a broader base of support for their initiatives. And they both experimented with new organizational capacity-building efforts—PWC's work in founding the CDWC and WDP's expansion into Dallas and Houston and its establishment of a 501(c)(4)—that broadened their reach. Both cases also yielded similar outcomes: although the policy campaigns were successful, the groups were ultimately dissatisfied with the results. In California, the Domestic Worker Bill of Rights was ultimately watered down during the legislative process, and enforcement was found to be inadequate. In Texas, court rulings tying paid sick leave to the state's preemption law prevented it from being implemented. These disappointments prompted both groups to turn more forthrightly to political activism—to try to reconstruct their political contexts to be more hospitable to their members' concerns.

Altering the Political Environment

There are three primary ways alt-labor groups seek to alter their political environments: by building new electorates, influencing candidate selection processes, and expanding their state's enforcement capacity to facilitate policy "fit." This section considers each in turn, leveraging the groups' heterogeneity to draw out patterns common to all. The examples that follow illustrate how differently situated alt-labor groups—operating within distinct industries in varying political contexts and organizing workers with diverse racial and ethnic identities—are drawing upon the individual- and group-level capacities they have built to undertake similar types of political activities.

Building New Electorates

The political context in which alt-labor groups are situated powerfully shapes how they engage with their broader communities. In more heavily Republican and politically mixed localities, where elected officials tend to be less responsive to low-wage immigrant workers and workers of color, politically engaged alt-labor groups are working assiduously to build new electorates, conduct year-round voter engagement, and expand their bases to new geographies. In more heavily Democratic areas, many groups are growing their field operations in efforts to strengthen their connection to, and pull with, key electoral constituencies. In both cases, the groups are working to develop more active and engaged citizenries and make policymakers more responsive to their collective demands.

Most alt-labor groups are registered under the 501(c)(3) section of the tax code. Although they are legally permitted to devote unlimited resources to civic engagement activities, they are strictly prohibited from endorsing or even implying an endorsement of candidates for public office. Similarly, they must be strictly nonpartisan and cannot explicitly campaign for or against particular candidates. And legislative lobbying cannot constitute a "substantial part" of their activities (to be safe, less than 5 percent of their budget).[42] Yet, there are many ways in which 501(c)(3) organizations can act politically, so long as those activities remain nonpartisan. They can organize policy-centered issue education campaigns, hold public forums, organize public demonstrations, publish voter guides, field candidate questionnaires, commission polls, undertake leadership development, canvas and organize communities, and partake in a wide range of other civic engagement initiatives. These activities leave considerable room for 501(c)(3) alt-labor groups to shape the political context without running afoul of Internal Revenue Service tax exemption requirements.

The primary way alt-labor groups in red and purple political contexts seek to build new electorates is through year-round voter engagement. Rather than try to mobilize communities in the months leading up to an election—as in an electoral campaign—and then cease those activities thereafter, year-round voter engagement (sometimes called integrated voter engagement) aims to organize communities on an ongoing basis and encourage residents to participate in politics continuously. Alt-labor groups leverage their expertise in organizing to engage voters throughout the year via door-to-door canvassing and community outreach programming in which they listen to community members' concerns and priorities, discuss issues, encourage civic participation, and counteract disinformation and voter intimidation. Elections are treated as milestones in a longer-term strategy to transform the electorate and "reshape notions of citizenship and civic participation among those whose voices are often suppressed or overlooked."[43] Rather than emphasize the persuasion of "likely voters," year-round voter engagement seeks to change who participates, targeting first-time and "low-propensity" voters—those often ignored by the major parties, who are disproportionately low-income people of color and immigrants.[44] Groups conduct naturalization, nonpartisan registration, and voter mobilization drives; encourage community members to get politically engaged by regularly attending county, city, and town council meetings; ask candidates to state their positions on issues (also known as "bird-dogging"); and organize their neighbors. Year-round voter engagement can lead to higher voter turnout, a more engaged citizenry, and altered election outcomes at the margins, which can be decisive in close races.[45]

The groups also look for opportunities to expand their reach—typically across the county or state—to activate new populations of like-minded voters. Strategically speaking, an expanded community of interest that spans multiple representatives' districts can demonstrate to officeholders the breadth of support for the group's issue agenda and establish additional points of leverage on the policymaking process. More active and engaged citizenries that demand responsiveness from government officials constitute dynamic sources of power. Let us consider a few examples.

First, take the yeoman's work undertaken by Heartland Workers Center, headquartered in South Omaha, Nebraska. Heartland also has 8 locations in the eastern part of the state, including in Schuyler, a very small city 73 miles west of Omaha. According to the 2020 Census, Schuyler had a population of 6,547, 73.2 percent of which was "Hispanic or Latino."[46] Its largest employer was the food corporation Cargill, which has about 2,000 employees. In 2014, Heartland began organizing meatpacking workers in Schuyler. After about 9 months of door knocking, Heartland had built a base and was ready to undertake a program of civic engagement and non-partisan voter mobilization ahead of the midterm elections. It learned that, of the 1,200 Latinos who were eligible to vote in Schuyler, only 14 had voted in the previous election: "Fourteen: one-four," said executive director Sergio Sosa. Given time constraints, an extensive get-out-the-vote operation was not feasible, so Heartland resolved to "use the Latin American technique."[47] The Schuyler team pulled together a list of 250 friends and family who were eligible to vote and urged them to go "with your family and your compadres to vote—to hold them to account."[48] In the election, the number of Latinx voters in Schuyler increased almost tenfold, to 136 voters. Turnout increased again in 2016, and by 2018 there were 900 Latinx people voting in Schuyler.

Heartland's Schuyler group then mapped out the power structure in the city and discussed where it might be able to make inroads if community members were to run for elective office. It identified two open seats on the city council, seats on the board of education, and a board position on the chamber of commerce, among others. The group encouraged leaders from within its communities to run, aware that their candidacies would attract more community members to vote and that the more Latinx voters turned out, the more attractive it would be for quality candidates to run in subsequent elections. "It is a long-term strategy, voting and electing," Sosa said. "But we got the first Mexican Latina elected to city council in the whole state, in Schuyler. We got the first Salvadoran Latino to become a city councilor in Schuyler, and we got two on the school board of education."[49] Building a new electorate from scratch and developing leaders from within, Heartland was working to alter the political landscape in eastern Nebraska one small city at a time.

Like many alt-labor groups, Heartland began its political and civic engagement work on a shoestring budget, drawing solely on its members' determination to fuel its work. In 2010, for example, members decided they wanted to add a nonpartisan voter mobilization component to their regular community organizing activities. Sosa approached a foundation with whom the group had a relationship and asked for support. Funders quizzed Sosa on how much Heartland knew about get-out-the-vote (GOTV) efforts, how many times it had carried out such efforts in the past, and so forth. They were skeptical, given the organization's lack of experience. Heartland's members "hadn't done it before, but they wanted to do it," Sosa told the foundation. "We have people who know how to organize, and they want to get people to vote." The funders offered to pay a consultant to teach Heartland how to conduct GOTV drives and manage the campaign. Sosa politely refused, explaining, "I think we are ready to do things for ourselves."[50]

Determined to boost voter participation using their own methods in the mostly low-income Latinx population of South Omaha, Heartland organizers pooled their own money—collectively, they had about $2,000—and designed a plan to maximize their funds, emphasizing canvassing and one-on-one organizing.[51] They devised some rules: all canvassers had to have relationships with people in the community; they had to understand the issues that community members cared about; and they had to communicate a new theme to community members, many of whom lived in mixed-status families—"vote for your family." As Sosa explained: "If you are a citizen, but three other people in your family might be undocumented, then you have that responsibility as a leader to take care of business for your family . . . and you should vote."[52]

After two months of intensive community canvassing, issue education, and nonpartisan voter registration and mobilization, word of Heartland's efforts got out, and it got a call from the foundation. "'I heard that you are doing GOTV,'" Sosa recalled one of the funders asking him. "Where did you get the money? We didn't give you the money." Sosa explained: "I told you, just because you didn't give us the money doesn't mean we're not going to do it. Because we do things. We got a couple thousand from workers, and that's the budget we have."[53] Impressed, the foundation gave Heartland an additional $25,000, which enabled it to ramp up its field program prior to the midterm elections. Thereafter, "I Vote for My Family" became an institutionalized program housed within the group. Heartland had created a funding stream for voter engagement on its own terms (what Tom of CPA called "building self-determination" in the last chapter). Thereafter, Heartland continued to run GOTV campaigns in the way the group knew best—"the community organizing way," said Sosa.[54]

Alongside its workers' rights and leadership development initiatives, Heartland continues to run its nonpartisan I Vote for My Family initiative throughout the greater Omaha metro area to promote civic participation and education. Young volunteers—many of them children of undocumented immigrants—canvass their neighborhoods to educate eligible voters on how to register and vote on behalf of their mixed-status families. Some of the organizers are themselves undocumented: "But I voted maybe a hundred times!" one organizer told me, describing his efforts to get one hundred eligible voters to register and commit to voting.[55] In 2020, Heartland's I Vote for My Family initiative reported knocking on 14,000 doors, making 120,000 phone calls, and getting over 12,000 people to commit to voting. Biden's 2020 victory in the Second Congressional District of Nebraska— thought to be a potentially pivotal electoral vote—was owed in part to Heartland's efforts to register and mobilize thousands of first-time voters.[56]

Alt-labor groups also leverage their skills in grassroots organizing to expand their bases—and the new electorates they are building—to different areas of their states. Broadening their reach to include rural and suburban areas, for example, can help to highlight the universality of the issues workers face. Somos Un Pueblo Unido, headquartered in the liberal, urban state capital of Santa Fe, for example, has grown into a statewide political force by expanding its presence to rural areas across New Mexico. "Not only were we not getting what we need in the Rio Grande corridor, but people are dealing with wage theft all across the state: in poor communities, in conservative communities, in high-Native-American-population communities, in Latino communities," Somos director Diaz explained.[57] Over the past ten years, Somos has strategically established membership teams in the small cities of Espanola, Clovis, Portales, and Gallup and in the rural counties of Lea, Chaves, and San Juan. Now, with a diverse membership base that includes Latinx, Hispano ("Nuevomexicano"), Black, Native American, and White workers across urban, suburban, and rural areas, Somos has challenged the notion that workers' rights are strictly urban issues. It has also been running a citizenship outreach program in the four southeastern counties of the state, targeting the roughly eight thousand lawful permanent residents who are eligible to become citizens, and in Santa Fe County, where approximately four thousand legal permanent residents are eligible. Said Diaz: "We've been doing (c)(3) electoral work in those communities for years. And it's small, but it's 'small but mighty!' We're building our base, we're building the base of voters, we're doing issue education in these communities—we're building an electorate slowly."[58]

CWJ similarly has been conducting year-round voter engagement for more than a decade. One of the center's key objectives has been to get members to regularly attend city council and county board meetings and to make their voices heard. "The first time immigrants started coming to the council was *after* we founded this organization," Salih recalled. "Because we started mobilizing people there. We [explained that] you have to go and talk, you have to tell them. We [helped them] prepare their speeches, we helped them out really to have the courage enough to go and speak in front of the council."[59] As an ever-greater number of non-White immigrants began to attend the normally quiet, sparsely attended city council and county board meetings to ask questions and raise concerns about matters to their community, complaints were filed requesting that the workers' citizenship status be checked. "Where are those people coming from? Do they live here in Iowa City?" people would ask. "But all of them were citizens!" Salih said. Over time, elected officials began to respond to some of the citizens' concerns. "This community was really looking ugly before. But it's become very, very good now, just by going out and advocating."[60]

In 2017, the low-wage immigrant worker community urged Salih to run for an open at-large seat on the city council. She won handily with 77 percent of the vote and became the first immigrant and the first Muslim to serve on the council and the first Sudanese American woman elected to public office in the United States.[61] Forging a coalition with two other council members, Salih worked to ensure that many of the issues facing the low-wage immigrant community—be it workers' rights, tenants' rights, or transportation—received the council's attention. By 2021, she had become mayor pro tem (vice mayor). "I never thought I would be a politician, by the way. I don't know how to play those games," Salih said. "I'm a grassroots community organizer. I do things from scratch. . . . Sometimes people look at me as if I came from another planet. It is hard. But I don't give up. I say hey, you are a community organizer, you can do this."[62]

For most of CWJ's history, the Republican Party has enjoyed unified control of the Iowa state government. This has limited the ability of progressive groups to make headway in state politics. The legislature also hamstrung local governments' ability to raise labor standards in their communities by enacting preemption laws in 2016 and 2017 covering minimum wage, fair scheduling, project labor agreement, paid leave, and gig economy ordinances.[63] Despite these constraints, year-round voter engagement has paid off for the center, enabling it to win material gains for low-wage workers. Consider the minimum wage. In 2015, Johnson County raised its minimum wage to $10.10 per hour at the urging of CWJ and other groups; two years later, state preemption moved the wage floor back to $7.25, cutting workers' wages by 28 percent. In response, CWJ members went door-to-door asking business owners to pledge to keep paying their minimum wage workers $10.10 per hour. As an enticement, the center would present them with a certificate of their pledge along with a picture to hang in the front window of their business. By 2019, almost 170 businesses in Iowa City had voluntarily committed to paying the higher wage.[64] CWJ then worked to hold those employers accountable. "If I find out they did not pay the person $10.10," Salih said with a glint in her eye, "I treat that as a wage theft case, and say, 'You did not pay this person right.'"[65] Salih, backed by strong and vocal community support, also successfully pushed the city council to raise the minimum pay for city employees to $10.10 and then to $15.00, indexed to inflation.[66] The key to all these efforts was "community pressure," Salih explained. "One person cannot do anything. But a lot of people can do a lot of things together."[67] The Johnson County Board of Supervisors now "recommends" an annual minimum wage increase to all area business owners based on the consumer price index and publishes its recommendations widely. Even without a 501(c)(4) side organization and with limited resources (the center last reported only $250,000 in revenue),[68] the group's dedicated membership, staff, and allies built a new electorate in Iowa City comprised of low-wage immigrant workers and deepened the support they received from the broader community, resulting in an altered political environment.

ACE and LUCHA in Arizona have similarly undertaken year-round voter engagement since their founding in 2010; their extensive canvassing operation has grown each year. Targeting immigrant families, the groups' members go door-to-door to help residents navigate the naturalization process, register to vote, discuss issues, and build their civic capacities. These efforts have produced a more knowledgeable and active electorate that can be determinative in any given local election—which in turn can have up-ballot effects. New constituencies have created incentives for elected officials to attend to their concerns, as their votes could potentially alter the outcomes of close state-level elections. Thanks in large part to ACE and LUCHA's efforts, Latinx turnout in Arizona has grown each election cycle:

from 47 percent in 2016 to 61 percent in 2020.[69] In 2020, LUCHA's coalition mobilized 359,000 voters in Arizona, 56,000 of whom were voting for the first time.[70] During the first wave of the Covid-19 pandemic, LUCHA was one of the only groups in the state doing in-person canvassing; it registered 47,000 new voters and made almost three million calls: journalists credited LUCHA with helping Joe Biden win the battleground state by a small margin in November.[71]

The dynamics in blue political contexts are different. Although many groups conduct voter engagement, their purpose is less to transform the electorate than to mobilize the disaffected and demonstrate to politicians their strong connections to key constituencies. PWC, for example, has developed its electoral field operation partly because it builds the "leadership capacity within [its] base" and partly because an effective electoral field campaign demonstrates to elected officials that they should pay attention to the group's concerns. Said Soriano-Versoza: "When you can go to a legislator and they know that you have a field campaign in terms of electoral work, that makes them think and consider you in a different way. It's also another lever of power. And it's a way to get the issues and our leadership on the radar of whoever is going to win."[72] PWC takes care to let politicians know about its active field program; its new 501(c)(4), Pilipino Action Center; and its sister civic engagement organization, and to remind them that the Asian American and Pacific Islander community is not just a swing population in Los Angeles County but also the fastest-growing racial and ethnic group in the country.

Although it rarely pays for groups in heavily Democratic areas to take sides in primary contests, there can be a benefit to demonstrating the group's organizational "muscle" through canvassing operations that take place concurrently: champions in government may view the group's ground game as potentially valuable to them, and it can give pause to policymakers who are not supportive of the group's agenda. In Santa Fe, where elections are officially nonpartisan but the area is heavily Democratic, for example, Somos does not endorse candidates or intervene in primaries, but it does undertake GOTV campaigns "to show them that look, we're willing to do the work, we're willing to knock on the doors when we ask you to do something controversial."[73]

In sum, by building new electorates, expanding their geographic footprint in red and purple areas, and developing field programs to deepen their engagement with key constituencies in blue areas, alt-labor groups are creating incentives for politicians to be responsive to the concerns of their members and their communities. To hold politicians accountable to these concerns and interests, however, the groups must remain politically vigilant. Increasingly, they have recognized a need to go a step further and try to influence candidate selection processes.

Influencing Candidate Selection Processes

Many groups report that their interest in shaping electoral dynamics—directly in the case of 501(c)(4) groups and via civic engagement and issue education for 501(c)(3) groups—grew out of many years of trying to cajole incumbent politicians to support the policy priorities of their members only to receive equivocal or tepid responses and inadequate follow-through. Elected officials from both parties have proved to be frustrating—perhaps none more so than mainstream Democrats, ostensible allies whom alt-labor groups often view as more responsive to other constituencies. The groups have learned the hard way that even officials with whom they have forged long-standing relationships are not necessarily reliable allies, especially on the most politically divisive issues that are most important to their members (for example, undocumented immigrants' rights, criminal justice reform, and penalties for the mistreatment of workers).

Group leaders have come to realize that their timing was off—they were seeking responsiveness from elected officials who were already "bought and paid for by someone else," as Friedman of CPD put it.[74] Given the power and wealth of their opponents, many groups have concluded that "changing the minds of the people at the table" will always be a struggle. Said José Garza of WDP, "What we started to understand is that we really needed to start changing the people at the table. We're better off trying to change who's at the table."[75]

In the best-case scenario, alt-labor groups can help to elevate those whom party theorists call "genuine friends" to elective office: not merely allies or supporters, but leaders who emerge from within the community and have "demonstrated their commitment through prior service."[76] Genuine friends in office are best-case scenarios because groups do not have to monitor them and hold their feet to the fire. They are not allies, they are them.

Alt-labor groups have had some success in this regard, as well as some near misses. For example, Greg Casar was a staffer at WDP before he was elected to the Austin City Council in 2014 and then to the U.S. House of Representatives in 2022. In 2020, WDP co-executive director José Garza was elected Travis County district attorney; former WDP special counsel Stephanie Gharakhanian now sits on the Austin Community College board of trustees; and WDP cofounder Cristina Tzinzún Ramirez placed a close third in the 2020 Democratic primary for U.S. Senate. Other genuine friends include Nikema Williams, the NDWA's deputy political director and state director for NDWA's 501(c)(4), Care In Action, who in 2020 was elected to the U.S. House of Representatives for Georgia's Fifth District (John Lewis's district); Salih, cofounder and director of CWJ, who served on the city council and as mayor pro tem in Iowa City, Iowa; and Ana Maria Archila of MRNY and CPD, who came in third in the Democratic primary for lieu-tenant governor of New York in 2022. Groups have also seen their staff rise to prominent appointed positions in government: Alvar Ayala, Working Hands Legal Clinic director, is now chief of the Workplace Rights Bureau in the Illinois attorney general's office; RTF director Sophia Zaman now sits on the Illinois governor's Labor Advisory Board; Yolanda Carrillo, staffer at RTF, served as the chief legal counsel at the Department of Labor; and Oswaldo Alvarez, former executive director of the CWC, is now the execu-tive director of the Illinois Legislative Latino Caucus Foundation, the orga-nization of the Latinx caucus in the Illinois General Assembly.

The groups mobilize vigorously for their genuine friends, but few such candidates run for office. The next-best solution is to try to influence party primaries and general elections in hope of changing the personnel of govern-ment. Groups do not need a large number of genuine friends or allies in office in order to influence decision-making processes in government: sometimes getting only one champion elected to a city or county council—which are typically small governing bodies—can be enough to substantially reshape the policy agenda, as we saw in the case of Salih.

Although nonprofit tax law and election law limit the extent of their political activities, 501(c)(3) groups can strategically use their nonpartisan issue education and civic engagement campaigns to alter electoral dynamics in their localities, as described earlier, and those with 501(c)(4) side organiza-tions can also endorse candidates and run independent electoral campaigns, so long as influencing elections is not the groups' "primary purpose." Neither type of group can coordinate with candidates' campaigns or political parties. Without risking their nonprofit status, then, alt-labor groups can still do quite a bit to affect the outcomes of primary and general election contests.

For example, WDAF, a 501(c)(4), hires and trains staff and volunteers to canvass heavily in the predominantly Latinx and Black working-class communities in and around Austin, Dallas, Houston, and San Antonio. Over the last few years, the group has talked to tens of thousands of residents in these communities who had historically been disengaged from the electoral process but who they believed were likely to participate if sufficiently motivated to do so (dubbed "high potential voters"). Canvassers listen to community members' concerns, discuss issues on the legislative agenda, and encourage residents to envision an alternative agenda centered on their issues. As word of WDAF's large field program has spread, aspirants for elective office have sought out information on what its canvassers are learning. "If we're talking to 20,000 people in Austin in a particular district," Timm said, "candidates want to be talking about the same issues we're talking to people about at the door."[77]

In 2016, conservative Republican Kenneth Sheets from Texas House District 107 introduced a bill to preempt the ability of cities to condition public projects or tax incentives on higher labor standards—a key tool used by WDP and the Austin City Council to strengthen workers' rights. The bill threatened to undercut WDP's primary policy workaround. When confronted about how his bill would affect low-wage workers in the state, Sheets' response was "Well, it's not like working people have a voice at the Capitol," Timm recalled.[78] WDAF ran an issue education campaign around the policy proposal and flooded town halls in his district, generating enough outrage to force Sheets to withdraw the bill. The group resolved to defeat Sheets in the next election, organizing a major canvassing effort in his district in support of his opponent Victoria Neave—a young Latina who grew up in a working-class family. Neave defeated Sheets by a slim margin and was reelected each subsequent cycle by successively wider margins, ultimately receiving 73 percent of the vote in 2022.

In 2018, in a reversal of conventional support seeking—whereby candidates issue policy platforms and interest groups choose which one to endorse—WDP put out a six-point policy platform, which twenty-one of the twenty-eight candidates for Austin City Council signed (figure 6.1).[79] WDP then consulted with its members and decided which candidates to support among those who had committed to its policy positions. "It's really

Figure 6.1 Workers Defense Project's 2018 Policy Platform Pledge

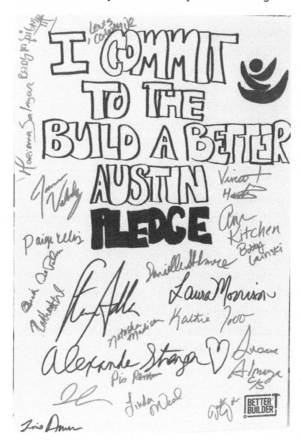

Source: Martin 2018. Reprinted with permission.

incredible to see how elected officials and people who either have power or are seeking power actually respond and shift their own issue agendas to include the issues that are important to working families that have historically been disenfranchised," said Timm.[80]

In 2020, despite the challenges of the Covid-19 pandemic, WDAF ran its largest nonpartisan voter mobilization program to date, primarily targeting young voters of color and first-time voters and ultimately reaching 378,000 voters in 5 counties. Due to the pandemic, the group started with a mostly remote strategy, relying on phone, text, email, and mail; but as the election approached, it shifted to door-to-door canvassing. The group also ran a digital campaign that it said reached 3.2 million young Latinx voters via Facebook, Instagram, and YouTube. Although Texas did not turn blue as some commentators suggested it might, Republican margins shrank and WDAF successfully helped to elect all the candidates it had endorsed. Its independent campaign efforts helped former WDP co-executive director José Garza become district attorney in Travis County and ally Delia Garza (no relation) win election as county attorney: both ran on decarceral agendas championed by WDP community. The group also helped elect José "Chito" Vela, former WDP board member, to replace Greg Casar on the Austin City Council in District 4; Tarsha Jackson, former organizer at Texas Organizing Project, to the Houston City Council; and allies Christian Menefee as Harris County attorney and Vikki Goodwin to Texas House District 47.

Democratic Party primaries can also be major sites of contestation. In Arizona, for example, LUCHA was caught off guard in the summer of 2020 when a group of well-funded moderate Democrats backed by Greater Phoenix Leadership (a group of CEOs that advocates for business-friendly policies) and Revitalize Arizona (the political arm of the Pipe Trades local union) challenged several LUCHA-backed progressives. Thanks to large campaign expenditures by those outside groups in the final weeks of the contest, the challengers seemed poised to win. Each of the closely watched contests was in a legislative district where LUCHA had established deep community ties over many years.[81] "This was an effort to undermine the years of work that our members had put into changing the legislative makeup—we were getting this close to a progressive majority—and this effort was going to put moderate blue-dog Democrats into these strong, progressive districts where if you are bold and courageous, your community will stand by you," said Gomez.[82]

About a month before the primary election, LUCHA learned that its favored candidates were being outspent 25 to 1 in some races.[83] LUCHA raised money, mobilized its membership and community allies, and spent a significant sum on radio ads, social media, and mailers to counteract the spending of its opponents (but was still outspent 5 to 1). The group relied most heavily on its field operation, tapping members' expertise in canvassing and organizing and their interpersonal networks throughout the districts. Rather than draw attention to the clash of personalities between candidates, LUCHA stressed policy issues that its endorsed candidates were committed to advancing on behalf of the community, including the "People's

Bailout," a set of policy demands that LUCHA had spent months putting together based on neighborhood canvassing and community forums. In the end, all six of LUCHA's endorsed candidates were victorious in the primaries and in the general election.

Most states that are labeled blue in presidential elections contain many red and purple congressional and state legislative districts. New Mexico, for example, is reliably Democratic in national elections but much more competitive in state-level and local elections. For example, New Mexico had a Republican governor from 2011 to 2018 and for decades until 2008 sent at least two Republicans to the U.S. House and one Republican to the Senate. New Mexico's 2nd District, covering the southern half of the state, was held by Republicans for 36 of 38 years prior to 2018. When Republican U.S. representative Steve Pearce announced his retirement that year, the Democratic Party did not consider the open-seat race competitive, as Pearce had won the previous two elections with over 62 percent of the vote, and did not devote significant resources to it. To help its favored candidate— Xochitl Torres Small, the granddaughter of migrant farmworkers—win the seat, Somos Un Pueblo Unido launched its 501(c)(4) group, Somos Acción. Although many towns in that portion of the state were majority Latinx, most Latinx residents had not previously voted. Somos Acción thus launched an ambitious door-knocking, mail, and media campaign to increase voter turnout, drawing on its rural membership groups described earlier. While the Torres Small campaign and other 501(c)(4) groups were turning out record numbers of voters in more urban areas of the district, Somos Acción was the only group canvassing voters in those rural areas. Many voters reacted with surprise, telling canvassers: "You're the only ones that have come—not even the candidate has come," Diaz reported. "The only money that was being invested was being invested through us—and we had a *medium*-sized operation as a (c)(4) in those communities."[84] Torres Small won by 3,722 votes, helping to give Democrats control of Congress midway through the Trump presidency.

Unlike WDAF, Somos Acción has not become directly involved in candidate recruitment or endorsements in those rural areas of the state, because it does not yet "have other forms of power in these communities— we have base and we have strategy and that's about it," said Diaz. Still, the 501(c)(4) operation has given Somos Un Pueblo Unido another channel through which to exert political leverage. "It puts us in a different position,"

Diaz explained. "We feel that it's a step in our power-building trajectory. . . . We always say, everything is helping us build power."[85]

A similar pattern is evident in Oregon, whose political geography is comparable to that of New Mexico, with some very liberal urban and suburban strongholds in the Northwest region of the state and the rest of the state almost exclusively rural, conservative, and dominated by Republicans. In 2016, PCUN's 501(c)(4), Acción Política PCUNista (APP), ran an independent campaign on behalf of state legislative candidate Teresa Alonso León, a close ally of the organization and a daughter of migrant farmworkers. Its members knocked on roughly 16,000 doors to mobilize predominantly Latinx workers and their families. Alonso León won by just over 1,000 votes, becoming the first Indigenous migrant Latina in the Oregon legislature. Over the next 4 years, APP ran more field programs on behalf of its favored candidates, mobilized voters around ballot initiatives affecting Latinx working families, and fought for several legislative changes. APP has since helped to elect and reelect several other Latinx and Latinx-friendly candidates to the state legislature, the Woodburn and Salem-Keizer School Board, and the mayoralty of Woodburn.

For the 2020 elections, APP developed a new technological infrastructure to coordinate its efforts and planned an extensive campaign around the census, state legislative races, and the presidential election. Although it had to scale back its field operation and do much of its work remotely during the pandemic, thereby undercutting its greatest strength in relational organizing, it still managed to organize 120 volunteers and send 3 new Latinx representatives to the Oregon state legislature.[86]

The most well-funded 501(c)(4) groups in my study were also the most vigorously engaged in efforts to shape electoral politics: MRA, CPDA, and NDWA's Care in Action—partly a reflection of their size and financial advantages, and partly a testament to their broad networks. MRA, for example, has locations in New York, Pennsylvania, New Jersey, Connecticut, and Nevada, a steady stream of funds, and long-standing partnerships with a wide range of progressive groups in each location. It regularly endorses the candidates who receive the greatest support from MRNY membership. In the presidential election of 2020, MRA reported making over 2.3 million phone calls and sending over 1.8 million texts in Pennsylvania, Nevada, New Jersey, and New York on behalf of its endorsed candidates.[87]

NDWA's 501(c)(4) group, Care in Action, has focused on growing the number of progressive women of color in elective office in geographically strategic states. Its first electoral field operation was organized in 2016 in Atlanta to engage more Black women domestic workers in electoral politics. Inspired by Stacey Abrams's gubernatorial campaign in 2018, Care in Action ramped up its field campaign in Georgia in the next electoral cycle. Although domestic workers had not traditionally engaged in electoral work, Abrams—"someone that looks like them, that had their lived experience"— and her campaign proved to be a powerful motivator.[88] The group focused on running multiracial, multilingual nonpartisan voter mobilization drives in smaller cities such as Macon and Savannah, where members "knocked on hundreds of thousands of doors, and sent over a million texts" and successfully elevated several women of color to positions of power.[89] In 2019, Care in Action also helped Virginia Democrats win control of the state legislature—which thereafter passed a bill to include domestic workers in the Virginia minimum wage. In 2020, the group endorsed seventy-six women of color candidates across seven states, including its own Nikema Williams in Georgia; and it played an important role in the ground campaigns for the January 2021 special and runoff elections for Democratic Senate candidates Raphael Warnock and Jon Ossoff, respectively, ultimately handing Democrats control of the U.S. Senate.[90]

Electoral politics is an arena in which alt-labor groups have been able to leverage their organizational innovations as well. In 2019, leaders from the regional movement hub in the Bay Area began discussions around how to make a difference in the 2020 elections. Noting that "there wasn't strategic local work to be done to defeat Trump" in San Francisco, movement leaders resolved to bring organizational capacity to battleground states in whatever way allied groups in those states wanted and to invest in the organizing skills of talented young people of color, in particular, Black and Indigenous youth, and nurture their networks.[91] Organizers thus created Seed the Vote, an ambitious, large-scale volunteer engagement program in which 1,250 activists campaigned in the battleground states of Arizona, Florida, Georgia, and Pennsylvania and 9,000 volunteers made phone calls at the direction of their allies in those states.[92] Quantifying the electoral impact of the effort is difficult, but the groups involved reported significant long-term coalition-building and movement-building gains.[93]

As we have seen, a hierarchy of preferred strategies plays out. Ideally, groups elevate genuine friends to positions of power. Short of that, they try to influence candidate selection processes to strengthen incentives for party nominees to be supportive of their agendas. And in general election campaigns, they run parallel independent campaigns to try to influence outcomes. Even if they only succeed in electing one genuine friend, securing policy commitments from a small number of legislators, or affecting general elections at the margins, their efforts can alter the legislative agenda and provide a foothold for their members to have greater voice in government. And when groups are not successful, driving up local turnout and having a visible ground game can still induce politicians to be responsive to their members.

Expanding State Enforcement Capacity to Facilitate Policy Fit

The final way alt-labor groups seek to reshape their political environments is by working to alter the regulatory capacities of the state. They aim to reconstruct the state's enforcement apparatus for two reasons: to ensure that existing policies will be properly enforced and to increase the likelihood that policymakers will view future policy proposals as feasible to implement because they "fit" existing state capacities.

Alt-labor's efforts to alter state capacities is part of a larger process of "policy feedback," whereby policies enacted in the present make certain outcomes more likely in the future by reconfiguring government capacities. As Theda Skocpol describes the process in her classic text: "Once instituted, policies have feedback effects in two main ways. In the first place, because of the official efforts made to implement new policies using new or existing administrative arrangements, policies transform or expand the capacities of the state. They therefore change the administrative possibilities for official initiatives in the future and affect later prospects for policy implementation. In the second place, new policies affect the social identities, goals, and capabilities of groups that subsequently struggle or ally in politics."[94] New policies thus have "effects on state capacities and politics that serve either to promote or to frustrate the further extension of that line of policymaking" in the future.[95]

Policy feedback is not an automatic or inevitable process, however. Policies do not transform state capacities on their own. There is a necessary middle step, in which interested groups seek to bolster, expand, and reorient the state's administrative capacities to ensure that enacted policies have their intended effects. Once expanded capacities are in place, future policies are more likely to be viewed as attractive by policymakers because they "fit" existing government institutions and are thus feasible to implement; supportive groups, meanwhile, become emboldened to push for them and leverage the new "opportunities that existing political institutions offer to the group or movement in question."[96]

Consider wage-and-hour laws. Because local wage-and-hour ordinances are not enforced by state or federal agencies, local jurisdictions must enforce their own policies. But existing local government regulatory capacities are rarely up to the task. Consequently, alt-labor groups and their allies have sought to create new local-level labor standards enforcement agencies for the purpose of policy enforcement—to investigate complaints of violations filed by workers, conduct outreach and educate businesses and workers about the new ordinances, and investigate problematic industries. Since 2001, new offices of labor standards have been created in at least thirty-one cities and counties, including Berkeley, Boston, Chicago, Denver, Duluth, Emeryville, Flagstaff, Los Angeles City, Los Angeles County, Minneapolis, New York City, Oakland, Pasadena, Philadelphia, San Francisco (the first such office), San Jose, Santa Fe, Santa Clara County, Seattle, St. Paul, St. Petersburg (since folded into the Pinellas County office), Tacoma, and Washington, D.C.; in Florida, wage theft enforcement offices have been established in Broward County, Miami-Dade County, and Pinellas County, and a wage dispute division exists in Palm Beach County. At the time of this writing, new offices were being established in San Diego County, San Diego (city), and Tucson.[97]

Many of these agencies are responsible for enforcing multiple local employment laws, but their enforcement capacities vary greatly. Some offices have dozens of investigators, considerable data to drive their operations, and significant autonomy to protect workers' rights; others have precious few staff and minimal resources, and many are under significant political pressure to make nice with business. Agencies' approaches vary as well: while some undertake "strategic enforcement" to maximize the use of their limited resources by proactively targeting industries high in violations but low in complaints, most respond exclusively to complaints received from workers, implicitly treating each complaint as an isolated event rather than a symptom of underlying problems in how industries operate. Alt-labor groups regularly seek to influence their work through pressure campaigns to promote strategic enforcement and the establishment of co-enforcement partnerships, which integrate alt-labor groups into the enforcement process.[98]

Consider the case of Chicago, where over the last decade alt-labor groups have worked not only to pass multiple policies, but also to build a new government regulatory apparatus capable of enforcing those policies. In January 2013, the worker centers Arise Chicago, Centro de Trabajadores Unidos, CWC, Latino Union, and ROC-Chicago led the campaign to enact an anti-wage-theft ordinance in Chicago.[99] The ordinance provided for the revocation of the business licenses of employers that were found liable for committing wage theft in willful or egregious cases.[100] The next year, the same Chicago-based worker centers, along with a coalition of non-profits, unions, and other community-based groups, successfully pressured the city council to raise the city's minimum wage from $8.25 to $13 by 2019. Two years later, alt-labor groups including Arise, CWC, ROC, NDWA, and UFR, in coalition with labor unions, public health groups, faith-based groups, and women's advocacy groups, succeeded in convincing the city council to enact a paid sick leave ordinance.[101]

The new ordinances constituted major wins. But if employers failed to pay their workers the minimum wage or allow them to take their accrued sick leave, workers' only recourse was to complain to the Chicago Department of Business Affairs and Consumer Protection (BACP). Historically, the BACP's main responsibilities included issuing business licenses and serving as a watchdog for consumer fraud; it had no experience working as a miniature Department of Labor. By 2018, it had become clear that the department did not have the capacity to enforce the newly enacted ordinances and that without enforcement, the policies provided no effective deterrence against noncompliance. Alt-labor groups found that low-wage workers continued to suffer wage theft at high rates and were routinely denied paid sick leave. With the minimum wage increasing each year, victims of wage theft were losing more and more money.[102] In response to this urgent and growing problem, Arise Chicago reassembled its coalition of allies from previous policy campaigns and set out to create a city-level Office of Labor Standards (OLS) that could be tasked with enforcing the new ordinances. Arise developed legislation to create the new office, identified champions in the city council, and organized around its enactment.

Said Kader: "The industries we organize in—they're basically zero percent compliant with employment law. So it does beg the question: Why are we passing these employment laws? We could pass a $50 minimum wage and it won't be enforced. We already have a minimum wage that's not enforced. That's a legitimate critique of the policy focus. So that's why we have this meta-policy policy—the OLS—to precisely address that question. It's a policy to enforce policy."[103]

Successfully enacted by the Chicago City Council on October 31, 2018 as an independently functioning unit within the BACP, Chicago's OLS was charged with enforcing the city's minimum wage, earned paid sick leave, and anti-wage-theft laws. It was given subpoena and audit powers, along with the power to revoke the business licenses of employers found guilty, and was tasked with responding to complaints, proactively investigating employers, and collecting and distributing back wages owed. Half of the fines it collected from violators would go toward funding the agency's operations.[104]

The relative ease with which Arise and its coalition partners managed to persuade the city council to create the OLS was a testament to the extensive political groundwork the coalition had laid in the years prior and to policymakers' investment in the policies they had already enacted. Whereas the groups' campaign for the anti-wage-theft ordinance in 2013 was combative and heated, their campaign for the new OLS was cooperative and relatively smooth. The groups and their policies now had multiple champions on the city council.[105] Staffing and funding would take more time, and effective enforcement remained a work in progress at the time of this writing. But the strong relationships forged between the alt-labor groups and OLS officials gave the groups reason for optimism.[106]

As new issues emerged, the existence of the OLS facilitated the enactment of even more worker-friendly ordinances. For example, Chicago-area worker centers and their allies began a new campaign for a fair workweek ordinance, also to fall under the OLS's purview, mandating that workers be given ten days advance notice in their scheduled work hours. The ordinance was championed by Arise, CWC, RTF, ROC-Chicago, WWJ, and CPD; the broader Fair Workweek Chicago campaign also included the United Food and Commercial Workers UFCW Local 881 union and a number of other groups.[107] The ordinance passed in July 2019 and was added to the OLS's list of responsibilities the following year.

At the height of the first Covid-19 wave in May 2020, the Chicago City Council passed an anti-retaliation ordinance to prohibit employers from retaliating against any employee who quarantined in compliance with the mayor's public health orders. The new OLS, now operational, was tasked with enforcing the law and helping workers and businesses understand their rights and responsibilities. The OLS was also charged with enforcing a new vaccine anti-retaliation ordinance enacted in April 2021, prohibiting employers from retaliating against workers for taking time during the workday to get a Covid-19 vaccine.

Later that year, Arise Chicago, the Latino Union of Chicago, NDWA, the Shriver Center on Poverty and Law, and Afire Chicago formed an innovative partnership campaign with the OLS called "Your Home Is Someone's Workplace" to promote and defend domestic workers' rights. The coalition succeeded in getting the city council to pass a new domestic workers' rights ordinance mandating that all Chicago employers of nannies, care workers, and home cleaners provide their employees with a written contract stipulating their wage and work schedule in their primary language. Complaints of violations would be received by the OLS, which had the authority to enforce the new ordinance and issue $500 penalties for each violation.[108] The existence of the OLS, in short, facilitated the creation of numerous new worker-friendly policies that "fit" the city's new enforcement capacities.

The strong relationships forged between alt-labor groups and OLS officials in Chicago created conditions that were ripe for co-enforcement—whereby government agencies contract with community-based worker organizations embedded in low-wage workers' communities to better identify, report, and enforce labor standards in high-violation sectors in which vulnerable low-wage workers are less likely to complain. Co-enforcement contracts vary but usually include the expectation that worker organizations draw upon their deep community ties, extensive networks of low-wage workers, and organizing skills to conduct public education campaigns, improve outreach to vulnerable populations of workers, assist in referring complainants to the agency, or help conduct "intakes" for the agency. In turn, their work educates enforcement agencies about the problems low-wage workers face and helps the agencies develop more effective and efficient methods of enforcing labor standards. As Fine describes in her pioneering work on co-enforcement, these arrangements draw upon each partner's "nonsubstitutable" capabilities, such as worker organizations' strong, trusted relationships with workers and state regulators' power to inspect worksites, demand information, and punish noncompliant businesses.[109]

In early September 2021, the Chicago OLS took the first steps toward establishing a co-enforcement partnership with Arise Chicago, awarding the group a $100,000 grant to conduct outreach and education to raise awareness about workers' rights and "increase access to the protections offered by the OLS" among workers in underserved communities, with specific activities earmarked for domestic worker training.[110] As alt-labor groups—in Chicago and elsewhere—continue to develop co-enforcement partnerships, they often look to the San Francisco Office of Labor Standards Enforcement (OLSE) as a model.

For over a decade, the OLSE has established co-enforcement partnerships with local groups; its annual funding commitment to co-enforcement has grown from $186,500 in its first phase (2010–2013) to $1,305,460 today (2022–2024).[111] In each phase, CPA, the leading alt-labor group in San Francisco, has been the lead contractor with the agency; it subcontracts with numerous community-based organizations that have deep roots in San Francisco's racially and ethnically diverse low-wage workforce through the Workers' Rights Community Collaborative (WRCC).

CPA, founded in 1972, has long been known for its expertise in relational organizing, leadership development training, and workplace justice campaigns. It has long-standing ties with labor unions and other community-based organizations in the area, and its staff has expertise in media relations and policy campaigns. For these reasons and more, CPA has developed into a formidable policy player in San Francisco: it was instrumental in enacting San Francisco's 2003 minimum wage, building up the OLSE, and launching the co-enforcement program. And as detailed in chapter 5, it has in recent years incubated a broader movement ecosystem around itself. Much of the group's political and organizational development was born of necessity, said former executive director Alex Tom:

> We won some things—for example, the minimum wage ordinance in San Francisco in 2003—and we were like, okay, we're done! We don't have to enforce minimum wage. And then we were like wait, the city doesn't have a fully staffed Office of Labor Standards and Enforcement—we have to help build it up! And then we were like wait, they want to cut OLSE funding! So what do we need? We need to build our governing power! People kept saying how this was so innovative—but no, we were just trying to win and maintain progressive governance on one critical working-class issue, which grew into a broader set of progressive demands.[112]

Quarterly meetings between the OLSE, CPA, and other community partners in the WRCC help to build trust between agency staff and organizers, as each side shares information and educates one another on their activities.[113] The collaboration has borne fruit: by 2015, 85 percent of back wages and interest collected by the OLSE came through co-enforcement, and analysts report that "co-enforcement norms have taken root" in San Francisco.[114] But challenges remain. The burden on worker center staff is high; time and resources are finite and intakes, casework, and other sundry co-enforcement work can compete with other core tasks such as organizing, leadership training, coalition building, and organization building—though sometimes these efforts are complementary, as when CPA and the OLSE collaborate in workplace justice campaigns.[115] Even when funding increases, in other words, the decision to devote resources to co-enforcement casework can trade off other work.

As Fine and Patel and Fisk have emphasized, co-enforcement partnerships must constantly negotiate jurisdictional frictions and procedural challenges as well.[116] Investigations invariably uncover confidential information that the agency cannot share with the worker organization, causing the alt-labor group to sometimes feel "left out of the loop" after the complaint has been filed. Sometimes the two entities' timetables do not align, and sometimes their missions are mismatched (for example, some agency officials find it inappropriate for the group to initiate a direct action campaign while an investigation is in process). Complaint-based systems also do not necessarily prioritize complaints that arrive via co-enforcement, despite the strong likelihood that prioritizing such complaints would incentivize workers to take advantage of the process. And some agency staff have expressed concerns that funding community organizations can threaten the agency's neutrality.

And yet, in places where co-enforcement has been implemented robustly, it has significantly augmented government enforcement capacities and substantively reoriented agencies' work in ways that further promote policy "fit" and increase alt-labor's political influence. From the government's perspective, co-enforcement gives agency staff an inside view of low-wage industries and helps them to see things from the perspective of the marginalized workers. It also "offers a way to embed a worker-oriented commitment throughout a bureaucracy so that enforcement is less subject to the vicissitudes of political swings in the executive branch."[117] By encouraging nonprofits to develop partnerships with community-based organizations that represent a variety of racial and ethnic groups, languages, industries, and occupations, co-enforcement arrangements also facilitate coalition building. And co-enforcement programs provide an important funding stream for under-resourced alt-labor groups and give the groups higher visibility in their communities and a proverbial "seat at the table" with powerful government regulators. In subsequent discussions around enforcement practices and policy campaigns, funded alt-labor groups are better positioned to have voice and influence.

Collaboration in San Francisco has clearly paid off. The OLSE has built significant capacity and an impressive track record recovering wages alongside the WRCC and has become a national model for cities across the city. Co-enforcement partnerships exist or have existed in various forms in Austin, Boston, Los Angeles, Miami-Dade County, Minneapolis, New York, Santa Clara County, Seattle, and the state of California, and are currently in development in numerous other states, cities, and counties, including Colorado, New Jersey, Oregon, Washington, and in the aforementioned Chicago.[118] Most co-enforcement initiatives are in their early stages, emphasizing outreach and education and starting with seed grants. But as Fine's research has shown, while funding outreach and education is an important first step in establishing relations between a government agency and community-based organizations, co-enforcement partnerships are most effective when they formalize the expected activities and the duration of the funding (as in San Francisco's three-year funded contracts with stipulated "deliverables"), target specific industries, receive strong support from key political actors, and recognize the unique capabilities that both the government agency and worker organization bring to the partnership.[119]

Alt-labor's efforts in this area—to create new city-level offices of labor standards, expand their purviews, and establish co-enforcement partnerships—thus offer illustrations of group-instigated positive policy feedback, whereby policy successes can alter the political environment, make future policy wins more likely, strengthen alt-labor groups' political standing, and improve policy effectiveness.

Part of alt-labor's motivation to influence electoral politics and reshape government capacities comes from the skepticism many leaders and organizers feel toward the ability of public policy to effectively solve the problems their members face. As Timm of WDP put it, "Policy is an organizing tool—it is a legal tool when you win it—but it's only a tool. It's never going to be the solution. It's never going to actually eradicate wage theft or dangerous and deadly conditions."[120] Or as Friedman of CPD said, "Law is a codification of power relations. So it is not going to be the thing that sets us free."[121] Policy campaigns are often viewed as more useful for organizing and movement-building than for what the policies will ultimately provide in terms of regulation. Most alt-labor groups hope the campaigns will be useful for both; but clearly their endeavors in the political arena are not driven only by their immediate policy goals. Campaigns are also part and parcel of the groups' long-term projects to disrupt status quo political dynamics and give more decision-making power to low-wage immigrant workers and workers of colors and their communities.

From alt-labor groups' policy campaigns to their year-round voter engagement programs to their co-enforcement partnerships, the examples in this chapter reveal that the groups are as concerned about how these activities strengthen them in the long run as they are about what these efforts accomplish in the near term. Groups routinely point to evidence of their resilience and versatility as markers of success—not because their goal is organizational persistence, per se, but because the persistence of their organizations advances the broader movement of which they are a part. Alt-labor groups view their fight for the rights of low-wage marginalized workers as continuous and never-ending. Because their overarching objective is to durably alter the balance of power across society and the economy, activities that result in more empowered workers, a deeper and wider base, stronger and more agile coalitions, and more flexibility and organizational capacity are celebrated because such activities enable their communities to persevere and adjust to changing conditions. This, they hope, will put them in a better position, going forward, to influence the decisions that shape their lives.

CHAPTER 7

Conclusion

FOR NEARLY THIRTY YEARS, PWC has been organizing low-wage Filipino immigrants in Southern California to fight for workers' and immigrants' rights and help its members secure access to vital services.[1] Its founders never anticipated that policy campaigns, political organizing, and building civic power would become so central to its mission. But by 2021, PWC had built a robust voter engagement field program, the Filipino Voter Empowerment Project, and launched a new 501(c)(4) "social welfare" sister organization, Pilipino Action Center, to further advance its foray into electoral politics.

One of the primary factors drawing PWC into the political arena was the fact that its policy and electoral work could simultaneously advance its organizing goals. As Soriano-Versoza, cofounder and executive director of PWC, explained:

> When we started, we thought the electoral realm was something we wouldn't be in at all. . . . We were just very focused on worker organizing—specific cases, specific worksites, building our muscle around that. But then seeing how much fundamentally needed to shift to make a real impact, our work grew from very worker organizing–focused to more policy-focused work—but in a way that was also in service of worker organizing—and then also electoral work, building power in the electoral and overall civic engagement space—while building in and creating new models that connected deeply with leadership development and base building and coalition building. That's what sold us—in addition to just seeing that these are

the next steps that we have to take in order to achieve the bigger changes that we want to make.[2]

PWC's political development illustrates the trajectory many alt-labor groups have taken over the past two decades. Founded to help low-wage workers organize collectively to redress wrongs committed against them, most groups started by emphasizing service provision and workplace justice campaigns—two highly responsive ways of helping workers address their most urgent problems. Services and direct actions are often successful: most groups have built long track records of winning workers' back wages, redressing other grievances, and helping members build valuable organizing and leadership skills. For groups that have become dependent on external funding for their survival, these strategies have the added benefit of ensuring that their primary constituency is, first and foremost, their members; they respond directly and authentically to members' needs rather than reflect the priorities of funders. But as strategies, they also have significant drawbacks, including their limited reach and impact.

For many groups, these drawbacks have led them to seek out new approaches, including campaigns for new and stronger public policies. To be sure, this is not a novel strategy; in their turn to policy, alt-labor groups have followed in the footsteps of labor unions. As detailed in chapter 2, starting in the early 1960s, labor unions played a central role in prompting state legislatures to enact a plethora of new and diverse laws to achieve many of the same substantive ends that might have otherwise been achieved through collective bargaining. In a remarkable historical juxtaposition, at the same time that labor law was drifting and union density was declining, state legislatures were creating thousands of new laws to regulate the workplace and provide legal pathways for workers to vindicate their rights. The resulting shift in the institutional locus of workers' rights—from labor law to employment law—thus began long before alt-labor emerged on the scene. But over the last two decades, alt-labor groups have made important contributions to this historical shift. They have led hundreds of subnational policy campaigns, taking advantage of the United States' decentralized federal system of governance to create new and parallel employment law regimes at the county, city, and local levels.

Drawing upon their efforts to build power for individuals and for the organization (described in chapter 5), alt-labor groups have successfully raised the wages of low-wage workers, improved workplace health and safety standards, obtained greater schedule flexibility for workers, established new channels for redressing grievances, and created new mechanisms to deter discrimination, harassment, and other forms of abuse and exploitation. They have also advanced policies affecting their members outside the workplace, such as protections for immigrants and regulations that pursue racial justice. To view these developments through a theoretical lens, we might say that labor law's drift has fostered a cycle of policy feedback: drift has led to organizational innovation, which has led to changes in the policy regime.

But even as they celebrate their policy successes, many alt-labor groups are disappointed by the results. Most policies are either watered down by the legislative process, poorly enforced, or both. Further, for groups that ultimately seek social, economic, and political transformation, most of these policies barely scratch the surface. Although their demands have grown bolder in recent years (for example, policies to end at-will employment and provide paid time off for all), the vast majority of their policy campaigns pursue only the most basic standards of fairness, decency, health, and dignity on the job—not the transformation of industries or the institutionalization of worker voice in the workplace or in society. Moreover, racially and economically marginalized low-wage workers continue to be treated as expendable and dismissed as second-class citizens—a fact that was brought into sharp relief by the disproportionate death toll among essential low-wage workers of color during the Covid-19 pandemic.[3]

The limits of policy, in other words, serve as a reminder of the unequal distribution of power and the formidable obstacles that stand in the way of fundamental change. Alt-labor groups have learned that no matter how loudly they protest—and no matter how compelling or tragic their members' stories of exploitation and abuse may be—their policymaking achievements will always be confined to what those who already have power deem acceptable. Until they can change the broader political context—the incentives that shape policymakers' behavior, prevailing notions of what ideas are legitimate, the issues that make it onto the agenda, and the capacity of government to implement and enforce its policies—their achievements will be limited to mostly minor and superficial changes that, in many cases, will exist only on paper.

This realization has prompted a growing number of groups to try to restructure their local political contexts. While many groups have long undertaken civic engagement activities in conjunction with their community organizing work, they now seek to go much further. Many endeavor to intervene directly in electoral politics by running year-round voter engagement campaigns and by intervening in candidate selection processes; they also work to augment the state's enforcement capacity to create conditions conducive to further policy change (all discussed in chapter 6). Perhaps the most concrete manifestation of alt-labor's political turn is the ongoing proliferation of 501(c)(4) entities that enable groups to endorse candidates and devote unlimited resources to lobbying.

I hasten to note that not every group has turned to policy and politics—some younger and less well-resourced groups have been reluctant to move beyond individual services, organizing, and workplace justice campaigns. But all the groups in my diverse sample readily acknowledge this general trend that has swept the alt-labor movement in recent years.[4] As one former organizer put it, "If you've built power in community organizations, you can use it in elections. It's crazy not to use it. Otherwise, you are a constant, low-level player. . . . There is a virtuous cycle: You organize, you seize political power, you pass laws and rules that create opportunities for more organizing and more power."[5]

Political engagement, however, brings new challenges of its own. To ensure ongoing political responsiveness from elected officials and effective enforcement of workers' rights and protections, alt-labor groups must monitor changing political conditions in their localities and engage continuously in politics and policymaking—even as they remain dedicated to carrying out their core service, organizing, and advocacy commitments. These new political responsibilities have been layered atop existing obligations, straining many resource-strapped groups. To be sure, policy and politics draw the attention of funders and prospective members, which can build capacity—and their campaigns can further build coalitions, develop organizational innovations, and deepen their bases—but there is little question that their dockets are starting to overflow.

The groups have strong incentives, however, to continue down this path—not least, because of the dramatic growth in the availability of political funding in recent years. One study found that between 2008 and 2020, funding for 501(c)(3) groups' nonpartisan voter education and voter registration initiatives grew sixteen-fold, reaching over half a billion dollars in the most recent presidential election year—and this figure did not even include so-called dark money funding for 501(c)(4) groups.[6] Clearly, this opening of the financial floodgates has incentivized groups to ramp up their political engagement activities and launch 501(c)(4) side organizations to take advantage of the new funding streams. Electoral work also fits comfortably with foundations' desire to see quantifiable accomplishments; there is more enthusiasm to fund this work than, say, organizing and individual- and group-level power building, which are inherently long-term propositions.

But the receipt of this funding is not costless for the groups. Recent changes in the progressive foundation landscape have created problematic pressures and reinforced inequalities in the alt-labor field. For example, when social justice foundations ally with progressive political networks such as the Democracy Alliance, as many have done in recent elections, their goals and strategies tend to converge and the kinds of community-based organizations selected for funding tend to narrow. "Consolidation can become a de facto vehicle for homogenization of principles and practice," writes Fellner, "where donor-driven brokers at the top of the food chain dictate the conditions for support and often the manner in which the work should be done by groups on the ground."[7] Groups that are affiliated with well-connected national networks often have easier access to political funding, while many stand-alone groups, no less experienced or effective, remain relatively resource poor. Meanwhile, the process and criteria for joining national networks often remain opaque. What is more, because progressive political donors tend to prioritize groups that operate in competitive swing states and districts, those in less competitive political contexts generally receive less attention, irrespective of their progress in building power and shifting dynamics in their communities. The timing of political funding also pairs awkwardly with alt-labor's strategic outlook; the tendency of political donors to pour large amounts of money into competitive races at the end of electoral cycles conflicts with alt-labor's commitment to year-round voter engagement and the pursuit of incremental structural change.[8]

While alt-labor groups clearly benefit from their unique position in progressive networks—they can legitimately claim to be the primary groups that organize and advocate for low-wage nonunionized workers—these dynamics affect their ability to secure funding and can therefore become "part of the calculus that worker centers face in determining their futures."[9] Alt-labor's goal of self-determination (developing programs and strategies on their own terms and then soliciting funding to support them) is thus becoming both more difficult to achieve and more critical than ever.[10]

Although the vast majority of alt-labor groups are small and relatively poor, a few have grown substantially and now draw millions in revenue; many more are on their way to achieving significant scale. While having more staff and resources enables groups to take on a wider variety of functions, it also puts them at risk of "becoming too institutional," as Bell of CWC put it, and "losing our grassroots activism." With greater resources comes the need to maintain substantially more back-end infrastructure—human resources, finance departments, legal compliance offices, and the like—and to be prepared for government audits and litigation, as per our discussion of 501(c)(4)s and regional multi-entity movement hubs in chapter 5. But the more they come to resemble traditional nonprofits, the further they may be pulled from being member-driven community organizing groups.[11] The fear, said Bell, is "that we end up with two 'clients,' in a way—those who we're feeding reports to and those who are on the ground—and we're treating both like clients rather than treating the community as our power and our strength that has say over what we do."[12] The generosity of external funding, in other words, has created complex cross-pressures as the groups seek to be responsive to both their members and their funders.

In addition to the pressure alt-labor groups have long felt to demonstrate that they are truly member driven, they now also feel pressure to demonstrate that they legitimately represent the broader communities for whom they advocate in the political arena. As Soriano-Versoza noted earlier, most politically engaged alt-labor groups endeavor to integrate their political work with their community organizing, base-building, and other power-building work—both out of principle and because it offers the best response to the "nonelected representative" critique.[13] But it can be difficult to execute. Keeping workers engaged after campaigns have concluded, for example, continues to be a significant challenge.

But "that is the work," as one organizer put it. In the study of U.S. politics, scholars tend to think of political engagement as organized around elections and, to a lesser extent, policy campaigns. But for alt-labor groups, organizing low-wage workers and their communities and building power at the individual and group levels are never-ending pursuits. The groups' time horizons thus differ fundamentally from those of myopic, election-focused politicians.[14] Their members are not going anywhere, their problems are deeply rooted, and they are determined to keep up the fight. Policy and electoral campaigns, in this perspective, are but periodic milestones in a long-term effort to shift the balance of power in society, the economy, and the political system. The campaigns provide valuable organizing opportunities while slowly chipping away at their adversaries' outsize power and giving their community incrementally more power and influence over the decisions that shape their lives.

One of the primary objectives of alt-labor groups, therefore, is simply to persevere, grow, and continuously build more capacity—again, not for the purpose of self-perpetuation, per se, but for the sake of the broader workers' rights movement, for which their organizations serve as critical vehicles. Their goal is not to win every battle—it is to stay in the fight. After all, alt-labor faces formidable opposition, and many groups have not survived. Worker centers have been smeared as illegal UFOs—"union front organizations"—and erroneously charged with skirting labor law in order to do work that is "outsourced" to them by labor unions.[15] During the Obama presidency, the Republican-led House Labor and Workforce Committee conducted a four-year oversight investigation into whether alt-labor groups such as WDP, ROC, and OUR Walmart (now United for Respect) should be treated as "labor organizations," forced to comply with onerous regulations governing their internal practices and financial reporting requirements, and prohibited from engaging in secondary activities.[16] At the same time, former corporate lobbyist Richard Berman's Center for Union Facts filed a complaint with the Internal Revenue Service asking to revoke the CIW's tax-exempt status. And under Trump, Labor Secretary Alex Acosta leveled similar threats against alt-labor groups, targeting CTUL in Minneapolis in particular.[17] Several groups have been subject to SLAPP suits (strategic lawsuits against public participation) designed to silence their speech on issues of public concern, restrain their activities, and bankrupt them. Sharon Block notes that these sorts of attacks are "backhanded compliments" that implicitly acknowledge alt-labor's success in helping workers. That may be true, but they have also had what Kate Griffith and Leslie Gates call a "chilling effect," especially on low-capacity groups that are unable to afford lawsuits or compliance with more onerous regulations, dampening their enthusiasm for bolder campaigns.[18]

To remain resilient, alt-labor groups therefore must think constantly about how to stockpile their power resources, nurture their strengths, learn from setbacks, adapt, and, most of all, develop "grit," says Friedman of CPD:

> It is a battle for power and it doesn't stop. It's not like: Oh, we won! It's like: We won today. We are constantly fighting, and the fight isn't going to go away, I don't think. So we're just trying our best and we're trying to look around and learn. What I am more mindful of, with time, is how totally complicated it is, and the role of creativity, courage, persistence, and luck in this is. So we're trying to build an institution that can stay in the fight, that gets a bunch of people who have those characteristics in the same fight—and then we've just gotta stay. And when we have a horrible, annoying disaster happen, we try and learn from it. It's like when educators talk about grit—that's the most important thing, more important than math, more important than reading. It's the ability to learn and go on.[19]

Part of this determination stems from the groups' recognition that their future prospects are likely to hinge on events that are almost entirely outside their control. They are, to a significant degree, dependent on variable external forces—be they structural changes in the economy, technological advances that shape the nature of low-wage work, changes in the philanthropic landscape, the prospect of significant labor law reform (which could alter alt-labor's raison d'être), or changes in the rules governing nonprofit group behavior. Alt-labor groups exist in relation to these variables. That is why so many groups emphasize perseverance: they have internalized the instability of the broader environment in which they exist and recognize the critical importance of their own organizational resilience to sustaining the broader movement of which they are a part.

Perseverance is also necessitated by the ephemeral and dynamic nature of power, which as Diaz explains, requires continuous attention to the ebb and flow of power relations:

> The number-one job of the organizer is to help our members, in any given moment, assess our power at that moment. That's it. Because it changes every day, depending on a whole host of issues that sometimes has nothing to do with us. . . . The goal is to continue to build as much power as we can—and it's going to look different at different moments—so that we can continue to be able to alter the relations of power and be able to change things fundamentally over time, knowing that that's a never-ending job, and also knowing that we can pass these really great policies that we worked hard for, and they can disappear if we don't actually have the power to sustain them.[20]

We still have much to learn about best practices in this regard. But it is important to keep in mind that what works in one context may not work in another. Organizing and power building are inherently local processes, and different groups have different capacities and face different challenges. Thankfully, case studies of grassroots organizing and power building are accumulating—but many open questions remain. How, for example, ought differently situated groups build strategic capacity?[21] Are different types of decision-making processes more effective than others in helping groups resolve the membership/funding dilemma? The micro-dynamics of power building at the individual and group levels (discussed in chapter 5) also require more exploration. How economically and racially marginalized people can best develop political capacities in oppressive settings remains an urgent question, both for those who wish to replicate the successes of others and for the prospect of democratic renewal more broadly. The opportunities for further research in this area, in other words, are many.

This study has emphasized the commonalities among groups, notwithstanding their many differences, while drawing out some of the major determinants of their behavior. As more groups turn to policy and politics, new questions will arise that will require flipping the analysis back to explaining the differences across groups, given their similar trajectories. For example, how will differently situated groups endeavor to balance their many (and sometimes competing) commitments—such as service provision, community organizing, leadership development, policy campaigns, and civic and electoral engagement—as their political profiles grow? As more groups embrace the role of political intermediary, and as more groups gain more experience with the role, will their core commitments change? How best to square responsiveness to their base, to the foundations and other external sources that fund them, and to the larger communities they seek to represent and support? At what point might politically engaged worker centers become more like "citizen centers" or special interest groups? How to measure and evaluate the trade-offs as the groups continue to change, grow, and adapt? Variation across contexts should provide useful analytical leverage in exploring these issues.

Of course, one must not lose sight of the forest for the trees. Although alt-labor groups face countless challenges and their organizational model is filled with tensions, they have proved remarkably successful at navigating the new volatile legal, political, and resource environment that has emerged in the wake of labor law's drift. They have provided indispensable support and served as critical organizational vehicles for a broad cross section of low-wage workers in disparate industries who would have otherwise remained atomized and disconnected. And they have played a vital role in advancing the promise of multiracial democracy in the United States. In their civic engagement work, these small, scrappy groups have expanded the electorate to include tens of thousands of people who have long been overlooked, ignored, or cynically demobilized or disenfranchised. By helping these communities channel their voices through collective action, alt-labor groups have broken down ideational barriers, challenged the status quo, and taken steps toward creating systemic change. In their fight for workers' rights, immigrants' rights, racial justice, and gender equality, they reveal the promise of organized action to repair the foundations of democratic self-governance.

Research Methods

BRIEF DISCUSSIONS OF the research methods used in this book appear throughout the text. For example, my "diverse case" selection strategy is discussed in chapter 1; chapter 2 reviews how I assemble and analyze data on state employment laws and provides descriptions of the variables used in my statistical analyses; and chapter 3 contains a brief discussion of my wage theft analyses. In this appendix, I offer further details on methods and provide some additional statistical analyses. Throughout the book, I use both qualitative and quantitative data; this appendix addresses each in turn. However, note that the distinction is somewhat artificial, as several analyses involve coding and statistically analyzing qualitative data and others use an integrative multi-method design.[1]

Qualitative Research

This book uses several types of qualitative data, including in-depth interviews with leaders, organizers, and members of alt-labor groups; internal documents, memos, and white papers; subnational employment laws and minimum wage statutes; and local newspapers. Each is analyzed differently.

Case Selection and Interviews

In seeking to construct a "diverse" sample of alt-labor groups, I intentionally selected groups with characteristics that varied along several key criteria (age, region, geographic reach, state partisan context, industrial focus, network affiliation, revenue, and whether they self-identified as a "worker center"). See tables 1.1 and A.1. To identify the groups, I started with the lists of worker centers mentioned in Fine's large body of work, Bobo and Pabellón, Fine and Nik Theodore's map, and journalistic accounts that mentioned other types of alt-labor groups.[2] I reached out to three dozen groups by email and phone calls and through messages on Facebook, Twitter, and LinkedIn. Six groups did not respond or the interviews fell through (five in the Midwest, one in the South), leaving thirty organizations and a response rate of thirty out of thirty-six, or 83 percent.

I conducted semi-structured, in-depth interviews with leaders, organizers, and members of each group, as well as direct observation to the extent possible prior to Covid-19. During the Covid-19 pandemic, interviews were conducted over Zoom or on the phone. Most interviews were with executive directors and organizers (paid or volunteer); I also interviewed "rank-and-file" members whenever possible. In all, I interviewed forty-three leaders and organizers and approximately fifteen members across thirty organizations. Among the interviewed leaders and organizers, approximately two-thirds were apparently non-White—which is noted only in relation to the (evidently erroneous) critique that such nonprofits are led predominantly by White staff (discussed in chapter 3). A majority of interviewees were women. Quotes from leaders and organizers are attributed when permission was granted. Some interviewees chose to remain anonymous or to keep certain quotes anonymous. Interviews with low-wage workers were wide-ranging but usually not recorded and are treated here as "off the record" or "on background" in compliance with Northwestern University institutional review board guidelines.

In the "semi-structured" interviews with leaders and organizers, I asked the same set of questions while allowing for follow-up questions and extended digressions. The common questions inquired into the groups' origins and development; how they are structured and how they operate, including questions about funding, their legal status, and the racial/ethnic, gender, and occupational composition of their membership; what their goals are and how they pursue them; how their approaches to serving and organizing their members have changed over the years; how they have confronted challenges that have arisen; and where the groups are looking to go in the future. I also asked specifically about how they relate to other groups and entities (such as funders, allies, and opponents) and how the political context in which they are situated affects their work. Interviewees were thus able to raise whatever issues were most important to them and I could follow their lead as the conversation unfolded. Throughout, I requested as many concrete examples as possible. I recorded and transcribed the interviews when permission was granted and used the qualitative analysis software NVivo to help identify categories and themes that cut across groups.

Subnational Employment Laws

With a small team of research assistants, I used the Bureau of Labor Statistics' *Monthly Labor Review* (*MLR*) to construct a dataset of every employment law enacted in all fifty states and Washington, D.C., between 1960 and 2014 (the last year of systematic recording), categorized the laws according to the topics listed in the reports (for example, "wages," "hours of work," "plant closings," "child labor," and "whistleblower"), and hand-coded them to gauge whether the laws were more worker-friendly or more employer-friendly.

The *MLR* dataset includes only legislative enactments; executive orders, judicial rulings, and ballot initiatives are excluded. Automatic "triggered" updates mentioned in the reports (for example, annual increase in minimum wage as a result of prior legislation) are also excluded. Starting in 1992, the *MLR* ceased tracking occupational safety and health, employment and training, labor relations, employee background clearance, and economic development legislation; laws in those categories were therefore excluded from the entire dataset. The *MLR* publishes separate articles on unemployment insurance and workers' compensation; those policies are excluded as well.

To distinguish employer-friendly from worker-friendly laws, three independent researchers coded 6,420 laws enacted between 1960 and 2010 (two coded 1960–1972, three coded 1973–2010), yielding an 89 percent

Table A.1 List of Alt-Labor Groups Included in Study

Name	Headquarters	Year Founded	Worker Center?	Geographic Reach	State Partisan Context	Sectoral Focus	Total Revenue (from Most Recent 990 Available)
Chinese Progressive Association (CPA)	San Francisco, CA	1972	Amalgam	Local	Democratic	Multiple	$6,806,727
Pineros y Campesinos Unidos del Noroeste (PCUN)	Woodburn, OR	1977	Amalgam	Local	Democratic	Agriculture	$403,781
Arise Chicago	Chicago, IL	1991	Worker center	Local	Democratic	Multiple	$949,384
Somos Un Pueblo Unido	Santa Fe, NM	1995	Amalgam	State	Democratic	Multiple	$1,733,075
Pilipino Workers Center (PWC)	Los Angeles, CA	1997	Worker center	Local	Democratic	Multiple	$1,825,784
Make the Road New York (MRNY)	New York, NY	1997	Amalgam	Local	Democratic	Multiple	$24,939,711
Chicago Workers' Collaborative (CWC)	Chicago, IL	2000	Worker center	Local	Democratic	Temp staffing	$839,208
New Labor	New Brunswick, NJ	2000	Worker center	State	Democratic	Multiple	$492,439
Workers Defense Project (WDP)	Austin, TX	2002	Worker center	State	Republican	Construction	$2,277,932
Restaurant Opportunities Center United (ROC)	New York, NY	2004	Worker center	Multistate	Mixed	Restaurant	$5,727,743
New Orleans Workers' Center for Racial Justice (NOWCRJ)	New Orleans, LA	2006	Worker center	State	Republican	Multiple	$1,787,260
WeCount!	Homestead, FL	2006	Worker center	Local	Republican	Multiple	$279,464
National Domestic Workers Alliance (NDWA)	New York, NY	2007	Alliance	Multistate	Mixed	Domestic work	$12,457,744

Organization	Location	Year	Type	Geographic reach	State partisan context	Worker center?	Budget
El Centro de Igualdad y Derechos	Albuquerque, NM	2009	Other	Local	Democratic	Multiple	$685,876
Heartland Workers Center (HWC)	Omaha, NE	2009	Worker center	State	Republican	Multiple	$1,706,997
Living United for Change in Arizona (LUCHA)	Phoenix, AZ	2010	501(c)(4)	State	Republican	Multiple	$1,693,113
Arizona Center for Empowerment (ACE)	Phoenix, AZ	2010	Other	State	Republican	Multiple	$915,057
United for Respect (UFR)	Oakland, CA	2011	Other	Multistate	Mixed	Retail	$809,139
Center for Popular Democracy (CPD)	New York, NY	2012	Alliance	Multistate	Mixed	Multiple	$28,906,156
Center for Worker Justice of Eastern Iowa (CWJ)	Iowa City, IA	2012	Other	Local	Mixed	Multiple	$250,443
Needham Area Immigration Justice Task Force	Needham, MA	2012	Other	Local	Democratic	Multiple	$1,300
Adelante Alabama Worker Center	Birmingham, AL	2014	Worker center	Local	Republican	Multiple	$548,444
CPD Action (CPDA)	New York, NY	2014	501(c)(4)	Multistate	Mixed	Multiple	$6,883,526
Make the Road Action (MRA)	New York, NY	2014	501(c)(4)	Multistate	Mixed	Multiple	$918,054
Raise the Floor Alliance (RTF)	Chicago, IL	2014	Alliance	State	Democratic	Multiple	$1,732,015
Workers Defense Action Fund (WDAF)	Austin, TX	2014	501(c)(4)	State	Republican	Multiple	$466,181
Acción Política PCUNista	Woodburn, OR	2016	501(c)(4)	State	Democratic	Multiple	$1,436,416
Center for Empowered Politics (CEP)	San Francisco, CA	2017	501(c)(4)	Multistate	Mixed	Multiple	$1,029,177
Somos Acción	Santa Fe, NM	2018	501(c)(4)	State	Democratic	Multiple	$126,250
Worker Justice Wisconsin (WJW)	Madison, WI	2018	Worker center	Local	Republican	Multiple	$102,833

Source: Author's compilation.

Note: "State partisan context" indicates which political party controlled state government during most years of the group's existence, with emphasis placed on control of both houses of the state legislature. "Mixed" indicates divided/alternating control or that the organization works in multiple states with varying partisan contexts. "Geographic reach" indicates the group's organizing purview. "Worker center?" indicates whether the group self-identifies as a worker center.

agreement score and a Cohen's Kappa coefficient of 0.77, which is on the high end of the "substantial" agreement range (0.61–.80).[3] Nevertheless, I use all the laws in my analyses, including employer-friendly laws, as discussed below.

Figure 2.2 sorts all employment laws into four categories. These include the following types of laws (categories are from *MLR*). Wages: minimum wage, overtime, prevailing wage, wages, and wages paid. Hours and leave: family issues, hours of work, offsite work, parental leave, family leave, time off, and women's laws. Discrimination and retaliation: discharge, discrimination, employee testings, equal employment opportunity, genetic testing, workers with disabilities, workplace security and violence, whistleblower. Terms and conditions of employment: child labor, department of labor, displaced homemakers, employee leasings, garment industry, apparel, independent contractor, plant closings, private employment agencies, undocumented workers (includes human trafficking, immigrant protection, immigration legislation, and migrant workers), and worker privacy.

Alt-Labor Policy Campaigns

To determine the extent of alt-labor group involvement in subnational minimum wage, paid sick, and fair workweek campaigns (table A.2), my research team conducted systematic searches of thousands of full-text local newspaper articles using the NewsBank database. Search terms included the jurisdiction in question and broad search terms (for example, "minimum wage"), and encompassed the years prior to and after policy enactment. If no results were found, Google News was searched as well. For each campaign, a narrative was written in which all political actors named as pushing for or against the policy were recorded, along with other pertinent details. The Internet Archive was used to identify coalition partners where necessary. All newspaper stories were saved.

Quantitative Research

I analyze several types of quantitative data in this book, including the aforementioned data on employment law enactments at the state level; employment law data collected by third-party sources; data on state legislative enactments; Current Population Survey-Merged Outgoing Rotation

Table A.2 Local Fair Workweek, Minimum Wage, and Paid Sick Leave Laws and Participation by Alt-Labor Groups, 2003–2019

	City/County	Year	Alt-Labor Group Cited as Leader in Campaign?	Group Name (Ad Hoc Coalition Name)
Fair Workweek	Santa Clara County, CA	2014	✓	EBASE, IWJ
	San Francisco, CA	2015	✓	CPA
	New York, NY	2017	✓	MRNY, CPD
	Philadelphia, PA	2017	✓	UFR, CPD (Fair Workweek Initiative)
	San Jose, CA	2017	✓	EBASE
	Seattle, WA	2017	✓	CPD (Fair Workweek Initiative)
	Emeryville, CA	2018	✓	EBASE, CPD
	Chicago, IL	2019	✓	Arise, CPD, CWC, RTF, ROC, WWJ (Fair Workweek Chicago)
Paid Sick Leave	San Francisco, CA	2006	✓	CPA
	Washington, DC	2008	✓	ROC (Paid Sick Days for All Coalition)
	Seattle, WA	2011	✓	Casa Latina (Seattle Coalition for a Healthy Workforce)
	New York, NY	2013	✓	DWU, MRNY, CPD, ROC (New York Paid Sick Days Coalition)
	Washington, DC	2013	✓	ROC (Paid Sick Days for All Coalition)
	New York, NY	2014	✓	DWU, MRNY, CPD, ROC (New York Paid Sick Days Coalition)
	Oakland, CA	2014	✓	EBASE, ROC (Lift Up Oakland)
	Montgomery County, MD	2015	✓	CASA de Maryland, IWJ (Working Matters Coalition)
	Philadelphia, PA	2015	✓	ROC, TWA-PA (PA Coalition for Healthy Families and Workplaces)
	Pittsburgh, PA	2015	✓	Hill District Consensus Group (Pittsburgh United)
	Tacoma, WA	2015	✓	El Comite (Healthy Tacoma)
	Berkeley, CA	2016	✓	EBASE (Berkeley Minimum Wage Initiative Coalition)
	Chicago, IL	2016	✓	Arise, UFR, ROC, NDWA (Paid Sick Time Chicago Coalition)
	Cook County, IL	2016	✓	Arise, UFR, ROC, NDWA (Paid Sick Time Chicago Coalition)
	Los Angeles, CA	2016	✓	Black Worker Center, CARECEN, KIWA, ROC (Raise the Wage LA)

(Table continues on p. 228)

Table A.2 *(Continued)*

	City/County	Year	Alt-Labor Group Cited as Leader in Campaign?	Group Name (Ad Hoc Coalition Name)
	Minneapolis, MN	2016	✓	CTUL
	San Diego, CA	2016	✓	IWJ, Employee Rights Center (Raise Up San Diego)
	Santa Monica, CA	2016		
	St. Paul, MN	2016	✓	CTUL
	Austin, TX	2018	✓	WDP (Working Texans for Paid Sick Time, Work Strong Austin)
	Duluth, MN	2018		
	San Antonio, TX	2018	✓	WDP (Working Texans for Paid Sick Time)
	Westchester, NY	2018	✓	MRNY (WCLC)
	Dallas, TX	2019	✓	WDP (Working Texans for Paid Sick Time)
	Emeryville, CA	2019	✓	EBASE
Minimum Wage	San Francisco, CA	2003	✓	CPA, LRCL, POWER
	Santa Fe, NM	2003	✓	Somos
	Santa Fe, NM	2007	✓	Somos
	Albuquerque, NM	2012	✓	El Centro, Ole, ROC
	San Jose, CA	2012		
	Bernalillo County, NM	2013	✓	El Centro
	Montgomery County, MD	2013	✓	CASA
	Prince George's County, MD	2013	✓	CASA
	Seatac, WA	2013		
	Chicago, IL	2014	✓	ROC, Arise (Raise Chicago Coalition)
	Las Cruces, NM	2014		
	Louisville, KY	2014		
	Mountain View, CA	2014	✓	EBASE, WPU (Santa Clara County–wide campaign)

Location	Year		Organization
Oakland, CA	2014	✓	EBASE, ROC (Lift Up Oakland)
Richmond, CA	2014		
San Francisco, CA	2014	✓	CPA (Coalition for a Fair Economy)
Sante Fe County, NM	2014	✓	Somos (Santa Fe Living Wage Network)
Seattle, WA	2014	✓	Casa Latina (15 Now)
Sunnyvale, CA	2014		
Bangor, ME	2015		
Birmingham, AL	2015		
El Cerrito, CA	2015		
Emeryville, CA	2015	✓	EBASE
Johnson County, IA	2015	✓	CWJEI
Kansas City, MO	2015	✓	Stand Up KC
Lexington, KY	2015		
Los Angeles County, CA	2015		
Los Angeles, CA	2015	✓	BWC, CARECEN, KIWA, ROC (Raise the Wage LA)
Mountain View, CA	2015	✓	EBASE, WPU (Santa Clara County–wide campaign)
Palo Alto, CA	2015	✓	EBASE, WPU (Santa Clara County–wide campaign)
Portland, ME	2015		
Santa Clara, CA	2015		
St. Louis, MO	2015		
Tacoma, WA	2015		
Berkeley, CA	2016		
Cook County, IL	2016	✓	Arise
Cupertino, CA	2016	✓	EBASE, WPU (Santa Clara County–wide campaign)
Flagstaff, AZ	2016	✓	LUCHA (Flagstaff Needs a Raise)
Linn County, IA	2016		
Los Altos, CA	2016	✓	EBASE, WPU (Santa Clara County–wide campaign)
Malibu, CA	2016		

(Table continues on p. 230)

Table A.2 (*Continued*)

City/County	Year	Alt-Labor Group Cited as Leader in Campaign?	Group Name (Ad Hoc Coalition Name)
Pasadena, CA	2016	✓	NDLON
Polk County, IA	2016	✓	CCI
San Diego, CA	2016	✓	IWJ (Raise Up San Diego)
San Jose, CA	2016	✓	EBASE, WPU (Santa Clara County–wide campaign)
San Leandro, CA	2016	✓	EBASE
San Mateo, CA	2016		
Santa Monica, CA	2016	✓	SMART
Sunnyvale, CA	2016	✓	EBASE, WPU (Santa Clara County–wide campaign)
Wapello County, IA	2016		
Washington, DC	2016	✓	ROC
Belmont, CA	2017		
Milpita, CA	2017	✓	EBASE, WPU (Santa Clara County–wide campaign)
Minneapolis, MN	2017	✓	CTUL
Montgomery County, MD	2017		
Richmond, CA	2017		
Santa Clara, CA	2017	✓	EBASE, WPU (Santa Clara County–wide campaign)
Alameda, CA	2018		
Mountain View, CA	2018	✓	EBASE, WPU (Santa Clara County–wide campaign)
Redwood City, CA	2018		
St. Paul, MN	2018	✓	CTUL

Location	Year		Organization
Daly City, CA	2019		COPA, UNE (Work Here Thrive Here)
Denver, CO	2019	✓	ROC
Emeryville, CA	2019	✓	
Fremont, CA	2019		
Menlo Park, CA	2019	✓	EBASE
Novato, CA	2019	✓	Comite Vida (North Bay Jobs with Justice)
Petaluma, CA	2019	✓	Comite Vida (North Bay Jobs with Justice)
South San Francisco, CA	2019	✓	EBASE

Source: Author's calculations.

Note:

Abbreviations

Arise = Arise Chicago

BWC = Black Worker Center

CARECEN = Central American Resource Center

CASA = Casa de Maryland

CCI = Iowa Citizens for Community Improvement

COPA = Colorado People's Alliance

CPA = Chinese Progressive Association (San Fran)

CPD = Center for Popular Democracy

CTUL = Centro de Trabajadores Unidos en la Lucha

CWC = Chicago Workers Collaborative

CWJEI = Center for Worker Justice of Eastern Iowa

DWU = Domestic Workers United

EBASE = East Bay Alliance for a Sustainable Economy

El Centro = El Centro de Igualdad y Derechos

IWJ = Interfaith Worker Justice

KIWA = Koreatown Immigrant Worker Alliance

LRCL = La Raza Centro Legal

MRNY = Make the Road New York

NDLON = National Day Labor Organizing Network

NDWA = National Domestic Workers Alliance

POWER = People Organized to Win Employment Rights

ROC = Restaurant Opportunities Center

RTF = Raise the Floor Alliance

SMART = Santa Monicans Allied for Responsible Tourism

Somos = Somos Un Pueblo Unido

TWA-PA = Taxi Workers Alliance for Pennsylvania

UFR = United for Respect/OUR Walmart

UNE = United for a New Economy

WCLC = Westchester Community/Labor Coalition for Earned Sick Time

WDP = Workers Defense Project

WPU = Working Partnerships USA

WWJ = Warehouse Workers for Justice

Group (CPS-MORG) data; Internal Revenue Service 990 tax returns from tax-exempt organizations; and a variety of data drawn from other sources.

Employment Law Analyses

In estimating the relationship between state-level employment law enactments and union density (chapter 2), I use all employment laws—not only employee-friendly laws—both because the direction of some laws is difficult to discern and because it is preferable to bias the analyses against finding that more liberal states with stronger labor unions enacted more laws. To standardize employment law enactments across states, I use state legislative enactments by year, as recorded in the Book of the States, as the denominator.[4] My panel analyses use John Driscoll and Aart Kraay's standard errors, which are heteroskedasticity- and autocorrelation-consistent and robust to general forms of cross-sectional dependence.[5]

For the purposes of cross-validation, I also tested three alternative dependent variables that theoretically capture the same phenomenon of interest (variation in the strength of state employment laws) (table A.3). The first uses a Chamber of Commerce study in which researchers examined thirty-four types of laws on the books in 2009 and graded each state on the extent to which its laws increased the regulatory burden on business and opened the door to litigation.[6] The second uses the Index of Worker Freedom compiled by the conservative Alliance for Worker Freedom in 2009, which tracked fifteen laws that it claimed obstructed workers' freedom and drove away high-quality workers.[7] The third measures the number of major state-level employment laws on the books in each state in 2014, as tracked by two authoritative sources: the National Conference of State Legislatures and the Department of Labor. All three alternative measures are highly correlated with the distribution of employment laws as measured by the *MLR* data, and union density is strongly related to each.

Chapter 2 mentions that I also flipped the analysis around, regressing union density on employment laws plus controls, as in Freeman's initial analysis of the government substitution hypothesis, to examine in a panel analysis whether employment laws contributed to union decline.[8] I find a strong and positive statistical relationship, which does not support the notion that employment laws contributed to union decline (table A.4).

Table A.3 Estimating the Relationship between Union Density and
Employment Law Enactments (Alternative Dependent Variables)

	NCSL and DOL (1)	Chamber of Commerce (2)	IWF (3)
Union density baseline	0.231***	0.655**	0.157**
	(0.0606)	(0.285)	(0.0706)
Union density change	0.224**	0.135	0.0769
	(0.0856)	(0.402)	(0.0998)
Income	4.60e-05	0.00102**	0.000123
	(8.73e-05)	(0.000410)	(0.000102)
Manufacturing	0.633	−2.391	6.500*
	(3.225)	(15.17)	(3.759)
Legislative productivity	8.72e-06	0.000308*	2.38e-05
	(3.35e-05)	(0.000158)	(3.91e-05)
State policy liberalism	2.809	−8.309	3.798
	(1.986)	(9.337)	(2.314)
Right to work	−1.298*	−15.81***	−3.582***
	(0.699)	(3.285)	(0.814)
Constant	3.389	43.59***	−11.88***
	(2.394)	(11.26)	(2.790)
Observations	50	50	50
Adjusted R-squared	0.624	0.725	0.760

Source: Galvin 2019.

Note: DOL, Department of Labor; IWF, Index of Worker Freedom; NCSL, National Conference of State Legislatures.

* $p < .05$; ** $p < .01$; *** $p < .001$

My integrative multi-method approach to exploring the relationship between labor union activity and employment law enactments (using the statistical model to select the "deviant" and "extreme-on-X" case studies of Maine, Pennsylvania, and Missouri) draws upon previously published work, in which further methodological details are available.[9] Toward the end of chapter 2, I discuss incorporating the new information gained through this iterative process into an improved, better specified model featuring previously omitted variables (partisan control of legislature and a reconstructed right-to-work variable).[10] This model offers further confirmation of the strong relationship between union density and state-level employment laws (table A.5).

Table A.4 Regressing Union Density on Employment Laws

	(1)	(2)	(3)	(4)
Employment Laws	0.218***	0.161***	0.0751***	0.0348**
	(0.0612)	(0.0406)	(0.0198)	(0.0151)
Manufacturing	1.398	−0.440	26.38***	12.89***
	(3.119)	(3.936)	(4.872)	(4.219)
Income	−0.000253***	0.000274***	−0.000235***	8.42e-05***
	(4.81e-05)	(6.40e-05)	(4.44e-05)	(1.81e-05)
Right to work	−8.282***	−7.002***	−2.628***	−1.137*
	(0.243)	(0.226)	(0.548)	(0.611)
Legislative productivity	−0.00161**	−0.00164***	−0.00136***	−0.000575**
	(0.000715)	(0.000488)	(0.000399)	(0.000236)
State policy liberalism	3.567***	2.662***	0.231	−0.0233
	(1.232)	(0.821)	(2.140)	(0.714)
Year fixed effects	No	Yes	No	Yes
State fixed effects	No	No	Yes	Yes
Constant	24.74***	24.47***	19.09***	21.18***
Observations	1,000	1,000	1,000	1,000
R-squared	0.549	0.653		
Number of groups	50	50	50	50

Source: Galvin 2019.

$* p < .1; ** p < .05; *** p < .01$

Wage Theft Analyses

Measuring the scope and depth of wage theft is difficult. No single data source systematically and reliably tracks the incidence of wage theft and records the precise amounts of money that are not being paid. Early studies of minimum wage compliance used data provided voluntarily by employers to the Bureau of Labor Statistics, but employer-reported data are not reliable, as employers who violate the law cannot be trusted to report that information to government agencies.

Workers can report wage theft by filing lawsuits or lodging complaints with federal, state, and local enforcement agencies. But lawsuits are often too expensive for minimum-wage workers and the costs of litigation frequently exceed the amounts of back pay owed. Complaints are also problematic measures of the incidence of wage theft because the workers who are more likely to be exploited are also more likely to be unaware of their right to complain (whether due to language barriers, lack of information and

Table A.5 Estimating the Relationship between Union Density and Employment Law Enactments (Improved Model)

	(1)	(2)	(3)	(4)
Union density	0.113***	0.0989***	0.115***	0.0929**
	(0.0193)	(0.0143)	(0.0341)	(0.0349)
Manufacturing	−9.122***	−8.626***	−10.75***	−8.570*
	(2.067)	(2.166)	(3.899)	(4.285)
Income	8.85e-05***	9.86e-05**	7.75e-05***	−7.67e-05**
	(1.25e-05)	(3.76e-05)	(1.63e-05)	(3.07e-05)
Right to work	−1.872***	−2.228***	1.355*	0.805
	(0.198)	(0.272)	(0.764)	(0.839)
Legislative productivity	0.00546***	0.00569***	0.00349***	0.00311***
	(0.000627)	(0.000675)	(0.000434)	(0.000573)
State policy liberalism	−1.780***	−3.105***	0.0236	2.080
	(0.441)	(1.018)	(0.609)	(1.254)
Democratic control	1.109***	1.213***	1.639***	1.739***
	(0.262)	(0.318)	(0.404)	(0.414)
Constant	−0.956	0.0661	−0.477	0.504
	(0.817)	(0.634)	(0.732)	(1.068)
Year fixed effects	No	Yes	No	Yes
State fixed effects	No	No	Yes	Yes
Observations	980	980	980	980
R-squared/within R-squared	0.414	0.440	0.1383	0.1969
Number of groups	49	49	49	49

Source: Author's calculations.

Note: Standard errors in parentheses.

* $p < .1$; ** $p < .05$; *** $p < .01$

knowledge, or fear of retaliation, termination, or deportation). Lawsuits and the complaints government agencies receive thus provide inaccurate and unreliable portraits of the actual number of violations. We must therefore turn to alternative methods to more accurately detect and measure violations. Survey data on hours and earnings are invaluable in this regard, as they enable us to estimate the underlying incidence of wage violations indirectly.

Most useful is the Current Population Survey's Merged Outgoing Rotation Groups (CPS-MORG) data, which the U.S. Department of Labor's Wage and Hour Division uses to conduct "priority setting by industries" for proactive investigations and triaging complaint investigations and which remains the top choice of every social scientist who has sought to develop national or industry-specific estimates of FLSA noncompliance since the 1970s.[11]

The CPS-MORG data has many advantages: it is gathered via extensive interviews with around 60,000 households per month; it is representative at the state and national levels (unlike other survey data, such as the Survey of Income and Program Participation [SIPP]); and its individual-level responses permit us to estimate earnings and minimum wage violations relatively easily. The biggest downside is measurement error, as with any survey. I discuss the steps taken to address measurement error below.

Wage Variable

To ensure my estimates of wage violations are conservative underestimates, I follow Cooper and Kroeger in taking the higher of the reported wage (hourly wage or weekly pay divided by hours worked) for hourly workers who report both hourly and weekly earnings.[12] I also use wage variables that include wages earned from overtime, tips, and commissions (OTC) for both hourly and nonhourly workers. This is preferable to the alternative, which excludes OTC for hourly workers while including it for nonhourly workers (for whom different sources of wages are not distinguished). Efforts to estimate and subtract OTC from nonhourly workers adds unknown quantities of additional measurement error to this key variable and is not recommended.[13] Wage estimates are therefore conservative overestimates that effectively downward-bias the estimated minimum wage violation rates.

Estimating Minimum Wage Violations

Minimum wage violations are dichotomous measures of whether an individual's estimated hourly wage was lower than the applicable legal minimum as of the date (month) effective. For the minimum wage, I use the lowest applicable wage rate (such as the state rate rather than the city or county rate, the small business rate rather than the large business rate, and so on). When a state lacks its own minimum, I use the federal rate.[14]

Note that the point estimates for minimum wage violation rates are entirely a function of how one chooses to cut the data. If one uses a larger pool of workers (say, all covered workers),[15] or a smaller pool (say, only those earning at or below their state's minimum wage),[16] the resulting point esti-mates will be much lower or higher, respectively.

Exemptions

For all wage theft analyses, I endeavored to include only those workers who were covered and nonexempt from their state's applicable minimum wage laws. Each state has many different exemptions and coverage exclusions— some minor, some major. Using VitalLaw's state-by-state minimum wage law summaries and consulting statutes directly, I worked with my research team to catalog and code every exemption listed in the minimum wage laws in all fifty states and the District of Columbia. About half of the 969 exemptions could be identified in the CPS-MORG data and excluded from the analysis while the other half could not—usually because CPS-MORG data do not provide information on employers beyond the industry and occupation in which the employee works. (Some examples of exemptions that could not be identified: those working for an agricultural employer that did not use more than five hundred man-days of agricultural labor in any calendar quarter of the preceding calendar year or who are immediate family members of their agricultural employer, those working at amusement or recreational establishments having seasonal peaks, and those operating vehicles or vessels on behalf of a motor carrier company under specific conditions.) Point estimates and confidence intervals are extremely similar, however, irrespective of whether exemptions are taken into account.

Survey Weights and Standard Errors

All analyses, including population estimates, use the survey weights sug-gested by Davern and colleagues which are necessary given the sampling method of the CPS.[17]

Measurement Error

There is reason to believe that measurement error in the CPS may downward-bias the estimates of minimum wage violations.[18] First, despite going to great lengths to reach them, both Hispanics (Latinx) and undocu-mented immigrants are underrepresented in the CPS.[19] Because workers in these groups are at higher risk of experiencing minimum wage violations, the estimates of violations reported here should be considered conservative estimates. Second, in Bollinger's study of measurement error in the CPS, he finds a "high over reporting of income for low-income men" driven by "about 10% of the reporters who grossly over report their income," thus potentially biasing estimates downward even further.[20] Third, CPS data have a shortage of low-wage workers and an excess of high-wage workers relative to comparable survey data like SIPP; one effect of this imbalance could be to bias downward estimates of minimum wage violations.[21] Roemer does find that the CPS reaches more "underground" workers than other large-scale surveys and is less biased than alternatives.[22] But given the high rates of violation discovered in the 2009 innovative survey by Bernhardt and colleagues of hard-to-reach workers in the "informal" labor market—higher than the estimates presented here—there is reason to suspect that these findings underestimate the prevalence of minimum wage violations across the board.[23] The fact that measurement error surely exists recommends using caution when working with the point estimates reported.

To address measurement error and further err on the side of undercounting minimum wage violations, I exclude from the analyses all workers not specifying hourly/nonhourly status, nonhourly workers with weekly earnings less than $10, workers with hourly wages less than $1, and respondents with imputed hours.[24] Unemployed, self-employed, and self-incorporated workers are also excluded. I conduct several sensitivity tests, including analyses excluding proxy respondents and analyses in which violations were calculated as hourly wages less than the applicable minimum wage minus $0.25 and $0.50. Relative violation rates remain extremely similar in all sensitivity tests.

Low-Wage Workers

Low-wage workers are operationalized as all eligible workers in the bottom quintile of their state's wage distribution in a given year.

Race Variable

Racial and ethnic categories are mutually exclusive. I follow the Center for Economic and Policy Research (CEPR) and the Economic Policy

Institute (EPI) in the construction of the race variable.[25] "Black" includes those who identify as Black-White; Black-American Indian; Black-Asian; Black-Hawaiian/Pacific Islander; White-Black-American Indian; White-Black-Asian; White-Black-Hawaiian/Pacific Islander; Black-American Indian-Asian; and White-Black-American Indian-Asian. "Asian" includes those who identify as Asian and Hawaiian/Pacific Islander; White-Asian; White-Hawaiian/Pacific Islander; American Indian-Asian; American Indian-Hawaiian/Pacific Islander; Asian-Hawaiian/Pacific Islander; White-American Indian-Asian; White-American Indian-Hawaiian/Pacific Islander; White-Asian-Hawaiian/Pacific Islander; White-American Indian-Asian-Hawaiian/Pacific Islander. "Other" includes American Indian (only); White-American Indian; other three races; other four and five races. "Hispanic" includes those who identify as Mexican, Mexican-American, Mexicano/Mexicana, Chicano/Chicana, Mexican (Mexicano), Mexicano/Chicano, Puerto Rican, Cuban, Dominican, Salvadoran, Other Hispanic, Central/South American, Central American, (excluding Salvadoran), South American, and any of these categories and White, Black, Asian, or Other.

In the comparative analyses of minimum wage violations by demographic group in chapter 3, the term "Hispanic" corresponds to the label used by CPS. According to the CPS, "noncitizen" refers to any person born outside the United States who is not a naturalized U.S. citizen (for example, a refugee, asylee, undocumented immigrant, or legal permanent resident), was not born in Puerto Rico, and does not have parents who are U.S. citizens.

Data

For all these analyses, I use the IPUMS CPS-MORG abstracts generated by Flood et al. 2020.

Membership Dues

Only eighteen of thirty alt-labor groups reported "membership dues" or unmarked "miscellaneous" revenue separately in their Internal Revenue Service 990 tax returns. The average revenue from amounts designated as "membership dues" alone was 0.38 percent (ten of thirty groups). When we include the eight additional groups that reported "miscellaneous" or "other" revenue, the average only rises to 0.39 percent. The highest share was 1.2 percent and the lowest was 0.02 percent. It is possible, however, that if membership dues were considered "contributions" or "donations"—terms used by several alt-labor leaders—groups may have reported this revenue as part of the catchall category that also includes foundation funding ("other contributions, gifts, grants, and similar amounts"), which is always the largest category.

NOTES

Chapter 1: Introduction: The New Politics of Workers' Rights

1. *Lucas, Davis, and Green v. Gold Standard Baking, MVP*, 13 CV 1524 N.D. Ill. (2017); *Zollicoffer and Green v. Gold Standard Baking, MVP*, 13 C 1524 N.D. Ill. (2018), https://cases.justia.com/federal/district-courts/illinois/ilndce/1:2013cv01524/280596/786/0.pdf?ts=1585732984; Elejalde-Ruiz 2016; Evans 2016.
2. Gold Standard Baking Linkedin, https://www.linkedin.com/company/gold-standard-baking (accessed March 11, 2021).
3. *Zollicoffer and Green v. GSB*, 5.
4. Evans 2016; Chan 2016.
5. Elejalde-Ruiz 2016. Seven years and many court dates later, Green settled his class-action lawsuit for just over half a million dollars (U.S. Equal Employment Opportunity Commission 2020).
6. Evans 2016.
7. *Zollicoffer and Green v. GSB*.
8. Bernhardt et al. 2009; Fine et al. 2020; BLS 2021b; and see wage theft analysis in chapter 3.
9. Morris and Mitchell 2012.
10. Krista Kjellman Schmidt (ProPublica), "Raani OSHA Documents," https://www.documentcloud.org/documents/714378-raani-osha-documents (accessed June 1, 2023); Mitchell 2013. The Occupational Safety and Health Administration (OSHA) ultimately cited Raani with fourteen safety violations, including willfully failing to provide proper protective clothing and eye, face, and hand protection and willfully failing to use available emergency care. OSHA's investigation revealed that

Centeno's injuries were not isolated; injuries in Raani's factory were "abundant" and the employer's "lack of concern for employee safety was tangible." Of Raani's 150 employees, 40 percent were temp workers. Because temps were short-term workers and technically employed by temp agencies, the companies that hired them did "not have the same commitment to providing a safe workplace, to providing the proper training," said former OSHA director David Michaels. OSHA 2012; Morris and Mitchell 2012; Grabell 2013.

11. Murthy 2013.
12. Amendment to the Day and Temporary Labor Services Act, SB0047, 99th Illinois General Assembly (2015).
13. Evans 2016.
14. Ganz 2000.
15. Tim Bell (executive director of the CWC), interview with the author, December 2017.
16. Evans 2016.
17. Formally, HB 690, the Responsible Job Creation Act, a set of amendments to Illinois' Day and Temporary Labor Services Act, 100th Illinois General Assembly (2015). Kacich 2017; Contreras 2017; Ammons 2017.
18. Bell, 2017 interview.
19. Sophia Zaman (executive director of RTF), interview with the author, July 2019. Also pivotal, of course, was the bill's lead sponsor and champion, freshman Rep. Carol Ammons, a member of the Black Caucus and former community organizer.
20. Schuhrke 2017; Evans 2017.
21. Roeder 2021.
22. Roeder 2019.
23. Scott 2021; Elejalde-Ruiz 2021; Carden and Gormley 2021.
24. On co-enforcement, see Fine 2017; Fine and Bartley 2018.
25. Scott 2021.
26. Bell, interview with the author, April 2022. In 2023, CWC successfully got both houses of the Illinois legislature to pass most of its remaining "wish list" items in the Temp Worker Fairness and Safety Act (HB 2862), including additional support for enforcement. As this book was going to press, the bill was sent to the governor for his signature. It mandated equal pay for equal work by temps who worked at the same job for longer than ninety days, improved safety training and more rigorous notification requirements, higher penalties for violations, and increased funding for enforcement. It also gave "interested parties," including worker centers, a private right of action to strengthen enforcement of the law (*Illinois Business Journal* 2023).
27. Weil 2014; Kalleberg 2009, 2011; Howell and Kalleberg 2019; Standing 2014; Osterman 2014; Milkman 2014.
28. Weil 2014; Piore and Schrank 2018; Schrank 2019.
29. Bernhardt, Spiller, and Theodore 2013; Pager, Bonikowski, and Western 2009.
30. Part of the problem was the National Labor Relations Board's ever-changing definition of "joint employment" (Andrias 2016, 58–63; Hatton 2011, 134–41; Greenhouse 2021).

31. Fine and Piore 2021, 1086; Lambert and Haley 2021, 1232.
32. Gleeson 2009, 2016; Griffith 2011; Weil and Pyles 2005.
33. Berrey, Nelson, and Nielsen 2017; Gleeson 2016; Gordon 2005.
34. Galvin 2019. On the perils of federalism, see Grumbach 2022.
35. For an alternate view, see Sachs 2008.
36. Ashenfelter and Smith 1979; Weil 2005; Galvin 2016.
37. Weil 2018; Fine et al. 2020; Fine and Bartley 2018.
38. The term "alt-labor" was coined by Josh Eidelson (2013). Although "alt-labor" is sometimes used by journalists to describe any worker movement that is not explicitly tied to a labor union—including the (Service Employees International Union–funded) Fight for $15 movement, online platforms such as coworker.org, and the wildcat teacher strikes of 2018—I use the term more narrowly here. I define "alt-labor groups" as registered nonprofit organizations that organize low-wage workers to fight for workers' rights and economic justice. This categorization includes all "worker centers"; similar community-based groups, alliances, and organizations that do not identify as worker centers (and/or explicitly reject the "worker center" label) but pursue the same core priorities; groups that organize at a regional or national scale; sister organizations registered under the 501(c)(4) "social welfare" section of the tax code; and "amalgams" (McAlevey 2013) such as Make the Road New York that pursue a wide range of issues, but fighting for workers' rights and economic justice remains central to their mission. For more on the range of alt-labor groups, see chapter 3; for decision rules and research methods for this study, see discussion below and in the appendix. On worker centers, see Fine 2006; Fine et al. 2018; Gordon 2005; Narro 2005; Theodore, Valenzuela, and Melendez 2006; Theodore 2007; Milkman 2007; Milkman, Bloom, and Narro 2010; Cordero-Guzmán, Izvănariu, and Narro 2013; Griffith and Gates 2019.
39. Olson 1965.
40. Fine 2006; Kochan et al. 2022, 6, 32, find that the number of worker centers reached "at least 246" by the end of 2021. Including alt-labor groups that do not identify as worker centers brings the total number up to the 250–300 range. See chapter 3 for more discussion of this growth.
41. Hertel-Fernandez 2019; Hacker et al. 2022b.
42. For example, Piven and Cloward 1977; Baumgartner and Leech 1998; Strolovitch 2007; Gilens and Page 2014. But see Gause 2022.
43. Soss and Weaver 2017.
44. Berry and Arons 2005. For example, CWC, as a 501(c)(3) organization, was prohibited from engaging in any hint of electioneering—endorsing candidates, engaging in partisan activities, or being involved, even indirectly, in any candidate's campaign for elective public office—and had to carefully limit the extent of its direct lobbying activities as well.
45. Smith (2007) 2017; Francis 2019; Frantz and Fernandes 2018; Teles 2016.
46. Alt-labor's political and electoral engagement may thus be understood as an effort to escape the paradox identified by Jeffrey Berry and David Arons (2005, 4) whereby

the legal limit on 501(c)(3) lobbying activities "harms the most vulnerable populations, who are denied effective representation in the political system." See also Marwell 2004.

47. Levine 2016, 2017.

48. For example, Marwell 2007.

49. Dubofsky and McCartin 2017. For an overview of the labor question, see Fraser 2022.

50. Roosevelt 1940; Dubofsky and McCartin 2017.

51. Huthmacher 1968.

52. In 2022, 71 percent of Americans approved of labor unions (McCarthy 2022).

53. For example, Goldfield 1987; Estlund 2002; Cowie 2010; Frymer 2008; Lichtenstein 2013; Rosenfeld 2014; Windham 2017; Eidlin 2018; Mishel, Rhinehart, and Windham 2020; Swenson 2002; Brady 2007; Bronfenbrenner 2009; Logan 2006.

54. For example, Block and Sachs 2020; Andrias and Sachs 2021; Andrias and Rogers 2018; Madland 2016, 2021; Rolf 2016.

55. Hall and Soskice 2001.

56. King and Rueda 2008.

57. Thelen 2014, 13–16.

58. Hacker 2004, 2019; see also Hacker and Pierson 2010.

59. Hacker 2004, 2005; Hacker and Pierson 2010; Galvin and Hacker 2020.

60. Bartels 2016; Béland, Rocco, and Waddan 2016; Galvin 2016, 2019; Piore and Schrank 2018.

61. Galvin and Hacker 2020.

62. Hacker et al. 2022b; Hacker 2004; Stepan and Linz 2011.

63. Although many policy effects diminish over time due to the lack of what Suzanne Mettler (2016) calls "policy maintenance," policy drift typically involves the deliberate choice of policymakers not to make formal revisions that would prevent those diminished effects and often finds those opposed to policy updates leveraging institutional veto points to hold the policy in place and obstruct proposed reforms.

64. Hacker and Pierson 2010.

65. Ibid., 59; Galvin 2019; Galvin and Hacker 2020; Snead 2023.

66. Save the minor expansion of coverage to health care workers in 1974.

67. These efforts included Lyndon B. Johnson's effort to repeal section 14b (right-to-work laws) of the Taft-Hartley Act in 1965, the Labor Law Reform Act of 1978, the Workplace Fairness Act of 1993, the Employee Free Choice Act of 2009, and the Protect the Right to Organize Act of 2021.

68. As Andrias 2016 shows, the NLRA does not facilitate self-organization and collective action across multiple employers (thereby ignoring the complexities of subcontracting, franchising, temp work, and outsourcing within modern supply chains and economic networks); it fails to require employers to bargain with multiple units of organized employees; as amended by the Taft-Hartley Act of 1947, it forbids "cross-employer economic action" like secondary boycotts—including pickets at the corporate headquarters of a franchiser; and it fails to cover nontraditional work relationships, such as independent contractors and gig workers.

69. As Warren Snead (2023) has recently shown, the Supreme Court played a central role in facilitating these developments through its statutory interpretations of labor law, which have strengthened the hand of employers and made union elections more difficult to win. National Labor Relations Board rulings have impacted union strategies as well—for example, by disallowing, then allowing, then again disallowing "joint employers." These mechanisms of drift have helped employers, aided by the union-avoidance industry, to exploit, evade, or break the law to thwart union drives.

70. Estlund 2002, 1527; Sachs 2007, 376; Sachs 2008, 2686; Summers 1988, 10; Weiler 1983, 1769.

71. Hirsch and Macpherson 2003; BLS 2023b. The recent uptick was outpaced by growth in the overall workforce.

72. BLS 2023a.

73. Bernhardt et al. 2008; Bernhardt et al. 2009; Maltby 2009; Grabell and Berkes 2015; Kalleberg 2011; Galvin 2016; Bobo 2009; Hertel-Fernandez 2018a.

74. Galvin and Hacker 2020.

75. It also may mean turning to the courts or administrative agencies. Ibid.

76. Schattschneider 1960, 71.

77. Hacker et al. 2022b.

78. As Elisabeth Clemens (2006) has argued, policies featuring "a complex tangle of indirect incentives, crosscutting regulations, overlapping jurisdictions, delegated responsibility and diffuse accountability" (187) are a defining characteristic of the American state. Reactions to policy drift may be considered among "the diversity of the political projects that have combined to produce our oft-maligned tangle of governance" (209).

79. Galvin and Hacker 2020.

80. Galvin 2019; Snead 2023; *San Diego Bldg. Trades Council v. Garmon*, 359 U.S. 236 (1959). Subsequent Court decisions narrowed the ability of states and localities to intervene further still—for example, the 1976 *Machinists v. Wisconsin Employment Relations Committee* case (427 U.S. 132) ruled that subnational regulation of labor-management relations was preempted even in areas Congress ostensibly meant to leave to "the free play of economic forces," thereby "virtually banish[ing] states and localities from the field of labor relations" (Estlund 2002), with precious few exceptions.

81. Public-sector labor laws are the most well known, as is California's Agricultural Labor Relations Act of 1975, which extended collective bargaining rights to farmworkers in the state.

82. Estlund 2002.

83. Galvin and Seawright 2021.

84. Galvin and Hacker 2020.

85. Pierson 1993.

86. Howell and Kalleberg 2019; Weil 2014, 15–18.

87. To be sure, some unions developed innovative organizing campaigns and successfully unionized thousands of low-wage immigrant workers of color (as the well-known

Justice for Janitors campaign across dozens of cities attests). But most low-wage workers remained unaffiliated with unions (Waldinger et al. 1996; Milkman 2006, 2011).

88. Fine 2006, 14–15.
89. Ibid.
90. Fine 2006; Griffith and Gates 2019.
91. Fisk 2016. Until 2018, both 501(c)(3) and 501(c)(4) nonprofits had to disclose identifying information about donors who gave $5,000 or more to the Internal Revenue Service, but the IRS was prohibited from revealing the c4s' information. Since 2020, identifying information about donations to 501(c)(4) organizations no longer needs to be reported. 501(c)(3) groups must still disclose their donations over $5,000, but identifying information is not reported publicly.
92. Smith (2007) 2017; Ahn (2007) 2017; Gilmore (2007) 2017; Piven and Cloward 1977.
93. Griffith 2015.
94. For example, Vernuccio 2013.
95. Greenhouse 2020.
96. Reskin 2012.
97. Lieberman 1998; Mettler 1998; Michener 2018; Thurston 2018, 2021; SoRelle 2020.
98. Alonso-Villar, del Rio Otero, and Gradín 2012; Alonso-Villar and del Rio Otero 2013; Trounstine 2018, 2021.
99. Soss and Weaver 2017. See also Trounstine 2018.
100. Soss and Weaver 2017, 567.
101. Ibid.; Desmond 2016.
102. Bergmann 1971, 1974; Altonji and Blank 1999; Pitts 2018; see also the wage theft analysis in chapter 3. In highly competitive low-wage labor markets in which the exploitation of people of color, immigrants, and women is rampant, the long history of occupational segregation and discrimination has dovetailed with underenforcement of the law to create especially disadvantaged populations.
103. Hacker et al. 2022a, 205.
104. Michener 2020; Soss and Weaver 2017. See also SoRelle and Michener 2022; Pitts 2018.
105. Soss and Weaver 2017. Alt-labor groups are not alone. In recent years, social scientists have identified a number of community organizing groups that are also helping racially and economically marginalized low-wage workers come together to build power and contest their exploitation, including the faith-based and immigrant-led community organizing groups in Hahrie Han, Elizabeth McKenna, and Michelle Oyakawa's (2021) study, the local membership-driven community-based organizations in Michener's (2020) work, and the tenant-rights organizations studied by Mallory SoRelle and Michener (2022).
106. Fine 2005.
107. Schattschneider 1960, 16, 40. Italics in the original.
108. "Private government" is from Anderson 2017.
109. Milkman 2010, 15–16. See also, for example, Fine, Narro, and Barnes 2018; Jacobs 2018.

110. See table A.2. Methods discussed in the appendix.

111. Baumgartner and Jones 1993; Kingdon 1984; Bawn et al. 2012.

112. Fine 2005.

113. Fine 2005, 2006.

114. Chun 2011; Bobo 2009; Fine 2011a; Mattoni 2012; Rhomberg 2018; Rosado Marzán 2018.

115. Marcela Diaz (executive director of Somos Un Pueblo Unido), interview with the author, July 2019.

116. Gerring 2006; Seawright and Gerring 2008. Interviews were conducted in person, and I engaged in direct observation to the extent possible prior to the Covid-19 pandemic. In all, I interviewed forty-three leaders and organizers and approximately fifteen members across thirty organizations. Quotes from leaders and organizers are attributed when permission was granted. Some interviewees chose to remain anonymous or to keep their quotes anonymous. Interviews with low-wage workers were treated as off the record or on background, in compliance with Northwestern University institutional review board guidelines. Six groups either did not respond to interview requests or were unable to participate in the interviews (five in the Midwest, one in the South), leaving thirty organizations and a response rate of thirty out of thirty-six, or 83 percent. A more extensive discussion of methods can be found in the appendix. Group names and abbreviations can be found in table A.1.

117. Though less often used in political science, the concept of generative power is commonly invoked among feminist scholars and development practitioners. For example, Rowlands 1995, 1997; Hartsock 1983; VeneKlasen et al. 2002; Gaventa and Cornwall 2008; Kabeer 1994; Williams 1994; Gaventa 1982; Lukes 2021; see also Wright 2000.

118. Lesniewski and Gleeson 2022; Minkler et al. 2014; Lipscomb et al. 2006.

119. Han 2014; Tapia 2019.

120. Grumbach and Michener 2022.

121. Michener 2023 shows how preemption causes local tenant groups to temper their goals, expend precious resources on policy adaptation, and strain their limited capacities.

122. On policy fit, see Skocpol 1992.

123. Gaventa 1982; see also Lawless and Fox 2001; Walker 2020; Piven and Cloward 1977.

124. Problems of sustainability and legitimacy are common for the new groups that emerge in the context of policy drift (Galvin and Hacker 2020).

125. Levine 2016, 2017.

126. Strolovitch 2007.

127. Interview with the author (anonymous).

128. Cited in Andrias 2016, 37n190.

Chapter 2: The Changing of the Guard from Labor Law to Employment Law

1. Estlund 2002; Hacker and Pierson 2010; Galvin 2019.

2. Summers 1988.

3. Anderson 2017.

4. Huthmacher 1968, 204.

5. Schattschneider 1935, 288; Pierson 1993; Béland, Campbell, and Weaver 2022.

6. Sachs 2008 makes a similar argument, which parts of this analysis explicitly build on, but the focus here is different. Benjamin Sachs's innovative account emphasizes how employment law can serve as a substitute for labor law by providing legal cover for workers' collective actions; he draws attention to the fact that workers are "relying on employment statutes, not only for the traditional purpose of securing the substantive rights provided by those laws, but also as the legal architecture that facilitates their organizational and collective activity—a legal architecture we conventionally call labor law" (2687). My focus is on the form and substantive content of these laws (what Sachs calls their "traditional purpose") and on the new kinds of organizational politics that have emerged around them.

7. Thelen 2014; Hacker 2019, 249.

8. Gleeson 2016; Gordon 2005.

9. Berrey, Nelson, and Nielsen 2017.

10. Ibid., 263.

11. Summers 1988, 10–11.

12. Stone 1992, 593.

13. Estlund 2005, 321, 326.

14. St. Antoine 2003, 526–27.

15. Andrias 2016, 37.

16. Sachs 2008, 2687.

17. St. Antoine focuses on the role state courts played in reshaping the doctrine of at-will employment (2003, 508).

18. Bales 1993, 1876.

19. Jacobs 2018, 271.

20. Fine and Piore 2021, 1086.

21. St. Antoine 2003, 495.

22. Bureau of Labor Statistics 1960–2014.

23. For more on methods, see the appendix.

24. See the appendix for laws included in each category.

25. Epp 1998.

26. The statewide average was 142 laws and a 59 percent rate of private-sector union density decline.

27. Bureau of Labor Statistics 1960–2014.

28. For more on methods, see the appendix.

29. Grumbach 2018, 2022.

30. Ashenfelter and Smith 1979; Weil 2005; Weil and Pyles 2005; Galvin 2016; Fine and Bartley 2018.

31. Tsoukalas et al. 2022.

32. For example, in California, see Su 2016; in New York, see Fine and Gordon 2010, 569; in Illinois, see Illinois Office of the Governor 2022. See also Galvin 2016; Fine 2017.

33. See, for example, Brudney 2005; Estlund 2005; Secunda 2007.

34. For example, the California Agricultural Labor Relations Act (CA Labor Code § 1140.2 [2018]); Seattle Independent Contractor Protections Ordinance (SMC § 14.34 [2021]); Gerstein and Gong 2022.

35. St. Antoine 2003, 495; Summers 1988.

36. Sachs 2008, 2688; Andrias 2016, 37–40.

37. Sachs 2008, 2688–89, citing Brudney 1996 and Estlund 2002.

38. Brudney 1996, 1564.

39. Lichtenstein 2013, x.

40. Stone 1992, 638. See also Bales 1993, 1997.

41. Frymer 2008.

42. Galvin 2019; Weiler 1990.

43. Neumann and Rissman 1984.

44. Moore and Newman 1988; Hauserman and Maranto 1988; Moore, Newman, and Scott 1989; Bennett and Taylor 2001; Coombs 2008.

45. Gottschalk 2000; Jamison 2016.

46. Freeman and Medoff 1984.

47. Ahlquist and Levi 2013, 2.

48. Moore, Newman, and Scott 1989, 539.

49. Freeman and Medoff 1984, 202; Western and Rosenfeld 2011; Rosenfeld 2014.

50. Freeman 1986.

51. Ibid., 265.

52. Ibid., 262.

53. Ibid., 265.

54. Southern Labor Institute 1986, 2.

55. To be as conservative as possible, the analyses here include all employment laws— not only employee-friendly laws—effectively biasing the analyses against finding that more liberal states with stronger labor unions enacted more laws.

56. Hirsch and Macpherson 2003.

57. Freeman 1986.

58. Chen 2009.

59. Ibid., 158; Dixon 2007.

60. Council of State Governments 1935–2017.

61. Caughey and Warshaw 2018.

62. George and Bennett 2005; Gerring 2006; Seawright 2016a, 2016b.

63. Seawright 2016a.

64. Galvin 2021.

65. Galvin and Seawright 2021.

66. Collier, Brady, and Seawright 2004, 227–28.

67. See table A.4 and discussion in the appendix for more information.

68. Freeman and Medoff 1984; Rosenfeld 2014.

69. Hacker and Pierson 2010; Kalleberg 2011; Western and Rosenfeld 2011; Rosenfeld 2014; Ahlquist 2017; Bucci 2018; Hertel-Fernandez 2018a.

70. Galvin 2021.
71. Fine 2013, 2017.
72. Colvin 2017; Staszak 2015, 2020.

Chapter 3: Vulnerable Workers, the Rise of Alt-Labor, and the Funding Dilemma

1. CWJ found that the men also had not received paystubs or written statements for the number of hours they had worked, the amount of money they had earned, or the deductions that had been made; Ramirez had not been registered as a subcontractor in Iowa; they had received threats of retaliation for exercising their wage payment rights under federal and Iowa law and their concerted activity rights under section 7 of the NLRA; and their employer had failed to provide personal protection equipment to protect them from Covid-19 or medical care for their workplace injuries (Morgenson and Cavazuti 2021; Jordan 2020; Mercado 2020; Kuhlenbeck 2020; LiUNA 2021; Cadwell 2021).
2. Clark-Bennett 2020; LiUNA 2021.
3. Mercado 2020.
4. Estlund 2002; Andrias 2016; Galvin 2019.
5. Stone 2004; Dobbin 2009; Edelman 2016; Berrey, Nelson, and Nielsen 2017.
6. Berrey, Nelson, and Nielsen 2017; Gleeson 2016.
7. Bernhardt et al. 2008; Bernhardt et al. 2009; Bernhardt, Spiller and Theodore 2013; Weil 2014; Ji and Weil 2015; Galvin 2016; Kim 2021; Fine et al. 2021b.
8. Lichtenstein 2013, 264; Bobo 2009; Gleeson 2012, 2016.
9. Kalleberg 2011; Howell and Kalleberg 2019; Appelbaum, Bernhardt, and Murnane 2003; Families and Workers Fund 2022.
10. Appelbaum, Bernhardt, and Murnane 2019; Anderson et al. 2021.
11. Howell 2019; Zipperer et al. 2022.
12. Piore and Schrank 2018.
13. King and Rueda 2008.
14. Greico 2014; Straut-Eppsteiner 2022.
15. Farhang and Katznelson 2005.
16. Appelbaum, Bernhardt, and Murnane 2003; Kalleberg 2011.
17. Garcia 2012, 3–4.
18. Pitts 2018; Berrey, Nelson, and Nielsen 2017; Gleeson 2016.
19. Gleeson 2016, 2.
20. Chen 2021.
21. Crenshaw 1990; Strolovitch 2007; Hancock 2016. As we will see, workers who check multiple demographic boxes have significantly higher probabilities of experiencing wage theft than each subgroup.
22. The share of the labor force that is Black grew from 9.9 percent in 1976 to 12.6 percent in 2020; the share of women in the labor force grew from 45.7 percent

to 57.4 percent (Rolen and Toossi 2018; BLS 2021a, 2021c, 2022; Newburger and Gryn 2009).

23. Budiman et al. 2020.

24. Passel and Cohn 2019.

25. Soss and Weaver 2017, 567; Milkman 2020a; Trounstine 2018.

26. Gleeson 2016, 10–12.

27. Although retaliation is illegal, it is not necessarily costly for employers. In *Hoffman Plastic Compounds, Inc. v. National Labor Relations Board* (2002), the Supreme Court ruled that undocumented immigrants who are retaliated against—in this case, terminated—for attempting to unionize are not entitled to back pay.

28. On the complex relationship between immigration law and workplace policies— termed by Kati Griffith "immmployment law"—see Griffith 2009, 2011.

29. For example, Bernhardt et al. 2009.

30. Cooper and Kroeger 2017; Prins et al. 2021; Eisenberg-Guyot et al. 2022.

31. "Low-wage" is defined as those in the bottom quintile of their state's wage distribution.

32. This does not take into account that some workers who were paid less than the minimum wage were likely promised higher wages than the statutory minimum. Workers who experienced minimum wage violations during this period would have made $9.31 per hour, on average, had they been paid their state's minimum wage.

33. About 35 percent of these workers were also married. For poverty thresholds, see U.S. Census Bureau 2023.

34. David Cooper and Teresa Kroeger (2017) conducted a similar analysis, also with CPS-MORG data, using similar methods to Galvin (2016) and here, but confined their analyses to the ten most populous states in 2013 through 2015. They estimate that 17 percent of eligible low-wage workers suffered a minimum wage violation and lost $3,300 per year, which is comparable to what I find here (in those ten states, I find a 16 percent violation rate and $2,765 lost per year on average between 2013 and 2015). They estimate $8 billion stolen annually between 2013 and 2015; I estimate $6 billion in those ten states. Hence, my estimates are comparable but more conservative, likely due to differing measures of hours worked and state-level exemptions from minimum wage laws. See the appendix for further discussion.

35. These were determined using three-digit industry codes, industries with $N > 5,000$ between 2010 and 2022, from CPS-MORG data.

36. These were determined using three-digit occupation codes, occupations with $N > 2,000$ between 2010 and 2022, from CPS-MORG data.

37. The use of the term "Hispanic" in this section corresponds to the label used by CPS.

38. Noncitizens are also far more likely to get hurt or killed on the job than U.S. citizens (see Grabell and Berkes 2017).

39. Galvin and Hacker 2020.

40. The term was coined by Josh Eidelson (2013) and is now widely used. For example, Walsh 2018; Oswalt and Rosado Marzán 2020; Milkman 2020b; Fisk 2020; Griffith and Gates 2020; *American Prospect* 2021–22.

41. Fine 2006, 11. See also Gordon 2005; Theodore 2007; Milkman 2007, 2011, 2013; Milkman, Bloom, and Narro 2010; Fine et al. 2018; Narro 2005; Theodore, Valenzuela, and Melendez 2006; Cordero-Guzmán, Izvănariu, and Narro 2013; Griffith and Gates 2019.

42. "Amalgam" is from McAlevey 2013. See also the list of groups in table 1.2.

43. Fine 2006.

44. Ibid.

45. Fine 2005, 2006, 2011a; Fine, Narro and Barnes 2018; Milkman, Bloom, and Narro 2010; Milkman and Ott 2014; Rosado Marzán 2018; Theodore, Gutelius, and Gonzalez 2019; Fisk 2020; Griffith and Gates 2019.

46. Fine et al. 2018; Kochan et al. 2022, 6, 32.

47. Fine 2006, 9.

48. Ibid., 9–11; Chen 2021.

49. Pitts 2018; National Black Worker Center, "Our Story," https://nationalblackworker centers.org/about/ (accessed June 1, 2023).

50. *American Prospect* 2021. See also Pitts 2018.

51. Fine and Theodore 2012.

52. Fine 2006.

53. Ibid., 14.

54. Ibid.

55. Ibid., 14–15.

56. Marwell 2004; Levine 2016.

57. Gilmore (2007) 2017, 47.

58. Tilly 2010.

59. McAdam and Tarrow 2010.

60. Fine 2006, 12; see also Minkoff 2002.

61. Fine 2006, 35–36; Milkman 2013, 2014.

62. Narro and Fine 2018.

63. Fine, Narro, and Barnes 2018.

64. Fine 2011b; Romero-Alston and Gupta 2021.

65. Fine 2007; Narro and Fine 2018; Luce et al. 2014; Milkman and Ott 2014; Milkman, Bloom, and Narro 2010.

66. Juravich 2018.

67. Kader 2020, 8.

68. But on unions' expanding purviews, see Sneiderman and McCartin 2018 for a discussion of the "Bargaining for the Common Good" union movement.

69. Berry and Arons 2005.

70. Ganz 2000; Theodore, Gutelius, and Gonzalez 2019, 6.

71. Chen 2021.

72. Donations to 501(c)(4) organizations are generally not tax deductible but are anonymous; 501(c)(3) donations over $5,000 have only been anonymous (to the public but not to the Internal Revenue Service) since 2020.

73. Greenhouse 2020.

74. Wright 2000; Silver 2003.

75. Fine, Narro, and Barnes 2018, 25, write: "While garment workers were once able to build significant structural power despite their position at the bottom of multilevel labor and product supply chains, we have few contemporary models of widespread successful unionization among unskilled private sector workers beyond construction laborers, janitors and security guards."

76. Rhomberg 2018; Andrias 2016.

77. Milkman 2010, 13.

78. Mazahir Salih (executive director and cofounder of CWJ), interview with the author, December 2019.

79. Jessica Vosburgh (executive director of Adelante Alabama), interview with the author, July 2020.

80. Ursula Price (executive director of NOWCRJ), interview with author, August 2020.

81. Rachel LaZar (executive director of El Centro de Igualdad y Derechos), interview with author, July 2019.

82. Gilmore (2007) 2017, 50.

83. Fine 2006, 2011b; Fellner 2021a; Romero-Alston and Gupta 2021.

84. Fine, Narro, and Barnes 2018, 26; Kuttner 2023; Ganz 2009; Fine 2006, 233, 255, 296n8, citing Aldon Morris.

85. Interview with the author.

86. Fine 2006, 217–23, 231–39, 254–55.

87. "We don't want to be beholden to powers that can pull our money and use that as leverage against us," one worker center director said. Interview with the author.

88. Gates et al. 2018, 40.

89. Data from Internal Revenue Service 990 forms, "membership dues" revenue category. See the appendix for more detail. It is quite possible, however, that some groups treat membership dues as "contributions" or "donations" and report them as part of the catchall category that also includes foundation funding ("other contributions, gifts, grants, and similar amounts")—which is always the largest revenue category.

90. For example, Fine 2006, 219–23, 231–39; Fine 2011b; Teles 2016; Fine, Narro, and Barnes 2018; Gates et al. 2018; Frantz and Fernandes 2018; Francis 2019; Fellner 2021a; Romero-Alston and Gupta 2021.

91. Smith (2007) 2017. Gilmore ([2007] 2017, 50) reminds us that foundations are "repositories of twice-stolen wealth—(a) profit sheltered from (b) taxes."

92. LaMarche 2021.

93. Teles 2016.

94. Fine 2011b.

95. Kuttner 2023.

96. Han et al. 2021, 18.

97. Ibid., 18. See also Ganz 2009.

98. Han, McKenna, and Oyakawa 2021, 17.

99. Fine 2006; Milkman 2010.

100. Sen 2003 discusses the model of community organizing associated with Saul Alinsky's writings and teachings and reviews some of the critiques this model has generated, including the "antiracist critique" (xlix–l). In light of this critique, it is worth noting that among the forty-three group leaders and staff organizers I interviewed, only about one-third were apparently White.
101. Jenkins 2002, 64.
102. Ibid., 80.
103. For a thoughtful examination of democratic modes of worker center governance and the legal implications, see Fisk 2016.
104. Ibid.; Sen 2003; Pyles 2013; Lesniewski 2013.
105. For more on these models, see the workplace justice lab@RU's "Build the Base, Grow the Movement" program (https://smlr.rutgers.edu/wjl-build-base, accessed June 17, 2023).
106. Aquilino Soriano-Versoza (cofounder and executive director of the PWC), interview with the author, April 2021.
107. McAlevey 2014a.
108. Gilmore (2007) 2017, 51, 41.
109. Ford Foundation 2023.
110. W. K. Kellogg Foundation 2023b.
111. W. K. Kellogg Foundation 2023a.
112. Public Welfare Foundation, "Grants," https://www.publicwelfare.org/grants/ (accessed June 17, 2023).
113. Interview with the author.
114. Smith (2007) 2017, 10–11.
115. Ahn (2007) 2017, 64.
116. Giridharadas 2019; Smith (2007) 2017; Gupta 2021.
117. Francis and Kohl-Arenas 2021.
118. Francis and Kohl-Arenas 2021; Francis 2019; Ahn (2007) 2017; Smith (2007) 2017.
119. Smith (2007) 2017, 15.
120. Lift Fund, "Labor Innovations for the 21st Century," https://theliftfund.org/ (accessed May 31, 2023).
121. Romero-Alston and Gupta 2021.
122. Also see Gupta 2021.

Chapter 4: The Logic of Alt-Labor's Political Development

1. Han, McKenna, and Oyakawa 2021; Michener 2020; Levine 2016.
2. These characteristic challenges are found not only in the case of labor law's drift but also in the cases of disability insurance, health care, housing, and welfare. See Galvin and Hacker 2020.
3. Jenkins 2002.
4. In some senses, this is an advantage alt-labor has relative to unions, which, fairly or not, are often accused of looking out for their members at the expense of broader constituencies of workers. Alt-labor does not face that critique.

5. Levine 2016.
6. Gleeson 2010.
7. Interview with the author.
8. Reyna Lopez (executive director of PCUN), interview with the author, July 2020.
9. Supporting workers in these ways also serves as a crucial recruitment tool, as even individual lawsuits can be effective tools in building social movements. McCann 1994.
10. Adam Kader (former worker center director and current public policy director of Arise Chicago), interview with the author, April 2019.
11. Bell, 2017 interview.
12. Deborah Axt (co-executive director of MRNY), interview with the author, September 2019.
13. Kader, interview.
14. Diaz, interview.
15. Warren 2001, 111.
16. Lucia Pedroza (organizer at Heartland Workers Center), interview with the author, August 2019.
17. See, for example, Milkman 2010, 12–13. But it has always been the case that some groups offer services and others downplay them (Fine 2006, 72–99).
18. LaZar, interview.
19. Pedroza, interview.
20. Diaz, interview.
21. Theodore, Gutelius, and Gonzalez 2019, 11; Milkman 2014; Fine 2005, 2006; Rosado Marzán 2018; Lesniewski 2013; Chun 2005, 2011.
22. Interview with the author.
23. 29 U.S.C. §157.
24. Chun 2011, 17–18; Rosado Marzán 2018.
25. Fine 2011a, 609; Greenhouse 2020.
26. Stephen 2012.
27. Meyer 2017; Meyer and Fine 2017.
28. Bell, 2017 interview.
29. Kader, interview.
30. Singh 2016.
31. Alex Tom (former executive director of CPA and current director of CEP), interview with the author, January 2022.
32. Ibid.
33. Kader, interview.
34. Andrew Friedman (former co-executive director of MRNY and current co-executive director of the CPD), interview with the author, September 2019.
35. Axt, interview.
36. Brady 2014, 234.
37. One Fair Wage, "Our Work," https://onefairwage.site/our-work (accessed June 1, 2023).
38. Saru Jayaraman (former co-executive director of ROC), interview with the author, September 2019.

39. See also Bernhardt, Spiller, and Theodore 2013.
40. Fine 2005, 1; Fine 2006. See also Gordon 2005.
41. Fine 2011a, 614.
42. Fine, Narro, and Barnes 2018, 10.
43. Doussard and Gamal 2015; Galvin 2016.
44. See the appendix for more on methods.
45. For example, see Worker Centers, https://workercenters.com/ (accessed June 1, 2023).
46. Saru Jayaraman, in *American Prospect* 2021.
47. Milkman 2010, 15–16; see also Jacobs 2018.
48. Fine 2005; Gordon 2005.
49. Kader, interview.
50. Zaman, interview.
51. Anderson 2017, 54.
52. Schattschneider 1960, 39–40, also 9–10. Emphasis in the original.
53. McAlevey 2014a, 185.
54. Block and Sachs 2020.
55. Kader, interview.
56. For a critique along these lines, see Jenkins 2002.
57. Bell, 2017 interview.
58. Ashenfelter and Smith 1979; Weil 2005; Galvin 2016. But see Hardy 2021.
59. Galvin 2016.
60. H.R. 7701, 117th Cong. (2022), Sec. 103 (b)(3)(A)(iii).
61. Eisenbrey 2016. For recent state-level initiatives, see Pokorny 2019; McGuireWoods 2020.
62. Quoted in Centro de Trabajadores Unidos en la Lucha 2021, 11.
63. Sergio Sosa (executive director of Heartland Workers Center), interview with the author, August 2019.
64. Economic Policy Institute 2019.
65. Jenkins 2002, 62.
66. Ibid., 63.
67. Ibid., 61–62.
68. Frymer 2010.
69. Hacker et al. 2022b, 2.
70. On policy fit, see Skocpol 1992.
71. Fine 2006, 254.
72. Ibid.
73. Ibid., 256.
74. Gordon 2005, 220–21.
75. Working Families Party, "Working Families National Committee," https://working families.org/working-families-national-committee/ (accessed June 21, 2023).
76. See also Levine 2016; Marwell 2004.
77. Jenkins 2002, 57.

78. Milkman, 2010, 13.
79. See chapter 6 for more illustrations and analysis.
80. Gordon (2005) calls this "noncitizen citizenship."

Chapter 5: Building Power, Forging Capacity

1. For example, Hertel-Fernandez 2019; Hacker et al. 2022b; Gilens and Page 2014.
2. Nancy Hartsock describes this type of power "as energy and competence rather than dominance" (1983, 224).
3. Rowlands 1997, 122, 14.
4. Gaventa 1982; Lukes (1975) 2021.
5. Gaventa 1982, 23–24. Emphasis in the original.
6. Quoted in Theodore, Gutelius, and Gonzalez 2019, 14.
7. Han 2014, 10, 91–92. See also Woodly 2021; Bobo et al. 2001; Warren 2001; Smock 2004; Alinsky 1989.
8. Han 2014, 96. See also Woodly 2021; Ganz 2009.
9. Han 2014, 96.
10. On the evolving role of the community organizer, see Petitjean 2023.
11. Freire 2018; Fine 2006, 206–08.
12. Alex Gomez (executive director of Arizona Center for Empowerment and organizing director of LUCHA), interview with the author, August 2020.
13. Han, McKenna, and Oyakawa 2021; Han 2014.
14. Garza 2020, 57; Petitjean 2023, 16–18.
15. Zitha 2014. See also Han 2014; Han, McKenna, and Oyakawa 2021.
16. Sosa, interview.
17. Ana Maria Archila (former co-executive director of MRNY and current co-executive director of the CPD), interview with the author, September 2019.
18. Vosburgh, interview.
19. Gomez, interview.
20. Salih, interview.
21. Ibid.
22. Marwell 2004.
23. Salih, interview.
24. Rogers and Kim 2022.
25. McAlevey 2014b, 14.
26. Gaventa 1982, 257.
27. Some issues are identified by leaders who see an important behind-the-curtain policy problem emerging that members may not—for example, MRNY's campaign around forced arbitration or United for Respect's campaign against the role of private equity in the "financialization" of retail. But in the overarching main, the groups tackle issues that their members identify as the most pressing and important in their lives.

28. Chen 2021.
29. Burnham and Theodore 2012.
30. Anna Duncan (director of affiliate engagement of NDWA), interview with the author, January 2020.
31. This emergent understanding is reflected in new developments across the labor movement, including the Bargaining for the Common Good movement, the Fight for $15, and the Red for Ed teachers' union strikes. See, for example, Oswalt 2016.
32. Price, interview.
33. Ibid.
34. Schattschneider 1960.
35. Interfaith Worker Justice was dissolved on December 31, 2021.
36. Hojnacki 1997, 1998; Mahoney 2008; Hojnacki et al. 2012; Heaney and Lorenz 2013.
37. Bill Okerman (vice president and treasurer of the Needham Area Immigration Justice Task Force), interview with the author, June 2020.
38. Rebecca Meier-Rao (executive director of WJW), interview with the author, July 2020.
39. Friedman, interview.
40. Center for Popular Democracy, "About," https://www.populardemocracy.org/about-us (accessed June 1, 2023).
41. Vosburgh, interview.
42. Mahoney 2008.
43. Schattschneider 1960, 5, 10, 40.
44. Tattersall 2010. See also Van Dyke and Amos 2017; Levi and Murphy 2006; Hojnacki 1997; Obach 2004.
45. José Garza (former co-executive director of WDP), interview with the author, July 2019.
46. Van Dyke and McCammon 2010; Strolovitch 2007; Tattersall 2005.
47. Price, interview.
48. *American Prospect* 2021.
49. Fekkak Mamdouh (senior director at One Fair Wage), interview with the author, September 2019.
50. Jayaraman, interview.
51. Greenhouse 2021.
52. Greenhouse 2021; Meyerson 2015.
53. Fine 2007.
54. Ibid., 341.
55. For example, Veronica Mendez Moore, CTUL's codirector, said: "Having a union is the ideal. It creates the highest standard" (Greenhouse 2021).
56. Narro and Fine 2018, 70.
57. Greenhouse 2021.
58. Temp Worker Union Alliance Project, "Contact," https://www.twuap.org/contact8 (accessed June 1, 2023).
59. Pattison 2021; Greenhouse 2021.

60. Quoted in Greenhouse 2021.
61. Zaman, interview.
62. McAlevey 2016.
63. Andrias 2016; Andrias and Rogers 2018; Madland 2021.
64. McAlevey 2016; Tattersall 2008.
65. Sneiderman and McCartin 2018.
66. Fine et al. 2018; Kochan et al. 2022; Milkman 2020b.
67. Organizer, interview with the author, July 2019.
68. Ganz 2000, 1005.
69. Diaz, interview.
70. For a scathing critique of the UFR model, see Leo 2020.
71. Dan Schlademan (co-executive director of UFR), interview with the author, March 2020. See also Schlademan 2017.
72. Brafman and Beckstrom 2006.
73. Schlademan, interview.
74. See City News Service 2016.
75. Schlademan, interview.
76. See Lieber 2018.
77. Schlademan, interview.
78. Wartzman 2019.
79. Warren 2021.
80. For example, Leo 2020.
81. JPAC included Chicago Workers Collaborative, Centro de Trabajadores Unidos, and Latino Union of Chicago. The other five groups in RTF are Arise Chicago, Worker Center for Racial Justice, Warehouse Workers for Justice, Chicago Community and Workers' Rights, and ROC-Chicago.
82. Kader, interview.
83. Zaman, interview.
84. Okere et al. 2021; Schuhrke 2021.
85. Fellner 2020.
86. Garza, interview.
87. Care in Action, "About Care in Action," https://careinaction.us/about/ (accessed May 31, 2023); Romero-Alston and Gupta 2021.
88. Axt, interview.
89. Ibid.
90. Ibid.
91. Tom, interview.
92. Ibid.
93. CEP 2021.
94. Tom 2019.
95. Tom, interview.
96. Tom, interview.

Chapter 6: Policy and Politics: Illustrations

1. Han, McKenna, and Oyakawa 2021.
2. Hacker et al. 2022a.
3. Soss and Weaver 2017; Michener 2020; Michener and SoRelle 2022.
4. Soriano-Versoza, interview.
5. Ibid.
6. Boris and Klein 2015.
7. Shah 2014, 1.
8. Constante 2016; Wolfe et al. 2020, 7.
9. Wang 2015, 30.
10. Soriano-Versoza, interview.
11. Ibid.
12. Employment: Minimum Wage and Overtime Compensation, AB 2536 (2006), https://leginfo.legislature.ca.gov/faces/billTextClient.xhtml?bill_id=200520060AB2536.
13. Wang 2015, 38.
14. Wolfe et al. 2020.
15. Shah 2014.
16. Wang 2015, 41.
17. Mason 2013.
18. WDP first engaged in the policymaking process with a successful effort to block the enactment of an anti-solicitation ordinance in 2005 that would have criminalized day labor in Austin and undercut the livelihood of many of its members.
19. Cox, Timm, and Tzintzún 2009.
20. Toohey 2010. Research later showed that the ordinance was successful at increasing construction workers' access to rest breaks (Scott, Boggess, and Timm 2018).
21. Fine 2017.
22. Better Builder, https://www.betterbuildertx.org/en/our-standards/; Hasan 2017.
23. Cantu 2017; Bernier 2021.
24. Block and Sachs 2020, 92; Better Builder, https://www.betterbuildertx.org/en (accessed June 1, 2023).
25. Spencer 2019.
26. Garza, interview.
27. Ibid.
28. Feltz 2018.
29. Freer 2018.
30. Platoff 2018; Palacios 2018.
31. Young 2018.
32. Samuels 2019.
33. Bova 2021.
34. Timm 2021.
35. Bova 2021.

36. *Tex. Ass'n of Bus. v. City of Austin,* 565 S.W.3d 425 (Tex. App. 2018); *Washington v. Associated Builders & Contractors of S. Tex. Inc.,* No. 04-20-00004-CV, 621 S.W.3d 305; *ESI/Emp. Sols. v. City of Dallas,* 531 F. Supp. 3d 1181 (E.D. Tex. 2021).

37. Timm, interview with the author, April 2022.

38. Norimine 2020.

39. Austin's new Wage Theft Prevention ordinance, however, passed in December 2022 at WDP's urging, seemed likely to escape most preemption restrictions (Fisher 2023).

40. Garza, interview. On "successful failures," see Weinbaum 2004, cited in Milkman 2010, 16.

41. Timm, interview.

42. See Internal Revenue Service 2022.

43. Lin et al. 2019.

44. Hajnal and Lee 2011.

45. Winkelman and Malachowsky 2009; Pastor, Perera, and Madeline 2013; Han 2014; Paschall et al. 2015; Lin et al. 2019.

46. U.S. Census Bureau 2020.

47. Sosa, interview.

48. Ibid.

49. Ibid.

50. Ibid.

51. Ibid.

52. Ibid.

53. Ibid.

54. Ibid.

55. Heartland organizer, interview with the author, August 2019.

56. See Burbach 2020.

57. Diaz, interview.

58. Ibid.

59. Salih, interview.

60. Ibid.

61. Davis 2017a, 2017b.

62. Salih, interview.

63. Economic Policy Institute 2019.

64. Gruber-Miller 2017; CWJ 2019.

65. Salih, interview.

66. Oren Smith 2018; Broxton 2021.

67. Salih, interview.

68. In 2019, CWJ was in dire financial straits and sought help from Johnson County (Scheinblum 2019).

69. Bergad and Miranda 2021.

70. Loper 2021.

71. For example, Cháves 2020.

72. Soriano-Versoza, interview.

73. Diaz, interview.

74. Friedman, interview.

75. Garza, interview.

76. Bawn et al. 2012.

77. Timm, interview, 2019.

78. Ibid.

79. Martin 2018.

80. Timm, interview, 2019.

81. Kimbel-Sannit 2020.

82. Gomez, interview.

83. Ibid.

84. Diaz, interview.

85. Ibid.

86. Fellner 2021b.

87. See Make the Road Action 2020.

88. Fellner 2021b.

89. Care in Action, "About Care in Action," https://careinaction.us/about/ (accessed May 31, 2023).

90. Fellner 2021b.

91. Seed the Vote 2021, 21.

92. Ibid.

93. Ibid., 23.

94. Skocpol 1992, 58.

95. Ibid. See also Pierson 1993; Mettler and SoRelle 2014.

96. Skocpol 1992, 54.

97. See Gerstein and Gong 2022; Fine and Bartley 2018, 4; Fine and Shepherd 2022.

98. Fine 2017.

99. Kader 2013.

100. Eidelson 2013; Kader 2013.

101. Paid Sick Time Chicago Coalition, "About the Laws," http://sicktimechicago.org /about/#the-coalition (accessed June 30, 2022).

102. Galvin et al. 2023.

103. Kader, interview.

104. Elejalde-Ruiz 2018.

105. For example, Selvam 2018.

106. Oswalt and Rosado Marzán 2018; Rosado Marzán 2021; Doussard and Lesniewski 2017.

107. Fair Workweek Chicago, "Our Coalition," https://www.chicagofairworkweek.com /our-coalition/ (accessed August 15, 2020).

108. Kang 2022.

109. Fine and Gordon 2010; Fine 2017; Patel and Fisk 2017; Fine and Bartley 2018; Fine et al. 2020, 2021a.

110. See Business Affairs and Consumer Protection 2021.

111. Ibid., 8; OLSE 2022.
112. Tom, interview.
113. Patel and Fisk 2017, 13–14; CPA 2017.
114. Fine 2017, 21; Patel and Fisk 2017, 12.
115. CPA 2017.
116. Fine 2017; Patel and Fisk 2017.
117. Patel and Fisk 2017, 20.
118. Low-Wage Worker Legal Network 2020; Gerstein and Gong 2022; Fine and Bartley 2018.
119. Fine 2017.
120. Timm, interview 2019.
121. Friedman, interview.

Chapter 7: Conclusion

1. Ghandnoosh 2010.
2. Soriano-Versoza, interview.
3. Wolfe, Harknett, and Schneider 2021.
4. See also Fellner 2020, 2021a, 2021b.
5. Kuttner 2023.
6. McArthur 2023.
7. Fellner 2021a.
8. Ibid.
9. Fellner 2021a. See also Teles 2016.
10. McArthur 2023.
11. Fisk 2016.
12. Bell, 2022 interview.
13. Levine 2016.
14. Mayhew (1974) 2004.
15. Vernuccio 2013; Griffith 2015; Griffith and Gates 2019; Gottheil 2014; Worker Centers, "Union Front Groups," https://workercenters.com/union-front-groups (accessed June 13, 2023).
16. Griffith and Gates 2019.
17. Block 2017.
18. Ibid.; Griffith and Gates 2019.
19. Friedman, interview.
20. Diaz, interview.
21. Ganz 2000, 2009; Han, McKenna, and Oyakawa 2021.

Appendix: Research Methods

1. On integrative multi-method research, see Seawright 2016.
2. Bobo and Pabellón 2016; Fine and Theodore 2012.

3. Landis and Koch 1977.
4. Council of State Governments 1935–2017.
5. Driscoll and Kraay 1998.
6. Eisenach 2011.
7. Johnson and Hollenbeck 2009.
8. Freeman 1986.
9. Galvin 2021; Galvin and Seawright 2021.
10. Based on Galvin and Seawright 2021.
11. "Priority setting by industries" is from Weil 2018, 441. For other social science research, see Ashenfelter and Smith 1979; Ehrenberg and Schumann 1982; Sellekaerts and Welch 1984; Trejo 1991, 1993; Fry and Lowell 1997; Weil and Pyles 2005; Eastern Research Group 2014; Galvin 2016; Cooper and Kroeger 2017.
12. Cooper and Kroeger 2017.
13. Eastern Research Group 2014.
14. See Vaghul and Zipperer 2021 for state minimum wage data.
15. As in Eastern Research Group 2014.
16. As in Ashenfelter and Smith 1979.
17. Davern et al. 2007.
18. For an excellent discussion of the advantages and limitations of using the CPS data to estimate minimum wage violations given the existence of measurement error and other issues, see Eastern Research Group 2014, appendix B.
19. McKay 1992. As Bernhardt et al. 2009 write: "standard surveying techniques—phone interviews or census-style door-to-door interviews—rarely are able to fully capture the population that we are most interested in: low-wage workers who may be hard to identify from official databases, who may be vulnerable because of their immigration status, or who are reluctant to take part in a survey because they fear retaliation from their employers. Trust is also an issue when asking for the details about a worker's job, the wages they receive, whether they are paid off the books or not, and their personal background" (56).
20. Bollinger 1998.
21. Roemer 2002; Eastern Research Group 2014.
22. Roemer 2002.
23. Bernhardt et al. 2009.
24. These adjustments follow Eastern Research Group 2014, Galvin 2016, and Cooper and Kroeger 2017.
25. See Economic Policy Institute 2023.

REFERENCES

Ahlquist, John S. 2017. "Labor Unions, Political Representation, and Economic Inequality." *Annual Review of Political Science* 20(1): 409–32.

Ahlquist, John S., and Margaret Levi. 2013. *In the Interest of Others: Organizations and Social Activism*. Princeton, N.J.: Princeton University Press.

Ahn, Christine E. (2007) 2017. "Democratizing American Philanthropy." In *The Revolution Will Not Be Funded*, edited by INCITE! Durham, N.C.: Duke University Press.

Alinsky, Saul. 1989. *Rules for Radicals: A Pragmatic Primer for Realistic Radicals*. New York: Vintage.

Alonso-Villar, Olga, and Coral del Rio Otero. 2013. "The Occupational Segregation of Black Women in the United States: A Look at Its Evolution from 1940 to 2010." Verona, Italy: Society for the Study of Economic Inequality, September 2013. http://econpapers.repec .org/paper/inqinqwps/ecineq2013-304.htm.

Alonso-Villar, Olga, Coral del Rio Otero, and Carlos Gradín. 2012. "The Extent of Occupational Segregation in the United States: Differences by Race, Ethnicity, and Gender." *Industrial Relations: A Journal of Economy and Society* 51(2): 179–212.

Altonji, Joseph G., and Rebecca M. Blank. 1999. "Race and Gender in the Labor Market." In *Handbook of Labor Economics*, vol. 3, edited by Orley C. Ashenfelter and David Card. Amsterdam: Elsevier.

American Prospect. 2021. "Building a Just Economy: Insights from Worker Center Leaders." *American Prospect*, September 3, 2021. https://prospect.org/videos/building-a-just-economy -insights-from-worker-center-leaders-event-video/.

———. 2021–22. "The Alt-Labor Chronicles: America's Worker Centers." *American Prospect*. Accessed May 25, 2023. https://prospect.org/labor/the-alt-labor-chronicles-america-s -worker-centers.

Ammons, Carol. 2017. "Hearing in House to Move Responsible Job Creation Act." Press release, March 14, 2017. http://www.staterepcarolammons.com/news/2017/3/14/hearing -in-house-to-move-responsible-job-creation-act.

Anderson, Elizabeth. 2017. *Private Government: How Employers Rule Our Lives (and Why We Don't Talk about It)*. Princeton, N.J.: Princeton University Press.

Anderson, Monica, Colleen McClain, Michelle Faverio, and Risa Gelles-Watnick. 2021. "The State of Gig Work in 2021." Pew Research Center, December 8, 2021. https://www .pewresearch.org/internet/2021/12/08/the-state-of-gig-work-in-2021.

Andrias, Kate. 2016. "The New Labor Law." *Yale Law Journal* 126(1): 2–100.

Andrias, Kate, and Brishen Rogers. 2018. *Rebuilding Worker Voice in Today's Economy*. New York: Roosevelt Institute. https://rooseveltinstitute.org/publications/rebuilding-worker -voice-in-todays-economy.

Andrias, Kate, and Benjamin Sachs. 2021. "Constructing Countervailing Power: Law and Organizing in an Era of Political Inequality." *Yale Law Journal* 130(3): 546–635.

Appelbaum, Eileen, Annette Bernhardt, and Richard J. Murnane, eds. 2003. *Low-Wage America: How Employers Are Reshaping Opportunity in the Workplace*. New York: Russell Sage Foundation.

Ashenfelter, Orley, and Robert S. Smith. 1979. "Compliance with the Minimum Wage Law." *Journal of Political Economy* 87(2): 333–50.

Bales, Richard. 1993. "A New Direction for American Labor Law: Individual Autonomy and the Compulsory Arbitration of Individual Employment Rights." *Houston Law Review* 30(5): 1863–914.

———. 1997. "The Discord between Collective Bargaining and Individual Employment Rights: Theoretical Origins and a Proposed Solution." *Boston University Law Review* 77(4): 687–760.

Bartels, Larry M. 2016. *Unequal Democracy: The Political Economy of the New Gilded Age*. Princeton, N.J.: Princeton University Press.

Baumgartner, Frank R., and Bryan D. Jones. 1993. *Agendas and Instability in American Politics*. Chicago: University of Chicago Press.

Baumgartner, Frank R., and Beth L. Leech. 1998. *Basic Interests: The Importance of Groups in Politics and in Political Science*. Princeton, N.J.: Princeton University Press.

Bawn, Kathleen, Martin Cohen, David Karol, Seth Masket, Hans Noel, and John Zaller. 2012. "A Theory of Political Parties: Groups, Policy Demands and Nominations in American Politics." *Perspectives on Politics* 10(3): 571–97.

Béland, Daniel, Andrea Louise Campbell, and R. Kent Weaver. 2022. *Policy Feedback: How Policies Shape Politics*. Elements in Public Policy. Cambridge: Cambridge University Press.

Béland, Daniel, Philip Rocco, and Alex Waddan. 2016. *Obamacare Wars: Federalism, State Politics, and the Affordable Care Act*. Lawrence: University Press of Kansas.

Bennett, James T., and Jason E. Taylor. 2001. "Labor Unions: Victims of Their Political Success?" *Journal of Labor Research* 22(2): 261–73.

Bergad, Laird W., and Luis Miranda Jr. 2021. *Latino Voter Registration and Participation Rates in the 2020 Presidential Election*. New York: Center for Latin American, Caribbean, and Latino Studies.

Bergmann, Barbara R. 1971. "The Effect on White Incomes of Discrimination in Employment." *Journal of Political Economy* 79(2): 294–13.

———. 1974. "Occupational Segregation, Wages and Profits when Employers Discriminate by Race or Sex." *Eastern Economic Journal* 1(2): 103–10.

Bernhardt, Annette, Heather Boushey, Laura Dresser, and Chris Tilly, eds. 2008. *The Gloves-Off Economy: Workplace Standards at the Bottom of America's Labor Market.* Champaign, Ill.: Labor and Employment Relations Association.

Bernhardt, Annette, Ruth Milkman, Nik Theodore, Douglas Heckathorn, Mirabai Auer, James DeFilippis, Ana Luz González, Victor Narro, Jason Perelshteyn, and Diana Polson. 2009. *Broken Laws, Unprotected Workers: Violations of Employment and Labor Laws in America's Cities.* New York: National Employment Law Project.

Bernhardt, Annette, Michael W. Spiller, and Nik Theodore. 2013. "Employers Gone Rogue: Explaining Industry Variation in Violations of Workplace Laws." *ILR Review* 66(4): 808–32.

Bernier, Nathan. 2021. "Leaders to Cement Austin's Multibillion-Dollar Transit Rollout Amid Concerns from Local Advocates." KUT, October 29, 2021. https://www.kut.org /transportation/2021-10-29/leaders-to-cement-austins-multibillion-dollar-transit-rollout -amid-concerns-from-local-advocates.

Berrey, Ellen, Robert L. Nelson, and Laura Beth Nielsen. 2017. *Rights on Trial: How Workplace Discrimination Law Perpetuates Inequality.* Chicago: University of Chicago Press.

Berry, Jeffrey M., with David F. Arons. 2005. *A Voice for Nonprofits.* Washington, D.C.: Brookings Institution Press.

Block, Sharon. 2017. "Backhanded Compliment: Acosta Threatens Workers Centers." OnLabor, November 20, 2017. https://onlabor.org/backhanded-compliment-acosta -threatens-workers-centers.

Block, Sharon, and Benjamin Sachs. 2020. *Clean Slate for Worker Power: Building a Just Economy and Democracy.* Cambridge, Mass.: Labor and Worklife Program, Harvard Law School. https://uploads-ssl.webflow.com/5fa42ded15984eaa002a7ef2/5fa42ded 15984ea6a72a806b_CleanSlate_SinglePages_ForWeb_noemptyspace.pdf.

Bobo, Kimberley A. 2009. *Wage Theft in America: Why Millions of Working Americans Are Not Getting Paid—and What We Can Do about It.* New York: New Press/W. W. Norton.

Bobo, Kim, and Marién Casillas Pabellón. 2016. *The Worker Center Handbook: A Practical Guide to Starting and Building the New Labor Movement.* Ithaca, N.Y.: Cornell University Press.

Bollinger, Christopher R. 1998. "Measurement Error in the Current Population Survey: A Nonparametric Look." *Journal of Labor Economics* 16(3): 576–94.

Boris, Eileen, and Jennifer Klein. 2015. *Caring for America: Home Health Workers in the Shadow of the Welfare State.* New York: Oxford University Press.

Bova, Gus. 2021. "Again, Texas Republicans Fail to Gut Local Labor Protections." *Texas Observer*, June 3, 2021. https://www.texasobserver.org/again-texas-republicans-fail-to -gut-local-labor-protections.

Brady, David. 2007. "Institutional, Economic, or Solidaristic? Assessing Explanations for Unionization Across Affluent Democracies." *Work and Occupations* 34(1): 67–101.

Brady, Marnie. 2014. "An Appetite for Justice: The Restaurant Opportunities Center of New York." In *New Labor in New York: Precarious Workers and the Future of the Labor Movement*, edited by Ruth Milkman and Ed Ott. Ithaca, N.Y.: Cornell University Press.

Brafman, Ori, and Rod A. Beckstrom. 2006. *The Starfish and the Spider: The Unstoppable Power of Leaderless Organizations*. New York: Penguin.

Bronfenbrenner, Kate. 2009. "No Holds Barred: The Intensification of Employer Opposition to Organizing." *EPI Briefing Paper* 235. Washington, D.C.: Economic Policy Institute. https://hdl.handle.net/1813/74292.

Broxton, Deion. 2021. "Iowa City Gov't Set to Make Minimum Wage for City Jobs $15 an Hour." CBS 2 Iowa, January 26, 2021. https://cbs2iowa.com/news/local/iowa-city-govt -set-to-make-minimum-wage-for-city-jobs-15-an-hour.

Brudney, James J. 1996. "Reflections on Group Action and the Law of the Workplace Symposium: The Changing Workplace." *Texas Law Review* 74: 1563–99.

———. 2005. "Neutrality Agreements and Card Check Recognition: Prospects for Changing Paradigms." *Iowa Law Review* 90(3): 819–86.

Bucci, Laura C. 2018. "Organized Labor's Check on Rising Economic Inequality in the U.S. States." *State Politics and Policy Quarterly* 18(2): 148–73.

Budiman, Abby, Christine Tamir, Lauren Mora, and Luis Noe-Bustamante. 2020. "Facts on U.S. Immigrants, 2018." Pew Research Center, August 20, 2020. https://www.pewresearch .org/hispanic/2020/08/20/facts-on-u-s-immigrants/.

Burbach, Christopher. 2020. "Omaha Blacks, Latinos Played Major Role in Biden Winning Electoral Vote in Nebraska." *Omaha World-Herald*, November 13, 2020. https://starherald .com/news/state-and-regional/omaha-blacks-latinos-played-major-role-in-biden-winning -electoral-vote-in-nebraska/article_ac611913-cfe3-543a-93e4-a13bb6455311.html.

Bureau of Labor Statistics (BLS). 1960–2014. "State Labor Legislation Enacted in [Previous Year]." *Monthly Labor Review*. Volumes 83–136.

———. 2021a. "Four States and D.C. Had Labor Force That Was More Than 30 Percent African American in 2020." February 19, 2021. https://www.bls.gov/opub/ted/2021/four -states-and-dc-had-labor-force-that-was-more-than-30-percent-african-american-in -2020.htm.

———. 2021b. *National Census of Fatal Occupational Injuries in 2020*. Washington: Bureau of Labor Statistics. https://www.bls.gov/news.release/pdf/cfoi.pdf.

———. 2021c. "Women in the Labor Force: A Databook." *BLS Reports* 1092. Washington: Bureau of Labor Statistics. https://www.bls.gov/opub/reports/womens-databook/2020 /home.htm.

———. 2022. "Labor Force Characteristics of Foreign-born Workers Summary." May 18, 2022. https://www.bls.gov/news.release/forbrn.nr0.htm.

———. 2023a. "Annual Work Stoppages Involving 1,000 or More Workers, 1947 - Present." February 22, 2023. https://www.bls.gov/web/wkstp/annual-listing.htm.

———. 2023b. "Union Members – 2022." January 19, 2023, https://www.bls.gov/news .release/pdf/union2.pdf.

Burnham, Linda, and Nikolas Theodore. 2012. *Home Economics: The Invisible and Unregulated World of Domestic Work.* New York: National Domestic Workers Alliance. DOI: https://doi.org/10.13140/RG.2.1.4018.6648.

Business Affairs and Consumer Protection. 2021. "BACP Awards Grant to Arise Chicago to Raise Awareness of Chicago's Labor Laws." Business Affairs and Consumer Protection, September 2, 2021. https://www.chicago.gov/city/en/depts/bacp/provdrs/business_support_tools/news/2021/september/awardsgrants.html.

Cadwell, Joe. 2021. "Wage Theft - The Blusky Files." *Grit Nation* podcast. October 3, 2021. https://gritnw.buzzsprout.com/1320718/8821369-stolen-wage-theft-in-construction-blusky-expose.

Cantu, Tony. 2017. "Workers Defense Project Outlines 2016 Accomplishments, Victories in Central Texas." Patch, January 3, 2017. https://patch.com/texas/eastaustin/workers-defense-project-outlines-2016-accomplishments-victories-central-texas.

Carden, Tommy, and Elena Gormley. 2021. *The COVID Jungle: Chicagoland's Essential Food Workers and the Need for Vaccination Priority.* Joliet, Ill.: Warehouse Workers for Justice. http://www.ww4j.org/uploads/7/0/0/6/70064813/wwj_food_workers_report-2-1.pdf.

Caughey, Devin, and Christopher Warshaw. 2018. "Policy Preferences and Policy Change: Dynamic Responsiveness in the American States, 1936–2014." *American Political Science Review* 112(2): 249–66.

Center for Empowered Politics. 2021. "Center for Empowered Politics (CEP) and Center for Empowered Politics Education Fund (CEPEF) Overview and Priorities." Information sheet given to the author by the center's director.

Center for Worker Justice of Eastern Iowa (CWJ). 2019. "Center for Worker Justice of Eastern Iowa Seven-Year Retrospective and Vision for the Future." October 2019. Report obtained from the center by the author.

Centro de Trabajadores Unidos en la Lucha. 2021. *Annual Report.* Minneapolis: Centro de Trabajadores Unidos en la Lucha. https://ctul.net/wp-content/uploads/2021/10/annual_report.pdf.

Chan, Julia B. 2016. "Decoding the Language of Discrimination." Reveal, January 11, 2016. https://revealnews.org/blog/decoding-the-language-of-discrimination/.

Chávez, Aida. 2020. "If Arizona Goes Blue, Look to Joe Arpaio and the Latinos Who Organized Against Him." Intercept, November 2, 2020. https://theintercept.com/2020/11/02/arizona-latino-voters-joe-arpaio/.

Chen, Anthony S. 2009. *The Fifth Freedom: Jobs, Politics, and Civil Rights in the United States, 1941–1972.* Princeton, NJ: Princeton University Press.

Chen, Michelle. 2021. "How the Powerless Win Power." *American Prospect,* April 19, 2021. https://prospect.org/labor/the-alt-labor-chronicles-america-s-worker-centers/how-the-powerless-win-power.

Chinese Progressive Association (CPA). 2017. *Organizing Wins! How Yank Sing Workers Transformed Their Workplace and Their Entire Industry.* San Francisco: CPA. https://cpasf.org/wp-content/uploads/2018/11/Yank_Sing_report_14_print.pdf.

Chun, Jennifer Jihye. 2005. "Public Dramas and the Politics of Justice: Comparison of Janitors' Union Struggles in South Korea and the United States." *Work and Occupations* 32(4): 486–503.

———. 2011. *Organizing at the Margins.* Ithaca, N.Y.: Cornell University Press.

City News Service. 2016. "Walmart to Close 7 Stores in Southern California." *Los Angeles Daily News,* January 15, 2016, https://www.dailynews.com/2016/01/15/walmart-to-close -7-stores-in-southern-california.

Clark-Bennett, Robin. 2020. "Workers' Rights Abuses and Community Response on BluSky Jobsite, Cedar Rapids." Center for Worker Justice of Eastern Iowa, December 1, 2020. https://www.mkldc.org/wp-content/uploads/2020/12/BluSky-Working-conditions -Summary.pdf.

Clemens, Elisabeth S. 2006. "Lineages of the Rube Goldberg State: Building and Blurring Public Programs, 1900–1940." In *Rethinking Political Institutions: The Art of the State,* edited by Daniel J. Galvin, Stephen Skowronek, and Ian Shapiro. New York: NYU Press.

Collier, David, Henry E. Brady, and Jason Seawright. 2004. "Sources of Leverage in Causal Inference: Toward an Alternative View of Methodology." In *Rethinking Social Inquiry: Diverse Tools, Shared Standards.* Lanham, Md.: Rowman and Littlefield.

Colvin, Alexander J. S. 2017. "The Growing Use of Mandatory Arbitration." Economic Policy Institute, September 27, 2017. https://www.epi.org/publication/the-growing-use -of-mandatory-arbitration.

Constante, Agnes. 2016. "California Governor Signs Bill Granting Overtime to Domestic Workers into Law." NBC News, September 13, 2016. https://www.nbcnews.com/news /asian-america/california-governor-signs-bill-granting-overtime-to-domestic-workers -law-n647816.

Contreras, Daisy. 2017. "Illinois Issues: The Trouble with Temp Work." NPR Illinois, April 20, 2017. https://www.nprillinois.org/statehouse/2017-04-20/illinois-issues-the -trouble-with-temp-work?fbclid=IwAR3erUXV5K2687aaz79MuZi6oNaAwkWoBih 7ctSW3D5oDmGxtGJdYaPWGVk.

Coombs, Christopher K. 2008. "The Decline in American Trade Union Membership and the 'Government Substitution' Hypothesis: A Review of the Econometric Literature." *Journal of Labor Research* 29(2): 99–113.

Cooper, David, and Teresa Kroeger. 2017. "Employers Steal Billions from Workers' Paychecks Each Year: Survey Data Show Millions of Workers Are Paid Less Than the Minimum Wage, at Significant Cost to Taxpayers and State Economies." Economic Policy Institute, May 10, 2017. https://www.epi.org/publication/employers-steal-billions-from-workers -paychecks-each-year.

Cordero-Guzmán, Héctor R., Pamela A. Izvănariu, and Victor Narro. 2013. "The Development of Sectoral Worker Center Networks." *Annals of the American Academy of Political and Social Science* 647(1): 102–23.

Council of State Governments, American Legislators' Association. 1935–2017. *The Book of the States.* Lexington, Ky.: Council of State Governments.

Cowie, Jefferson. 2010. *Stayin' Alive: The 1970s and the Last Days of the Working Class.* New York: New Press.

Cox, Lauren, Emily Timm, and Cristina Tzintzún. 2009. *Building Austin, Building Injustice: Working Conditions in Austin's Construction Industry.* Austin: Workers Defense Project. https://workersdefense.org/wp-content/uploads/2020/10/research/Building%20Austin%20Building%20Injustice.pdf.

Crenshaw, Kimberle. 1990. "Mapping the Margins: Intersectionality, Identity Politics, and Violence against Women of Color." *Stanford Law Review* 43(6): 1241–99.

Davern, Michael, Arthur Jones Jr., James Lepkowski, Gestur Davidson, and Lynn A. Blewett. 2007. "Estimating Regression Standard Errors with Data from the Current Population Survey's Public Use File." *Inquiry* 44 (Summer): 211–24.

Davis, Andy. 2017a. "Making History: Mazahir Salih Is the Press-Citizen Person of the Year." *Iowa City Press-Citizen,* December 29, 2017. https://www.press-citizen.com/story/news/local/2017/12/29/making-history-mazahir-salih-press-citizen-person-year/982176001.

———. 2017b. "Mazahir Salih, Iowa City's Newest Councilwoman, Makes History." *Iowa City Press-Citizen,* November 8, 2017. https://www.press-citizen.com/story/news/local/2017/11/08/mazahir-salih-iowa-citys-newest-councilwoman-makes-history/846379001/.

Desmond, Matthew. 2016. *Evicted: Poverty and Profit in the American City.* New York: Crown.

Dixon, Marc. 2007. "Limiting Labor: Business Political Mobilization and Union Setback in the States." *Journal of Policy History* 19(3): 313–44.

Dobbin, Frank. 2009. *Inventing Equal Opportunity.* Princeton, N.J.: Princeton University Press.

Doussard, Marc, and Ahmad Gamal. 2016. "The Rise of Wage Theft Laws: Can Community-Labor Coalitions Win Victories in State Houses?" *Urban Affairs Review* 52(5): 780–807.

Doussard, Marc, and Jacob Lesniewski. 2017. "Fortune Favors the Organized: How Chicago Activists Won Equity Goals under Austerity." *Journal of Urban Affairs* 39(5): 618–34.

Driscoll, John C., and Aart C. Kraay. 1998. "Consistent Covariance Matrix Estimation with Spatially Dependent Panel Data." *Review of Economics and Statistics* 80(4): 549–60.

Dubofsky, Martin, and Joseph A. McCartin. 2017. *Labor in America: A History.* New York: Wiley Blackwell.

Eastern Research Group. 2014. "The Social and Economic Effects of Wage Violations: Estimates for California and New York." *Final Report Prepared for the US Department of Labor.* Lexington, Mass.: Eastern Research Group.

Economic Policy Institute. 2019. "Workers' Rights Preemption in the U.S.: A Map of the Campaign to Suppress Workers' Rights in the States." Updated August 2019. Accessed June 23, 2022. https://www.epi.org/preemption-map/#:~:text=Cities%252C%2520counties%252C%2520and%2520other%2520local,that%2520target%2520key%2520worker%2520rights.

Economic Policy Institute 2023. Current Population Survey Extracts, Version 1.0.40, Microdata Extracts, wbhao: Race/ethnicity, including Asian. https://microdata.epi.org/variables/demographics/wbhao/.

Edelman, Lauren B. 2016. *Working Law: Courts, Corporations, and Symbolic Civil Rights.* Chicago: University of Chicago Press.

Ehrenberg, Ronald G., and Paul L. Schumann. 1982. "Compliance with the Overtime Pay Provisions of the Fair Labor Standards Act." *Journal of Law & Economics* 25(1): 159–81.

Eidelson, Josh. 2013. "Alt-labor." *American Prospect*, January 29, 2013. https://prospect.org /notebook/alt-labor.

Eidlin, Barry. 2018. *Labor and the Class Idea in the United States and Canada.* New York: Cambridge University Press.

Eisenach, Jeffrey A. 2011. *The Impact of State Employment Policies on Job Growth: A 50-State Review.* Washington: U.S. Chamber of Commerce.

Eisenberg-Guyot, Jerzy, Katherine M. Keyes, Seth J. Prins, Sarah McKetta, Stephen J. Mooney, Lisa M. Bates, Melanie M. Wall, and Jonathan M. Platt. 2022. "Wage Theft and Life Expectancy Inequities in the United States: A Simulation Study." *Preventive Medicine* 159 (June): 107068.

Eisenbrey, Ross. 2016. "New Legislation Could Help End Wage Theft Epidemic," Economic Policy Institute, March 16, 2016. https://www.epi.org/blog/new-legislation-could-help -end-wage-theft-epidemic/.

Elejalde-Ruiz, Alexia. 2016. "Discrimination Suit Alleges Black Temp Workers Passed over for Hispanics." *Chicago Tribune*, December 7, 2016. https://www.chicagotribune.com /business/ct-discrimination-temporary-staffing-1207-biz-20161206-story.html.

———. 2018. "Chicago to Create Office That Will Enforce City's Minimum Wage, Sick Leave Laws." *Chicago Tribune*, October 31, 2018. https://www.chicagotribune.com/business /ct-biz-chicago-office-labor-laws-standards-1101-story.html.

———. 2021. "Temp Agencies Have Long Been Accused of Discriminating against Black Job Applicants. An Experiment Set Out to Prove It." *Chicago Tribune*, February 23, 2021. https://www.chicagotribune.com/business/ct-biz-temporary-staffing-agencies-racial -discrimination-20210223-34sof3i56rhjxhzu42xtcshx44-story.html.

Epp, Charles R. 1998. *The Rights Revolution: Lawyers, Activists, and Supreme Courts in Comparative Perspective.* Chicago: University of Chicago Press.

Estlund, Cynthia L. 2002. "The Ossification of American Labor Law." *Columbia Law Review* 102(6): 1527–612.

———. 2005. "Rebuilding the Law of the Workplace in an Era of Self-Regulation." *Columbia Law Review* 105(2): 319–404.

Evans, Will. 2016. "Kill Bill: How Illinois' Temp Industry Lobbying Quashed Reform." *Reveal*, June 13, 2016. https://revealnews.org/article/kill-bill-how-illinois-temp-industry -lobbying-quashed-reform/.

———. 2017. "Illinois Temp Workers Win New Protections." Reveal, September 26, 2017. https://revealnews.org/blog/illinois-temp-workers-win-new-protections/.

Families and Workers Fund. 2022. *Reimagining Job Quality Measurement.* New York: Families and Workers Fund. https://familiesandworkers.org/web-jqmi-full-report/.

Farhang, Sean, and Ira Katznelson. 2005. "The Southern Imposition: Congress and Labor in the New Deal and Fair Deal." *Studies in American Political Development* 19(1): 1–30.

Fellner, Kim. 2020. "From Voice to Vote: Worker Centers Enlarge their Political Footprint." *Worker Centers in Retrospect and Prospect Research Paper* 1. New York: Ford Foundation.

———. 2021a. "The Funding Dilemma," *American Prospect*, April 26, 2021. https://prospect
.org/labor/the-alt-labor-chronicles-america-s-worker-centers/the-funding-dilemma.

———. 2021b. "Voices to Votes: Worker Centers Meet the Political Moment." *American
Prospect*, April 26, 2021. https://prospect.org/labor/the-alt-labor-chronicles-america-s
-worker-centers/voices-to-votes-worker-centers-meet-the-political-moment.

Feltz, Reneé. 2018. "Koch-Backed Group Fights Paid Sick Leave Laws as Flu Sweeps US."
Guardian, February 11. https://www.theguardian.com/us-news/2018/feb/11/paid-sick
-leave-koch-brothers-nfib.

Fine, Janice. 2005. "Community Unions and the Revival of the American Labor Movement."
Politics and Society 33(1): 153–99.

———. 2006. *Worker Centers: Organizing Communities at the Edge of the Dream*. Ithaca,
N.Y.: ILR Press/Cornell University Press.

———. 2007. "A Marriage Made in Heaven? Mismatches and Misunderstandings between
Worker Centres and Unions." *British Journal of Industrial Relations* 45(2): 335–60.

———. 2011a. "New Forms to Settle Old Scores: Updating the Worker Centre Story in the
United States." *Relations Industrielles/Industrial Relations* 66(4): 604–30.

———. 2011b. "Worker Centers: Entering a New Stage of Growth and Development." *New
Labor Forum* 20(3): 45–53.

———. 2013. "Solving the Problem from Hell: Tripartism as a Strategy for Addressing Labour
Standards Non-compliance in the United States." *Osgoode Hall Law Journal* 50(4): 813–43.

———. 2017. "Enforcing Labor Standards in Partnership with Civil Society: Can
Co-enforcement Succeed Where the State Alone Has Failed?" *Politics and Society* 45(3):
359–88.

Fine, Janice, and Tim Bartley. 2018. "Raising the Floor: New Directions in Public and Private
Enforcement of Labor Standards in the United States." *Journal of Industrial Relations*
61(2): 252–76.

Fine, Janice, Linda Burnham, Kati Griffith, Minsun Ji, Victor Narro, and Steven Pitts, eds.
2018. *No One Size Fits All: Worker Organization, Policy, and Movement in a New Economic
Age*. Champaign: University of Illinois at Urbana-Champaign.

Fine, Janice, Daniel J. Galvin, Jenn Round, and Hana Shepherd. 2020. *Maintaining Effective U.S. Labor Standards Enforcement through the Coronavirus Recession*. Washington:
Washington Center for Equitable Growth. https://equitablegrowth.org/wp-content
/uploads/2020/09/090320-labor-enforcement-report.pdf.

———. 2021a. "Strategic Enforcement and Co-enforcement of U.S. Labor Standards Are
Needed to Protect Workers through the Coronavirus Recession." Washington Center for
Equitable Growth, January 14, 2021. https://equitablegrowth.org/strategic-enforcement
-and-co-enforcement-of-u-s-labor-standards-are-needed-to-protect-workers-through-the
-coronavirus-recession.

———. 2021b. "Wage Theft in a Recession: Unemployment, Labour Violations, and
Enforcement Strategies for Difficult Times." *International Journal of Comparative
Labour Law and Industrial Relations* 37(2/3): 107–32.

Fine, Janice, and Jennifer Gordon. 2010. "Strengthening Labor Standards Enforcement
through Partnerships with Workers' Organizations." *Politics and Society* 38(4): 552–85.

Fine, Janice, Victor Narro, and Jacob Barnes. 2018. "Understanding Worker Center Trajectories." In *No One Size Fits All: Worker Organization, Policy, and Movement in a New Economic Age*, edited by Janice Fine, Linda Burnham, Kati Griffith, Minsun Ji, Victor Narro, and Steven Pitts. Champaign: University of Illinois at Urbana-Champaign.

Fine, Janice, and Michael Piore. 2021. "Introduction to a Special Issue on the New Labor Federalism." *ILR Review* 74(5): 1085–102.

Fine, Janice, and Hana Shepherd. 2022. "Business Power and the Turn toward the Local in Employment Standards Policy and Enforcement." Economic Policy Institute, May 19, 2022. https://www.epi.org/unequalpower/publications/local-employment-standards -policy-and-enforcement.

Fine, Janice, and Nik Theodore. 2012. *Worker Centers 2012: Community Based and Worker Led Organizations.* Washington: Center for Faith-Based and Community Partnerships, U.S. Department of Labor. http://smlr.rutgers.edu/news/worker-centers-community -based-and-worker-led-organizations.

Fisher, Lina. 2023. "Austin Tries to Address Wage Theft, Texas Tries to Make It Harder." *Austin Chronicle*, April 28. https://www.austinchronicle.com/news/2023-04-28/austin -tries-to-address-wage-theft-texas-tries-to-make-it-harder/.

Fisk, Catherine L. 2016. "Workplace Democracy and Democratic Worker Organizations: Notes on Worker Centers." *Theoretical Inquiries in Law* 17(1):101–30.

———. 2020. "Sustainable Alt-Labor." *Chicago-Kent Law Review* 95(1): 7–36.

Flood, Sarah, Miriam King, Renae Rodgers, Steven Ruggles, J. Robert Warren, and Michael Westberry. 2022. Integrated Public Use Microdata Series, Current Population Survey: Version 10.0 [dataset]. Minneapolis, Minn.: IPUMS. DOI: https://doi.org/10.18128 /D030.V10.0.

Ford Foundation. 2023. "Grantee: New Orleans Workers' Center for Racial Justice." Accessed May 31, 2023. https://www.fordfoundation.org/work/our-grants/awarded-grants/awarded -grant/general-support-to-build-the-power-and-participation-of-workers-and-communities -and-project-support-/129012.

Francis, Megan Ming. 2019. "The Price of Civil Rights: Black Lives, White Funding, and Movement Capture." *Law and Society Review* 53(1): 275–309.

Francis, Megan Ming, and Erica Kohl-Arenas. 2021. "Here We Go Again: Philanthropy & Movement Capture." *The Forge*, June 17. https://forgeorganizing.org/article/here-we-go -again-philanthropy-movement-capture.

Frantz, Courtney, and Sujatha Fernandes. 2018. "Whose Movement Is It? Strategic Philanthropy and Worker Centers." *Critical Sociology* 44(4/5): 645–60.

Fraser, Steve. 2022. "The 'Labor Question' Is about Life during and after Capitalism." Jacobin, November 16, 2022. https://jacobin.com/2022/11/us-history-labor-slavery-freedom -capitalism.

Freeman, Richard B. 1986. "Unionism and Protective Labor Legislation." In *Proceedings of the Thirty-Ninth Annual Meeting.* Edited by Barbara D. Dennis. Madison, Wis.: Industrial Relations Research Association.

Freeman, Richard B., and James L. Medoff. 1984. *What Do Unions Do?* New York: Basic Books.

Freer, Emma. 2018. "Paid Sick Days Measure for Austin Workers Passes Early Friday Morning after Hours of Tinkering, Testimony." *Community Impact*, February 16. https://communityimpact.com/austin/central-austin/city-county/2018/02/16/austin-city-council-paid-sick-days-austin-workers-passes-early-friday-morning-hours-tinkering-testimony/.

Freire, Paulo. 2018. *Pedagogy of the Oppressed*. New York: Bloomsbury.

Fry, Richard, and B. Lindsay Lowell. 1997. "The Incidence of Subminimum Pay among Native and Immigrant Workers." *Population Research and Policy Review* 16(4): 363–81.

Frymer, Paul. 2008. *Black and Blue: African Americans, the Labor Movement, and the Decline of the Democratic Party*. Princeton, N.J.: Princeton University Press.

———. 2010. *Uneasy Alliances: Race and Party Competition in America*. Princeton, N.J.: Princeton University Press.

Galvin, Daniel J. 2016. "Deterring Wage Theft: Alt-labor, State Politics, and the Policy Determinants of Minimum Wage Compliance." *Perspectives on Politics* 14(2): 324–350.

———. 2019. "From Labor Law to Employment Law: The Changing Politics of Workers' Rights." *Studies in American Political Development* 33(1): 50–86.

———. 2021. "Labor's Legacy: The Construction of Subnational Work Regulation." *ILR Review* 74(5): 1103–31.

Galvin, Daniel J., Jake Barnes, Jenn Round, and Janice Fine. 2023. "Wage Theft in Chicago: Minimum Wage Violations," Workplace Justice Lab, February 2023.

Galvin, Daniel J., and Jacob S. Hacker. 2020. "The Political Effects of Policy Drift: Policy Stalemate and American Political Development." *Studies in American Political Development* 34(2): 216–38.

Galvin, Daniel J., and Jason N. Seawright. 2021. "Surprising Causes: Propensity-Adjusted Treatment Scores for Multimethod Case Selection." *Sociological Methods and Research*. Published online May 19, 2021. DOI: https://doi.org/10.1177/00491241211004632.

Ganz, Marshall. 2000. "Resources and Resourcefulness: Strategic Capacity in the Unionization of California Agriculture, 1959–1966." *American Journal of Sociology* 105(4):1003–62.

———. 2009. *Why David Sometimes Wins: Leadership, Organization, and Strategy in the California Farm Worker Movement*. Oxford: Oxford University Press.

Garcia, Ruben J. 2012. *Marginal Workers: How Legal Fault Lines Divide Workers and Leave Them without Protection*. New York: NYU Press.

Garza, Alicia. 2020. *The Purpose of Power: How We Come Together when We Fall Apart*. New York: One World.

Gates, Leslie C., Kati L. Griffith, Jonathan L. Kim, Zane Mokhiber, Joseph C. Basler, and Austin Case. 2018. "Sizing Up Worker Center Income (2008–2014): A Study of Revenue Size, Stability, and Streams." In *No One Size Fits All: Worker Organization, Policy, and Movement in a New Economic Age*, edited by Janice Fine, Linda Burnham, Kati Griffith, Minsun Ji, Victor Narro, and Steven Pitts. Champaign: University of Illinois at Urbana-Champaign.

Gause, LaGina. 2022. *The Advantage of Disadvantage: Costly Protest and Political Representation for Marginalized Groups*. New York: Cambridge University Press.

Gaventa, John. 1982. *Power and Powerlessness: Quiescence and Rebellion in an Appalachian Valley*. Champaign: University of Illinois Press.

Gaventa, John, and Andrea Cornwall. 2008. "Power and Knowledge." In *The SAGE Handbook of Action Research*, edited by Peter Reason and Hilary Bradbury. New York: SAGE.

George, Alexander L., and Andrew Bennett. 2005. *Case Studies and Theory Development in the Social Sciences*. Cambridge, Mass.: MIT Press.

Gerring, John. 2006. *Case Study Research: Principles and Practices*. New York: Cambridge University Press.

Gerstein, Terri, and LiJia Gong. 2022. "The Role of Local Government in Protecting Workers' Rights." Economic Policy Institute, June 13, 2022. https://www.epi.org/publication /the-role-of-local-government-in-protecting-workers-rights-a-comprehensive-overview -of-the-ways-that-cities-counties-and-other-localities-are-taking-action-on-behalf-of -working-people.

Ghandnoosh, Nazgol. 2010. "Organizing Workers along Ethnic Lines." In *Working for Justice: The LA Model of Organizing and Advocacy*, edited by Ruth Milkman, Joshua Bloom, and Victor Narro. Ithaca, N.Y.: ILR Press/Cornell University Press.

Gilens, Martin, and Benjamin I. Page. 2014. "Testing Theories of American Politics: Elites, Interest Groups, and Average Citizens." *Perspectives on Politics* 12(3): 564–81.

Gilmore, Ruth Wilson. (2007) 2017. "In the Shadow of the Shadow State." In *The Revolution Will Not Be Funded*, edited by INCITE! Durham, N.C.: Duke University Press.

Giridharadas, Anand. 2019. *Winners Take All: The Elite Charade of Changing the World*. New York: Vintage.

Gleeson, Shannon M. 2009. "From Rights to Claims: The Role of Civil Society in Making Rights Real for Vulnerable Workers." *Law and Society Review* 43(3): 669–700.

———. 2010. "Labor Rights for All? The Role of Undocumented Immigrant Status for Worker Claims Making." *Law and Social Inquiry* 35(3): 561–602.

———. 2012. *Conflicting Commitments: The Politics of Enforcing Immigrant Worker Rights in San Jose and Houston*. Ithaca, N.Y.: Cornell University Press.

———. 2016. *Precarious Claims: The Promise and Failure of Workplace Protections in the United States*. Oakland: University of California Press.

Goldfield, Michael. 1987. *The Decline of Organized Labor in the United States*. Chicago: University of Chicago Press.

Gordon, Jennifer. 2005. *Suburban Sweatshops: The Fight for Immigrant Rights*. Cambridge, Mass.: Harvard University Press.

Gottheil, Tim. 2014. "Not Part of the Bargain: Worker Centers and Labor Law in Sociohistorical Context." *New York University Law Review* 89(6): 2228–64.

Gottschalk, Marie. 2000. *The Shadow Welfare State: Labor, Business, and the Politics of Health-Care in the United States*. Ithaca, N.Y.: Cornell University Press.

Grabell, Michael. 2013. "The Expendables: How the Temps Who Power Corporate Giants Are Getting Crushed." ProPublica, June 27, 2013. https://www.propublica.org/article /the-expendables-how-the-temps-who-power-corporate-giants-are-getting-crushe.

Grabell, Michael, and Howard Berkes. 2015. "The Demolition of Workers' Comp." ProPublica, March 4, 2015. https://www.propublica.org/article/the-demolition-of -workers-compensation.

———. 2017. "They Got Hurt at Work. Then They Got Deported." *ProPublica*, August 16, 2017. https://www.propublica.org/article/they-got-hurt-at-work-then-they-got-deported.

Greenhouse, Steven. 2020. *Beaten Down, Worked Up: The Past, Present, and Future of American Labor*. New York: Anchor.

———. 2021. "Embracing and Resisting: The Variable Relationships Between Worker Centers and Unions." *American Prospect*, April 22, 2021. https://prospect.org/labor/the -alt-labor-chronicles-america-s-worker-centers/embracing-resisting-variable-relationships -between-worker-centers-unions.

Greico, Elizabeth M. 2014. "The 'Second Great Wave' of Immigration: Growth of the Foreign-Born Population Since 1970." U.S. Bureau of the Census, February 26, 2014. https://www.census.gov/newsroom/blogs/random-samplings/2014/02/the-second -great-wave-of-immigration-growth-of-the-foreign-born-population-since-1970.html.

Griffith, Kate, and Leslie Gates. 2019. "Why the DOL Should Keep its Hands Off of Worker Centers." *OnLabor*, November 26, 2019. https://onlabor.org/why-the-dol-should-keep -its-hands-off-of-worker-centers.

Griffith, Kati L. 2009. "U.S. Migrant Worker Law: The Interstices of Immigration Law and Labor and Employment Law." *Comparative Labor Law and Policy Journal* 31(1):125–62.

———. 2011. "Undocumented Workers: Crossing the Borders of Immigration and Work-place Law." *Cornell Journal of Law and Public Policy* 21(3): 611–40.

———. 2015. "Worker Centers and Labor Law Protections: Why Aren't They Having Their Cake?" *Berkeley Journal of Employment and Labor Law* 36(2): 331–49.

Griffith, Kati L., and Leslie C. Gates. 2019. "Worker Centers: Labor Policy as a Carrot, Not a Stick." *Harvard Law and Policy Review* 14(1): 231–57.

———. 2020. "Milking Outdated Laws: Alt-Labor as a Litigation Catalyst." *Chicago-Kent Law Review* 95(1): 245–69.

Gruber-Miller, Stephen. 2017. "In Johnson County, More Than 140 Businesses Pledge $10.10 Minimum Wage." *Iowa City Press-Citizen*, September 18, 2017. https://www.press-citizen .com/story/news/local/2017/09/18/johnson-county-minimum-wage-group-claims-over -140-businesses-committed-paying-10-10/676725001/.

Grumbach, Jacob M. 2018. "From Backwaters to Major Policymakers: Policy Polarization in the States, 1970–2014." *Perspectives on Politics* 16 (2): 416–35.

———. 2022. *Laboratories against Democracy: How National Parties Transformed State Politics*. Princeton, N.J.: Princeton University Press.

Grumbach, Jacob M., and Jamila Michener. 2022. "American Federalism, Political Inequality, and Democratic Erosion." *Annals of the American Academy of Political and Social Science* 699(1): 143–55.

Gupta, Sarita. 2021. "Donor Collaboration Is Necessary to Fund Movements at Scale." *The Forge*, June 17. https://forgeorganizing.org/article/donor-collaboration-necessary -fund-movements-scale.

Hacker, Jacob S. 2004. "Privatizing Risk without Privatizing the Welfare State: The Hidden Politics of Social Policy Retrenchment in the United States." *American Political Science Review* 98(2): 243–60.

———. 2005. "Policy Drift: The Hidden Politics of US Welfare State Retrenchment." In *Beyond Continuity: Institutional Change in Advanced Political Economies*, edited by Wolfgang Streeck and Kathleen Thelen. New York: Oxford University Press.

———. 2019. *The Great Risk Shift: The New Economic Insecurity and the Decline of the American Dream*. Oxford: Oxford University Press.

Hacker, Jacob S., Alexander Hertel-Fernandez, Paul Pierson, and Kathleen Thelen. 2022a. "The American Political Economy: Markets, Power, and the Meta Politics of U.S. Economic Governance." *Annual Review of Political Science* 25: 197–217.

———. 2022b. "Introduction: The American Political Economy: A Framework and Agenda for Research." In *The American Political Economy: Politics, Markets, and Power*, edited by Jacob Hacker, Alexander Hertel-Fernandez, Paul Pierson, and Kathleen Thelen. New York: Cambridge University Press.

Hacker, Jacob S., and Paul Pierson. 2010. *Winner-Take-All Politics: How Washington Made the Rich Richer and Turned Its Back on the Middle Class*. New York: Simon and Schuster.

Hajnal, Zoltan L., and Taeku Lee. 2011. *Why Americans Don't Join the Party*. Princeton, N.J.: Princeton University Press.

Hall, Peter, and David Soskice. 2001. *Varieties of Capitalism: The Institutional Foundations of Comparative Advantage*. New York: Oxford University Press.

Han, Hahrie. 2014. *How Organizations Develop Activists: Civic Associations and Leadership in the 21st Century*. Oxford: Oxford University Press.

Han, Hahrie, Elizabeth McKenna, and Michelle Oyakawa. 2021. *Prisms of the People: Power and Organizing in Twenty-First-Century America*. Chicago: University of Chicago Press.

Hancock, Ange-Marie. 2016. *Intersectionality: An Intellectual History*. Oxford: Oxford University Press.

Hardy, Tess. 2021. "Digging into Deterrence: An Examination of Deterrence-Based Theories and Evidence in Employment Standards Enforcement." *International Journal of Comparative Labour Law and Industrial Relations* 37(2/3): 133–60.

Hartsock, Nancy. 1983. *Money, Sex and Power: Toward a Feminist Historical Materialism*. New York: Longman.

Hasan, Syeda. 2017. "Austin's Faster Permitting Program Will Include Construction Worker Protections." KUT, February 8, 2017. https://www.kut.org/austin/2017-02-08/austins-faster-permitting-program-will-include-construction-worker-protections.

Hatton, Erin. 2011. *The Temp Economy: From Kelly Girls to Permatemps in Postwar America*. Philadelphia: Temple University Press.

Hauserman, Nancy R., and Cheryl L. Maranto. 1988. "The Union Substitution Hypothesis Revisited: Do Judicially Created Exceptions to the Termination-at-Will Doctrine Hurt Unions?" *Marquette Law Review* 72 (3): 317–48.

Heaney, Michael T., and Geoffrey M. Lorenz. 2013. "Coalition Portfolios and Interest Group Influence over the Policy Process." *Interest Groups and Advocacy* 2(3): 251–77.

Hertel-Fernandez, Alexander. 2018a. *Politics at Work: How Companies Turn Their Workers into Lobbyists*. New York: Oxford University Press.

———. 2019. *State Capture: How Conservative Activists, Big Businesses, and Wealthy Donors Reshaped the American States, and the Nation*. New York: Oxford University Press.

Hirsch, Barry T., and David A. Macpherson. 2003. "Union Membership and Coverage Database from the Current Population Survey: Note." *Industrial and Labor Relations Review* 56(2): 349–54. See http://www.unionstats.com for updated calculations.

Hojnacki, Marie. 1997. "Interest Groups' Decisions to Join Alliances or Work Alone." *American Journal of Political Science* 41(1): 61–87.

———. 1998. "Organized Interests' Advocacy Behavior in Alliances." *Political Research Quarterly* 51(2): 437–59.

Hojnacki, Marie, David C. Kimball, Frank R. Baumgartner, Jeffrey M. Berry, and Beth L. Leech. 2012. "Studying Organizational Advocacy and Influence: Reexamining Interest Group Research." *Annual Review of Political Science* 15: 379–99.

Howell, David R. 2019. "From Decent to Lousy Jobs: New Evidence on the Decline in American Job Quality, 1979–2017." Washington Center for Equitable Growth, August 30, 2019. https://equitablegrowth.org/working-papers/from-decent-to-lousy-jobs-new -evidence-on-the-decline-in-american-job-quality-1979-2017/.

Howell, David R., and Arne L. Kalleberg. 2019. "Declining Job Quality in the United States: Explanations and Evidence." *RSF: The Russell Sage Foundation Journal of the Social Sciences* 5(4): 1–53. DOI: https://doi.org/10.7758/RSF.2019.5.4.01.

Huthmacher, J. Joseph. 1968. *Senator Robert F. Wagner and the Rise of Urban Liberalism.* New York: Atheneum.

Illinois Business Journal. 2023. "Labor Groups Celebrate Passage of Landmark Temp Worker Fairness & Safety Act." *Illinois Business Journal,* May 22. https://www.ibjonline.com/2023 /05/22/labor-groups-celebrate-passage-of-landmark-temp-worker-fairness-safety-act/.

Illinois Office of the Governor. 2022. "Workplace Rights Attorney Jane Flanagan to Serve as Acting Director of Illinois Department of Labor." EIN Presswire, February 26, 2022. https://www.einnews.com/pr_news/564143196/workplace-rights-attorney-jane-flanagan -to-serve-as-acting-director-of-illinois-department-of-labor.

Internal Revenue Service. 2022. "Exemption Requirements - 501(c)(3) Organizations." February 17, 2022. https://www.irs.gov/charities-non-profits/charitable-organizations /exemption-requirements-501c3-organizations.

Jacobs, Ken. 2018. "Governing the Market from Below: Setting Labor Standards at the State and Local Levels." In *No One Size Fits All: Worker Organization, Policy, and Movement in a New Economic Age,* edited by Janice Fine, Linda Burnham, Kati Griffith, Minsun Ji, Victor Narro, and Steven Pitts. Champaign: University of Illinois at Urbana-Champaign.

Jamison, Peter. 2016. "Outrage after Big Labor Crafts Law Paying Their Members Less Than Non-union Workers." *Los Angeles Times,* April 9, 2016. https://www.latimes.com/local /cityhall/la-me-union-minimum-wage-20160410-story.html.

Jenkins, Steve. 2002. "Organizing, Advocacy, and Member Power: A Critical Reflection." *Working USA* 6(2): 56–89.

Ji, MinWoong, and David Weil. 2015. "The Impact of Franchising on Labor Standards Compliance." *ILR Review* 68(5): 977–1006.

Johnson, Brian M., and Todd Hollenbeck. 2009. *Index of Worker Freedom: A National Report Card.* Washington, D.C.: Alliance for Worker Freedom.

Jordan, Erin. 2020. "Texas Workers Say They Haven't Been Paid for Cedar Rapids Construction Work after Derecho." *Gazette*, November 16, 2020. https://www.thegazette.com/government-politics/texas-workers-say-they-havent-been-paid-for-cedar-rapids-construction-work-after-derecho.

Juravich, Tom. 2018. "Constituting Challenges in Different Arenas of Power: Worker Centers, the Fight for $15, and Union Organizing." *Labor Studies Journal* 43(2): 104–17.

Kabeer, Naila. 1994. *Reversed Realities: Gender Hierarchies in Development Thought.* New York: Verso.

Kacich, Tom. 2017. "Ammons Introduces Bill to Improve Conditions for Temp Workers." *News-Gazette*, January 25, 2017. https://www.news-gazette.com/news/ammons-introduces-bill-to-improve-conditions-for-temp-workers/article_92fdcea0-5f73-5ca2-9f37-b367b0201a40.html.

Kader, Adam. 2013. "Arise Chicago Leads Campaign to Pass Anti-Wage Theft Ordinance." *Dignity at Work: Workers' Struggles for Dignity in Chicago and Beyond*, January 24, 2013. https://dignityatwork.wordpress.com/2013/01/24/arise-chicago-behind-chicagos-anti-wage-theft-campaign.

———. 2020. "Worker Centers and the Future of the Labor Movement." *LERA Perspectives on Work*. Champaign, Ill.: Labor and Employment Relations Association. https://lerawebillinois.web.illinois.edu/index.php/PFL/article/download/3386/3350.

Kalleberg, Arne L. 2009. "Precarious Work, Insecure Workers: Employment Relations in Transition." *American Sociological Review* 74(1): 1–22.

———. 2011. *Good Jobs, Bad Jobs: The Rise of Polarized and Precarious Employment Systems in the United States, 1970s to 2000s.* New York: Russell Sage Foundation.

Kang, Esther Yoon-Ji. 2022. "Five Things to Know about a New Chicago Law for Domestic Workers and the People Who Hire Them." WBEZ, January 12, 2022. https://www.wbez.org/stories/domestic-workers-in-chicago-must-have-written-contracts/c542eco1-f781-4d2b-9dbe-c90276498207.

Kim, Joy Jeounghee. 2021. "Violations of the U.S. Minimum Wage Laws: A Method of Wage Theft." *Journal of Economic Issues* 55(4): 977–98.

Kimbel-Sannit, Arren. 2020. "LUCHA Emerges as Key PAC in Arizona Progressive Movement." *Arizona Capitol Times*, August 14, 2020. https://azcapitoltimes.com/news/2020/08/14/lucha-emerges-as-key-pac-in-arizona-progressive-movement/.

King, Desmond, and David Rueda. 2008. "Cheap Labor: The New Politics of 'Bread and Roses' in Industrial Democracies." *Perspectives on Politics* 6(2): 279–97.

Kingdon, John W. 1984. *Agendas, Alternatives, and Public Policies*, vol. 45. Boston: Little, Brown.

Kochan, Thomas A., Janice R. Fine, Kate Bronfenbrenner, Suresh Naidu, Jacob Barnes, Yaminette Diaz-Linhart, Johnnie Kallas, Jeonghun Kim, Arrow Minster, Di Tong, Phela Townsend, and Danielle Twiss. 2022. *U.S. Workers' Organizing Efforts and Collective Actions: A Review of the Current Landscape.* Worker Empowerment Research Network. https://mitsloan.mit.edu/sites/default/files/2022-06/Report%20on%20Worker%20Organizing%20Landscape%20in%20US%20by%20Kochan%20Fine%20Bronfenbrenner%20Naidu%20et%20al%20June%202022.pdf.

Kuhlenbeck, Mike. 2020. "BlueSky Workers in Cedar Rapids Win Victory against Wage Theft." *Workers World*, November 27, 2020. https://www.workers.org/2020/11/52742/.

Kuttner, Robert. 2023. "Countervailing Powers: Community Organizing and Electoral Politics." *The Forge*, March 8. https://forgeorganizing.org/article/community-organizing -and-electoral-politics.

LaMarche, Gara. "Philanthropy and Organizing: My Journey." *The Forge*, June 17. https:// forgeorganizing.org/article/philanthropy-and-organizing-my-journey.

Lambert, Susan J., and Anna Haley. 2021. "Implementing Work Scheduling Regulation: Compliance and Enforcement Challenges at the Local Level." *ILR Review* 74(5): 1231–57.

Landis, Richard J., and Gary G. Koch. 1977. "The Measurement of Observer Agreement for Categorical Data." *Biometrics* 33(1): 159–74.

Lawless, Jennifer L., and Richard L. Fox. 2001. "Political Participation among the Urban Poor." *Social Problems* 48(3): 265–82.

Leo, United for Respect. 2020. "Burnout Culture, Workers as Props: Organizers at United for Respect Speak Out." Organizing Work, May 16, 2020. https://organizing.work/2020/05 /burnout-culture-workers-as-props-organizers-at-united-for-respect-speak-out.

Lesniewski, Jacob. 2013. "Constant Contestation: Dilemmas of Organizing, Advocacy, and Individual Interventions at a Worker Center." PhD diss., University of Chicago.

Lesniewski, Jacob, and Shannon Gleeson. 2022. "Mobilizing Worker Rights: The Challenges of Claims-Driven Processes for Re-Regulating the Labor Market." *Labor Studies Journal* 47(3): 241–61.

Levi, Margaret, and Gillian H. Murphy. 2006. "Coalitions of Contention: The Case of the WTO Protests in Seattle." *Political Studies* 54(4): 651–70.

Levine, Jeremy R. 2016. "The Privatization of Political Representation: Community-Based Organizations as Nonelected Neighborhood Representatives." *American Sociological Review* 81(6): 1251–75.

———. 2017. "The Paradox of Community Power: Cultural Processes and Elite Authority in Participatory Governance." *Social Forces* 95(3): 1155–79.

Lichtenstein, Nelson. 2013. *State of the Union: A Century of American Labor*, revised and expanded ed. Princeton, N.J.: Princeton University Press.

Lieber, Chavie. 2018. "Thousands of Toys R Us Workers Are Getting Severance, following Months of Protests." Vox, November 21, 2018, https://www.vox.com/the-goods/2018 /11/21/18106545/toys-r-us-retail-workers-severance.

Lieberman, Robert C. 1998. *Shifting the Color Line: Race and the American Welfare State*. Cambridge, Mass.: Harvard University Press.

Lin, May, Jennifer Ito, Madeline Wander, and Manuel Pastor. 2019. *Vote, Organize, Transform, Engage: New Frontiers in Integrated Voter Engagement (IVE)*. Los Angeles: University of Southern California Program for Environmental and Regional Equity.

Lipscomb, Hester J., Dana Loomis, Mary Anne McDonald, Robin A. Argue, and Steve Wing. 2006. "A Conceptual Model of Work and Health Disparities in the United States." *International Journal of Health Services* 36(1): 25–50.

LiUNA, Midwest Region. 2021. "Not-So-Blue-Sky." Accessed May 31, 2023. https://www .midwestlaborers.org/not-so-blue-sky/.

Logan, John. 2006. "The Union Avoidance Industry in the United States." *British Journal of Industrial Relations* 44(4): 651–75.

Loper, Collen. 2021. "Data to Win: How 2020 Shapes 2022." Way to Win. Accessed June 1, 2023. https://waytowin.docsend.com/view/fh4c97yfdx24smzt.

Luce, Stephanie, Jennifer Luff, Joseph A. McCartin, and Ruth Milkman. 2014. *What Works for Workers? Public Policies and Innovative Strategies for Low-Wage Workers*. New York: Russell Sage Foundation.

Lukes, Steven. (1975) 2021. *Power: A Radical View*. 3rd ed. London: Bloomsbury.

Low-Wage Worker Legal Network. 2020. "Low-Wage Workers' Priorities for the Biden/Harris Administration." December 20, 2020. Document sent to the author.

Madland, David. 2016. *The Future of Worker Voice and Power*. Washington, D.C.: Center for American Progress.

———. 2021. *Re-Union: How Bold Labor Reforms Can Repair, Revitalize, and Reunite the United States*. Ithaca, N.Y.: Cornell University Press.

Mahoney, Christine. 2008. *Brussels versus the Beltway: Advocacy in the United States and the European Union*. Washington, D.C.: Georgetown University Press.

Make the Road Action. 2020. "Make the Road Action Members Delivered!" Facebook, November 4, 2020. https://www.facebook.com/maketheroadaction/posts/3742147852470661.

Maltby, Lewis. 2009. *Can They Do That? Retaking Our Fundamental Rights in the Workplace*. New York: Portfolio.

Martin, Ken. 2018. "Workers Defense Seeks Committed Candidates." Austin Bulldog, August 27, 2018. https://theaustinbulldog.org/workers-defense-seeks-committed-candidates.

Marwell, Nicole P. 2004. "Privatizing the Welfare State: Nonprofit Community-Based Organizations as Political Actors." *American Sociological Review* 69(2): 265–91.

———. 2007. *Bargaining for Brooklyn: Community Organizations in the Entrepreneurial City*. Chicago: University of Chicago Press.

Mason, Melanie. 2013. "Gov. Brown Signs Bill Making Domestic Workers Eligible for Overtime." *Los Angeles Times*, September 26, 2013. https://www.latimes.com/politics/la-xpm-2013-sep-26-la-me-pc-domestic-workers-overtime-20130926-story.html.

Mattoni, Alice. 2012. *Media Practices and Protest Politics: How Precarious Workers Mobilise*. London: Routledge.

Mayhew, David R. (1974) 2004. *Congress: The Electoral Connection*. New Haven, Conn.: Yale University Press.

McAdam, Doug, and Sidney Tarrow. 2010. "Ballots and Barricades: On the Reciprocal Relationship between Elections and Social Movements." *Perspectives on Politics* 8(2): 529–42.

McAlevey, Jane. 2013. "Make the Road New York: Success through 'Love' and 'Agitation.'" *Nation*, May 22, 2013. https://www.thenation.com/article/archive/make-road-new-york-success-through-love-and-agitation.

———. 2014a. "The High-Touch Model: Make the Road New York's Participatory Approach to Immigrant Organizing." In *New Labor in New York: Precarious Workers and the Future of the Labor Movement*, edited by Ruth Milkman and Ed Ott. Ithaca, N.Y.: Cornell University Press.

————. 2014b. *Raising Expectations (and Raising Hell): My Decade Fighting for the Labor Movement*. New York: Verso.

————. 2016. *No Shortcuts: Organizing for Power in the New Gilded Age*. New York: Oxford University Press.

McArthur, Loren. 2023. "To Save Democracy, Fund Organizing." *Stanford Social Innovation Review* 21(2): 77–78.

McCann, Michael W. 1994. *Rights at Work: Pay Equity Reform and the Politics of Legal Mobilization, Language and Legal Discourse*. Chicago: University of Chicago Press.

McCarthy, Justin. 2022. "U.S. Approval of Labor Unions at Highest Point Since 1965." Gallup, August 30, 2022. https://news.gallup.com/poll/398303/approval-labor-unions -highest-point-1965.aspx.

McGuireWoods. 2020. "Virginia Enacts New 'Wage Theft Law,' Creating Private Right of Action for Unpaid Wages." April 28. https://www.mcguirewoods.com/client-resources /Alerts/2020/4/virginia-enacts-new-wage-theft-law.

McKay, Ruth B. 1992. "Cultural Factors Affecting within Household Coverage and Proxy Reporting in Hispanic (Salvadoran) Households. A Pilot Study." *Proceedings of the Section on Survey Research Methods*. Alexandria, Va.: American Statistical Association.

Mercado, Melody. 2020. "Construction Workers Repairing Derecho Damage Will Receive More Than $30,000 in Unpaid Wages." *Des Moines Register*, November 20, 2020.

Mettler, Suzanne. 1998. *Dividing Lines: Gender and Federalism in New Deal Public Policy*. Ithaca, N.Y.: Cornell University Press.

————. 2016. "The Policyscape and the Challenges of Contemporary Politics to Policy Maintenance." *Perspectives on Politics* 14(2): 369–90.

Mettler, Suzanne, and Mallory SoRelle. 2014. "Policy Feedback Theory." In *Theories of the Policy Process*, edited by Paul Sabatier and Christopher M. Weible. Boulder, Colo.: Westview Press.

Meyer, Rachel. 2017. "Precarious workers and collective efficacy." *Critical Sociology* 43(7/8): 1125–41.

Meyer, Rachel, and Janice Fine. 2017. "Grassroots Citizenship at Multiple Scales: Rethinking Immigrant Civic Participation." *International Journal of Politics, Culture, and Society* 30(4): 323–48.

Meyerson, Harold. 2015. "Raising Wages from the Bottom Up: Three Ways City and State Governments Can Make the Difference." *American Prospect*, April 6.

Michener, Jamila. 2018. *Fragmented Democracy: Medicaid, Federalism, and Unequal Politics*. New York: Cambridge University Press.

————. 2020. "Power from the Margins: Grassroots Mobilization and Urban Expansions of Civil Legal Rights." *Urban Affairs Review* 56(5): 1390–422.

————. 2023. "Entrenching Inequity, Eroding Democracy: State Preemption of Local Housing Policy." *Journal of Health Politics, Policy and Law* 48(2): 157–85.

Michener, Jamila, and Mallory SoRelle. 2022. "Politics, Power, and Precarity: How Tenant Organizations Transform Local Political Life." *Interest Groups and Advocacy* 11(2): 209–36.

Milkman, Ruth. 2006. *L.A. Story: Immigrant Workers and the Future of the U.S. Labor Movement*. New York: Russell Sage Foundation.

———. 2007. "Labor Organizing among Mexican-Born Workers in the United States: Recent Trends and Future Prospects." *Labor Studies Journal* 32(1): 96A–112.

———. 2010. "Introduction." In *Working for Justice: The L.A. Model of Organizing and Advocacy*, edited by Ruth Milkman, Joshua Bloom, and Victor Narro. Ithaca, N.Y.: ILR Press/Cornell University Press.

———. 2011. "Immigrant Workers and the Future of American Labor." *ABA Journal of Labor and Employment Law* 26(2): 295–310.

———. 2013. "Back to the Future? U.S. Labour in the New Gilded Age." *British Journal of Industrial Relations* 51(4): 645–65.

———. 2014. "Introduction: Toward a New Labor Movement? Organizing New York City's Precariat." In *New Labor in New York: Precarious Workers and the Future of the Labor Movement*, edited by Ruth Milkman and Ed Ott. Ithaca, N.Y.: ILR Press/Cornell University Press.

———. 2020a. *Immigrant Labor and the New Precariat*. New York: John Wiley and Sons.

———. 2020b. "Union Decline and Labor Revival in the 21st Century United States." *Chicago-Kent Law Review* 95 (1): 273–95.

Milkman, Ruth, Joshua Bloom, and Victor Narro. 2010. *Working for Justice: The L.A. Model of Organizing and Advocacy*. Ithaca, N.Y.: ILR Press/Cornell University Press.

Milkman, Ruth, and Ed Ott. 2014. *New Labor in New York: Precarious Workers and the Future of the Labor Movement*. Ithaca, N.Y.: ILR Press/Cornell University Press.

Minkler, Meredith, Alicia L. Salvatore, Charlotte Change, Megan Gaydos, Shaw San Liu, Pam Tau Lee, Alex Tom, Rajiv Bhatia, and Niklas Krause. 2014. "Wage Theft as a Neglected Public Health Problem: An Overview and Case Study from San Francisco's Chinatown District." *American Journal of public Health* 104(6): 1010–20.

Minkoff, Debra C. 2002. "The Emergence of Hybrid Organizational Forms: Combining Identity-Based Service Provision and Political Action." *Nonprofit and Voluntary Sector Quarterly* 31(3): 377–401.

Mishel, Lawrence, Lynn Rhinehart, and Lane Windham. 2020. "Explaining the Erosion of Private-Sector Unions." Economic Policy Institute, November 18, 2020. https://www.epi.org/unequalpower/publications/private-sector-unions-corporate-legal-erosion/.

Mitchell, Chip. 2013. "Company: Temporary Worker to Blame for His Fatal Burns." WBEZ Chicago, January 7, 2013. https://www.wbez.org/stories/company-temporary-worker-to-blame-for-his-fatal-burns/a6bb5a46-2b23-4249-ac8b-ced105d8c3b2.

Moore, William J., and Robert J. Newman. 1988. "A Cross-Section Analysis of the Postwar Decline in American Trade Union Membership." *Journal of Labor Research* 9(2): 19–32.

Moore, William J., Robert J. Newman, and Loren C. Scott. 1989. "Welfare Expenditures and the Decline of Unions." *Review of Economics and Statistics* 71(3): 538–42.

Morgenson, Gretchen, and Lisa Cavazuti. 2021. "The Hidden Scourge of 'Wage Theft': When Higher Profits Come Out of Workers' Pockets." NBC News, September 6, 2021. https://www.nbcnews.com/business/business-news/hidden-scourge-wage-theft-when-higher-profits-come-out-workers-n1272238.

Morris, Jim, and Chip Mitchell. 2012. "They Were Not Thinking of Him as a Human Being." Center for Public Integrity, December 20, 2012. https://publicintegrity.org

/inequality-poverty-opportunity/workers-rights/they-were-not-thinking-of-him-as-a
-human-being/.

Murthy, Karla, producer. 2013. "Organizing Workers to Bring Down Barriers." Filmed
October 2013 at Moyers and Company, Chicago. Video, 3:27. https://billmoyers.com
/content/organizing-workers-to-bring-down-barriers/.

Narro, Victor. 2005. "Impacting Next Wave Organizing: Creative Campaign Strategies of
the Los Angeles Worker Centers." *New York Law School Law Review* 50 (2): 465–514.

Narro, Victor, and Janice Fine. 2018. "Labor Unions/Worker Center Relationships, Joint
Efforts, Experiences." In *No One Size Fits All: Worker Organization, Policy, and Move-
ment in a New Economic Age*, edited by Janice Fine, Linda Burnham, Kati Griffith,
Minsun Ji, Victor Narro, and Steven Pitts. Champaign: University of Illinois at Urbana-
Champaign.

Neumann, George R., and Ellen R. Rissman. 1984. "Where Have All the Union Members
Gone?" *Journal of Labor Economics* 2(2): 175–92.

Newburger, Eric, and Thomas Gryn. 2009. "The Foreign-Born Labor Force in the United
States: 2007." U.S. Census Bureau American Community Survey Reports ACS-10.
https://www.census.gov/library/publications/2009/acs/acs-10.html.

Norimine, Hayat. 2020. "Federal Judge Stops Dallas from Endorsing Ordinance That Requires
Paid Sick Leave." Dallas Morning News, March 30, 2020. https://www.dallasnews.com
/news/public-health/2020/03/31/federal-judge-stops-dallas-from-enforcing-ordinance
-requiring-paid-sick-leave/.

Obach, Brian K. 2004. *Labor and the Environment Movement: The Quest for Common
Ground*. Cambridge, Mass.: MIT Press.

Occupational Safety and Health Administration (OSHA). 2012. "Region 5 News Release:
12-901-CHI." U.S. Department of Labor, May 16, 2012. https://www.osha.gov/news
/newsreleases/region5/05162012-0.

Office of Labor Standards Enforcement (OLSE), City and County of San Francisco. 2022.
"Request for Proposals: Worker Rights Protection and Labor Law Outreach Services."
March 21, 2022. https://sfgov.org/olse/sites/default/files/P-690%20%287-21%29_RFP
_Worker%20Rights%20%26%20Labor%20Law%20Outreach.pdf.

Okere, Ugo, Paul Sonn, Sophia Zaman, Kara Rodriguez, and Irene Tung. 2021. "Secure Jobs,
Safe Workplaces, and Stable Communities: Ending At-Will Employment in Illinois."
National Employment Law Project, March 31, 2021. https://www.nelp.org/publication
/secure-jobs-safe-workplaces-stable-communities-ending-will-employment-illinois/.

Olson, Mancur. 1965. *The Logic of Collective Action: Public Goods and the Theory of Groups*.
Cambridge, Mass.: Harvard University Press.

Oren Smith, Zachary. 2018. "City Council Sets 'Ambition' for $15 Minimum Wage in Three
Years." *Iowa City Press-Citizen*, September 18, 2018. https://www.press-citizen.com/story
/news/2018/09/18/city-council-directs-city-plan-15-3-year/1352815002/.

Osterman, Paul. 2014. *Securing Prosperity: The American Labor Market: How It Has Changed
and What to Do about It*. Princeton, N.J.: Princeton University Press.

Oswalt, Michael M. 2016. "Improvisational Unionism." *California Law Review* 104(3):
597–670.

Oswalt, Michael M., and César Rosado Marzán. 2018. "Organizing the State: The 'New Labor Law' Seen from the Bottom-Up." *Berkeley Journal of Employment and Labor Law* 39(2): 415–80.

———. 2020. "Alt-Labor Law: Symposium Introduction." *Chicago-Kent Law Review* 95(1): 3–6.

Pager, Devah, Bart Bonikowski, and Bruce Western. 2009. "Discrimination in a Low-Wage Labor Market: A Field Experiment." *American Sociological Review* 74(5): 777–99.

Palacios, Joey. 2018. "San Antonio City Clerk Certifies Petition Signatures for Mandatory Paid Sick Leave." Texas Public Radio, August 2, 2018. https://www.tpr.org/san-antonio /2018-08-02/san-antonio-city-clerk-certifies-petition-signatures-for-mandatory-paid -sick-leave.

Paschall, Kristee, Michelle Penson, Joy Cushman, Hahrie Han, and Paul Speer. 2015. "Integrated Voter Engagement Research Report." PICO National Network, Fall 2015. Accessed in 2020. http://www.piconetwork.org.

Passel, Jeffrey S., and D'Vera Cohn. 2019. "Mexicans Decline to Less Than Half the U.S. Unauthorized Immigrant Population for the First Time." Pew Research Center, June 12, 2019. https://www.pewresearch.org/fact-tank/2019/06/12/us-unauthorized-immigrant -population-2017/.

Pastor, Manuel, Gihan Perera, and W. Madeline. 2013. *Moments, Movements, and Momentum: Engaging Voters, Scaling Power, Making Change.* Los Angeles: USC Program for Environmental and Regional Equity.

Patel, Seema N., and Catherine L. Fisk. 2017. "California Co-Enforcement Initiatives that Facilitate Worker Organizing." *Harvard Law and Policy Review Online* 12. https:// heinonline.org/HOL/LandingPage?handle=hein.journals/hlpron12&div=4&id=&page=.

Pattison, Mark. 2021. "Illinois Success Story Shows Strength of CCHD Grant Funding." Crux, September 19, 2021, https://cruxnow.com/church-in-the-usa/2021/09/illinois -success-story-shows-strength-of-cchd-grant-funding.

Petitjean, Clément. 2023. *Occupation: Organizer: A Critical History of Community Organizing in America.* Chicago: Haymarket Books.

Pierson, Paul. 1993. "When Effect Becomes Cause: Policy Feedback and Political Change." *World Politics* 45(4): 595–628.

Piore, Michael J., and Andrew Schrank. 2018. *Root-Cause Regulation: Protecting Work and Workers in the Twenty-First Century.* Cambridge, Mass.: Harvard University Press.

Pitts, Steven. 2018. "The National Black Worker Center Project: Grappling with the Power-Building Imperative." In *No One Size Fits All: Worker Organization, Policy, and Movement in a New Economic Age,* edited by Janice Fine, Linda Burnham, Kati Griffith, Minsun Ji, Victor Narro, and Steven Pitts. Champaign: University of Illinois at Urbana-Champaign.

Piven, Frances Fox, and Richard A. Cloward. 1977. *Poor People's Movements: Why They Succeed, How They Fail.* New York: Vintage.

Platoff, Emma. 2018. "San Antonio Passes Paid Sick Leave Ordinance, Joining Austin in Fight Against Top Texas Republicans." *Texas Tribune,* February 16, 2018. https://www .texastribune.org/2018/08/16/san-antonio-paid-sick-leave-ordinance/.

Pokorny, Bill. 2019. "Stiff New Employer Penalties Included in Illinois $15 Minimum Wage Law." Franczek, February 19, 2019. https://www.wagehourinsights.com/2019/02/stiff-new-employer-penalties-included-in-illinois-15-minimum-wage-bill.

Prins, Seth J., Sarah McKetta, Jonathan Platt, Carles Muntaner, Katherine M. Keyes, and Lisa M. Bates. 2021. "The Serpent of Their Agonies": Exploitation as Structural Determinant of Mental Illness." *Epidemiology* 32(2): 303–09.

Pyles, Loretta. 2013. *Progressive Community Organizing: Reflective Practice in a Globalizing World*. New York: Routledge.

Reskin, Barbara. 2012. "The Race Discrimination System." *Annual Review of Sociology* 38: 17–35.

Rhomberg, Chris. 2018. "'$15 and a Union': Searching for Workers' Power in the Fight for $15 Movement." In *No One Size Fits All: Worker Organization, Policy, and Movement for a New Economic Age*, edited by Janice Fine, Linda Burnham, Kati Griffith, Minsun Ji, Victor Narro, and Steven Pitts. Champaign: University of Illinois at Urbana-Champaign.

Roeder, David. 2019. "'Seal of Approval' Sought to Curb Abuses at Temporary Staffing Firms." *Chicago Sun-Times*, May 26, 2019. https://chicago.suntimes.com/2019/5/26/18639069/temp-agencies-temporary-staffing-seal-approval-worker-abuse.

———. 2021. "Groups Accuse Temp Agencies of Bias in Hiring." *Chicago Sun-Times*, February 23, 2021. https://chicago.suntimes.com/business/2021/2/23/22297720/temp-agencies-warehouse-industry-hiring-bias.

Roemer, Marc. 2002. "Using Administrative Earnings Records to Assess Wage Data Quality in the March Current Population Survey and the Survey of Income and Program Participation." Washington: U.S. Bureau of the Census, November 19, 2002. https://www.census.gov/library/working-papers/2002/demo/asa2002.html.

Rogers, Reuel R., and Jae Yeon Kim. 2022. "Rewiring Linked Fate: Bringing Back History, Agency, and Power." *Perspectives on Politics* 21(1): 288–301.

Rolen, Emma, and Mitra Toossi. 2018. "Blacks in the Labor Force." Bureau of Labor Statistics, February 2018. https://www.bls.gov/careeroutlook/2018/article/blacks-in-the-labor-force.htm.

Rolf, David. 2016. "Toward a 21st-Century Labor Movement." *American Prospect*, April 18, 2016. https://prospect.org/power/toward-21st-century-labor-movement/.

Romero-Alston, Laine, and Sarita Gupta. 2021. "Worker Centers: Past, Present, and Future." *American Prospect*, August 30, 2021. https://prospect.org/labor/the-alt-labor-chronicles-america-s-worker-centers/worker-centers-past-present-and-future.

Roosevelt, Franklin D. 1940. "Address at Teamsters Union Convention, Washington, D.C." Speech, Washington, D.C., September 11, 1940. American Presidency Project. https://www.presidency.ucsb.edu/documents/address-teamsters-union-convention-washington-dc.

Rosado Marzán, César F. 2018. "Worker Centers and the Moral Economy: Disrupting through Brokerage, Prestige, and Moral Framing." *University of Chicago Legal Forum* 2017: 409–34.

———. 2021. "How Co-enforcement Shapes Informal Generalism." Presentation at the American Bar Foundation, March 31, virtual.

Rosenfeld, Jake. 2014. *What Unions No Longer Do*. Cambridge, Mass.: Harvard University Press.

Rowlands, Jo. 1995. "Empowerment Examined." *Development in Practice* 5(2): 101–07.

———. 1997. *Questioning Empowerment: Working with Women in Honduras*. Boston: Oxfam.

Sachs, Benjamin I. 2007. "Labor Law Renewal." *Harvard Law and Policy Review* 1(2): 375–400.

———. 2008. "Employment Law as Labor Law." *Cardozo Law Review* 29(6): 2685–748.

Samuels, Alex. 2019. "Dallas to Require Employers to Offer Paid Sick Leave as Texas Lawmakers Debate Banning Such Ordinances." *Texas Tribune*, April 24, 2019. https://www.texastribune.org/2019/04/24/dallas-paid-sick-leave-ordinance/.

Schattschneider, Elmer Eric. 1935. *Politics, Pressures and the Tariff*. New York: Prentice-Hall.

———. 1960. *The Semi-Sovereign People: A Realist's View of Democracy in America*. New York: Holt, Rinehart and Winston.

Scheinblum, Aaron. 2019. "Iowa City Nonprofit Asks Board of Supervisors for $70,000, Citing Potential to Close." KCRG, May 6, 2019. https://www.kcrg.com/content/news/Iowa-City-nonprofit-asks-Board-of-Supervisors-for-70000-citing-potential-to-close-509561291.html.

Schlademan, Daniel. 2017. "A Reborn American Labor Movement Is Coming—If Unions Are Bold Enough to Change." Quartz, April 6, 2017, https://qz.com/951268/a-reborn-american-labor-movement-is-coming-if-unions-are-bold-enough-to-change/.

Schrank, Andrew. 2019. "Rebuilding Labor Power in the Postindustrial United States." *Annals of the American Academy of Political and Social Science* 685(1): 172–88.

Schuhrke, Jeff. 2017. "A Trailblazing New Law in Illinois Will Dramatically Expand Temp Workers' Rights." In *These Times*, October 4, 2017. https://inthesetimes.com/article/a-trailblazing-new-law-in-illinois-will-dramatically-expand-temp-workers-ri.

———. 2021. "The Movement to End At-Will Employment Is Getting Serious." *In These Times*, April 6, 2021. https://inthesetimes.com/article/at-will-just-cause-employment-union-labor-illinois.

Scott, Brittany. 2021. *Opening the Door: Ending Racial Discrimination in Industrial Temp Hiring through Innovative Enforcement*. New York: Partners for Dignity and Rights. https://faofbce7-d85e-4925-af7c-4b7d25478b8c.filesusr.com/ugd/3b486b_1a0b55bob90b4ca99d63a057406c4b96.pdf.

Scott, Jennifer, Bethany Boggess, and Emily Timm. 2018. "Ensuring the Right to Rest: City Ordinances and Access to Rest Breaks for Workers in the Construction Industry." *Journal of Occupational and Environmental Medicine* 60(4): 331–36. https://journals.lww.com/joem/Abstract/2018/04000/Ensuring_the_Right_to_Rest__City_Ordinances_and.6.aspx.

Seawright, Jason. 2016a. "The Case for Selecting Cases That Are Deviant or Extreme on the Independent Variable." *Sociological Methods and Research* 45(3): 493–525.

———. 2016b. *Multi-method Social Science: Combining Qualitative and Quantitative Tools*. Cambridge: Cambridge University Press.

Seawright, Jason, and John Gerring. 2008. "Case Selection Techniques in Case Study Research: A Menu of Qualitative and Quantitative Options." *Political Research Quarterly* 61(2): 294–308.

Secunda, Paul M. 2007. "Toward the Viability of State-Based Legislation to Address Workplace Captive Audience Meetings in the United States." *Comparative Labor Law and Policy Journal* 29(2): 209–46.

Seed the Vote. 2021. "It Took All of Us. Organizing Works: A Report on Seed the Vote's 2020 Elections Experiment to Help Defeat Trump and Build Our Movements." Accessed June 1, 2023. https://www.seedthevote.org/read-our-report-on-the-work-we -did-in-2020/?fbclid=IwAR1R8Am78kPJkWt9Epwr1z3OMoRlDoq-M-DunYKYXg VnvvkGUKipno2PjzA.

Sellekaerts, Brigitte H., and Stephen W. Welch. 1984. "An Econometric Analysis of Minimum Wage Noncompliance." *Industrial Relations: A Journal of Economy and Society* 23 (2): 244–59.

Selvam, Ashok. 2018. "Chicago Establishes City Hall Watchdog Office to Protect Restaurant/ Bar Workers." Chicago Eater, October 31, 2018. https://chicago.eater.com/2018/10/31 /18045182/chicago-office-labor-management-alderman-arise-chicago-low-wage-workers.

Sen, Rinku. 2003. *Stir It Up: Lessons in Community Organizing and Advocacy.* New York: John Wiley and Sons.

Shah, Hina. 2014. "Grassroots Policy Advocacy and the California Domestic Worker Bill of Rights." Shriver Center Publications, April 9, 2014. https://digitalcommons.law.ggu .edu/pubs/623.

Silver, Beverly J. 2003. *Forces of Labor: Workers' Movements and Globalization Since 1870.* New York: Cambridge University Press.

Singh, Sonia. 2016. "How to Beat Retaliation, Even without a Union." *Labor Notes*, January 6. https://labornotes.org/2016/01/how-beat-retaliation-even-without-union.

Skocpol, Theda. 1992. *Protecting Soldiers and Mothers: The Political Origins of Social Policy in the United States.* Cambridge, Mass.: Belknap Press of Harvard University Press.

Smith, Andrea. (2007) 2017. "Introduction." In *The Revolution Will Not Be Funded*, edited by INCITE! Durham. N.C.: Duke University Press.

Smock, Kristina. 2004. *Democracy in Action: Community Organizing and Urban Change.* New York: Columbia University Press.

Snead, Warren. 2023. "The Supreme Court as an Agent of Policy Drift: The Case of the NLRA." *American Political Science Review* 117(2): 661–74.

Sneiderman, Marilyn, and Joseph A. McCartin. 2018. "Bargaining for the Common Good: An Emerging Tool for Rebuilding Worker Power." In *No One Size Fits All: Worker Organization, Policy, and Movement in a New Economic Age*, edited by Janice Fine, Linda Burnham, Kati Griffith, Minsun Ji, Victor Narro, and Steven Pitts. Champaign: University of Illinois at Urbana-Champaign.

SoRelle, Mallory E. 2020. *Democracy Declined: The Failed Politics of Consumer Financial Protection.* Chicago: University of Chicago Press.

SoRelle, Mallory, and Jamila Michener. 2022. "Methods for Applying Policy Feedback Theory." In *Methods of the Policy Process*, edited by Christopher M. Weible and Samuel Workman. New York: Routledge.

Soss, Joe, and Vesla Weaver. 2017. "Police Are Our Government: Politics, Political Science, and the Policing of Race–Class Subjugated Communities." *Annual Review of Political Science* 20: 565–91.

Southern Labor Institute. 1986. *The Climate for Workers in the United States: A Study and Report by the Southern Labor Institute*. Appendix II. Atlanta, Ga.: Southern Regional Council.

Spencer, Bridget. 2019. "'Freedom City' Policies Bring Misdemeanor Arrests Down by More Than 60 Percent." Fox 7 Austin, June 19, 2019, https://www.fox7austin.com/news /freedom-city-policies-bring-misdemeanor-arrests-down-by-more-than-60-percent#/.

Standing, Guy. 2014. *A Precariat Charter: From Denizens to Citizens*. London: A&C Black.

St. Antoine, Theodore J. 2003. "Labor and Employment Law in Two Transitional Decades." *Brandeis Law Journal* 42(3): 495–527.

Staszak, Sarah L. 2015. *No Day in Court: Access to Justice and the Politics of Judicial Retrenchment*. New York: Oxford University Press.

———. 2020. "Privatizing Employment Law: The Expansion of Mandatory Arbitration in the Workplace." *Studies in American Political Development* 34(2): 239–68.

Stepan, Alfred, and Juan J. Linz. 2011. "Comparative Perspectives on Inequality and the Quality of Democracy in the United States." *Perspectives on Politics* 9(4): 841–56.

Stephen, Lynn. 2012. *The Story of PCUN and the Farmworker Movement in Oregon*. Eugene: University of Oregon, Center for Latino/a and Latin American Studies (CLLAS). https://cllas.uoregon.edu/wp-content/uploads/2010/06/PCUN_story_WEB.pdf.

Stone, Katherine Van Wezel. 1992. "The Legacy of Industrial Pluralism: The Tension between Individual Employment Rights and the New Deal Collective Bargaining System." *University of Chicago Law Review* 59(2): 575–644.

———. 2004. *From Widgets to Digits: Employment Regulation for the Changing Workplace*. Cambridge: Cambridge University Press.

Straut-Eppsteiner, Holly. 2022. "Citizenship and Immigration Statuses of the U.S. Foreign-Born Population." Congressional Research Service, July 18, 2022. https://crsreports .congress.gov/product/pdf/IF/IF11806.

Strolovitch, Dara Z. 2007. *Affirmative Advocacy: Race, Class, and Gender in Interest Group Politics*. Chicago: University of Chicago Press.

Su, Julie A. 2016. "Enforcing Labor Laws: Wage Theft, the Myth of Neutrality, and Agency Transformation." *Berkeley Journal of Employment and Labor Law* 37(1): 143–56.

Summers, Clyde W. 1988. "Labor Law as the Century Turns: A Changing of the Guard." *Nebraska Law Review* 67(1): 7–27.

Swenson, Peter A. 2002. *Capitalists against Markets: The Making of Labor Markets and Welfare States in the United States and Sweden*. New York: Oxford University Press.

Tapia, Maite. 2019. "'Not Fissures but Moments of Crises That Can Be Overcome': Building a Relational Organizing Culture in Community Organizations and Trade Unions." *Industrial Relations* 58(1): 229–50.

Tattersall, Amanda. 2005. "There Is Power in Coalition." *Labour and Industry: A Journal of the Social and Economic Relations of Work* 16(2): 97–112.

———. 2008. "Coalitions and Community Unionism: Using the Term Community to Explore Effective Union-Community Collaboration." *Journal of Organizational Change Management* 21(4): 415–32.

————. 2010. *Power in Coalition: Strategies for Strong Unions and Social Change*. New York: Routledge.

Teles, Steven. 2016. "Foundations, Organizational Maintenance, and Partisan Asymmetry." *PS: Political Science and Politics* 49(3): 455–60.

Thelen, Kathleen. 2014. *Varieties of Liberalization and the New Politics of Social Solidarity*. Cambridge: Cambridge University Press.

Theodore, Nik. 2007. "Closed Borders, Open Markets: Day Laborers' Struggle for Economic Rights." In *Contesting Neoliberalism: Urban Frontiers*, edited by Helga Leitner, Jamie Peck, and Eric S. Sheppard. New York: Guilford Press.

Theodore, Nik, Beth Gutelius, and Ana Luz Gonzalez. 2019. *The Worker Center Ecosystem in California: Organizing to Transform Low-Wage Industries*. LIFT. DOI: https://doi.org /10.13140/RG.2.2.34993.63847.

Theodore, Nik, Abel Valenzuela Jr., and Edwin Meléndez. 2006. "La Esquina (The Corner): Day Laborers on the Margins of New York's Formal Economy." *Working USA: The Journal of Labor and Society* 9(4): 407–23.

Thurston, Chloe N. 2018. *At the Boundaries of Homeownership: Credit, Discrimination, and the American State*. New York: Cambridge University Press.

————. 2021. "Racial Inequality, Market Inequality, and the American Political Economy." In *The American Political Economy: Politics, Markets, and Power*, edited by Jacob Hacker, Alexander Hertel-Fernandez, Paul Pierson, and Kathleen Thelen. New York: Cambridge University Press.

Tilly, Charles. 2010. *Regimes and Repertoires*. Chicago: University of Chicago Press.

Timm, Emily. 2021. "Construction Workers Are Essential Workers: An Interview with Workers Defense Project." Rice Design Alliance, April 27, 2021. https://www.ricedesignalliance .org/wdp-interview.

Tom, Alex. 2019. "Building Healthy and Durable Movement Ecosystems: A 'Workforce Development Plan' for the 21st Century." Center for Empowered Politics, June 18. White paper shared with the author.

Toohey, Marty. 2010. "Construction Workers Must Get Rest Breaks, City Council Says." *Austin American-Statesman*, July 30, 2010.

Trejo, Stephen J. 1991. "The Effects of Overtime Pay Regulation on Worker Compensation." *American Economic Review* 81(4): 719–40.

————. 1993. "Overtime Pay, Overtime Hours, and Labor Unions." *Journal of Labor Economics* 11(2): 253–78.

Trounstine, Jessica. 2018. *Segregation by Design: Local Politics and Inequality in American Cities*. New York: Cambridge University Press.

————. 2021. "The Production of Local Inequality: Race, Class, and Land Use in American Cities." In *The American Political Economy: Politics, Markets, and Power*, edited by Jacob Hacker, Alexander Hertel-Fernandez, Paul Pierson, and Kathleen Thelen. New York: Cambridge University Press.

Tsoukalas, Alexis P., Jenn Round, Janice Fine, and Daniel J. Galvin. 2022. "Minimum Wage Enforcement: The Unfinished Business of Florida's Constitutional Amendment." *Florida Journal of Law and Public Policy* 32(3): 463–90.

U.S. Census Bureau. 2020. "QuickFacts: Schuyler City, Nebraska." April 1, 2020. https://www.census.gov/quickfacts/schuylercitynebraska.

———. 2023. "Historical Poverty Tables: People and Families—1959 to 2021," Table 1: Weighted Average Poverty Thresholds for Families of Specified Size: 1959 to 2021. January 20. https://www.census.gov/data/tables/time-series/demo/income-poverty/historical-poverty-people.html.

U.S. Equal Employment Opportunity Commission. 2020. "Most Valuable Personnel and MVP Workforce to Pay $568,500 to Settle EEOC Race and Sex Discrimination Suit." Press release, June 29, 2020. https://www.eeoc.gov/newsroom/most-valuable-personnel-and-mvp-workforce-pay-568500-settle-eeoc-race-and-sex.

Vaghul, Kavya, and Ben Zipperer. 2021. "Historical State and Sub-state Minimum Wages." Version 1.3.0, 2021. https://github.com/benzipperer/historicalminwage/releases/tag/v1.3.0.

Van Dyke, Nella, and Bryan Amos. 2017. "Social Movement Coalitions: Formation, Longevity, and Success." *Sociology Compass* 11(7): 1–17.

Van Dyke, Nella, and Holly J. McCammon. 2010. *Strategic Alliances: Coalition Building and Social Movements*. Minneapolis: University of Minnesota Press.

VeneKlasen, Lisa, Valerie Miller, Debbie Budlender, and Cindy Clark. 2002. *A New Weave of Power, People and Politics: The Action Guide for Advocacy and Citizen Participation*. Oklahoma City: World Neighbors.

Vernuccio, F. Vincent. 2013. "Attack of the UFOs." *Labor Watch*, Capital Research Center, September 4, 2013. https://capitalresearch.org/article/attack-of-the-ufos-alt-labor-worker-centers-and-the-rise-of-united-front-organizations.

Waldinger, Roger D., Chris Erickson, Ruth Milkman, Daniel Mitchell, Abel Valenzuela, Kent Wong, and Maurice Zeitlan. 1996. "Helots No More: A Case Study of the Justice for Janitors Campaign in Los Angeles." Los Angeles: UCLA: The Ralph and Goldy Lewis Center for Regional Policy Studies, April 1996. https://escholarship.org/uc/item/15z8f64h.

Walker, Hannah L. 2020. *Mobilized by Injustice: Criminal Justice Contact, Political Participation and Race*. New York: Oxford University Press.

Walsh, Dylan. 2018. "Alt-Labor, Explained." MIT Sloan School of Management, October 29, 2018. https://mitsloan.mit.edu/ideas-made-to-matter/alt-labor-explained.

Wang, Catherine Suzanne. 2015. "'We Still Have a Long Ways to Go': The Pilipino Workers Center's Past and Ongoing Work on the California Domestic Worker Bill of Rights and Temporary Protected Status Campaigns." M.A. thesis, University of California, Los Angeles.

Warren, Elizabeth. 2021. "Warren, Baldwin, Brown, Pocan, Jayapal, Colleagues Reintroduce Bold Legislation to Fundamentally Reform the Private Equity Industry." Office of United States Senator Elizabeth Warren, October 20, 2021, https://www.warren.senate.gov/newsroom/press-releases/warren-baldwin-brown-pocan-jayapal-colleagues-reintroduce-bold-legislation-to-fundamentally-reform-the-private-equity-industry.

Warren, Mark. 2001. *Dry Bones Rattling: Community Building to Revitalize American Democracy.* Princeton, N.J.: Princeton University Press.

Wartzman, Rick. 2019. "How a Few Former Toys 'R' Us Employees Are Helping Lead the Brand's Comeback and Putting Workers First." *Fast Company*, November 13, 2019, https://www.fastcompany.com/90429425/how-a-few-former-toys-r-us-employees-are-leading-the-brands-comeback-and-putting-workers-first.

Weil, David. 2005. "Public Enforcement/Private Monitoring: Evaluating a New Approach to Regulating the Minimum Wage." *Industrial and Labor Relations Review* 58(2): 238–57.

———. 2014. *The Fissured Workplace: Why Work Became So Bad for So Many and What Can Be Done to Improve It.* Cambridge, Mass.: Harvard University Press.

———. 2018. "Creating a Strategic Enforcement Approach to Address Wage Theft: One Academic's Journey in Organizational Change." *Journal of Industrial Relations* 60(3): 437–60.

Weil, David, and Amanda Pyles. 2005. "Why Complain? Complaints, Compliance, and the Problem of Enforcement in the U.S. Workplace." *Comparative Labor Law and Policy Journal* 27(1): 59–92.

Weiler, Paul. 1983. "Promises to Keep: Securing Workers' Rights to Self-Organization under the NLRA." *Harvard Law Review* 96(8): 1769–827.

———. 1990. *Governing the Workplace: The Future of Labor and Employment Law.* Cambridge, Mass.: Harvard University Press.

Weinbaum, Eve S. 2004. *To Move a Mountain: Fighting the Global Economy in Appalachia.* New York: The New Press.

Western, Bruce, and Jake Rosenfeld. 2011. "Unions, Norms, and the Rise in U.S. Wage Inequality." *American Sociological Review* 76(4): 513–37.

Williams, Suzanne. 1994. *The Oxfam Gender Training Manual.* Boston: Oxfam.

Windham, Lane. 2017. *Knocking on Labor's Door: Union Organizing in the 1970s and the Roots of a New Economic Divide.* Chapel Hill: University of North Carolina Press.

Winkelman, Lee, and Jeff Malachowsky. 2009. *Integrated Voter Engagement: A Proven Model to Increase Civic Engagement.* New York: Funders' Committee For Civic Participation. https://funderscommittee.org/wp-content/uploads/2017/01/fccp_integrated_voter_engagement_case_studies_2009_final.pdf.

W. K. Kellogg Foundation. 2023a. "Grants: National Domestic Workers Alliance." Accessed June 1, 2023. https://www.wkkf.org/grants/grant/2022/06/general-operating-support-6008705.

———. 2023b. "Grants: Pilipino Workers Center of Southern California." Accessed June 1, 2023. https://www.wkkf.org/grants/grant/2022/06/general-operating-support-6008705.

Wolfe, Julia, Jori Kandra, Lora Engdahl, and Heidi Shierholz. 2020. "Domestic Workers Chartbook." Economic Policy Institute, May 14, 2020. https://www.epi.org/publication/domestic-workers-chartbook-a-comprehensive-look-at-the-demographics-wages-benefits-and-poverty-rates-of-the-professionals-who-care-for-our-family-members-and-clean-our-homes/.

Wolfe, Rebecca, Kristen Harknett, and Daniel Schneider. 2021. "Inequalities at Work at Work and the Toll of COVID-19," *Health Affairs*, June 4, 2021. https://www.healthaffairs.org/do/10.1377/hpb20210428.863621/full/.

Woodly, Deva R. 2021. *Reckoning: Black Lives Matter and the Democratic Necessity of Social Movements.* New York: Oxford University Press.

Wright, Erik Olin. 2000. "Working-Class Power, Capitalist-Class Interests, and Class Compromise." *American Journal of Sociology* 105(4): 957–1002.

Young, Stephen. 2018. "Activists Fall Just Short of Sick Leave Petition Signature Requirement." *Dallas Observer*, July 17, 2018. https://www.dallasobserver.com/news/dallas-sick-leave-initiative-fails-10914592.

Zipperer, Ben, Celine McNicholas, Margaret Poydock, Daniel Schneider, and Kristen Harknett. 2022. "National Survey of Gig Workers Paints a Picture of Poor Working Conditions, Low Pay." Economic Policy Institute, June 1, 2022. https://www.epi.org/publication/gig-worker-survey.

Zitha, Xolani. 2014. "Frontiers of Democracy Research: The Gettysburg Project." Medium, Harvard Ash Center, April 11, 2014. https://medium.com/challenges-to-democracy/frontiers-of-democracy-research-the-gettysburg-project-f81e0dc17eec.

INDEX

Tables and figures are listed in **boldface**.